Historical Dictionaries of Literature and the Arts
Jon Woronoff, Series Editor

1. *Science Fiction Literature*, by Brian Stableford, 2004.
2. *Hong Kong Cinema*, by Lisa Odham Stokes, 2007.
3. *American Radio Soap Operas*, by Jim Cox, 2005.
4. *Japanese Traditional Theatre*, by Samuel L. Leiter, 2006.
5. *Fantasy Literature*, by Brian Stableford, 2005.
6. *Australian and New Zealand Cinema*, by Albert Moran and Errol Vieth, 2006.
7. *African-American Television*, by Kathleen Fearn-Banks, 2006.
8. *Lesbian Literature*, by Meredith Miller, 2006.
9. *Scandinavian Literature and Theater*, by Jan Sjåvik, 2006.
10. *British Radio*, by Seán Street, 2006.
11. *German Theater*, by William Grange, 2006.
12. *African American Cinema*, by S. Torriano Berry and Venise Berry, 2006.
13. *Sacred Music*, by Joseph P. Swain, 2006.
14. *Russian Theater*, by Laurence Senelick, 2007.
15. *French Cinema*, by Dayna Oscherwitz and MaryEllen Higgins, 2007.
16. *Postmodernist Literature and Theater*, by Fran Mason, 2007.
17. *Irish Cinema*, by Roderick Flynn and Pat Brereton, 2007.
18. *Australian Radio and Television*, by Albert Moran and Chris Keating, 2007.
19. *Polish Cinema*, by Marek Haltof, 2007.
20. *Old Time Radio*, by Robert C. Reinehr and Jon D. Swartz, 2008.
21. *Renaissance Art*, by Lilian H. Zirpolo, 2008.
22. *Broadway Musical*, by William A. Everett and Paul R. Laird, 2008.
23. *American Theater: Modernism*, by James Fisher and Felicia Hardison Londré, 2008.
24. *German Cinema*, by Robert C. Reimer and Carol J. Reimer, 2008.
25. *Horror Cinema*, by Peter Hutchings, 2008.
26. *Westerns in Cinema*, by Paul Varner, 2008.
27. *Chinese Theater*, by Tan Ye, 2008.
28. *Italian Cinema*, by Gino Moliterno, 2008.
29. *Architecture*, by Allison Lee Palmer, 2008.

30. *Russian and Soviet Cinema*, by Peter Rollberg, 2008.
31. *African American Theater*, by Anthony D. Hill, 2009.
32. *Postwar German Literature*, by William Grange, 2009.
33. *Modern Japanese Literature and Theater*, by J. Scott Miller, 2009.
34. *Animation and Cartoons*, by Nichola Dobson, 2009.
35. *Modern Chinese Literature*, by Li-hua Ying, 2010.
36. *Middle Eastern Cinema*, by Terri Ginsberg and Chris Lippard, 2010.
37. *Spanish Cinema*, by Alberto Mira, 2010.
38. *Film Noir*, by Andrew Spicer, 2010.
39. *French Theater*, by Edward Forman, 2010.
40. *Choral Music*, by Melvin P. Unger, 2010.
41. *Westerns in Literature*, by Paul Varner, 2010.
42. *Baroque Art and Architecture*, by Lilian H. Zirpolo, 2010.
43. *Surrealism*, by Keith Aspley, 2010.
44. *Science Fiction Cinema*, by M. Keith Booker, 2010.
45. *Latin American Literature and Theater*, by Richard A. Young and Odile Cisneros, 2010.
46. *Children's Literature*, by Emer O'Sullivan, 2010.

Historical Dictionary of Science Fiction Cinema

M. Keith Booker

Historical Dictionaries of
Literature and the Arts, No. 44

The Scarecrow Press, Inc.
Lanham • Toronto • Plymouth, UK
2010

Published by Scarecrow Press, Inc.
A wholly owned subsidiary of The Rowman & Littlefield Publishing Group, Inc.
4501 Forbes Boulevard, Suite 200, Lanham, Maryland 20706
http://www.scarecrowpress.com

Estover Road, Plymouth PL6 7PY, United Kingdom

British Library Cataloguing in Publication Information Available

Library of Congress Cataloging-in-Publication Data

Booker, M. Keith.
Historical dictionary of science fiction cinema / M. Keith Booker.
    p. cm. — (Historical dictionaries of literature and the arts)
Includes bibliographical references.
ISBN 978-0-8108-5570-0 (cloth : alk. paper) — ISBN 978-0-8108-7462-6 (ebook)
1. Science fiction films—Dictionaries. I. Title.
PN1995.9.S26B566 2010
791.43'615—dc22   2010016612

*For Benjamin Booker, Skylor Booker,
and Adam Booker.*

Contents

Editor's Foreword

Although it has actually been around since the early days of filmmaking, science fiction cinema is a contemporary and futuristic genre. It deals with events that usually take place at a far-off time and often far-off place; thus it appeals to the human desire to understand and perhaps predict the future. It also helps to explain science and technology and where they could be leading us. Science fiction cinema tackles prickly problems, often in a context that make them more real than reality—problems such as environmental degradation; overpopulation and pressure on space and goods; friction between the sexes, races, and nations; and the coming and substantially greater difficulties in dealing with rogue computers, robots, clones, and possibly even aliens (if we can believe what we see in the movies). Although science fiction cinema is often termed escapism, it is also an attempt to come to terms with a rapidly changing world. Consider the words of the great science fiction author Arthur C. Clarke: "We all want to escape occasionally. But science fiction is often very far from escapism, in fact you might say that science fiction is escape into reality. . . . It's a fiction which does concern itself with real issues: the origin of man; our future. In fact I can't think of any form of literature which is more concerned with real issues, reality."

This *Historical Dictionary of Science Fiction Cinema* is an excellent guide to the field. The chronology illustrates how long the movies have been around and charts some of the major advances—and films—over the years. The introduction then provides an overview, reminding us that science fiction cinema is hardly monolithic; rather, it consists of different genres, produced in an increasing range of countries, and using varying techniques. The bulk of the information, as usual, appears in the dictionary, with entries on directors, actors, and films. Other entries deal with topics such as monsters, alien invasions, utopia, and dystopia, as well as production sites (half a dozen countries), technical aspects, and new technologies (computer-generated imagery). The bibliography provides resources for further information.

It was written by M. Keith Booker, who is the James E. and Ellen Wadley Roper Professor of English at the University of Arkansas. He is also the director of the university's Program in Comparative Literature and Cultural Studies. Therefore, Dr. Booker does not simply deal with science fiction in the abstract; he shows how films and their writers, directors, actors, and genres fit into a historical context and relate to us in the present. He has also written dozens of books on literature and popular culture—more broadly and more specifically, half a dozen books on science fiction, with two recent publications dealing with science fiction cinema: *Alternative Americas: Science Fiction Film and American Culture* and *The Science Fiction Handbook*. This volume, therefore, presents a wealth of experience and knowledge for a variety of audiences.

Jon Woronoff
Series Editor

Preface

The first film I ever saw in a theater, at the age of five, was *Queen of Outer Space* (1958)—exactly the sort of film that, in some circles, has given science fiction cinema a bad name. Among other things, I know that the film was being offered as a "Saturday-morning children's matinee" at a reduced admission, which I supposed answers the question of why my parents took me to see such a film in the first place. It also indicates the way in which, by 1958, science fiction film was being regarded as childish. Still, seeing the big screen for the first time, I was mesmerized and still vividly remember the texture of the experience, if not the details of what I actually saw. I've been fascinated by film—and especially by science fiction film—ever since. Much of my work as a professional cultural critic has been devoted to the topic, particularly to exploring the ways in which science fiction film can be a serious and sophisticated cultural phenomenon that is not kid's stuff at all.

Science fiction as a whole is distinctive in its ability to take viewers into new settings from which they can potentially gain new perspectives on their own world. As such, it has political and intellectual potential that goes beyond that of virtually any other genre, and critics of written science fiction have, in recent years, made much of this potential. Science fiction film, however, remains a cultural form widely regarded as being for entertainment only, works that might impress audiences with their groundbreaking special effects but that are unlikely to make audiences think differently about the real world—or to think at all. This view of science fiction film has specific historical roots in phenomena such as the pulpy science fiction serials of the 1930s, low-budget productions of the 1950s (often geared toward teen audiences), and increasing emphasis on special effects (rather than thoughtful exploration of serious issues) that has plagued science fiction film since *Star Wars*. I hope that this historical dictionary will both document the processes through which science fiction cinema has come to be regarded as something of a "light" entertainment and also indicate the richness and diversity with which science fiction film has, at its best, demonstrated a potential to be something much more.

Reader's Note

For films originally released with a title in a language other than English, that title is generally given first throughout the dictionary, followed by the English-language title. However, in cases where the film is important enough to have its own entry in the dictionary, the entry appears under the title by which the film is most widely known, which is usually the English title. Any words in boldface lead to other entries in the dictionary.

Chronology

1818   Great Britain: Mary Shelley's *Frankenstein,* often considered the first science fiction (sf) novel, is published. It will later prove to be the direct or indirect inspiration for numerous films that straddle the boundary between sf and horror.

1895   Great Britain: H. G. Wells publishes *The Time Machine,* the first of his major "scientific romances," which together will help to form the foundation of modern sf, inspiring numerous later film adaptations.

1898   Great Britain: Wells publishes *The War of the Worlds,* another major scientific romance that will later be adapted to film multiple times.

1902   France: Georges Méliès's *Le voyage dans la lune (A Trip to the Moon),* an adaptation of an 1867 novel by Jules Verne, features some of the first sf special effects footage.

1907   France: Méliès's *20,000 lieues sous les mers (20,000 Leagues Under the Sea)* is the first of what will be several film adaptations of the 1870 Verne novel. Hand-tinted, frame by frame, it is also one of the first color films, though a few color effects had been included in *Voyage dans la lune.*

1910   United States: The Edison company releases the first film adaptation of *Frankenstein.*

1920   Germany: *Das Kabinett des Doktor Caligari (The Cabinet of Dr. Caligari)* features a mad scientist and employs a German expressionist style that will influence numerous later sf films.

1924   Soviet Union: *Aelita* adapts Alexei Tolstoy's similarly titled novel to silent film, dramatizing socialist ideals in an adventure set on Mars.

1925 United States: The silent film adaptation of Sir Arthur Conan Doyle's *The Lost World* features special effects by Willis O'Brien that foreshadow his work on *King Kong* (1933).

1927 Germany: Fritz Lang's dystopian *Metropolis,* sometimes considered the first full-fledged sf film, represents one of the high points of the German expressionist style in cinema.

1928 Germany: *Alraune* spans the boundary between sf and horror and anticipates a later sf interest in genetics.

1929 Germany: Lang's *Frau im Mond* (*Woman in the Moon*) is a serious sf film about a trip to the moon that introduces a number of future conventions for the cinematic representation of rocket launches. **Great Britain:** *High Treason* depicts a future London—with visuals being clearly influenced by *Metropolis.*

1930 Germany: *Alraune* is remade, with sound and with the same star (Brigitte Helm). **United States:** The lighthearted sf musical *Just Imagine* brings technological fantasy to Depression-era audiences in the first American sf feature film.

1931 France: Abel Gance's *La fin du monde* (*End of the World*), about a comet hurtling toward the earth, is one of the first sf disaster films. **United States:** British director James Whale helms the first sound-era film adaptation of *Frankenstein.*

1933 France/Germany: The pro-Nazi film *Der Tunnel* (*The Tunnel*) focuses on building a transatlantic tunnel, simultaneously made in parallel German- and French-language versions. **United States:** A 10-minute film featuring pulp sf hero Buck Rogers premieres at the World's Fair in Chicago. The original *King Kong* features the most complex special effects yet put on film. *It's Great to Be Alive* is an sf musical comedy, Fox's follow-up to *Just Imagine.*

1934 Germany: *Gold* anticipates many later sf films as a tycoon attempts to hijack a major scientific discovery for profit. **Great Britain:** *Once in a New Moon* uses the planetary disaster film to promote British liberal democratic values.

1935 Great Britain: *Der Tunnel* is completely remade in an English-language version, moving the action into the future and dropping the pro-Nazi (and anti-Semitic) propaganda. **United States:** Whale's *Bride of Frankenstein* is a worthy sequel to the original *Frankenstein*.

1936   Great Britain: *Things to Come* adapts H. G. Wells's *The Shape of Things to Come* (1933) to film, becoming the first major Anglophone sf film. **Soviet Union:** Scientist Konstantin Tsiolkovsky's visions of the possibilities of future space flight come to life in *Kosmicheskiy reys: Fantasticheskaya novella* (generally known in English as *The Space Ship* or *The Space Voyage*). **United States:** *Flash Gordon* becomes the first of three film serials featuring the comic-strip sf hero.

1939   United States: A 12-part *Buck Rogers* serial is released.

1940   United States: A mad scientist shrinks his antagonists to tiny size in *Dr. Cyclops*.

1941   United States: A mad scientist seeks to create an army of electrically charged zombies in *Man Made Monster*.

1949   United States: *Mighty Joe Young* is a virtual remake of *King Kong*, by the same creative team that made the original.

1950   United States: *Destination Moon* and *Rocketship X-M* become the first works of the American sf explosion of the 1950s. Though a less notable film, *The Flying Saucer* more directly reflects the era's cold war tensions.

1951   Great Britain: *The Man in the White Suit* (1951) is a thoughtful exploration of the economic ramifications of the scientific discovery of a cloth that never wears out, thus threatening the textile industry. **United States:** *The Thing from Another World* becomes the first of the many alien-invasion films of the 1950s. Arch Oboler's *Five* is the first cold war film to depict the after-effects of a nuclear apocalypse. *When Worlds Collide* treats the catastrophic destruction of the earth as a chance for a new start. *The Day the Earth Stood Still* demonstrates the potential of sf film to address complex contemporary issues in a thoughtful manner. Edgar Ulmer's ultra–low budget *The Man from Planet X* joins it in warning against the kind of paranoia and xenophobia that fuels many of the alien-invasion films of the decade. *Lost Continent* is an early example of the sf adventure film.

1952 Austria: *April 1, 2000* is a political satire that comments on the weakness of Austria after World War II. **United States:** Jesus Christ contacts earth from his Martian base in the truly strange *Red Planet Mars.* **West Germany:** *Alraune* remakes the pioneering film of 1928 and 1930.

1953 Great Britain: Hammer Films' *Spaceways* (co-produced with the American Lippert Productions) becomes the studio's first sf film. **United States:** *War of the Worlds* becomes one of the more successful adaptations of the sf writings of H. G. Wells. *Invaders from Mars* makes clear the potential of alien-invasion narratives to allegorize the perceived communist threat to the United States. *It Came from Outer Space,* on the other hand, counsels against paranoid fear of the Other. *The Beast from 20,000 Fathoms* uses state-of-the-art special effects from Ray Harryhausen.

1954 Japan: *Gojira* (*Godzilla*) initiates the Japanese monster-movie genre; significantly, the giant monster is a byproduct of atomic-weapons testing. **United States:** *20,000 Leagues Under the Sea* is a glossy, relatively big-budget undersea adventure from Disney. Jack Arnold's *Creature from the Black Lagoon* initiates a major sf monster movie sequence. In *Them!* radiation produces giant ants that threaten the southwest United States. *Tobor the Great* is a boy-and-his-robot story that warns against the evils of Soviet agents.

1955 Great Britain: *The Quatermass Xperiment,* a film adaptation of a British television serial, brings Hammer Films further into the realm of sf film. **United States:** Arnold returns to direct the *Black Lagoon* sequel *Revenge of the Creature.* Arnold also directs the giant-spider monster movie *Tarantula. This Island Earth* (1955) is an ambitious space opera that lacks the special-effects technology to be truly successful but looks forward to bigger and better things. *Conquest of Space* breaks new ground in the depiction of travel in outer space. *Day the World Ended* is Roger Corman's low-budget take on the nuclear postapocalyptic film. *It Came from Beneath the Sea* makes good use of Ray Harryhausen's monster effects.

1956 United States: Science fiction film gestures toward literariness with *Forbidden Planet. Invasion of the Body Snatchers* becomes for many the quintessential cold war paranoid alien-invasion film of the

1950s. The alien-invasion film *Earth vs. the Flying Saucers* contains some of the most memorable images from 1950s sf film. *Godzilla, King of the Monsters* brings the Japanese monster-movie icon to widespread American audiences. *It Conquered the World* is the first of the low-budget sf films directed by Roger Corman for American International Pictures. *The Creature Walks Among Us* completes the *Creature from the Black Lagoon* sequence.

1957   Great Britain: Hammer Films' *Curse of Frankenstein* combines sf and Gothic horror. Val Guest's *Quatermass 2* is a sequel to the 1955 original. **Japan:** The alien-invasion narrative comes to Japan in *Chikyû Bôeigun* (*The Mysterians*). **Mexico:** In *La momia azteca contra el robot humano* (*The Aztec Mummy vs. The Human Robot*) a mummy seeks to defend an Aztec burial site from a plundering mad scientist. **United States:** *The Incredible Shrinking Man* initiates a cycle of late-1950s "size-change" films and addresses a number of issues related to threatened masculinity in the 1950s. *The Amazing Colossal Man*, released six months later, takes the size change in the opposite direction. *Kronos* is an alien-invasion narrative that foretells the energy crises of later decades. Nathan Juran's *20 Million Miles to Earth* combines the alien-invasion narrative with the monster movie, with stop-motion special effects from Harryhausen. *The Monolith Monsters* is a good example of the 1950s sf-monster movie, as is Bert I. Gordon's *Beginning of the End*.

1958   Italy/France: *La morte viene dallo spazio* (*The Day the Sky Exploded*) is the first Italian sf film. **United States:** *Attack of the 50 Foot Woman* is a low-budget camp classic that addresses some profound gender-related concerns of the era, as does *I Married a Monster from Outer Space*. *Attack of the Puppet People* features a doll maker who shrinks humans to the size of his dolls. *The Fly* memorably combines science fiction and horror. *Earth vs. the Spider* is a typical 1950s monster movie. Teenagers save the world in *The Blob*. Roger Corman's *Teenage Caveman* also seeks the youth market.

1959   United States: *Plan 9 from Outer Space* (which went on to gain cult status as possibly the worst film ever made) epitomizes the bad, low-budget sf films of the 1950s. *Journey to the Center of the Earth* takes a more mainstream approach to sf adventure. *The Angry Red Planet* expands the monsters-on-Mars subgenre. Survivors of a nuclear war poignantly await death in *On the Beach*.

1960   East Germany/Poland: *Der schweigende Stern* (*The Silent Star*) adapts Stanisław Lem's novel to the screen. An expurgated version was released in the United States in 1962 as *First Spaceship on Venus*. **Soviet Union:** *Nebo zovyot* is a space-race drama that is remade by Roger Corman in the United States in 1963 as *Battle Beyond the Sun*. **United States:** *The Time Machine* is a classic adaptation of the novel by H. G. Wells. Irwin Allen's *The Lost World* becomes the best-known adaptation of Sir Arthur Conan Doyle's original story.

1961   Great Britain: *The Day the Earth Caught Fire* is a science fiction disaster film. **Great Britain/United States:** *Mysterious Island,* based on a novel by Jules Verne, is a retro science fiction adventure set in the civil war era. **Italy:** *Battle of the Worlds* is a new twist on the alien-invasion narrative. **Japan:** *Mothra* features a new movie monster in the vein of Godzilla. **United States:** Irwin Allen's *Voyage to the Bottom of the Sea* is a relatively big-budget undersea adventure. Disney's *The Absent-Minded Professor* is lighthearted science fiction for kids.

1962   France: Constructed almost entirely of a sequence of still photos, Chris Marker's *La jetée* is a haunting evocation of a postapocalypse world. **Great Britain:** In *The Day of the Triffids,* murderous plants from outer space are defeated by exposure to salt water. **Japan/United States:** Two classic movie monsters square off in *Kingu Kongu tai Gojira* (*King Kong vs. Godzilla*). **Soviet Union:** *Planeta Bur* is a monsters-on-Venus film, later reworked as an English-language version for American audiences as *Voyage to the Prehistoric Planet* (1965), then again as *Voyage to the Planet of Prehistoric Women* (1968). **United States:** *Panic in Year Zero!* is a post–nuclear holocaust drama.

1963   Great Britain: *The Damned* addresses a number of key cold war issues in its portrayal of a group of radioactive mutant children being held captive by the authorities in preparation for the day when their resistance to radiation can help them repopulate a postapocalyptic earth. **United States:** Roger Corman's low-budget *X: The Man with the X-Ray Eyes* is a surprising success.

1964 Great Britain: *First Men in the Moon* is a relatively high-budget adaptation of H. G. Wells's novel of the same title. Stanley Kubrick's *Dr. Strangelove or: How I Learned to Stop Worrying and Love the Bomb* becomes the definitive film about the folly of the cold war arms race. **Italy/United States:** Vincent Price is the lone survivor of a vampire plague in the first of three film adaptations of Richard Matheson's 1954 novel *I Am Legend.* **Japan:** *Mothra vs. Godzilla* pits the two well-known movie monsters against each other. **United States:** *Robinson Crusoe on Mars* is a reworking of Defoe's original novel in an outer-space setting.

1965 France/Italy: Jean-Luc Godard's *Alphaville* brings French New Wave cinema to sf. **Great Britain:** Terence Fisher's *The Earth Dies Screaming* brings a horror sensibility to the alien-invasion film. *Invasion* uses Asian actors to represent alien invaders. The popular British sf television series comes to the big screen in *Dr. Who and the Daleks.* *It Happened Here* depicts an alternative England occupied by the Germans during World War II. **Italy:** Mario Bava's *Terrore nello spazio* (released in the United States as *Planet of the Vampires*) effectively combines horror and space opera, influencing later films such as *Alien* (1979). Elio Petri's *The 10th Victim* stars Marcello Mastroianni and Ursula Andress in a satire of violence in entertainment that becomes a cult classic. **Mexico:** In *El planeta de las mujeres invasoras* (*Planet of the Female Invaders*) alien women try to steal the lungs of humans so they can breathe on earth. **United States:** Bert I. Gordon's *Village of the Giants* is one of the less distinguished film adaptations of the work of H. G. Wells.

1966 Great Britain: France's François Truffaut directs *Fahrenheit 451,* an adaptation of Ray Bradbury's dystopian novel of the same title. Runaway science creates monsters in Terence Fisher's *Island of Terror.* **Mexico:** In *Santo Enmascarado de Plata vs. "La invasión de los marcianos"* (*Santo the Silver Mask vs. The Martian Invasion*) a masked Mexican wrestler battles scantily clad female Martian invaders. **United States:** Tiny adventurers explore the interior of the human body in Richard Fleischer's *Fantastic Voyage.*

1967 Great Britain: *Night of the Big Heat* is another horror-inflected alien-invasion film from Terence Fisher. *Quatermass and the Pit* extends the British sf franchise from the 1950s. **Soviet Union:** The space opera *Tumannost Andromedy* (*Andromeda Nebula*) adapts Ivan Yefremov's 1957 novel *Andromeda.*

1968 France/Italy: Roger Vadim's *Barbarella* is erotic sf with a campy touch. **Great Britain/United States:** Stanley Kubrick's *2001: A Space Odyssey* brings sf film into the realm of high art. **United States:** The hugely successful (and satirically smart) *Planet of the Apes* helps to resurrect American sf film from the doldrums of the 1960s.

1969 Great Britain: *Journey to the Far Side of the Sun* (aka *Doppelgänger*) is an interesting parallel-world narrative. **United States:** American astronauts have trouble getting back to earth in *Marooned.* Disney's *The Computer Wore Tennis Shoes* is sf for the teen market that oddly foreshadows the themes of cyberpunk. *The Illustrated Man* adapts some of the short stories of Ray Bradbury.

1970 Great Britain: Val Guest's *Toomorrow* is a whimsical sf musical. **United States:** *Beneath the Planet of the Apes* is the first of four *Planet of the Apes* sequels. A sinister computer tries to take over the world in *Colossus: The Forbin Project.*

1971 Great Britain/United States: Kubrick's *A Clockwork Orange* is a dystopian classic. **United States:** *The Andromeda Strain* combines plague, alien invasion, and nuclear disaster scenarios in an effective thriller. *The Omega Man* is the second adaption of Richard Matheson's *I Am Legend,* with Charlton Heston in the role of the last man on earth. The dystopian film *THX 1138* is the first film by George Lucas.

1972 East Germany: *Eolomea* is a science fiction thriller produced by Deutsche Film-Aktiengesellschaft Studios in East Germany. **Great Britain:** *Z.P.G.* focuses on the dangers of overpopulation. **Soviet Union:** Andrei Tarkovsky's *Solaris* brings Stanisław Lem's meditative sf novel to the screen in a highly successful adaptation. **United States:** *Silent Running* is one of the first major sf films to focus on environmental concerns. *Slaughterhouse-Five* adapts Kurt Vonnegut's quirky time-travel novel to film. *Now You See Him, Now You Don't* is another Disney foray into sf.

1973 Czechoslovakia/France: The animated *La planète sauvage* (*Fantastic Planet*) features surreal imagery and political allegory; it wins the special jury prize at the 1973 Cannes Film Festival. **Soviet Union:** Leonid Gaidai's *Ivan Vasilevich menyaet professiyu* (*Ivan Vasilevich Changes Professions*, released in the West as *Ivan Vasilevich: Back to the Future*) is based on a play by master satirist Mikhail Bulgakov. **United States:** *Soylent Green* is one of the most memorable of the dystopian films of the early 1970s. Woody Allen's *Sleeper* spoofs those films. Michael Crichton's *Westworld* warns of the dangers of excessive automation, yet also employs computer animation for the first time in sf film. *The Day of the Dolphin* is a political thriller featuring intelligent dolphins. *Battle for the Planet of the Apes* continues that franchise.

1974   Mexico/United States: The postapocalyptic film *Chosen Survivors* is an international co-production. **United States:** *The Terminal Man* expresses contemporary concerns about the rising power of computers. John Carpenter's *Dark Star* is a quirky science fiction comedy. *Zardoz* is one of the stranger sf films of the decade.

1975   Great Britain: *Rollerball* is an effective dystopian film that seeks to critique our fascination with violence. *The Land that Time Forgot* is an entry in the dinosaur enclave subgenre. **Great Britain/ United States:** *The Rocky Horror Picture Show* is a campy musical romp through the alien-invasion narrative that becomes an all-time cult favorite. **United States:** *A Boy and His Dog* is a satirical postapocalyptic film with a twist ending. Robots replace suburban housewives in *The Stepford Wives*. *The Strongest Man in the World* completes Disney's trilogy of youth-oriented sf films featuring Kurt Russell. In *Escape to Witch Mountain* Disney moves into the realm of the alien-invasion narrative.

1976   East Germany: *Im Staub der Sterne* (*In the Dust of the Stars*) brings groovy 1970s sf film to the Soviet bloc. **Great Britain:** Nicolas Roeg's *The Man Who Fell to Earth* takes a new look at the alien-invasion narrative. **United States:** *Futureworld* is both a sequel to and a virtual remake of *Westworld*. *Logan's Run* is a postapocalyptic-dystopian film that becomes something of a cult classic.

1977   Great Britain/United States: *The People that Time Forgot* is a sequel to *The Land that Time Forgot*. **United States:** *Close Encounters of the Third Kind* and *Star Wars* initiate a major new wave of sf film, the former a thoughtful alien-invasion narrative, the latter an old-style space opera that is particularly important for beginning a special-effects revolution. In *Demon Seed* a rogue computer seeks to father a new strain of hybrid humans. *The Island of Dr. Moreau* adapts the 1896 H. G. Wells novel of that title.

1978 United States: *Invasion of the Body Snatchers* is an effective remake of the 1956 classic. With *Return from Witch Mountain* and *The Cat from Outer Space,* Disney produces two benevolent alien-invasion narratives in one year. *Capricorn One* features a hoax landing on Mars. Nazi scientists try to clone Hitler in *The Boys from Brazil.*

1979 Australia: *Mad Max* initiates an influential postapocalyptic sequence. **France/Great Britain:** *Moonraker* is the most science fictional of all the James Bond films. **Soviet Union:** Tarkovsky's *Stalker* is a haunting evocation of the strange "Zone," whose bizarre properties might have been the result of an earlier alien landing. **United States:** *Alien* brings a new gritty realism to sf film action and introduces a new feminist sf icon in Sigourney Weaver's Ripley. *Star Trek: The Motion Picture* brings the classic TV series to the big screen. Disney forays into big-budget adult science fiction with *The Black Hole. Meteor* is a science fiction disaster film. Robert Altman directs the offbeat postapocalyptic film *Quintet. Parts: The Clonus Horror* is a dystopian film with an emphasis on cloning.

1980 Great Britain/United States: *Flash Gordon* is a campy feature-length adaptation of the 1930s serials. **Japan:** The plague film *Virus* is the most expensive Japanese film to date, but is an international box-office failure. **United States:** The success of *The Empire Strikes Back* solidifies the status of the *Star Wars* franchise as an sf phenomenon. Roger Corman's *Battle Beyond the Stars* tries to cash in on the phenomenon. *Saturn 3* does likewise, with a bigger budget, but makes little impact. Playmate Dorothy Stratten stars in *Galaxina,* a parody of *Star Wars* and other recent sf hits.

1981 Australia: *Mad Max 2* (released in the United States as *The Road Warrior*) is a major hit, propelling Mel Gibson to stardom. **Canada:** David Cronenberg's *Scanners* is an sf film with a definite horror twist. **Canada/United States:** The animated *Heavy Metal* adapts the cult-favorite comic book of the same title. **United States:** John Carpenter's *Escape from New York* is an ultraviolent postapocalyptic action film featuring former Disney kid star Kurt Russell. *Outland* is something of a science fiction Western.

1982   Canada: David Cronenberg's *Videodrome* will become a cult classic. **Italy:** *1990: I guerrieri del Bronx* (*1990: The Bronx Warriors*) and *I nuovi barbari* (*The New Barbarians*) initiate a cycle of violent postapocalyptic films from Italy. **United States:** Ridley Scott's *Blade Runner* will become the model for virtually all cinematic depictions of the urban future. This year, perhaps the richest single year in the history of science fiction film, also sees the release of Steven Spielberg's *E.T. the Extra-Terrestrial* and *Star Trek: The Wrath of Khan.* Disney's *Tron* points toward computer-generated special effects of the future, while Clint Eastwood's *Firefox* demonstrates that special-effects technologies are already sufficiently advanced to generate effective sf action-thrillers. John Carpenter remakes *The Thing from Another World* as *The Thing.*

1983   Canada/United States: *Strange Invaders* gently spoofs the alien invasion subgenre. **France:** Luc Besson shows a special visual flair with the black-and-white postapocalyptic film *Le dernier combat* (*The Last Combat*). **France/Yugoslavia:** *Le prix du danger* (*The Danger Prize*) satirizes the media and is a forerunner of *The Running Man.* **Italy:** *2019—Dopo la caduta di New York* (*2019, After the Fall of New York*) and *Fuga dal Bronx* (*Escape from the Bronx*) are further entries in the spate of postapocalyptic films that marked the early 1980s. **United States:** *Return of the Jedi* completes the first *Star Wars* trilogy. Computers and human brains interface in *Brainstorm*, a proto-cyberpunk film. Lizzie Borden's *Born in Flames* is a radical feminist sf film.

1984   Great Britain: *1984* adapts George Orwell's dystopian classic to film. **Great Britain/United States:** James Cameron's *The Terminator* initiates a major new sf film franchise—and makes Arnold Schwarzenegger a star. **Japan:** Hayao Miyazaki's ambitious *Kaze no tani no Naushika* (*Nausicaä of the Valley of the Wind*) brings the postapocalyptic narrative to animated film. **Poland:** *Sexmission* is a satirical time-travel sex comedy. **United States:** *Star Trek III: The Search for Spock* continues that franchise. *2010* is a sequel to *2001: A Space Odyssey.* David Lynch's adaptation of Frank Herbert's classic sf novel *Dune* is not generally well received. *Night of the Comet, Repo Man,* and *The Adventures of Buckaroo Banzai Across the Eighth Dimension* all seem custom-designed to become cult hits. *The Brother from Another Planet* is similarly offbeat, but makes serious comments about racism. Michael Crichton's *Runaway* deals with some of the same themes as *The Terminator,* but less successfully.

1985   Australia/United States: *Mad Max Beyond Thunderdome* completes the important postapocalyptic sequence. **Great Britain:** *Brazil* is Terry Gilliam's off-beat take on the dystopian film. **Great Britain/ United States:** Tobe Hooper's *Lifeforce* combines the alien-invasion narrative with the vampire narrative. **New Zealand:** *The Quiet Earth* is New Zealand's version of the last-man-on-earth film. **United States:** The time-travel comedy *Back to the Future* becomes a major pop-cultural phenomenon. *Enemy Mine* uses outer-space adventure to promote racial tolerance. *Cocoon* is a kind and gentle take on the alien-invasion narrative. *Real Genius, My Science Project,* and *Weird Science* are sf comedies for the teen market.

1986   Canada/United States: David Cronenberg remakes *The Fly.* **Soviet Union:** *Kin-dza-dza!* is a comic dystopian film that satirizes numerous aspects of Soviet life, though it satirizes the capitalist alternative as well. **United States:** Cameron's *Aliens* proves the viability of the *Alien* concept as the basis for a franchise. *Star Trek IV: The Voyage Home* is one of the more successful films in that franchise. Tobe Hooper remakes *Invaders from Mars* with a horror twist. *Short Circuit* is a successful sf romantic comedy.

1987   United States: Paul Verhoeven's *Robocop* is one of the highlights of 1980s sf film, though its two sequels will be highly forgettable. Mel Brooks's *Spaceballs* effectively spoofs *Star Wars* and similar films. The Schwarzenegger vehicle *Predator* is a violent alien-invasion/combat narrative. The film **batteries not included* is a family-oriented alien-invasion narrative, somewhat in the tradition of *Cocoon. Cherry 2000* goes in the other direction with a violent postapocalyptic narrative.

1988   Australia: In *Incident at Raven's Gate* acclaimed Australian director Rolf de Heer tries his hand at a blend of horror and alien invasion. **Japan:** The dystopian-postapocalyptic manga series *Akira* is successfully adapted as an anime film. **United States:** John Carpenter's *They Live* is a low-budget alien-invasion film that manages some highly effective political satire. *Alien Nation* combines the alien invasion narrative with the police drama.

1989 Italy: Humans battle aliens for sport in *Arena*. **Japan:** *Kidô keisatsu patorebâ: The Movie* (*Patlabor: The Movie*) continues the output of anime sf. **United States:** James Cameron's *The Abyss* combines the alien-invasion narrative with the undersea adventure, and breaks new technical ground in underwater filmmaking. *Leviathan* is an undersea monster movie, as is *DeepStar Six*. The *Star Trek* franchise begins to show its age in *Star Trek V: The Final Frontier*. *Cyborg* tries to piggyback on the success of Cameron's earlier *The Terminator*. *Back to the Future Part II* continues the lighthearted time-travel sequence. *Millennium* is a more serious time-travel narrative. Disney re-enters the sf business with *Honey, I Shrunk the Kids*. *Bill & Ted's Excellent Adventure* is a successful teen-oriented time-travel comedy.

1990 Germany/United States: *Moon 44* is an early effort from Roland Emmerich. **Great Britain/United States:** *Hardware* attempts to bring cyberpunk to film. **Spain:** *The Rift* is an entry in the undersea monster movie subgenre. **United States:** *Back to the Future Part III* completes the *Back to the Future* sequence. Verhoeven's *Total Recall* is one of the more successful of the film adaptations of the work of Philip K. Dick. *The Handmaid's Tale* adapts Margaret Atwood's feminist dystopian novel. *Spaced Invaders* spoofs the alien-invasion narrative. *Robocop 2* is a widely panned sequel.

1991 Australia/France/Germany: Renowned filmmaker Wim Wenders tries his hand at cyberpunk in *Bis ans Ende der Welt* (*Until the End of the World*). **France/United States:** *Terminator 2: Judgment Day* is a highly successful continuation of the *Terminator* sequence. **Japan:** *Godzilla vs. King Ghidora* pits classic monsters against an invading alien. **United States:** *Eve of Destruction* is a less-than-successful effort at cyberpunk film. A classic franchise continues to decline in *Star Trek VI: The Undiscovered Country*.

1992 Hong Kong: *The Wicked City* is a high-action alien-invasion thriller. **United States:** David Fincher's *Alien³* brings a noir sensibility to the *Alien* sequence. *Freejack* is a time-travel, cyberpunk film with rocker Mick Jagger as a key villain. *Honey, I Blew Up the Kid* is another Disney size-change film.

1993 United States: The computer-generated dinosaurs of Spielberg's *Jurassic Park* are a special-effects sensation. *Body Snatchers* is a second remake of *Invasion of the Body Snatchers*. *Demolition Man* is a dystopian film with entertaining moments. *Fortress* is a dystopian film with an artificial-intelligence motif.

1994 United States: *Star Trek: Generations* passes the baton for the film franchise to the cast of *Star Trek: The Next Generation*. Roland Emmerich moves into the realm of big-budget sf with *Stargate*. *Death Machine* recalls both *Robocop* and *The Terminator* in its campy exploration of cyborg and robot themes. *No Escape* recalls the violent postapocalyptic films of the 1980s. *Timecop* is a hybrid of the time-travel and police action genres.

1995 Japan: *Kôkaku kidôtai* (*Ghost in the Shell*) successfully brings cyberpunk to anime. **United States:** Terry Gilliam's *Twelve Monkeys* brings the concepts of *La jetée* to mainstream film. *Johnny Mnemonic* attempts to bring the cyberpunk fiction of William Gibson to film. *Strange Days* also draws on cyberpunk. *Outbreak* is a big-budget, plague-scare film. *Species* is an erotic alien-invasion thriller. *Screamers* is an action film loosely based on a story by Philip K. Dick. *Waterworld* is a postapocalyptic film with most of the earth under water; it is a bust in the United States but a huge hit in Japan. *Virtuosity* is a thriller with a virtual-reality main theme.

1996 Great Britain/Ireland/United States: *Space Truckers* is an effective space opera that also spoofs its own genre, while satirically addressing a number of issues. **United States:** *Independence Day* is a blockbuster alien-invasion–disaster film hit, quickly followed by Tim Burton's *Mars Attacks!*, a highly successful spoof of the same genre. *The Arrival* is a competent alien-invasion film. *Star Trek: First Contact* is the first film in the franchise devoted entirely to the new cast. *Escape from L.A.* is John Carpenter's followup to the much earlier *Escape from New York*. *The Island of Dr. Moreau* features Marlon Brando, but little else of note. *Multiplicity* is a cloning comedy.

1997 France: Luc Besson's *The Fifth Element* is a stylish space opera–alien-invasion film with a liberal dose of campy humor. **Great Britain/United States:** *Event Horizon* is an ambitious combination of science fiction and horror. **Spain:** *Abre los ojos* (*Open Your Eyes*) is an effective alternative-reality film. **United States:** Jean-Pierre Jeunet's *Alien: Resurrection* is the quirkiest of the *Alien* films. *Gattaca* is a dystopian film that addresses issues related to genetic engineering. *Men in Black* becomes the most commercially successful sf comedy in cinema history. Verhoeven's *Starship Troopers* brings Robert A. Heinlein's most controversial novel to film. *Contact* is a philosophical alien-invasion narrative based on the novel by astronomer Carl Sagan. *The Postman* is a big-budget postapocalyptic film. *The Sticky Fingers of Time* is an interesting time-travel narrative.

1998 Australia/United States: Alex Proyas's *Dark City* questions the nature of reality with some of the most effective urban noir scenes since *Blade Runner*. **Japan:** *Andromedia* is a cyberpunk crime drama. **United States:** *Armageddon* is a big-budget, effects-driven disaster film from Michael Bay. Roland Emmerich's similarly effects-driven remake of *Godzilla* is similarly panned by critics. *Deep Impact* is another sf disaster film. *Sphere* brings Hollywood glamour to the undersea adventure. *Star Trek: Insurrection* suggests that the franchise is in decline. *The X-Files* brings the alien-invasion television drama to the big screen. Robert Rodriguez combines alien invasion, horror, and teen angst in *The Faculty*. *Six-String Samurai* is a truly original postapocalyptic narrative. *The Truman Show* is only marginally science fictional, but raises numerous important questions and gets a great deal of attention. *Lost in Space* attempts an adaptation of the 1960s television series. *New Rose Hotel* is another adaptation of the cyberpunk fiction of William Gibson.

1999 Australia/United States: *The Matrix* is the first truly successful cyberpunk film. **Canada/Great Britain:** Cronenberg's *eXistenZ,* focusing on video gaming, is one of several end-of-the-century films featuring virtual-reality motifs. **United States:** *Star Wars: Episode I— The Phantom Menace* begins the second *Star Wars* trilogy with a huge commercial success. *Bicentennial Man* probes the boundary between man and machine, but without the edgy sensibilities of cyberpunk. *The Thirteenth Floor* is another virtual reality film. *The Matrix* becomes the most successful virtual reality film of all, with strong cyberpunk elements. The animated children's film *The Iron Giant* engages in dialogue with the tradition of paranoid cold war alien-invasion narratives. *The Astronaut's Wife* is an alien-invasion thriller that looks back to the paranoid films of earlier years. *Deep Blue Sea* is another undersea monster movie. *Galaxy Quest* spoofs the fan culture, especially that surrounding *Star Trek*.

2000   United States: Brian De Palma tries his hand at outer-space adventure in *Mission to Mars,* a film with strong echoes of *2001: A Space Odyssey. Red Planet* also narrates a trip to Mars. The animated space opera *Titan A.E.* is a commercial failure, but points toward interesting possibilities. Verhoeven's *Hollow Man* is strong on special effects, but otherwise a critical failure. *Pitch Black* is an action thriller with some thoughtful elements.

2001   Japan: *Kaubôi bibappu: Tengoku no tobira (Cowboy Bebop: The Movie)* is a notable anime film based on the television series of the same title. **Japan/Poland:** *Avalon* is another take on the video game as alternative reality. **Japan/United States:** *Final Fantasy: The Spirits Within* brings the Japanese role-playing game to the big screen—and is the first attempt to make a photorealistic animated sf film. **United States:** Spielberg's *Artificial Intelligence: AI* brings Kubrick's original conception of a film about a sentient robot-child to the screen. Tim Burton remakes *Planet of the Apes* with a huge budget and spectacular visuals, but it still fails to measure up to the original. *Donnie Darko* is a time-travel reality bender that quickly becomes a cult favorite. Disney's *Atlantis: The Lost Empire* is an animated version of the retro sf adventure film. David Duchovny stars in the alien-invasion comedy *Evolution,* partly a spoof of *The X-Files,* in which he starred on television. John Carpenter's *Ghosts of Mars* is a violent entry in the monsters-on-Mars subgenre. *Vanilla Sky* remakes *Abre los ojos.*

2002   Great Britain: *28 Days Later* is Danny Boyle's take on the postapocalyptic zombie film. **South Korea:** *2009: Lost Memories* is an elaborate alternate history narrative; *Yesterday* is a slick, violent, big-budget sf thriller. Together, the films put Korea on the international map of sf film. **United States:** Spielberg's *Minority Report* is an effective dystopian thriller. *Men in Black II* is another commercial success, but adds little to the original. A remake of *Solaris* fails to capture the profundity of the Soviet original. *Star Trek: Nemesis* sends the franchise into a seven-year hiatus and ends the run of the *Next Generation* cast. *Star Wars: Episode II—Attack of the Clones* continues science fiction film's most lucrative franchise. *Equilibrium* is a stylish dystopian thriller with fight scenes influenced by *The Matrix*. *Resident Evil* is a zombie action film with strong science fiction elements. M. Night Shyamalan's *Signs* is an alien-invasion narrative with religious overtones. *Reign of Fire* is a postapocalyptic film in which the apocalypse is caused by dragons. Disney's *Treasure Planet* transplants *Treasure Island* into outer space. *Teknolust* is a cloning film with strong comic elements.

2003   Australia/United States: *The Matrix Reloaded* and *The Matrix Revolutions* complete the important cyberpunk sequence. **Germany/Great Britain/United States:** *Terminator 3: Rise of the Machines* is the low point of the *Terminator* sequence. **Great Britain:** *Code 46* is a dystopian film with cyberpunk elements. **South Korea:** The futuristic *Natural City* quickly gains a reputation as the "Korean *Blade Runner*." **United States:** John Woo's *Paycheck* is one of the least successful of the film adaptations of the work of Philip K. Dick. *Timeline* is a time-travel film based on a novel by Michael Crichton.

2004   France: *Immortel (ad vitam)* combines animation with live-action shot in front of green screens to break new technological ground in its depiction of a dystopian future. **Great Britain/Italy/United States:** The relatively big-budget *Sky Captain and the World of Tomorrow* is shot entirely in front of green screens, and includes one computer-generated character. **Japan:** *Casshern* employs much the same technology as the French *Immortel*. *Innocence: Ghost in the Shell* is a sequel to the anime classic, becoming the first animated film nominated for the Palme d'Or at the Cannes Film Festival. *Appurushîdo (Appleseed)* is another successful anime sf film. **United States:** Big-budget special effects dramatize the consequences of global warming in *The Day After Tomorrow*. *I, Robot* is a stylish special-effects thriller that has little to do with the Isaac Asimov book from which it takes its title. The low-budget *Able Edwards* joins the year's demonstration of the possibilities of green-screen technologies for sf filmmaking. *Primer* is an interesting, low-budget time-travel film. *The Butterfly Effect* is a less interesting time-travel film with a bigger budget. *Alien vs. Predator* combines two violent sf franchises. *The Chronicles of Riddick* is a violent sequel to *Pitch Black,* without the added nuances of the original.

2005 Austria/France/Germany/Great Britain: Werner Herzog's *The Wild Blue Yonder* is an unusual alien invasion narrative composed mostly of re-edited documentary footage. **Czech Republic/Germany/ Great Britain/United States:** *Doom* is a violent adaptation of a violent video game involving genetically engineered monsters on Mars. **Great Britain/United States:** *The Hitchhiker's Guide to the Galaxy* is a much-awaited adaptation that nevertheless makes little impact. **United States:** *Star Wars: Episode III—Revenge of the Sith* completes the second *Star Wars* trilogy. Steven Spielberg remakes *War of the Worlds* with state-of-the-art special effects to lukewarm critical response. A low-budget adaptation released in the same year as H. G. Wells's *The War of the Worlds,* is truer to the novel, but widely panned. Joss Whedon's *Serenity* brings the *Firefly* television series to the big screen. Michael Bay's *The Island* is a special-effects driven dystopian thriller that many saw as suspiciously similar to *Parts: The Clonus Horror* (1979). *Æon Flux* is a stylish dystopian thriller, with little substance, a live-action adaptation of an animated TV series. *Robots* is an animated children's film set in a world populated entirely by robots. The children's space adventure film *Zathura* is more fantasy than science fiction.

2006   Great Britain/Japan/United States: *Children of Men* is a stylish contemporary take on the postapocalyptic and dystopian genres. **Japan:** The animated, teen-oriented time-travel film *Toki o kakeru shôjo* (*The Girl Who Leapt through Time*) wins numerous awards. **United States:** *A Scanner Darkly* is an unusually faithful adaptation of a novel by Philip K. Dick. Richard Kelly's *Southland Tales* is a truly original near-future dystopian puzzler. Darren Aronofsky's *The Fountain* is a visually impressive but conceptually muddled narrative that weaves together three different narratives set in vastly different times. *Slither* combines horror and alien-invasion narratives. *V for Vendetta* is a controversial dystopian film that transplants Alan Moore's graphic novel into the 21st century. *Ultraviolet* is a fast-paced dystopian action film, designed to look as if it were based on a comic book, though it wasn't.

Mike Judge's *Idiocracy* is a mostly silly dystopian spoof that nevertheless makes some serious satirical points.

2007 France: *Chrysalis* is a near-future crime thriller. **Great Britain/Spain/United States:** *28 Weeks Later* continues the violent zombie action of *28 Days Later* (2002). **Great Britain/United States:** Danny Boyle's *Sunshine* is an ambitious space opera–disaster film. **United States:** Michael Bay's *Transformers* is a huge hit at the box office. *I Am Legend* features Will Smith as the last man on earth in the third film adaptation of the 1954 Richard Matheson novel of that title. *The Invasion* is basically the third remake of the original *Invasion of the Body Snatchers* (1956). Disney's *Meet the Robinsons* is a time-travel adventure for kids.

2008 Germany: *Far Cry* is a video-game adaptation about genetically engineered super soldiers. **Great Britain:** *Doomsday* looks back, with a wink, to the violent postapocalyptic films of the 1980s. **India:** *Love Story 2050* is a time-travel narrative from Bollywood. **Mexico:** The dystopian film *Sleep Dealer* effectively satirizes U.S. attitudes toward immigration. **United States:** A remake of *The Day the Earth Stood Still* (1951) attempts to recast the original warnings about the arms race into warnings about environmental destruction. M. Night Shyamalan's *The Happening* is another environmentalist cautionary tale. *Cloverfield* is an inventive alien-invasion–monster movie hybrid. *Jumper* is a high-action teleportation thriller. *The X-Files: I Want to Believe* leaves few believing in the future potential of that film franchise. The animated *Star Wars: The Clone Wars* adds another chapter to that franchise. Pixar's animated *WALL-E* provides a striking demonstration of the potential of computer-generated imagery for sf film.

2009 Germany/Great Britain/Italy/United States: *Terminator Salvation* reboots the franchise in the postapocalyptic future. **Great Britain/United States:** Alex Proyas's *Knowing* depicts the end of the earth, but aliens help relocate the survivors of the human species. **New Zealand/United States:** *District 9* is a thoughtful alien-invasion narrative that provides commentaries on racism and capitalist greed. **United States** J. J. Abrams's *Star Trek* prequel resurrects the film franchise with its biggest commercial success. Michael Bay's second *Transformers* film, *Transformers: Revenge of the Fallen,* again does big business at the box office but gets little respect from critics. *Moon* is an effective futuristic thriller. *The Time Traveler's Wife* is a romantic drama about an inadvertent time traveler. *Battle for Terra* (initially given a limited release in 2007, but released more widely in 2009) is an animated film for adults that provides serious reflections on colonialism and environmentalism. The visually inventive *9*, an animated postapocalyptic film, is also suitable mostly for adults. The animated alien-invasion film *Monsters vs. Aliens* is mostly for kids, however, as is the live-action *Aliens in the Attic*. The animated *Planet 51*, also for kids, reverses the alien-invasion theme as a human from earth lands on another planet. James Cameron's *Avatar*, the breakthrough 3-D sf epic, is released in December 2009, after more than four years of production (although the screenplay was written in 1994).

Introduction

The history of science fiction (sf) film now spans more than 100 years, during which time more than 1000 science fiction films of various kinds have been made, thanks to the contributions of filmmakers from around the world. Beginning with the work of pioneering French filmmaker Georges Méliès at the dawn of the 20th century (and of film itself) and moving through silent film highlights such as Fritz Lang's German expressionist classic *Metropolis,* sf film has had a long and eventful history that has taken it in many directions but that has moved the genre inexorably forward into a prominent place at the center of the film industry in the works of big-budget hitmakers such as George Lucas, Steven Spielberg, and Michael Bay. With European filmmakers initially on the forefront in the age of silent film, science fiction film has moved through a period of almost total dominance by Hollywood, beginning in the 1950s and continuing into the current era of intense globalization in which the emergence of new sf cinemas in Asia, Australia, and Europe has been accompanied by an increased tendency toward international co-production of science fiction films—partly because the films themselves have demonstrated a broad international box-office appeal. This movement has been accompanied by a gradual expansion of sf film into a wide variety of subgenres and into the exploration of numerous themes, many of which have fundamental social, political, and philosophical significance. At the same time, the versatility of science fiction film has allowed it to expand into a variety of different markets, appealing to age groups from small children to adults and to filmgoers of a variety of tastes, from those looking for simple, escapist entertainment to those looking to have their minds challenged and expanded. Finally, science fiction cinema has moved to the forefront of filmmaking technology, leading the way in technical advances that have enabled a new sophistication in the kind of visual effects for which sf film has become particularly well known in recent decades—but which have made important contributions to the evolution of other film genres as well.

SCIENCE FICTION FILM IN THE SILENT ERA

Méliès, a magician by trade, recognized early that images could be manipulated on film to create the kind of illusions that he could only dream of creating in the real world. Subsequently, Méliès made dozens of films that explored the potential of these illusions (what we now call *special effects*) to create visual fantasies for his audiences. In so doing, he made the first science fiction films. By 1902, he had made what is still his best-known film, the whimsical 14-minute fantasy *Le voyage dans la lune* (*A Trip to the Moon*), based on an 1865 novel by Jules Verne. Thus, given that Méliès was one of the very first filmmakers and that modern sf is often considered to have originated in the "scientific romances" of H. G. Wells in the period 1895–1905, it can fairly be said that science fiction film is essentially as old as film itself and virtually as old as science fiction itself. Meanwhile, in just over 100 years since the early work of Méliès, science fiction film has become one of the most important genres of world cinema, producing thrilling adventures, thoughtful explorations of serious social and political issues, and some of the biggest box-office hits of all time.

Following the work of Méliès, other films that might be described as *science fiction* quickly began to appear, though most early science fiction films spanned the boundary between sf and horror. Indeed, science fiction is notoriously hard to define as a genre, and the boundary between science fiction and other genres (especially horror and fantasy) can be vague and permeable. Still, most fans and scholars of sf have a fairly good working ability to distinguish works that they consider to be science fiction from works that are not. To a first approximation, one might say that science fiction is fiction that takes place in worlds that operate according to the same physical principles as our own but that differ from our own in ways that are rationally explicable, often (but not always) as the result of the discovery of scientific principles or the development of technologies unknown in our world. *Fantasy fiction,* meanwhile, typically takes place in worlds that operate according to a logic of their own; fantasy worlds thus need not obey the physical laws of our universe. As such, the boundary between sf and fantasy seems to be firm, and is essentially defined by the boundary between science and magic.

However, that boundary itself can sometimes be permeable, and it is certainly the case that images and motifs typically associated with fantasy (such as dragons or demons) can sometimes be found within works that would otherwise be categorized as science fiction, while the robots, spaceships, and other hardware typically associated with science fiction can sometimes appear within works that otherwise have the texture of fantasy. Horror fiction, one might say, also occurs in a world similar to our own, but involves monstrous and terrifying intrusions of supernatural (or at least extraordinary) forces that one would not expect to encounter in the real world. When these monstrous forces are unleashed as the result of scientifically explicable events (as is quite often the case with monster movies), then the boundary between horror and sf has been breached and the work involved belongs to both genres.

Many of the early science fiction films of the silent film era are hybrids of sf and horror, partly because science fiction as we know it did not fully develop as an identifiable genre until the 1930s. Thus, one of the first American science fiction films, produced by the Edison studio in 1910, was an adaptation of Mary Shelley's 1818 novel *Frankenstein,* often considered to be the first science fiction novel, but often associated with the horror genre as well. In 1920, the German expressionist movement in film reached one of its high points with the production of *Das Kabinett des Doktor Caligari* (*The Cabinet of Dr. Caligari*), which deals with a sort of mad scientist, but that, more importantly, features extreme lighting and distorted sets that effectively combine to create a mood of strangeness and horror.

Similar techniques were put to good use in Fritz Lang's *Metropolis* (1927), in many ways the culmination of German expressionist cinema and a film that is widely regarded as the first truly great work of science fiction cinema. *Metropolis* involves a towering futuristic city in which the rich live in utopian luxury while legions of poor workers slave away like automatons beneath the surface, tending the gigantic machines that power the golden world above. The film includes numerous visions of advanced technology, but also importantly explores the social and political consequences of that technology. The success of *Metropolis* led to the development of other science fiction films as well, including one,

Alraune, that was made as a silent film in 1928, then remade (with the same star, Brigitte Helm, who played the female lead in *Metropolis*) as a sound film in 1930.

Another science fictional highlight of the silent era in American film was *The Lost World,* based on a novel by Sir Arthur Conan Doyle and featuring some groundbreaking special effects in its vision of a lost enclave inhabited by dinosaurs. The other great science fiction film of the silent era was *Aelita: Queen of Mars,* released in the Soviet Union in 1924 during a period of exciting postrevolutionary activity in Soviet film as a whole. However, as the sound era arrived at the beginning of the 1930s, film received less and less priority in Soviet culture, while the rise of Adolf Hitler and the Nazis curtailed much of the most innovative activity in German cinema as well. Instead, the center of the film industry shifted to Hollywood, which began, during this dark and troubled decade, to exert its dominance in world cinema, even if that dominance did not really extend to science fiction film until the 1950s.

THE EARLY SOUND ERA AND THE
SCIENCE FICTION FILM BOOM OF THE 1950s

The first American science fiction film of the sound era was *Just Imagine* (1930), a musical comedy that features a mission to Mars but treats its science fictional material in a lighthearted manner that shows little real interest in the future potential for space exploration. *It's Great to Be Alive* (1933) had something of the same texture. Clearly, Hollywood was not at this time taking sf seriously as a potential film genre. The most important American science fiction films of the early 1930s were the series of monster movies produced in that period, especially *Frankenstein* (1931) and *King Kong* (1933), which had particularly strong science fictional elements, the monster in the first being produced as a result of scientific experimentation and in the second by evolution. These landmark films set the standard for the future development of the monster-movie genre and are still being viewed (and remade) in the 21st century. Also of particular note in the 1930s was the phenomenon of movie serials, which were particularly popular in the United States in the 1930s and which often featured science fictional themes, as in the Flash Gordon and Buck Rogers serials released between 1936 and 1940.

British science fiction films began to make a contribution to the development of the genre in the 1930s as well. Indeed, the British-produced *Things to Come* (1936), scripted by Wells and based on his own 1933 novel *The Shape of Things to Come,* is widely considered to be the first major science fiction film in English. All in all, however, the 1930s and 1940s were not particularly productive decades for science fiction film, even though the evolution of pulp magazines featuring sf stories, especially in the United States, made major contributions to the evolution of science fiction as a genre during this period.

Coming out of World War II and extending forward into the 1960s, science itself began to gain an unprecedented prominence in the popular consciousness, partly because of technologies developed during the war. The development of nuclear weapons during the war suddenly made the wholesale destruction of human civilization a more immediate threat than it had ever been before; meanwhile, advances in rocketry made during the war made space flight seem an impending reality as well. Computers, the technology for which developed rapidly during the war, were also becoming a more and more important part of modern life. Finally, continual advances in technology led to the development of home appliances and other devices that were changing the texture of day-to-day life, especially in the United States and other advanced Western nations, where booming postwar economies were also making such devices more and more affordable.

All of this occurred as written sf was moving into the latter stages of what came to be regarded as a Golden Age, with the science fiction novel becoming an important publishing phenomenon for the first time in the 1950s. It should come as no surprise, then, that science fiction film experienced an unprecedented boom during the 1950s as well. The decade got off to a fast start in 1950 as the space exploration dramas *Destination Moon* (scripted by Robert A. Heinlein and based on his 1947 novel *Rocket Ship Galileo*) and *Rocketship X-M* raced to get into theaters first, oddly anticipating the space race that was to come in the following years. These films also announced the beginning of an avalanche of sf films that for many came to be regarded as the most distinctive phenomenon in American film of the 1950s. In 1951 alone, three major sf films were released: the alien-invasion drama *The Thing from Another World;* the cosmic disaster film *When Worlds Collide;* and the thoughtful *The Day the Earth Stood Still,* which provided a rare statement against the cold war arms race. Arch Oboler's *Five,* also released in 1951, was a low-budget effort but was important as the first cold war–era film to depict the aftereffects of a nuclear apocalypse.

The coming years saw a continuation of this boom in the production of American science fiction films, the bulk of which had themes that were clearly related to the cold war–driven concerns of the time. Alien-invasion films—which echoed the paranoid fear that the United States was threatened by dangerous and nefarious enemies on all sides—were particularly prominent, as were postapocalyptic films that clearly related to the sense of a possible coming nuclear holocaust. This same paranoia informed the numerous monster movies produced during the decade, which often featured monsters created by radiation or some other form of scientific or technological mishap. On the other hand, other important films of the decade, while sometimes acknowledging the perceived external threats that exercised such a hold on the American imagination in the 1950s, also directly addressed more domestic anxieties, as when *The Incredible Shrinking Man* (1957) drew energy from the embattled state of American masculinity as traditional gender roles were more and more called into question. Meanwhile, *Invasion of the Body Snatchers* (1956), often seen as a paradigmatic expression of cold war anticommunist hysteria, could also be read as an expression of anxieties over other domestic threats, including anticommunism itself, as well as the growing routinization of life in America.

Over the course of the 1950s, American science fiction film came to be regarded by many in Hollywood as especially suitable fare for the teenage audiences that were becoming an increasingly important segment of the filmgoing demographic. This vein included interesting films such as *The Blob* (1958), but most of the films produced in the late 1950s for teen audiences were low-budget affairs, often laughably bad as films, quickly made and distributed for showings as double features in drive-ins. New companies, such as American International Pictures, became important players in the sf film industry as the result of their participation in this market. Some of the films produced by such companies showed flashes of genius (or at least gave experience to rising new talents on both sides of the camera). As a whole, though, the science fiction films of the 1950s are still often associated in the public mind (not entirely unfairly) with cheap effects, bad acting, and ludicrous scripts—as in the case of Ed Wood's *Plan 9 from Outer Space* (1959), often identified as the worst film ever made.

The output of British science fiction film also increased in the 1950s, though not nearly to the same extent as American sf film. This new output included several films produced by Hammer Film Productions, including the noir-inflected *Spaceways* (1953) and two spinoffs of a British sf television series, *The Quatermass Xperiment* (1955), and *Quatermass 2* (1957). Of course, Hammer's most important contribution came in the realm of horror, though many of their horror films, such as a revamped *Frankenstein* sequence, contained strong science fiction elements as well.

By the late 1950s, the sf film boom was becoming a truly international phenomenon. Beginning with *Godzilla* in 1954, Japanese monster movies gained a worldwide audience, and the Japanese began to make inroads into other genres of science fiction as well. Science fiction films were also being produced in the Soviet Union, East Germany, and Italy. The beginnings of the globalization of science fiction could also be seen in this period in the growing number of films that were international co-productions, involving financial support, talent, and distribution from two or more different countries. Thus, *La morte viene dallo spazio* (1958, *The Day the Sky Exploded*), which is generally regarded as the first Italian sf film, was actually a French-Italian co-production with important support from Compagnie Cinématagraphique de France. It also featured two Swiss actors in key roles. In addition, several Soviet, East German, and Italian films made during this period were later reworked into English versions (via dubbing, re-editing, and some added footage) for the low-budget American market.

1960S TO *STAR WARS*

Science fiction film in the 1960s was much less distinctive than in the 1950s and less dominated by the United States. As a whole, there were fewer films spread over a wider variety of genres, while international co-productions continued to be more and more common, somewhat diluting the differences between films from different nations. In the

United States, American International Pictures began to shift away from science fiction and into horror, beach movies, and other teen genres, while the major studies tended to stay away from science fiction. There were, however, some fairly expensive films for general audiences at the beginning of the decade. Disney, meanwhile, began to explore the science fiction film market for children and families. The British television series *Dr. Who* spread into theatrical film, while British studios also produced a number of alien-invasion films that were as much horror as science fiction, paralleling in this sense the continuing development of Italian science fiction film.

For a time in the mid-1960s, it might be argued that British science fiction film equaled American science fiction film in importance, though such comparisons are hard to make because the line between British and American sf film was increasingly diffuse. The most important British sf films of the first half of the 1960s, both released in 1964, were *First Men in the Moon,* a relatively high-budget adaptation of H. G. Wells's novel of the same title, and Stanley Kubrick's hilarious satire *Dr. Strangelove or: How I Learned to Stop Worrying and Love the Bomb,* which became the definitive film about the folly of the cold-war arms race. The first of these, set largely in late Victorian England, has a very British feel and includes a mostly British cast, though the female lead was an American actress (Martha Hyer) and the director, Nathan Juran, was an American, a veteran of the 1950s sf film boom. *Dr. Strangelove,* meanwhile, was officially a British production, filmed at Shepperton Studios in London and featuring British actor Peter Sellers as the lead cast member. However, it was made with financial backing from U.S.-based Columbia Pictures and set in the United States, with mostly American actors and an American director, though Kubrick spent much of his career living and working in the United Kingdom.

A similar complexity in nationality applies to *Fahrenheit 451* (1966), officially a British production, shot mostly at Pinewood Studios in England, but with a French director (François Truffaut). Meanwhile, it was based on an American novel and featured an Austrian star. In addition, the most important sf film made in Great Britain in the 1960s was officially a U.S.-UK co-production, Kubrick's *2001: A Space Odyssey* (1968). This landmark film was an important reminder of the aesthetic potential of science fiction film, while also looking all the way back to Méliès in its use of visual effects to introduce filmgoers to a world of wonder far beyond their everyday experience. *2001* combined with the American-produced *Planet of the Apes,* released in the same year, to suggest the possibility of a coming renaissance in science fiction film. That renaissance did, in fact, occur to some extent, as the early 1970s saw the release of such important sf films as Andrei Tarkovsky's haunting Soviet film *Solaris* (1972), based on the meditative sf novel by Polish sf master Stanisław Lem. Despite such examples, though, the early 1970s saw the return of American science fiction film to a position of global dominance. Disney produced a trilogy of lighthearted sf family films starring Kurt Russell in the period 1969–1975, but American sf films as a whole, responding to a Vietnam War– and Watergate-fueled darkness in the national mindset at the time, took a pessimistic turn toward emphasis on dystopian projections of the future. Pessimistic films of the early 1970s included four sequels to *Planet of the Apes* released between 1970 and 1973. Other key films of this period included Kubrick's *A Clockwork Orange* (1971), a British-American co-production. Other American films released in 1971 were the dystopian film *THX 1138,* the first film by George Lucas; *The Andromeda Strain,* a thriller that combines plague, alien invasion, and nuclear disaster scenarios; and *The Omega Man,* the second adaption of Richard Matheson's 1954 novel *I Am Legend,* a postapocalyptic vampire tale. Soon afterward, 1972 saw the release of *Silent Running,* one of the first major sf films to focus on environmental concerns, as well as the British production *Z.P.G.,* which focuses on the dangers of overpopulation. *Soylent Green* (1973), another dystopian film that focuses on overpopulation, ultimately became one of the most remembered of the dystopian films of the early 1970s, while Woody Allen's *Sleeper,* also released in 1973, is a spoof of those films. Meanwhile, Michael Crichton's *Westworld* (1973) also has a dystopian tone that warns of the dangers of excessive automation and computerization, while at the same time ironically making the first use of computer animation in sf film.

The pessimistic tone of sf film in the 1970s continued with the British dystopian release *Rollerball* (1975) and an additional flurry of American films: the postapocalyptic satire *A Boy and His Dog* (1975); *The Stepford Wives* (1975), which satirizes suburbia; the dystopian film *Futureworld* (1976), a sequel to *Westworld* with similar themes; and *Logan's Run* (1976), which combines the postapocalyptic and dystopian genres in what became something of a cult classic. All of that changed, however, with the release of Lucas's *Star Wars,* a film that looked back to the serials of the 1930s in its emphasis on pulpy adventure, while delivering a clear-cut victory of virtuous heroes over dastardly villains. It also employed groundbreaking special effects technologies that changed the course of science fiction film history forever.

1977–1989: A NEW GOLDEN AGE FOR SCIENCE FICTION FILM

Star Wars was a huge hit with science fiction fans of all ages and also attracted legions of new fans who had previously shown little interest in the genre. Meanwhile, even as its breakthrough special effects suggested new creative possibilities for science fiction film, its spectacular box-office success (with a domestic box-office gross of over $300 million on its first release, easily the highest of all time at that point) meant that studios of all sizes were suddenly scrambling to find promising science fiction projects. When Steven Spielberg's *Close Encounters of the Third Kind* followed later in the same year with another commercial hit that was also much more serious and aesthetically impressive, it was clear that a major renaissance in science fiction film was in full swing. This boom was particularly rich from 1977 through 1984, but really extended through the entire decade of the 1980s, especially in the United States.

Among other things, *Star Wars* is important in the history of science fiction film because it solidified the importance of franchises. Previous sequences (such as the *Creature from the Black Lagoon* films in the 1950s or the *Planet of the Apes* films in the period 1968–1973) had experienced success, but the branding effect of *Star Wars* (not only in triggering a string of hugely popular sequels, but also in founding a vast empire in other media and in the realm of licensing and merchandising) was unprecedented. Little wonder, then, that many of the films that immediately followed in the wake of *Star Wars* came with built-in franchising potential. For example, *Superman: The Movie,* released in 1978, continued a pop-culture franchise that had been in existence since the 1930s. Though not a science fiction film per se, *Superman* includes numerous science fictional elements (including the fact that Superman himself is an alien visitor from another planet). Moreover, this first film of the new *Superman* film franchise contains numerous elements that were clearly influenced by *Star Wars.*

The new science fiction film boom kicked into high gear in 1979 with the release of Ridley Scott's *Alien,* a film that originally seemed destined for low-budget treatment as a Roger Corman production, but was upgraded to A-level status as 20th Century Fox's followup to *Star Wars.* Featuring possibly the scariest sf monster ever put on film, along with the most interesting and realistic-looking spacecraft, *Alien* was a breakthrough film in a number of ways, including its focus on a physically and psychologically strong female protagonist. *Alien* looked back to earlier sf-horror hybrids, but it was an altogether original film. Ultimately, however, it participated in the new emphasis on science fiction film franchising by becoming the founding work in a franchise of its own. Meanwhile, 1979 also saw the release of *Star Trek: The Motion Picture,* a not entirely successful film that nevertheless announced the expansion of the *Star Trek* franchise into the realm of feature film, a phenomenon that, as of this writing, has produced a total of no less than 11 theatrical releases, making it the most extensive of all sf film franchises, especially if one adds in the 5 live-action television series as well as merchandising and works in a variety of other media.

The first *Star Trek* sequels, *The Wrath of Khan* (1982) and *The Search for Spock* (1984) made an important contribution to the sf film boom of 1977–1984, while *Star Trek IV: The Voyage Home* (1986) and *Star Trek V: The Final Frontier* (1989) appeared in the 1980s as well. Meanwhile, *Star Trek* became the most successful film franchise of the period with the release of *The Empire Strikes Back* (1980) and *The Return of the Jedi* (1983). The latter were again blockbuster hits, though the only film of this period to challenge the box-office success of the original *Star Wars* was Spielberg's *E.T. the Extra-Terrestrial* (1982), a sort of follow-up to *Close Encounters* that again featured benevolent aliens, but was aimed more at children and families. Of course, even during this period, science fiction films were not guaranteed to be successful, as can be seen from the case of Disney's big-budget, adult-oriented effort *The Black Hole* (1979), a critical and commercial bust.

Such failures aside, the coming few years nevertheless saw the release of an astonishing number of now-classic films. One of the crucial films of the era was a one-shot that did not initiate a franchise: Scott's *Blade Runner* (1982) exercised a powerful influence on numerous sf films that came after it. In particular, it made an indelible impression on our visions of how the future might look, especially in urban settings. *Blade Runner* combined stunning visuals with a rousing plot and a serious investigation of a number of crucial social, political, and philosophical issues, including the very definition of what it means to be human. In so doing, this important work made it clear that, whatever trends seemed to be underway, science fiction film still involved more than high-tech gun battles, impressive explosions, and other fancy special effects.

In addition to such major landmark films, the early 1980s also saw the production of a number of low-budget productions that attempted to join in on the new popularity of science fiction film. Some of these, such as the Corman-produced *Battle Beyond the Stars* (1980) were overtly derivative of major films such as *Star Wars,* yet provided moments of rousing entertainment. There were also distinctive trends outside the big-budget mainstream, such as the flurry of relatively inexpensive, but ultraviolent postapocalyptic thrillers that came out of Australia, Italy, and the United States during the first half of the 1980s.

James Cameron released *The Terminator* in 1984, a rather low-budget effort that employed an array of classic science fiction motifs in a mix that captured the popular imagination and set Arnold Schwarzenegger, who played the murderous title character, on his way to becoming the biggest star in science fiction and action films of the next decade. *The Terminator,* with its human-looking cyborg title character, followed *Blade Runner* in interrogating the boundary between humans and their technology, but managed to mix in time-travel, postapocalyptic, and horror elements as well. The "terminator" of the title was also a compelling figure that triggered a number of imitations, including Paul Verhoeven's *Robocop* (1987), a work that included a substantial amount of satire on the social and political situation in Reagan-era America, as well as providing ironic commentary on the science fiction genre itself. Indeed, one of the signs of the maturity of science fiction film as a cultural phenomenon was its growing self-consciousness during this era, as films frequently made references to other specific films or to specific science fictional traditions a key part of their content.

The Terminator also made Cameron a hot property among sf directors, leading him to become the director of *Aliens* (1986), which made *Alien* a franchise and in many ways surpassed the original film as a science fiction thriller with strong horror elements. Cameron also directed

The Abyss (1989), the sf film that topped off the decade with some of the genre's most impressive technical achievements ever, while also providing anti–arms race commentary that made it a sort of companion to *The Day the Earth Stood Still,* one film appearing near the beginning of the cold-war era and the other appearing near the end.

THE 1990s AND THE NEW MILLENNIUM

The major science fiction franchises established during the period 1977–1989 remained an important force in science fiction film over the next two decades. The *Alien* franchise, for example, continued with David Fincher's *Alien³* (1992), which added an extra noirish element to the franchise, and Jean-Pierre Jeunet's visually striking *Alien Resurrection* (1997), which added new touches of irony and humor to the sequence. The *Terminator* sequence rolled along as well. Cameron's *Terminator 2: Judgment Day* (1991) was in many ways superior to the original, though *Terminator 3: Rise of the Machines* (2003) was for many a sign that the franchise had run its course. However, a fourth film (and the first without Schwarzenegger) appeared in 2009, with *Terminator Salvation* moving the action of the sequence into the postapocalyptic future that was only hinted at in the first three films. *Star Trek* also extended into the new millennium, as *Star Trek VI: The Undiscovered Country* (1991), *Star Trek: Generations* (1994), *Star Trek: First Contact* (1996), *Star Trek: Insurrection* (1998), and *Star Trek: Nemesis* (2002) shifted the cast from that of the original 1960s television series to that of the 1987–1994 series *Star Trek: The Next Generation.* By this point, the sequence was clearly losing momentum. A 2009 prequel reboot, with the characters from the original series but set before the events of that series (and with new, younger actors), was a major hit, however, restoring the franchise to feature film health, even as it continued to have no contemporary television presence. The release of *Star Wars: Episode I—The Phantom Menace* in 1999 returned new *Star Wars* films to the theaters for the first time in 16 years; the film was a colossal hit, and two subsequent sequels—*Attack of the Clones* (2002) and *Revenge of the Sith* (2005)—were major box-office successes as well.

One of the biggest box-office successes in science fiction film of the 1990s was *Independence Day* (1996), an alien-invasion narrative with the structure of a disaster film that included a feel-good victory over the dastardly aliens by a coalition of virtuous Americans led by a heroic fantasy president. Another big hit was the alien-invasion spoof *Men in Black* the following year, one of whose stars, Will Smith, also starred in *Independence Day*. A 2002 sequel, *Men in Black II*, was also a hit but added little to the original, signaling an apparent dead-end for the franchise. Many of the nonfranchise highlights of the 1990s were especially quirky and unusual efforts, as science fiction film, after more than a decade of impressive achievement, seemed to be finding it harder and harder to break new ground. Philip K. Dick's stories and novels (one of which was the basis for *Blade Runner*) became particularly popular as source material for science fiction film during this period. The unusual Schwarzenegger vehicle *Total Recall* (1990), directed by Verhoeven, was based (very loosely) on a story by Dick, as were several relatively minor films of the next two decades, though Spielberg's *Minority Report* (2002) was the only other truly successful adaptation of Dick's writing. Other off-beat highlights of the 1990s included Terry Gilliam's postapocalyptic time-travel tale *Twelve Monkeys* (1995), Tim Burton's farcical alien-invasion narrative *Mars Attacks!* (1996), and Luc Besson's campy space opera *The Fifth Element* (1997). Alex Proyas's *Dark City* (1998) could definitely be placed in the off-beat category as well, while joining a spate of end-of-the-decade films dealing with virtual reality and the possibility that "true" reality is not nearly as well defined as we once thought. Among these films, the biggest success was *The Matrix* (1999), which was also striking for its combat scenes, adapted from martial arts films but with superb special effects, including super slow-motion.

The Matrix also founded a minifranchise, with two sequels appearing in 2003, but the sequence, based on a conflict between humans and their machines, seemed to run its course quickly. Nevertheless, this sequence was typical of the bulk of science fiction films in the first decade of the 21st century in its depiction of advanced technologies as potentially dangerous and sinister. Some narratives, however, were more complex in their exploration of the potential side-effects of technological progress. For example, *Bicentennial Man* (1999) is sentimentally sympathetic to its central figure, an artificially intelligent robot that becomes more and more indistinguishable from its human creators. Similarly, Spielberg's *Artificial Intelligence: AI* (2001) is sympathetic toward its human-looking boy-robot protagonist and negative in its depiction of antirobot activists, though pessimistic in its vision of a future human race wiped out by environmental devastation.

An environmentally devastated future seemed to become almost a given in the future worlds depicted in the science fiction films of the new millennium, though other sorts of postapocalyptic scenarios appeared as well, as in Danny Boyle's *28 Days Later* (2002), in which research into the biological bases of human violence lead to a plague of ultraviolent killer zombies. Meanwhile, films in all of the major science fiction genres continued to appear, some of which were quite distinctive and quite good, as in the case of Richard Kelly's *Donnie Darko* (2001) and Joss Whedon's *Serenity* (2005), and others of which were colossal hits at the box office, including the robot action narratives *I, Robot* (2004), *Transformers* (2007), and *Transformers: Revenge of the Fallen* (2009).

All in all, though, the major developments in science fiction film in the new millennium have not involved the production of striking landmark films so much as the rapid evolution of techniques of computer animation for use in the generation of special effects—or even entire films. In the long run, these technological advances may bode well for the future of science fiction film, though in the short term they seem to have led to an emphasis on action and special effects at the expense of serious and thoughtful explorations of serious issues. Of course, the use of computer-generated imagery in science fiction films dates back to the 1970s, but by 2004, with the release of such films as the Japanese *Casshern,* the French *Immortel (ad vitam)*, and the American *Able Edwards* and *Sky Captain and the World of Tomorrow* (the latter actually a joint British-Italian-American production), it was clear that science fiction film had reached the stage when entire films could be shot in front of green screens, with all backgrounds and science fictional devices added later by computer.

Meanwhile, the rapid increase in the percentage of scenery filled in by computer animation in science fiction film paralleled developments in animated film itself, where computer animation became the dominant technique, especially in America, where Pixar, a company dedicated from its beginnings to the production of computer-animated films, became the most successful producer of animated films for children. Pixar's films, meanwhile, frequently involved elements of sf, up to and including the 2008 film *WALL-E,* a purely science fictional film that employs a variety of science fiction motifs, including that of an environmentally devastated future earth.

Meanwhile, the case of Pixar is indicative of one additional important development in science fiction film during the period 1990–2009: the increasing importance of animated films in the world of sf. Many of these were children's films, and animated children's science fiction film gained an unprecedented prominence during this period, especially in the United States. Indeed, animated science fiction became so associated in American culture with children's films that animated science fiction films for more mature audiences, such as *Titan A. E.* (2000) or *Battle for Terra* (2007), struggled to find an audience. Even *The Iron Giant* (1999), a brilliant film that could appeal to both children and adults, was a box-office bust, finding no market niche though gaining considerable critical acclaim. However, animated science fiction films that seemed clearly aimed at children found considerable box-office success, with *WALL-E* leading the way with a worldwide gross of over $500 million. Meanwhile, the situation was somewhat different in Japan, where the rise of anime sf films—typically oriented toward mature audiences—represented probably the most important new contributions of Japanese film in the realm of science fiction since the early days of Godzilla. Meanwhile, though the world of science fiction film continued to be dominated by big-budget Hollywood blockbusters, there were signs by the early years of the 21st century of increased activity from a variety of countries around the world (such as France and South Korea), while international co-productions continued to be extremely common.

VARIETIES OF SCIENCE FICTION FILM

While science fiction film is often associated with a few iconic images (such as spaceships and robots), the historical evolution of sf film, traced previously, shows that the form is actually quite versatile and is able to respond quite directly to changing historical contexts. The most obvious example of this responsiveness is the boom in American science fiction film during the 1950s, when genres such as the alien invasion film, the monster movie, and the postapocalyptic film not only reflected but participated in the general paranoid tenor of the decade.

Even in this particularly distinctive period, however, sf film showed considerable versatility, responding not just to the twin cold-war fears of nuclear extermination and communist infiltration, but also reflecting anxieties that resulted from rapid changes in the texture of day-to-day life in the United States during the decade. Meanwhile, in subsequent decades, sf film has expanded into even more subgenres, while addressing a number of important social and political issues.

Science fiction film certainly does include rousing tales of outer-space adventure (in the subgenre of the "space opera") and numerous stories involving robots and other iconic forms of science fictional hardware. But science fiction adventure stories also include narratives of undersea exploration, as well as stories of the exploration of unusual enclaves on the earth, where, for example, dinosaurs and other unusual creatures can be found. In addition, the 1950s subgenres involving alien invasion, monsters, and postapocalyptic scenarios have remained popular, though they have often moved in new directions, as when the apocalyptic scenarios of recent sf films have replaced nuclear war with disease and environmental devastation as the prime threats to the continuation of human civilization as we know it. Meanwhile, sf film now also includes numerous low-tech or "soft" stories concerning the impact of scientific and technological changes on social structures and on the personal and emotional lives of specific individuals. Quite typically, these stories involve dystopian scenarios in which social changes have gone badly wrong, leading to oppressive political systems and impoverished individual lives. Such dystopian films serve as cautionary tales about the potential harmful consequences of a failure to deal properly with current-day problems and issues. Subgenres such as time-travel narratives open up a space for the exploration of numerous important philosophical ideas from fresh, new perspectives; similarly, the narratives in other science fiction films provide fresh insights into social categories such as race and gender. Other subgenres, such as cyberpunk, deal with the possibility that advances in technology might fundamentally change what it means to be human by blurring the boundary between humanity and the technology it creates. And stories involving genetic engineering suggest ways in which science and technology might bring about fundamental changes in the human race itself.

In short, science fiction film has a scope that is virtually as broad as that of film itself, running the gamut from musical comedy to serious political commentary, from lighthearted children's animated narratives to grim postapocalyptic warnings of potential coming disasters. As the entries in this dictionary (especially those on individual subgenres and themes) demonstrate, we now have a sizeable body of sf films in a variety of categories, ranging from the sublime (*2001: A Space Odyssey*) to the ridiculous (*Plan 9 from Outer Space*). We have films that deal with fundamental questions about what it means to be human (*Blade Runner*) and films that treat their science fictional scenarios as little more than opportunities for the generation of spectacular big-budget special effects and explosions (*Transformers*). Of course, seriousness and special effects need not be mutually exclusive, and a certain amount of inventive visual imagery is crucial to science fiction film as a whole, which uses special effects to help create believable alternative worlds in which to work their magic. Indeed, the history of science fiction film is inseparable from the history of the technologies that have been developed to create the special effects for the films.

THE TECHNOLOGY OF SCIENCE FICTION FILM

Science fiction film presents special challenges to filmmakers because it inherently involves the representation of a world that does not actually exist. Thus, sf filmmakers cannot simply rely on the photographic representation of the world as it is but must instead use various techniques to produce visual images of an imaginary world, filled with devices, landscapes, and creatures for which there is no direct real-world counterpart. Méliès set the tone early, producing special photographic effects by exposing his negatives to light and special chemicals during processing and by the simple expedient of having his assistants add paint effects onto his film one frame at a time. Such techniques continued to be used for the next several decades. Until the 1970s, however, the principal technique for the production of special effects in science fiction films involved the building and manipulating of physical sets and models (including puppets), allowing the camera merely to record what it saw, though in ways that often created the illusion that it saw much more. Thus, a few futuristic building fronts, supplemented by hand-painted backgrounds, could create the illusion that filmgoers were seeing an entire future city. Similarly, monsters and aliens were typically represented by actors wearing special costumes and makeup, often creating quite convincing exotic creatures.

These physical techniques for the creation of special visual effects have become more and more sophisticated over the years, as have techniques for filming these physical sets and models. Particularly prominent from the 1930s to the 1960s were techniques of stop-motion animation developed by artists such as Willis O'Brien and Ray Harryhausen, which involved photographing a series of still images of moveable models that could be manipulated between shots, creating the illusion of movement. Stop-motion is still used today for the creation of particular special effects, and sometimes even for the generation of entire films. From the 1970s onward, however, special effects in science fiction film have come more and more to be generated through the use of computer graphics.

A limited amount of crude computer-generated imagery (CGI) had already been used in films such as *Westworld* (1973) and *Futureworld* (1976), but the real breakthrough in CGI technology came with the advent of *Star Wars* in 1977, both because that film employed CGI with an unprecedented level of sophistication and because the technology of the filmmaking itself was foregrounded in the marketing of the film. From that point forward, filmgoing audiences have attended numerous science fiction films as much to see the effects of the technology used in making the films as to see the science fictional technologies represented in the films. In this sense, contemporary science fiction film represents a sort of throwback to the earliest days of film, when many attended showings of films primarily to be amazed by the very existence of moving pictures, regardless of what those pictures might contain. On the other hand, the increasing use of computerized techniques for the generation of effects in science fiction film (or of entire films) has placed science fiction film on the very forefront of 21st-century image-making technology, leading the way in the development of increasingly sophisticated techniques for the representation of science fictional worlds. Science fiction films themselves seem increasingly science fictional.

The Dictionary

20 MILLION MILES TO EARTH. (Dir. **Nathan Juran**, 1957.) A secret U.S. mission to Venus ends badly when the ship, apparently punctured by a meteor strike, crashes into the Mediterranean, killing all aboard except Colonel Robert Calder (William Hopper). The ship also returns with an egg recovered on Venus; the egg hatches into a cute little reptilian creature (that walks upright on its hind legs), but the creature (referred to as *the Ymir*) soon grows as big as an elephant. It also becomes dangerous and destructive, though the film treats the creature with considerable sympathy (furthered by the fact that audiences see it as a baby) and makes it clear that it is frightened and confused, acting largely in self-defense. The ultimate killing of the creature (after it climbs atop the Colosseum in Rome) is thus a moment of pathos rather than triumph. The sympathetic treatment of the creature (a sort of missing link between **dinosaurs** and primates) is one of the hallmarks of this film, a project that is furthered by the technically adept stop-motion animation with which the creature was created by **special-effects** master **Ray Harryhausen**. The highlight of this animation is probably a fight between the Ymir and an elephant late in the film, a scene graphic enough (it leaves the defeated elephant bleeding and unconscious) that it has been deleted from some television broadcasts of the film.

The Ymir is, in fact, one of the most effective of the many movie monsters created by Harryhausen in his long and productive career, even if it lacks the personality and expressiveness of the greatest film monsters, such as King Kong, who serves as a fairly obvious predecessor for the Ymir. Released in black and white, the film is also available on DVD in a colorized version, the processing of which was supervised by Harryhausen himself.

20th CENTURY FOX. Formed in 1935 via the merger of Fox Film Corporation and 20th Century Pictures, 20th Century Fox has been one of the major studios in the film industry ever since. The company has played a particularly important role in the history of sf film, beginning with their production of the romantic comedy *Just Imagine*, the first feature-length **American science fiction film** of the sound era, in 1930. They followed with *It's Great to Be Alive,* another musical comedy, in 1933. However, the company's first major sf film was the **alien-invasion** narrative *The Day the Earth Stood Still* (1951), a courageous film that counseled international cooperation and criticized the arms race during the height of cold-war hysteria. *Invaders from Mars* (1953), on the other hand, was an alien-invasion film that was much more in step with the paranoid tenor of the times. Fox mostly sat out the sf boom of the rest of the 1950s, producing only a couple of minor sf films until the 1959 sf **adventure** film *Journey to the Center of the Earth,* which was clearly aimed at broad, mainstream audiences, rather than at sf-genre audiences. They followed with a similar strategy in *The Lost World* (1960), but mostly stayed out of sf film in the 1960s, except for occasional service as a distributor for minor sf films made by others, including acting as the U.S. distributor for such British sf films as *The Earth Dies Screaming* (1964) and *Quatermass and the Pit* (1967).

In 1977, the history of Fox (and of sf film) moved in a dramatic new direction with the astonishing success of *Star Wars* (co-produced with **Lucasfilm**), easily the biggest hit in the company's long and illustrious history and perhaps their greatest contribution to the evolution of sf film. Fox followed with what became another sf classic with the release of *Alien* in 1979, establishing the studio as a leading player in the sf film boom of 1977 to 1984, during which time they also distributed the second and third *Star Wars* films. (All *Star Wars* films but the first have been produced by Lucasfilm and distributed by Fox.) Other Fox sf productions of the 1980s included *Enemy Mine* (1985), *Aliens* (1986), *Predator* (1987), *Alien Nation* (1988), and *The Abyss* (1989). Science fiction then remained a big part of Fox's film business with the release of two more *Alien* films and a huge blockbuster hit in *Independence Day* (1996). The decade then ended with *Star Wars: Episode I—The Phantom Menace* (1999), one of the biggest hits in film history and the beginning of a second trilogy of *Star Wars* films. Other Fox productions or co-productions of the early 2000s include *Minority Report* (2002), *Solaris* (2002), *I, Robot* (2004), and *The Day After Tomorrow* (2004). Their most recent productions include the 2008 remake of *The Day the Earth Stood Still*, the **children's science fiction** film *Aliens in the Attic* (2009), and **James Cameron**'s long-awaited *Avatar* (2009).

20,000 LEAGUES UNDER THE SEA. (Dir. **Richard Fleischer**, 1954.) Adapted from **Jules Verne**'s classic 1870 science fiction novel, *20,000 Leagues Under the Sea* was a full-color, relatively high-budget film that moved the **Disney** company into sf film for the first time, beginning a long association between the company and the genre. The film features unusually high-profile actors, starring James Mason as the mysterious Captain Nemo and Kirk Douglas as a colorful sailor who inadvertently joins the crew of the *Nautilus,* Nemo's high-tech submarine. It includes a number of underwater scenes that are reminiscent of the True-Life Adventures nature documentaries that Disney was making during this period. It also recasts Nemo's scientific discoveries as an anticipation of nuclear power and nuclear weapons, noting that he has tapped into the basic resources of the universe to produce a power source of unprecedented magnitude that also carries the threat of unmatched destructive potential. In the end, Nemo is killed after destroying all of his discoveries, having concluded that the 19th-century world in which the film is set is simply not ready for the power that his work could unleash. Someday ("in God's good time"), the film suggests, the world might be ready, though it leaves open the question of whether that time has been reached in 1954.

The question was particularly relevant at the time, not only because of the cold war in general, but because 1954 also saw the launch of the USS *Nautilus* (named after the high-tech sub in Verne's novel) as the first real-world nuclear-powered submarine. The film addresses other important issues as well, including the nature of scientific inquiry, which it explores by contrasting the brilliant but misanthropic and darkly obsessed Nemo with the optimistic and benevolent Professor Aronnax (Paul Lukas). Employing unusually good **special effects** for its time, *20,000 Leagues Under the Sea* was a pioneering film that paved the way for future sf-inflected **undersea adventure** narratives, from **Irwin Allen**'s *Voyage to the Bottom of the Sea* (1961) to the spate of such films that surrounded **James Cameron**'s groundbreaking *The Abyss* (1989). The heavily Americanized Disney film is still the classic movie version of Verne's novel, though it has been adapted numerous times, including a 1916 silent film; animated films in 1973, 1985, and 2002; and two made-for-TV movies in 1997. Still another remake, to be directed by McG, is tentatively slated for release in 2012.

2001: A SPACE ODYSSEY. (Dir. **Stanley Kubrick**, 1968.) Still widely regarded as the film that first demonstrated the potential of science fiction film to be genuine art, *2001: A Space Odyssey* has exercised a powerful influence on the look and feel of countless subsequent films in its genre. Though greeted with mixed reviews from critics on its initial release, the film has enjoyed a growing prestige over time and certainly helped to open the way for increased production of sf films in the 1970s, after a relatively slow decade in the 1960s. The striking classical music soundtrack of *2001* (including an overture and an intermission) openly declares its aspiration to the status of high art, but it is ultimately the visuals of the film that make it important. The film's representation of the futuristic technology of space travel remains effective and impressive even today, though the film was made without the aid of the kinds of **computer-generated imagery** that are indispensable to science fiction film in the 21st century. Images from the film (perhaps most importantly its renegade computer, HAL, and its central musical theme, Richard Strauss's *Also sprach Zarathustra*) have become an integral part of contemporary American popular culture.

Though the film relies far less on narrative than most sf films, it does tell a story, albeit one that leaves many aspects open to interpretation. Based on a short story by sf master **Arthur C. Clarke** (who co-wrote the script with director Kubrick), *2001* hints that a superhuman alien presence has been monitoring the evolution of the human race from its very beginning, perhaps subtly intervening when the time is right for the race to make a major new step in its development. In particular, the bulk of the film is set during one of those turning points, as an expedition into deep space apparently leads to an encounter with the aliens and a return to earth of an infant, seen by most as a Star Child who is supposed to help bring about the next stage in the evolution of the human species. The film thus deals with the kind of weighty matters that are appropriate to its considerable artistic merit, helping to open the way for a variety of serious issues to be dealt with in the sf films that followed it.

2009: LOST MEMORIES. (Dir. Lee Si-myung, 2002.) *2009: Lost Memories* is an ambitious South Korean–made **alternate history** in which the Japanese discover a mysterious time-travel device in an archaeological dig in Manchuria, then send an agent back in time to change history. In particular, the agent averts the 1909 assassination of Hirobumi Ito in Harbin, China. Ito then goes on to become a prime mover behind growing Japanese imperial power, leading the Japanese to ally with the United States against Germany in World War II and prolonging Japanese control of the Korean peninsula into the 21st century. The film's protagonist, Sakamoto (Jang Dong-kun), is a Korean who works as an agent of the Japanese Bureau of Investigation. Various events lead him to realize that history has been modified by Japanese intervention. He subsequently discovers the time-travel device and uses it to travel back to 1909 Harbin, where he ensures that Ito is, in fact, assassinated, restoring the original time line. The movie is a stylish thriller whose ultraviolent action punctuates a thoughtful narrative that takes time to build interesting characters and to address a number of political issues in a thoughtful way. However, *2009* never bothers to explain the mechanism of **time travel** used in the film and is in general a bit short on scientific conceptualization. *See also* KOREAN SCIENCE FICTION FILM.

28 DAYS LATER. (Dir. **Danny Boyle**, 2002.) The ultraviolent **postapocalyptic** film *28 Days Later* presents graphic images of a desolate London, devastated by a **plague** that turns the infected into murderous zombies within seconds. Though shot with a relatively small budget, the film is able to use innovative sound, camera work, and editing to create highly effective scenes of bloody violence, even without expensive **special effects**. The "Rage" virus is inadvertently released when animal rights activists attack a medical research facility in which chimps are being subjected to gruesome experiments, apparently designed to gain a better understanding of the violent impulses in humans. As a result, the crazed zombies become merely an extreme example of the kind of behavior that already informed human societies before the release of the virus, behavior of which we are reminded in the opening scenes of the film, which are composed of news footage of various violent atrocities from around the globe, footage that is apparently being shown to the chimps in the lab to gauge its effect on them. Indeed, when the film's protagonists, a group of survivors who band together in a positive image of community, finally escape London and are taken in by a group of soldiers who seemingly represent the last remaining vestiges of preplague authority, the soldiers turn out to be almost as dangerous and threatening as the zombies. As the film ends, the three remaining survivors have escaped the soldiers into the English countryside, where they spot a military plane that seems to promise rescue—though it is not at all clear that this "rescue" will be any better than the one from which they have just escaped.

Still, director Boyle was highly displeased with this studio-imposed "happy" ending and arranged that a more pessimistic alternate ending be added to the American theatrical release of the film. *28 Days Later* was a big enough success that the production of a sequel was no surprise. *28 Weeks Later* (2007), directed by Juan Carlos Fresnadillo, has even more frenetic action scenes than the original and ends as the virus spreads to France—thus possibly setting up another sequel.

– A –

ABLE EDWARDS. (Dir. Graham Robertson, 2004.) *Able Edwards* is a fascinating exercise in low-budget experimental filmmaking, made for $30,000 and with the help of the influence wielded by executive producer **Steven Soderbergh**. The film is essentially a science fiction remake of *Citizen Kane,* set in a future in which environmental catastrophe has forced the surviving members of the human race to abandon the earth and take up residence in an orbiting habitat called the "Civipod." It tells, in flashback, the story of the somewhat Kane-like media mogul Able Edwards (Scott Kelly Galbreath), in this case loosely modeled on Walt Disney rather than William Randolph Hearst. Actually, it tells the story of two different incarnations of Edwards: one who made a fortune in animation and theme parks back on earth and another who is the clone of the first, created to revive the flagging fortunes of the Edwards **Corporation** on the Civipod. The clone at first has considerable success, building new theme parks with "real" rides and attractions (as opposed to the virtual-reality entertainments to which the inhabitants of the Civipod have become accustomed), thus essentially reversing the strategy of the original Disney, whose simulated environments offered escape from reality. Disaster strikes, however, and a theme park accident leads to mass deaths, including that of Edwards's own son. Distraught, Edwards steals a spaceship and flies back to the surface of the earth, where he encounters a bronze statue of the first Edwards holding hands with his creation, Perry Panda; Disneyworld features a similar statue of Walt Disney and Mickey Mouse.

As interesting as this sf recasting of *Citizen Kane* might be, *Able Edwards* is probably most important as a demonstration of the possibilities of digital filmmaking. It was shot entirely in front of **green screens** using a handheld consumer-model video camera, thus helping to prove the viability of a process that would be used in bigger-budget 2004 films such as the British-Italian-American *Sky Captain and the World of Tomorrow,* the French *Immortel (ad vitam)*, and the Japanese **Casshern**. *See also* ENVIRONMENTALISM.

ABRAMS, J. J. (1966–). Known primarily as a key creative force behind the *Lost* television series and the resurrection of the *Star Trek* film franchise with the successful 2009 *Star Trek* film, J. J. Abrams has actually worked quite widely in science fiction. Early in his career, he wrote and executive produced (as Jeffrey Abrams) the romantic **time-travel** film *Forever Young* (1992), starring **Mel Gibson** as a test pilot who awakens after being cryogenically frozen for more than 50 years. In 1998, Abrams co-wrote the script for **Michael Bay**'s science fiction–**disaster** film *Armageddon*. His extensive television work in the early 21st century also includes the co-creation of *Fringe* (2008–), a science fiction–crime investigation series that is vaguely reminiscent of *The X-Files*. Abrams also produced the innovative **alien-invasion–monster movie** hybrid *Cloverfield*. He then turned his attention to *Star Trek* (2009), which he both produced and directed. He is now at work on still another *Star Trek* film, in addition to several other projects.

THE ABYSS. (Dir. **James Cameron**, 1989.) Both an **alien-invasion** narrative and an **undersea adventure**, *The Abyss* combines ground-breaking **special effects** with thoughtful content to produce one of the most important science fiction films of the late cold-war years. In the film, a submersible oil-drilling rig, the *Deepcore 2,* commanded by Virgil "Bud" Brigman (Ed Harris), embarks on a mission to rescue a damaged nuclear submarine that lies on the floor of the ocean. The crew of the rig is not really trained for such a mission, so the U.S. military, concerned that the wrecked sub might fall into Russian hands, sends a team of Navy Seals, led by Lieutenant Hiram Coffey (**Michael Biehn**), to lead the actual rescue and salvage operation. The Seals are accompanied by Lindsey Brigman (Mary Elizabeth Mastrantonio), Bud's estranged wife and the designer of *Deepcore 2.* The strain between Bud and Lindsey combines with friction between the Seals and the oil riggers to create interpersonal tensions within the rig that add to the political tensions without, as Russian and Cuban ships circle the area of the wreck, which is only 80 miles from Cuba. An approaching hurricane adds even more urgency to the mission. They find no survivors on the sub, though it quickly becomes clear that the Seals are more concerned with demolishing the high-tech sub than saving its crew.

Matters take a very different turn, however, when an alien ship is discovered in a deep trench (the "abyss" of the title) on the ocean floor. Coffey, now seemingly deranged, attempts to destroy the aliens, though eventually it becomes clear that the aliens, whose technology is largely based on the manipulation of water, are far more advanced than humans and probably have little to fear from human weapons. In something of an echo of *The Day the Earth Stood Still* (1951), the aliens step in and demand that the earth's military powers cease their confrontational tactics, lest the aliens be forced to intervene, wiping out much of humanity. Indeed, coming as it did at the end of the cold war, *The Abyss* combines with *The Day the Earth Stood Still* to bracket that era with narratives of alien intervention that serve to highlight the follies of the nuclear arms race. The undersea scenes of *The Abyss* are the most technically accomplished put on film at that time. Meanwhile, the film's most remembered scene is probably that in which the aliens send a tentacle of water aboard the oil rig to try to communicate with the crew; this tentacle has been identified as the first entirely computer generated "character" in film history.

ADVENTURE. While adventure of various kinds (such as the adventurous exploration of outer space) is quite often a central motif in science fiction, there is also a specific subgenre of science fiction that involves more earth-bound adventures—often in ways that are only marginally science fictional (usually because the adventure involves some sort of scientific discovery or exploration). The subgenre of the **undersea adventure** fits into this category to some extent, but it is still the case that the world beneath the seas is an alien one that, by definition, requires the use of a great deal of high-tech equipment for its exploration. In many ways, the prototype of science fiction adventure films is the 1959 big-budget production *Journey to the Center of the Earth,* based on **Jules Verne**'s 1864 novel. Science fiction adventure films are often set in a world of the present that differs only in slight ways from the real world of the audience. However, as in *Journey to the Center of the Earth,* such films are often set in the past, giving them a nostalgic quality somewhat similar to that found in "steampunk" science fiction. *Journey to the Center of the Earth* was remade in 2008 with state-of-the-art **special effects**, accompanied by a **mockbuster** of the same title. In basic concept, *Journey to the Center of the Earth* closely resembles the 1976 film *At the Earth's Core,* which was based on a 1914 novel of the same title by Edgar Rice Burroughs; indeed, the mockbuster version of *Journey* seems to owe as much to *At the Earth's Core* as to the film on which it was ostensibly based.

Verne's 1874 novel *The Mysterious Island* has been the source of several similarly titled film adaptations, the most prominent of which is the 1961 version directed by Cy Endfield and featuring special effects by **Ray Harryhausen**. Here, Union soldiers who escape from a Confederate prison camp find themselves on an island populated by giant animals (who turn out to be the result of experiments conducted by Captain Nemo from *20,000 Leagues Under the Sea.*) This notion of the discovery of a strange enclave where unusual wildlife abounds is central to the genre of science fiction adventure, exemplified by the discovery of the eponymous giant ape living among **dinosaurs** on a remote island in *King Kong* (1933). In many ways the classic example of such films is Irwin Allen' *The Lost World* (1960), probably the best of several film adaptations of Sir Arthur Conan Doyle's 1912 novel of the same name. Here, explorers encounter an exotic enclave inhabited by dinosaurs, which are, in fact, the favorite species for these sorts of films.

In this sense, **Steven Spielberg**'s *Jurassic Park* (1993) and its sequels can be considered members of the adventure subgenre of science fiction. *The Land that Time Forgot* (1975), based on a 1918 novel by Edgar Rice Burroughs and set during World War I, is a more conventional example of the subgenre, as survivors of a sinking British ship in World War I wind up marooned on an island inhabited by dinosaurs and other prehistoric animals. That film spawned a direct sequel, *The People that Time Forgot* (1977). *The Land that Time Forgot* was remade in 2009 as an Asylum films mockbuster, keyed to the release of the tongue-in-cheek sf adventure loosely based on the original Burroughs story, *Land of the Lost* (2009).

Finally, another variant of the science fiction adventure involves the discovery not of lost animal species but of lost human civilizations. The legendary lost city of Atlantis (first mentioned in Plato's dialogue *Timaeus and Critius*) has been a particularly prominent focus for such sf adventures, partly because Atlantis is rumored to have been a technologically advanced civilization. The most important sf film about adventurers discovering Atlantis is probably **George Pal**'s *Atlantis: The Lost Continent* (1961), remade in a kinder and gentler animated version for kids by **Disney** in 2001 as *Atlantis: The Lost Empire*.

AELITA. (Dir. Yakov Protazanov, 1924.) Still regarded as one of the classics of Soviet silent cinema and generally considered to be the first feature-length film about space travel, *Aelita* (aka *Aelita: Queen of Mars*) is an adaptation of Alexei Tolstoy's 1923 novel of the same title. In the film, a Soviet engineer, Los (Tsereteli), travels to **Mars** in a rocket ship. There, he helps instigate a popular revolt against the ruling king, with the help of Queen Aelita (Yuliya Solntseva). However, the real hero of the Martian revolution is the Bolshevik soldier Gusev (Nikolai Batalov), who leads the Martian workers in their effort to establish a socialist utopia on

Mars. As such, the film is often regarded as prosocialist and pro-Soviet propaganda, though it is in fact a complex work the political implications of which have been the subject of widely varying interpretations. For one thing, most of the film actually takes place in postrevolutionary Moscow, with a number of potential criticisms of the quality of life there. The film is further complicated because of the role played by the enigmatic Aelita, who supports the Martian revolt for her own purposes, then has to be killed by Los to prevent her from establishing a new tyranny on Mars. The fact that, in the end, the entire episode on Mars seems to have been a dream on the part of Los further adds ambiguity to the meaning of the film. In any case, *Aelita,* with its impressive futuristic Martian sets, was a groundbreaking film that exercised considerable influence on the look of science fiction film for decades to come.

AGAR, JOHN (1921–2002). John Agar was a Chicago-born American actor whose biggest claim to fame may be that he was married to Shirley Temple from 1945 to 1949. This marriage of the meatpacker's son to the Hollywood sweetheart put Agar in the public eye and quickly gained him a movie contract. His career in Hollywood got off to a good start with prominent roles in such films as the John Wayne war film *Sands of Iwo Jima* (1949) and the Western (also starring Wayne) *She Wore a Yellow Ribbon* (1949). Agar is best remembered today, however, for the low-budget science fiction movies in which he starred in the 1950s, including major roles in such sf films as *The Rocket Man* (1954), *Tarantula* (1955), *The Mole People* (1956), and *Attack of the Puppet People* (1958). In 1955, he had a major role as Dr. Clete Ferguson in *Revenge of the Creature,* the first sequel to **Creature from the Black Lagoon.** He descended into more forgettable sf films in the 1960s, including *Journey to the Seventh Planet* (1962) and *Women of the Prehistoric Planet* (1966), as well as the made-for-TV films *Curse of the Swamp Creature* (1966) and *Zontar: The Thing from Venus* (1966). Agar had a small role in the 1976 remake of *King Kong,* but most of his work from the 1970s onward involved guest roles on television. In 2005, he starred (again as Ferguson) posthumously in *The Naked Monster* (actually filmed in the mid-1980s), a campily nostalgic look back at the **monster movies** of the 1950s that also featured 1950s sf star **Kenneth Tobey.**

ALIEN **(AND SEQUELS).** (Dir. **Ridley Scott** et al., 1979–1997.) A key film in the science fiction boom of 1977 to 1984, *Alien* is a stylish thriller that combines elements of horror movie with some of the most convincing science fiction hardware ever put on film. In the film, the *Nostromo,* a lowly "commercial towing vehicle" belonging to the sinister **Weyland-Yutani Corporation** (here identified only as "The Company") is invaded by a murderous alien presence that memorably gets aboard by entering the body of a crew member (played by John Hurt) and then bursting out through his chest. The alien, rapidly growing larger and more deadly, kills off the crew of the ship one by one, until it is finally launched out into space by the efforts of the last surviving crew member, Ripley (**Sigourney Weaver**). The *Nostromo* itself is destroyed by the end of the film. However, depicted as a cluttered and claustrophobic industrial environment that differed dramatically from the sleek and gleaming spaceships to which sf fans had become accustomed, the ship became a landmark of science fiction film. The same can be said for the alien of the title, which went on to become one of the most successful monsters in sf film history. However, Ripley herself might have been the most important landmark in the film, a strong, courageous, capable female hero who became something of a feminist icon.

The commercial and artistic success of *Alien* made it the founding film in one of the most important sf film franchises of all time, though it took several years for the first sequel to appear. *Aliens* (1986) directly continues the action of the first film. However, under the direction of **James Cameron**, *Aliens* is a very different film, something like a combination of the original *Alien* with *The Terminator* (which Cameron directed in 1984) and *Rambo: First Blood Part II* (which Cameron wrote in 1985). *The Terminator,* in turn, was clearly influenced by *Alien,* so it made sense for Cameron to direct *Aliens,* a film that is scarier, more violent, and more overt in its criticism of the willingness of the Weyland-Yutani Corporation (now identified by name) to endanger human beings in the interest of extending its own profit.

As the film begins, Ripley (now identified as "**Ellen Ripley**") is recovered after drifting in space in an escape pod for 57 years while in hypersleep. Company officials do not appear to believe

Ripley's story of the destruction of the *Nostromo* (a valuable piece of hardware), but they nevertheless coerce her into going along as a consultant when they send a heavily armed expedition of "colonial marines" back to the planet where the alien was originally discovered to investigate the sudden cessation of communications from a human colony that has been placed there to terraform the dismal world. The colony, of course, has been destroyed by aliens, resulting in a gory battle between the aliens and the marines, most of whom are killed, though Ripley survives, saving a little girl left alive in the colony. As the film ends, Ripley, the girl, and one of the marines (played by **Michael Biehn**), head for home in hypersleep, secure in the notion that they have nuked the planet, which should presumably wipe out the aliens once and for all as well as nix the plan of the corporation to use the aliens as weapons and thus as a source of profit. Among other things, this film significantly extends our knowledge of the biology of the alien species, especially through the introduction of an alien queen, who has laid thousands of eggs on the planet, somewhat in the mold of a queen bee or ant.

The next sequel, *Alien³* (1992, directed by David Fincher) is a dark, brooding film that turns away from the frantic action of *Aliens*, depending more on atmosphere (it is set on a dismal prison planet with the atmosphere of a **postapocalyptic** film) for its effects. Here, it turns out that an alien (now described as a "xenomorph") has once again stowed away aboard the vessel that is presumably taking Ripley to earth and safety. The vessel crashes on the prison planet (run, of course, by the Weyland-Yutani Corporation, though essentially abandoned). In the crash, Hicks and Newt are killed, but Ripley survives; it eventually becomes clear that the alien has planted the embryo of a new queen inside Ripley herself, giving a dark twist to the motherly turn taken by Ripley in the previous film. This film is particularly interesting in its treatment of gender, as Ripley finally reveals herself as a woman with sexual needs, but adopts a unisex look by shaving her head and dressing like the (male) prisoners. Meanwhile, the alien escapes into the prison, wreaking much havoc until it is predictably killed by Ripley and a few surviving inmates, after which Ripley throws herself into a furnace full of molten led, thus killing herself and the gestating queen—and apparently ending the *Alien* sequence once and for all.

Both Ripley and the xenomorph nevertheless return in *Alien: Resurrection* (1997), set 200 years after *Alien³*. Weaver returns as a rebuilt clone of the original Ripley, constructed from a hybrid combination of the DNA of the original Ripley and the aliens—and only then after a series of ghoulish failed experiments have produced a sequence of monstrosities. This new Ripley is a dark and brooding character, her personality (and superhuman physical prowess) heavily influenced by her alien genes, though much of her new bitterness and hostility can be attributed to her resentment at having been created in the first place. Meanwhile, the government scientists who have created her (in a special lab on a craft in deep space, for added security) are also working to produce more xenomorphs, again for use as weapons, though this time they apparently plan to use them for "urban pacification" back on earth.

This film is in some ways the darkest of the entire series, though it also differs from its predecessors in its tendency toward quirky humor and one-liners, perhaps due to the contributions of screenwriter **Joss Whedon**. Moreover, the film is filled with references to earlier films, from *Frankenstein* to *Blade Runner* to the other *Alien* films themselves. It is also a gorgeous-looking film, clearly showing the visual touch of director **Jean-Pierre Jeunet**, who had established his elaborate, offbeat visual style in such earlier works as *Delicatessen* (1991) and *The City of Lost Children* (1995). In any case, the over-the-top visual style combines with the strange mixture of darkness and campy humor to make this by far the weirdest of all the *Alien* films. As the film ends, Ripley and her new robot sidekick, Call (Winona Ryder), have just landed on what seems to be a postapocalyptic earth (with a ruined Eiffel Tower in the background, much like the half-buried Statue of Liberty at the end of *Planet of the Apes*), very much leaving open the possibility of still another sequel. However, the only subsequent *Alien* films to appear as of this writing are *AVP: Alien vs. Predator* (2004) and *AVPR: Aliens vs. Predator—Requiem* (2007), which are not really sequels, but spin-offs from both the *Alien* and the *Predator* films. *See also* ALIEN INVASION; FEMINISM AND GENDER.

ALIEN INVASION. Stories of alien invasions from outer space first became popular in England at the end of the 19th century, with **H. G.**

Wells's *The War of the Worlds* (1898) emerging as the prototype for what became one of the key subgenres of science fiction. In the world of science fiction film, alien-invasion narratives became particularly popular in the 1950s, especially in **American science fiction film**, in which alien-invasion films became a central means for the expression of the sense of paranoia that permeated American society during the peak years of the cold war. Such prominent sf films from the 1950s as *The Thing from Another World* (1951), *Invaders from Mars* (1953), *The War of the Worlds* (1953, based on Wells's novel), *Earth vs. The Flying Saucers* (1956), *Kronos* (1957), *I Married a Monster from Outer Space* (1958), and *It! The Terror from Beyond Space* (1958) all deal with the theme of alien invasion from a paranoid perspective. Indeed, Don Siegel's *Invasion of the Body Snatchers* (1956) is often taken as one of the central cultural representations of 1950s cold-war paranoia, especially in the way it can be taken as an expression either of the fear of communist takeover or of anticommunist repression. British film also entered the fray with such efforts as *The Quatermass Xperiment* (1955).

If many of these films used the threat of an invasion from outer space as an allegorical stand-in for the perceived threat of communist invasion, other invasion films—including *Invasion U.S.A.* (1952), *Red Planet Mars* (1952), and *The 27th Day* (1957)—were much more overt in their thematization of 1950s paranoid fear (and hatred) of communism. On the other hand, other films took a much more conciliatory perspective, using the alien-invasion narrative as a warning against the dangers of militarism and xenophobia. Such films, including *The Day the Earth Stood Still* (1951) and *It Came from Outer Space* (1953) were among the most thoughtful and interesting sf films of the 1950s.

By the late 1950s, however, the alien-invasion film had joined the increasing effort to appeal to younger audiences. As early as 1953, *Invaders from Mars* featured a young boy who watched in horror as the authority figures around him (including his parents) became the mind-slaves of alien invaders. *The Space Children* (1958) then reversed this motif as horrified adults begin to realize that their children have fallen under the sway of alien mind control. Meanwhile, in *Teenagers from Outer Space* (1959), the aliens themselves are young hipsters, though the title (clearly designed to appeal to teenage filmgoers) exaggerates the extent to which this motif is actually central to the film. One the other hand, in *The Blob* (1958), teenagers lead the fight against a monstrous alien invader.

Alien-invasion films fell out of favor in the 1960s, with only an occasional entry, such as the British *The Day of the Triffids* (1962), appearing in the subgenre. *2001: A Space Odyssey* (1968), in which advanced aliens intervene in the evolution of the human race, is an alien-invasion film of sorts, as is *The Andromeda Strain* (1971), in which a microbe from outer space threatens to infect the population of the earth with a deadly plague. *The Man Who Fell to Earth* (1976) is a particularly interesting entry in the subgenre, though it was **Steven Spielberg**'s *Close Encounters of the Third Kind* (1977) that brought alien-invasion narratives back to true prominence in sf film. Spielberg's aliens were benevolent, though it was his *E.T. the Extra-Terrestrial* (1982) that featured what was perhaps the first truly loveable alien among major sf films. On the other hand, the *Alien* films, beginning with the original in 1979, portrayed a potential alien invader that was a genuinely frightening monster, though the **Weyland-Yutani Corporation** that attempts to exploit the alien for its own purposes is possibly even more monstrous. **Andrei Tarkovsky**'s *Stalker* (1979), from the Soviet Union, is also particularly worthy of mention during this period, with its portrayal of a genuinely strange landscape that might have been rendered so as the aftermath of an alien landing.

With the alien-invasion subgenre back on the sf film radar, remakes of the films of the 1950s began to appear. *Invasion of the Body Snatchers* has been remade no less than three times, including a film of the same title in 1978, as well as *Body Snatchers* (1993) and *The Invasion* (2007). Tobe Hooper remade *Invaders from Mars* as more of a horror movie in 1986. Meanwhile, though the *Body Snatchers* films are directly based on Jack Finney's 1954 novel *The Body Snatchers,* the real prototype of the alien mind control genre is **Robert A. Heinlein**'s 1951 novel *The Puppet Masters,* which was finally adapted directly in a film of the same title in 1994, though the 1958 novel *The Brain Eaters* was close enough to the novel that Heinlein filed a lawsuit.

The Faculty (1998) was an attempt to update this basic narrative for teen audiences at the end of the 20th century. **M. Night Shyama-**

lan's *Signs* (2002) is an ambitious effort that uses the alien-invasion narrative as a framework for a serious character study and an investigation of the nature of religious faith. Unfortunately, both the central character (played by **Mel Gibson**) and the film's aliens are ultimately uninteresting; in particular, the aliens both arrive (apparently in a hostile mode) and leave without explanation, though the film leaves open the possibility that their departure might have been the result of divine intervention, thus recalling the ending of the 1953 *The War of the Worlds,* to which one of the characters of *Signs* specifically compares their own situation midway through the film.

In the 1990s, television's *The X-Files* demonstrated the ongoing attraction of the paranoid alien conspiracy narrative, while **Roland Emmerich's** *Independence Day* (1996) demonstrated that the alien-invasion subgenre could still capture the public imagination of theater-goers. On the other hand, **Tim Burton's** *Mars Attacks!* (1996), released five months later, showed the potential of alien-invasion narratives (especially those from the 1950s) as objects of parody. Indeed, *Strange Invaders* had spoofed the subgenre as early as 1983, with special reference to *Invasion of the Body Snatchers.* Still, the alien-invasion narrative was used to serious effect in 2001, when the joint Japanese-U.S. production *Final Fantasy: The Spirits Within,* which was not made in the **anime** style and was loosely based on a popular Japanese role-playing game, was adapted to the big screen. It was the first attempt to make a photorealistic animated sf film. It featured an inadvertent invasion of ghosts from a destroyed planet and was not a box office success. In 2009, *District 9* related the story of a shipload of aliens who arrive on earth in a gigantic and highly advanced ship, but the ship becomes crippled, robbing them of their technological superiority to humans. The aliens are brought down to the earth's surface (in South Africa), then consigned to a ghetto (the "District 9" of the title), where they suffer considerable racist abuse in a motif that is further reinforced by their location in South Africa, a nation whose history is almost synonymous with racist oppression. Humans, meanwhile, scramble to unravel the secrets of the aliens' technology (hoping to gain both financial profits and military power), while the aliens struggle to find a way to escape and go home.

Meanwhile, narratives of alien invasion have also become a favorite subgenre in the world of **children's science fiction** film.

E.T. remains the most popular alien-invasion film that is often considered to be for children, though **Disney**, in particular, has made a number of such films, including the "Witch Mountain" sequence, beginning with *Witch Mountain* (1975). *The Cat from Outer Space* (1978) was also an early example of the children's alien-invasion film, with a cuddly alien who was something of a forerunner to E.T., indicating the tendency of the aliens in chidlren's films to be benevolent, a tendency that continued in such Disney films as *Lilo & Stitch* (2002). Disney's rewriting of the Chicken Little parable as an alien-invasion narrative in the computer animated *Chicken Little* (2005) depicts aliens who arrive on earth with a show of overwhelming force, but only because they mistakenly think they are saving a cute baby alien from abduction by earthlings. Warner's *The Iron Giant* (1999) is a particularly thoughtful example of the benevolent alien invader film that is accessible to children, while Nickelodeon's 2001 animated film *Jimmy Neutron: Boy Genius* (2001) and DreamWorks' *Monsters vs. Aliens* (2009) depict alien invaders who are sinister, but comically so.

ALLAND, WILLIAM (1916–1997). An actor, writer, producer, and director, William Alland is probably best remembered for playing Jerry Thompson, the reporter who attempts to unravel the facts of the life of William Foster Kane in *Citizen Kane*. But Alland also made a number of important contributions to science fiction film, especially as the producer of a series of films directed by **Jack Arnold** in the 1950s, including *It Came from Outer Space* (1953), *Creature from the Black Lagoon* (1954), *Revenge of the Creature* (1955), *Tarantula* (1955), and *The Space Children* (1958). Alland also produced *This Island Earth* (1955), *The Creature Walks Among Us* (1956), *The Mole People* (1956), *The Land Unknown* (1957), and *The Deadly Mantis* (1957). Except for *The Space Children* (Paramount), all of these sf productions were with Universal International Pictures.

ALLEN, IRWIN (1916–1991). Born in New York City, Irwin Allen was an American film and television producer and director who is best known for the spectacular disaster films *The Poseidon Adventure* (1972) and *The Towering Inferno* (1974). Such films earned him the nickname "Master of Disaster." However, Allen's first film work was in documentaries, and he also worked extensively in science fiction. For example, he both produced and directed *The Swarm* (1978), something of a disaster film (about killer bees) with sf elements. He also produced and directed the science fiction films *The Lost World* (1960) and *Voyage to the Bottom of the Sea* (1961), as well as the made-for-TV movie *City Beneath the Sea* (1971), intended as the pilot for a television series that never came into being. It is, however, for his work as a television producer that Allen is best known in science fiction. Series created and produced by Allen include *Voyage to the Bottom of the Sea* (1964–1967), *Lost in Space* (1965–1968), *The Time Tunnel* (1966–1967), and *Land of the Giants* (1968–1970).

ALPHAVILLE. (Dir. Jean-Luc Godard, 1965.) The **dystopian** film *Alphaville,* directed by Jean-Luc Godard, is a key film of the French New Wave. The film is set in a city of the same name, located in a distant galaxy and controlled by a giant computer, Alpha 60, which rules a totally rational, routinized society, suppressing all emotion and creativity. However, despite this typical science-fiction scenario, Godard eschews the futuristic look of many science-fiction films, opting to shoot the film on the streets of 1960s Paris and to dress his actors in clothing from the 1960s or even earlier. Protagonist Lemmy Caution (Eddie Constantine) is a trench coat–clad, hard-boiled detective derived from American film noir. He travels (by driving a Ford Mustang on an intergalactic highway) to Alphaville to try to apprehend the evil scientist Professor Vonbraun, designer of the Alpha 60 computer, before Alphaville can launch a war of conquest against the surrounding galaxies using new weapons of destruction more powerful than anything previously known to humanity. Caution succeeds by using poetry as a weapon against the coldly calculating Alpha 60. In the process, he also wins the love of Vonbraun's beautiful daughter, Natacha (Anna Karina), who rediscovers her humanity through her relationship with Caution.

The suggestion in *Alphaville* that love and art are key weapons against repression comes close to dystopian cliché, but this is a film that overtly plays with the conventions of the genre. Moreover, like the later *Blade Runner* (1982), *Alphaville* clearly draws much of its energy from its generic dialogue between a science-fiction vision of the future and an allusive nod to the past cinematic tradition of the film noir detective story. Meanwhile, Godard's use of present-day Paris to stand in for the city of Alphaville makes especially clear his desire to use the film to comment on the cold, inhuman conditions of life in modern cities of our own world. Through careful use of lighting, camera angles, and other technical strategies, Godard gives the city an eerily inhuman look, suggesting a similar dehumanization lying beneath the surface of 1960s Paris. The film's haunting soundtrack also makes a significant contribution to this effect, as a barrage of mechanical and monotonous noises enhances the haunting feel of the city. *See also* FRENCH SCIENCE FICTION FILM.

ALTERNATE HISTORY. The alternate (or "alternative") history narrative has typically been considered marginal to the enterprise of science fiction—perhaps because it usually involves little or no actual science. On the other hand, it is closely related to the well-established sf motif of **time travel**, in which time travelers are quite often involved in some sort of attempt to change the course of history. Alternate-history narratives, however, generally involve changes in large-scale social history rather than in the private lives of individuals, as is often the case with time-travel narratives. The alternate-history narrative typically looks at a single crucial turning point in history (the "point of divergence") and then attempts to explore the different ways history might have proceeded had that turning point played out differently. For example, numerous alternate-history novels have conjectured possible alternative paths that might have been taken by history had the South won the Civil War—as in Ward Moore's *Bring the Jubilee* (1953)—or the Axis powers won World War II—as in **Philip K. Dick**'s *The Man in the High Castle* (1962).

Such point-of-divergence narratives have been relatively rare in science fiction film. Kevin Brownlow's *It Happened Here* (1965) is set in an alternative 1944 England that has been invaded and occupied by the Germans during World War II. In *Timequest* (2000), a time-traveling agent prevents the assassination of U.S. president John F. Kennedy. That same year, South Korea's *2009: Lost Memories* became perhaps the most ambitious and elaborate alternate-history film yet produced. It involves changes to the history of Korea and the rest of Asia that occur when a time traveler goes back in time to prevent the 1909 assassination of Japanese envoy Hirobumi Ito in Harbin, China. Ito then goes on to become a prime mover behind growing Japanese imperial power, leading the Japanese to ally with the United States against Germany in World War II and prolonging Japanese control of the Korean peninsula into the 21st century.

Another form of the alternate-history narrative is the parallel world narrative, in which historical events proceed differently in an alternative version of our earth. A typical example is the 1969 film *Journey to the Far Side of the Sun* (aka *Doppelgänger*) in which an astronaut discovers a duplicate earth previously undetected because it is on the other side of the sun. Other films are less overt about the parallel-world theme, simply existing in a world that includes historical events or situations that are clearly different from our own. For example, reversing this Nazi-victory motif, Allied agents assassinate Adolf Hitler in Quentin Tarantino's *Inglourious Basterds* (2009). Again, however, this sort of parallel world film often deals more with personal experiences than with historical events, as in *Sliding Doors* (1998).

AMERICAN INTERNATIONAL PICTURES (AIP). Though a relatively small operation, AIP made a huge contribution to the **American science fiction film** boom of the 1950s, especially in the turn toward more teen-oriented fare in the latter half of the decade. The company was not, in fact, founded until 1956, when James H. Nicholson and Samuel Z. Arkoff decided to convert the existing American Releasing Corporation (which they had founded a year earlier) into a film production company that focused on low-budget films for mostly teen audiences. Using focus groups to determine what kinds of films would appeal to these audiences, it developed a very market-oriented approach that put more emphasis on working within formulas that had proven to be marketable than on creativity or artistic merit. Nevertheless, their typically tawdry productions sometimes had flashes of brilliance, especially in the hands of their leading producer, **Roger Corman**, who also often directed. Corman quickly showed a knack for producing highly marketable films very quickly and very cheaply, especially in the genres of horror and science fiction.

AIP made a variety of teen exploitation films in the late 1950s, often cashing in on contemporary fear about juvenile delinquency, but from a teen perspective that winked at the paranoia displayed by the older generation toward their own children. Teen culture films such as hot rod films and beach party films were also a staple of the company's output. In the realm of science fiction, Corman was definitely the company's leading light, though films such as *It Conquered the World* (1956) often contained horror elements as well, and Corman ultimately became better known for horror films—such as the cycle of eight Edgar Allan Poe adaptations that he did for AIP from 1960 to 1964. Director **Bert I. Gordon** also worked with AIP on most of his films of the late 1950s, beginning with *The Amazing Colossal Man* (1957), which the company distributed but did not produce. AIP also distributed the sequel, *War of the Colossal Beast* (1958), as well as *Attack of the Puppet People* (1958). They were the production company for Gordon's *Earth vs. the Spider* (1958).

In the mid-1960s, AIP also moved into television production, though without great success. By 1970, Corman founded his own production company, New World Pictures. Subsequently, AIP did less work with science fiction and instead explored new territory such as Blaxploitation films, including *Blacula* (1972), which combined this new endeavor with their traditional focus on horror. In science fiction, AIP moved in the latter part of the 1970s into bigger-budget, more mainstream science fiction with such films as *The Island of Dr. Moreau* (1977), based on the 1896 novel by **H. G. Wells** and starring Burt Lancaster and Michael York. They also produced *Meteor* (1979), a science fiction **disaster** film starring **Sean Connery**. AIP was the American distributor for a version of *Mad Max* (1979) that was dubbed into American English. Arkoff retired in 1979 and AIP was sold to Filmways, Inc., which was later bought by Orion Pictures. Most of the AIP library is now owned by Metro-Goldwyn-Mayer (M-G-M), which bought the financially troubled Orion in 1997.

AMERICAN SCIENCE FICTION FILM. Science fiction film got off to a slow start in the history of American cinema. Prior to the 1950s, the major entries in the genre from the United States included musical comedies from **20th Century Fox** such as *Just Imagine* (1930) and *It's Great to Be Alive* (1933), **monster movies** such as *Frankenstein* (1931) and *King Kong* (1933), serials such as the

Flash Gordon and **Buck Rogers** sequences of the 1930s, and the mad-scientist film *Dr. Cyclops* (1940). All of that changed in 1950, however, as the race between **Destination Moon** and **Rocketship X-M** to be the first major sf film released in the new decade was a sign of big things to come. The rest of the 1950s saw a major boom in the production of science fiction films in the United States, making sf film one of the key cultural phenomena of the decade.

The sf boom when into full swing in 1951, which was a particularly rich year. In this year, *The Thing from Another World* became the first of the many **alien-invasion** films of the 1950s, while **Arch Oboler**'s *Five* was the first cold-war film to depict the aftereffects of a nuclear apocalypse, while also commenting on such important themes as racism. *When Worlds Collide* treated the catastrophic destruction of the earth in a collision with another planet as a chance for a new start, in a disaster motif that also clearly reflected the nuclear fears of the time. *The Day the Earth Stood Still* was probably the most important sf film of the year, providing a warning against the cold-war arms race that demonstrated the potential of sf film to address complex contemporary issues in a thoughtful manner.

As the decade proceeded, a rich array of sf films began to appear, dominated by the alien-invasion narrative, the **postapocalyptic** film, and the **monster movie**, all reflecting in key ways the anxious, and often paranoid, tenor of the times. Yet some of these films were quite complex and nuanced, as when the *Creature from the Black Lagoon* trilogy (1954–1956) addressed concerns about unethical scientific research that can be related to concerns over the arms race, but also involved themes related to gender and domestic relations in the 1950s. *Invasion of the Body Snatchers* (1956), often seen as a paradigmatic expression of anticommunist hysteria, could also be read as an expression of anxieties over other threats, including anticommunism itself. In that same year, *Forbidden Planet* provided an especially sophisticated warning against the threat of nuclear weapons—and against the dangers posed by unrestrained technological development as a whole, laced with a liberal dose of Freudian psychology. That film also broke new ground in the development of visual effects, while attempting to give sf film a new cultural legitimacy by basing its narrative on Shakespeare's *The Tempest*. Meanwhile, *The Incredible Shrinking Man* (1957) addressed a number of the domestic anxieties of the 1950s, including the embattled state of American masculinity.

By the end of the 1950s, however, American science fiction film had come more and more to be regarded in Hollywood as especially suitable fare for the teenage audiences that were becoming an increasingly important segment of the filmgoing demographic. This vein included interesting and valuable films such as *The Blob* (1958), but most of the films produced in the late 1950s for teen audiences were low-budget affairs, often laughably bad as films. New studios such as **American International Pictures** began to dominate the genre, specializing in ultra-low-budget teen movies. As a result, the science fiction films of the 1950s as a whole are still often associated in the public mind with cheap effects, bad acting, and ludicrous scripts—as in the case of *Plan 9 from Outer Space* (1959), often identified as the worst film ever made. Relatively high-budget color films for fairly broad audiences, such as **George Pal**'s *The Time Machine* (1960), based on a novel by **H. G. Wells**, and Irwin Allen's *The Lost World* (1960), based on a novel by Sir Arthur Conan Doyle, did occasionally still appear, but became more and more rare as the new decade of the 1960s proceeded.

Disney's *The Absent-Minded Professor* (1961), a lighthearted **mad-scientist** film for children and families, suggested potential new directions for sf film, while films such as **Byron Haskin**'s *Robinson Crusoe on Mars* (1964) provided occasional highlights, but all in all the 1960s were a slow decade in American sf film until 1968, when *Planet of the Apes* was a major box-office hit that also provided thoughtful commentary on issues from the cold-war arms race to racism. Meanwhile, **Stanley Kubrick**'s *2001: A Space Odyssey*, a British-American co-production, broke new aesthetic ground, using a classical music soundtrack and special visual effects of unprecedented sophistication to help produce a film that was self-consciously intended to be a genuine work of art, rather than mere entertainment. The success of such films spurred a minor renaissance in American sf film in the coming years. However, with the Vietnam War and the Watergate scandal hovering over American society like twin dark clouds, the sf films of the early 1970s were almost universally dark in tone, dominated by such works of **dystopian** film as *A Clockwork*

Orange, another joint U.S./UK production directed by Kubrick, and *THX 1138,* the first film from future *Star Wars* creator **George Lucas,** both released in 1971. Other key works of this era included **Richard Fleischer's** *Soylent Green* (1973) and Michael Anderson's *Logan's Run* (1976). On the other hand, Woody Allen's farcical *Sleeper* provided a parodic rejoinder to the dystopian films of the early 1970s, though even it had certain dark undertones.

This darkness was lifted with the release of *Star Wars* in 1977, providing rollicking feel-good entertainment with vaguely mythical undertones, while looking nostalgically back on the serials of the 1930s. The "good versus evil" moral certainties of this film were clearly a major attraction for audiences, though it also helped that the film broke new ground in the use of high-tech **special effects,** pointing toward a bold new future in sf filmmaking. Meanwhile, **Steven Spielberg's** *Close Encounters of the Third Kind,* also re- leased in 1977, was one of the most sophisticated (both technically and thematically) alien-invasion films ever made, suggesting that the minor renaissance of the early 1970s was quickly becoming a major new boom. This suggestion was quickly verified with the release of *Alien* and *Star Trek: The Motion Picture* in 1979, followed by the first *Star Wars* sequel, *The Empire Strikes Back* in 1980, then by *Blade Runner* and *E.T. the Extra-Terrestrial* in 1982. Topped off with *The Return of the Jedi* in 1983 and *The Terminator* in 1984, the period from 1977 to 1984 was probably the richest in sf film his- tory. Indeed, though this boom slowed a bit after 1984, the release of *Aliens* in 1986, *Robocop* in 1987, and *The Abyss* in 1989 provided important high points through the rest of the 1980s. The *Back to the Future* trilogy (1985–1990) provided popular lighthearted sf fare during this period.

The 1990s got off to a good start as well, with films such as *Total Recall* (1990) and *Terminator 2: Judgment Day* (1991) providing thoughtfulness as well as rousing entertainment—and propelling **Arnold Schwarzenegger** to superstardom. Meanwhile, the *Alien* franchise continued to provide highlights with *Alien³* (1992) and *Alien: Resurrection* (1997). The **computer-generated imagery** that helped produce the dinosaurs of Spielberg's *Jurassic Park* (1993) provided another milestone in the history of special visual effects, while films such as *Twelve Monkeys* (1995) and *Dark City* (1998) demonstrated that there was still room for the quirky and the unusual in a field increasingly dominated by big-budget blockbusters. **Tim Burton's** *Mars Attacks!* (1996) and the first *Men in Black* film (1997) were successful sf comedies, the latter itself becoming a blockbuster hit. Meanwhile, *Independence Day* (1996), an alien-invasion narrative with the structure of a **disaster** film, was just behind *Jurassic Park* as the top-grossing sf film of the decade—the two were the highest grossing films of all time. And the decade ended on a high note, with the huge commercial success of *Star Wars: Episode I—The Phantom Menace* and the commercial and critical success of *The Matrix* (1999), a U.S.-Australian co-production now widely regarded as the first truly successful **cyberpunk** film. The underappreciated animated film *The Iron Giant* (1999) was another end-of-the-decade highlight.

Highlights of the new millennium in American sf film have included two more *Star Wars* sequels, two sequels to *The Matrix*, and two more *Terminator* films. Meanwhile, the *Star Trek* film franchise, which seemed on the verge of extinction with the failure of *Star Trek: Nemesis* (2002) gained renewed life with the success of the prequel/reboot of 2009, suggesting that the franchise effect remained strong in sf film. Non-franchise highlights of the first decade of the new millennium included Spielberg's *Artificial Intelligence: AI* (2001) and *Minority Report* (2002). Truly original sf films such as *Donnie Darko* (2001) and *Serenity* (2005) gained a cultish following, while big-budget effects-driven extravaganzas such as *I, Robot* (2004), *Transformers* (2007), and *Transformers: Revenge of the Fallen* (2009) raked in huge takes at the box office. **Children's science fiction** film became more and more prominent during the decade, culminating in **Pixar's** release of *WALL-E* in 2008, followed by an unprecedented spate of children's sf films in 2009. Another important phenomenon of this decade was a flurry of remakes of earlier classics, including *Planet of the Apes* (2001), *Solaris* (2002), *War of the Worlds* (2005), and *The Day the Earth Stood Still* (2008). However, though spiced up with state-of-the-art special effects, these remakes were generally less impressive and interesting than the originals. *See also* ARNOLD, JACK; BAY, MICHAEL; CARPENTER, JOHN; CORMAN, ROGER; GORDON, BERT I.; WISE, ROBERT.

ANDERSON, GERRY (1929–) AND SYLVIA (1937–). The British husband-and-wife production team of Gerry and Sylvia Anderson made a number of innovative contributions to science fiction (mostly in television) from the time of their marriage in 1960 to their separation in 1975. (They were formally divorced in 1980). They broke into science fiction television with the **space opera** *Fireball XL5* (1962), made with the "Supermarionation" process Gerry had developed beginning in the 1950s. Their first big hit, also made with marionettes, came in 1965 with the television series *Thunderbirds* in 1965, about a high-tech rescue team. The Andersons are best known, however, for the live-action television space adventures *UFO* (1970–1971) and *Space 1999* (1975–1978), though the latter series also marked the end of their partnership (and marriage). The *Thunderbirds* series inspired two feature films produced by the Andersons in the mid-1960s, but the only major sf film they produced was 1969's *Doppelgänger,* now better known by its U.S. title, ***Journey to the Far Side of the Sun.***

THE ANDROMEDA STRAIN. (Dir. **Robert Wise**, 1971.) Based on a novel by **Michael Crichton,** *The Andromeda Strain* is an effective techno-thriller that combines a twist on the **alien-invasion** narrative with a dramatization of concerns about germ warfare and the potential for germ warfare research to unleash a deadly **plague.** In the film, a U.S. space probe crashes back on earth, releasing a deadly microorganism that it has brought back (apparently inadvertently) to earth from outer space. Virtually all of the inhabitants of the small town of Piedmont, Arizona, are killed by the contagion almost immediately. The probe is quickly recovered and taken to a top-secret underground facility in Nevada; a crack team of scientists is then rushed to the facility in a desperate effort to figure out how to control the microorganism before it spreads across the planet. In the process, it becomes evident that the microorganism had actually been brought back from space intentionally, for use in the development of biological weapons. A nuclear holocaust theme is introduced in the film as well. The U.S. military nearly nukes Piedmont to try to wipe out the microorganism (now dubbed the "Andromeda strain"), but disaster is averted at the last moment when the scientists in Nevada realize that a nuclear explosion would only fuel the growth of the strain. Meanwhile, the Nevada facility is itself nearly nuked by its own self-destruct program, adding some last-minute suspense. That disaster is also averted. In the meantime, no cure for the Andromeda strain has been discovered, but the microorganism has by this time mutated into a noninfectious form. All is well for the time being, but the film ends with an ominous warning that more potential biological catastrophes might be on the way. A box-office hit as well as a critical favorite, *The Andromeda Strain* helped to fuel a minor early 1970s renaissance in the production of American sf films, almost all of which were pessimistic in tone.

ANIMATED SCIENCE FICTION FILMS. In the United States, animated science fiction films have been notably unsuccessful at the box office, with the exception of **children's science fiction** such as *WALL-E* (2008) and *Monsters vs. Aliens* (2009). The reason may be that, in the United States, animated films are perceived as being for children, even when they are not. Thus, science fiction films such as *Titan A.E.* (2000) and *Battle for Terra* (2007), which are not children's films, have had difficulty finding a marketing niche, while other films that can be considered children's films but that are perhaps more thoughtful and sophisticated than the typical children's film, such as *The Iron Giant* (1999), have had similar marketing difficulties. Internationally, the situation is somewhat different. In 1973, the joint Czechoslovakian-French production *La planète sauvage* (*Fantastic Planet*) featured surreal imagery and serious political allegory and won the special jury prize at the 1973 Cannes Film Festival. Animated science fiction has been especially successful in Japan, where the particular form of animation known as *anime* has produced a number of highly popular science fiction films designed for mature audiences. Films such as *Akira* (1988), *Kôkaku kidôtai* (1995, *Ghost in the Shell*), and *Toki o kakeru shôjo* (2006, *The Girl Who Leapt through Time*) have demonstrated that animated films can deal with sophisticated science fiction themes and narratives. Meanwhile, the Japanese-U.S. production *Final Fantasy: The Spirits Within,* not made in the anime style, was loosely based on a popular Japanese role-playing game—and was the first attempt to make a photorealistic animated sf film. It featured a big budget and a first-rate cast of American voice actors, but was not a box-office success. A subsequent film, *Final Fantasy*

VII: Advent Children (2005), was a Japanese production, more directly based on the *Final Fantasy VII* video game (thus the title). It had a much lower budget, but (thanks to advances in technology) achieved an animation style similar to that of the original *Final Fantasy* film.

Meanwhile, though animated science fiction films proper have not fared well in the United States, science fiction films from *Star Wars* (1977) onward have grown increasingly dependent on animation techniques involving **computer-generated imagery** to produce their **special effects**. This tendency reached a new level in 2004, when the French film *Immortel (ad vitam)*, the Japanese film **Casshern,** and the U.S.-British-Italian film *Sky Captain and the World of Tomorrow* employed live actors, but otherwise generated the entire film by computer animation. As a result, especially in the case of science fiction film, the line between animated film and live-action film has been considerably blurred.

While largely aimed at children, or at least families, *WALL-E* was a breakthrough in the realistic detail with which it represented science fiction scenarios, suggesting an extremely bright future for animated science fiction films. As if to bear that out, it was followed in 2009 by the richest year yet in that form. In addition to relatively light fare aimed at children—such as *Monsters vs. Aliens* and *Planet 51* (which reverses the alien-invasion scenario by having earthlings land on another planet)—that year saw more mature fare such as the **postapocalyptic** film *9,* as well as *Battle for Terra,* which received its first wide release in the United States, though it was originally released in 2007. Finally, **James Cameron's** *Avatar,* released in late 2009, makes extended use of highly sophisticated computer animation, though it includes live-action scenes as well. *See also* DISNEY; PIXAR.

ANIME. The term *anime* (essentially just a shortened form of the word *animation*) refers to a particular style of animation used in Japan in both film and television. While the history of anime dates back to the early decades of the 20th century, the form as it is now known has strong roots in the 1970s, when the growing popularity of Japanese comic books, or *manga,* exercised a powerful influence on Japanese animation styles, previously dominated by styles that were derivative of the films produced by the **Disney** company in the United States. By the end of the 1980s, the anime style had emerged as a fully developed art form, producing such groundbreaking works of animated science fiction film as the **dystopian-postapocalyptic** film *Akira,* adapted from the manga series of the same title. The anime style has enjoyed growing international popularity in recent years and now exerts a widespread influence on animation produced outside of Japan.

The manga of **Osamu Tezuka,** also an important animator, was particularly influential in the evolution of the modern anime style, and Tezuka himself was a pioneering director of anime, including extensive work on television adaptations of his own manga *Tesuwan Atom (Astro Boy),* which appeared from 1951 to 1968. In 2009, an American-produced, computer-animated *Astro Boy* feature-length film was released, bringing the **robot** hero to a new generation of viewers.

Internationally, the best-known anime artist is probably **Hayao Miyazaki,** renowned as the creator of a number of striking children's films translated into English and distributed in the West by the Disney company. Much of Miyazaki's work can be considered science fiction, including *Kaze no tani no Naushika* (1984, **Nausicaä of the Valley of the Wind**), regarded by many as his masterpiece. Though it contains important elements of the fantasy-adventure genre, *Nausicaä* is in fact a postapocalyptic film that resides firmly within the territory of science fiction and that is best suited for fairly mature audiences, treating very serious themes, such as **environmentalism**. *Mononoke-hime* (1997, *Princess Mononoke*), another of his most respected films, is primarily a fantasy film, but returns to many of the themes of *Nausicaä,* depicting a postapocalyptic world ravaged by militarism and environmental irresponsibility. *Hauru no ugoku shiro* (2004, *Howl's Moving Castle*) is another fantasy film, but one that contains an especially large amount of science fictional hardware.

Perhaps the most important anime director in the realm of science fiction film is **Mamoru Oshii,** who began his work as an anime director in the early 1980s with the *Urusei Yatsura* animated television series, which led him to direct two spinoff films of this **alien-invasion** story, *Urusei yatsura 1: Onri yû* (1983, *Urusei Yatsura: Only You*) and *Urusei Yatsura: Byûtifuru dorîmâ* (1984, *Urusei Yatsura:*

Beautiful Dreamer). In 1989, Oshii directed another anime science fiction film, *Kidô keisatsu patorebâ: The Movie* (*Patlabor: The Movie*), as part of an extensive franchise involving manga, serial television, and straight-to-video films, as well as this theatrical film; in 1993, he directed the sequel, *Kidô keisatsu patorebâ: The Movie 2* (*Patlabor 2: The Movie*). In the West, Oshii is probably best known as the director of the anime **cyberpunk** film *Kôkaku kidôtai* (1995, *Ghost in the Shell*), as well as its sequel, *Ghost in the Shell 2: Innocence* (2004), which became the first animated film to be nominated for the Palme d'Or at the Cannes Film Festival.

Other notable anime sf films include *Kaubôi bibappu: Tengoku no tobira* (2001, *Cowboy Bebop: The Movie*), *Appurushîdo* (2004, *Appleseed*), and *Toki o kakeru shôjo* (2006, *The Girl Who Leapt through Time*), and *Ekusu makina* (2007, *Appleseed: Ex Machina*). *See also* ANIMATED SCIENCE FICTION FILMS; *CASSHERN*; CHILDREN'S SCIENCE FICTION; CYBORG; JAPANESE SCIENCE FICTION FILM; VIRTUAL REALITY.

ARNOLD, JACK (1916–1992). Born Jack Arnold Waks in New Haven, Connecticut, Jack Arnold was one of the leading directors of the science fiction film explosion of the 1950s. Like many sf films of the period, Arnold's films were generally low-budget affairs, but several of his films stand out for their interesting cinematography, well-crafted scripts, and thoughtful exploration of contemporary social issues. Arnold's first directorial effort was the 1950 documentary *With These Hands,* which was nominated for an Academy Award for Best Documentary Feature. Its exploration of working conditions in the New York garment industry showed the social consciousness that continued to mark Arnold's later sf films, which began with *It Came from Outer Space* (1953), one of the most thoughtful (and least xenophobic) of the **alien-invasion** films of the 1950s. Arnold is perhaps best remembered for *Creature from the Black Lagoon* (1954) and its sequel *Revenge of the Creature* (1955), a pair of unusually cerebral examples of the **monster movie**. (A second sequel, 1956's *The Creature Walks Among Us,* was directed by John Sherwood.) Also particularly important in Arnold's directorial oeuvre is *The Incredible Shrinking Man* (1957), which effectively deals not only with cold-war nuclear fears, but also with anxieties about contemporary threats to traditional masculine roles. *Tarantula* (1955) was a better-than-average science-themed monster movie, though Arnold's later attempts to move into youth-market science fiction produced largely forgettable films such as *The Space Children* (1958) and *Monster on the Campus* (1958).

In 1959, Arnold went to England to direct the Peter Sellers vehicle *The Mouse that Roared.* In the 1960s and 1970s, he worked mostly in television, directing numerous episodes of such well-known series as *Gilligan's Island* and *The Brady Bunch.* In 1985 Arnold won the President's Award (for lifetime achievement) from the Academy of Science Fiction, Fantasy and Horror Films.

ARTIFICIAL INTELLIGENCE. *See* COMPUTERS AND ARTIFICIAL INTELLIGENCE.

ARTIFICIAL INTELLIGENCE: AI. (Dir. **Steven Spielberg**, 2001.) Based on a short story by Brian Aldiss, this Pinocchio-inspired **robot** narrative was scripted and directed by Spielberg, who took the helm when **Stanley Kubrick**, who had originally planned to do the film, died before he could begin the project. Set in a **postapocalyptic** world in which the natural human population has been decimated by the effects of environmental catastrophe, the film envisions a society in which artificial humans (here generally described as *robots,* or *Mechas*) play a more and more important role. Crack roboticist Allen Hobby (William Hurt) and his team develop a child robot that is capable of bonding with and genuinely loving human parents, so that it can serve as a surrogate child. The prototype of this new kind of robot, named David (Haley Joel Osment), goes to live with Henry and Monica Swinton (Sam Robards and Frances O'Connor), whose own child lies in a hospital in a vegetative state. After their natural child unexpectedly recovers and returns home, things begin to go badly for David, who is eventually left in the woods by Monica to avoid having it destroyed by his manufacturer. David's various adventures through subsequent dystopian and postapocalyptic settings make clear the animosity that many humans have toward Mechas, making the film something of an allegory about racism. David ends up in an underwater Manhattan, seeking the Blue Fairy in the hope that she can make it a real boy so that Monica will love it. An ice age follows, and David is recovered 2,000 years later by hyper-advanced robots, humans having since become extinct. They treasure the robot because of its direct memory of the human past and try to make its life as comfortable as they can, including giving it one last day with a Monica they have reconstructed from a DNA sample. Sometimes bordering on the overly sentimental, *Artificial Intelligence* is nevertheless an emotionally powerful film that deals with a number of issues: it not only explores the boundary between human and machine, but also projects a posthuman future actuated by environmental collapse. *See also* ENVIRONMENTALISM.

ASIMOV, ISAAC (1920–1992). Considered (along with **Robert A. Heinlein** and **Arthur C. Clarke**) to be one of the three great figures of the Golden Age of science fiction, Isaac Asimov is still one of the best known and most admired figures in the history of science fiction. Asimov's best-known fiction, such as the acclaimed *Foundation* trilogy of the early 1950s, has relatively little action and has proved difficult to adapt to film, though an adaptation of the first book in that trilogy is reportedly in development as of this writing, with **Roland Emmerich**, known mostly for the action and **special effects** in his films, paradoxically slated to direct. *Nightfall* (1988) was an unsuccessful film adaptation of an award-winning short story by Asimov. The film *Bicentennial Man* (1999) was based on a short story by Asimov and a followup novel—*The Positronic Man* (1993)—in which co-author Robert Silverberg helped to further develop Asimov's original ideas. The highest profile film adaptation of Asimov's work was **Alex Proyas**'s *I, Robot* (2004), though this film mainly just draws upon some of Asimov's basic ideas (such as the Three Laws of Robotics, which presumably ensure that **robots** will remain helpers, rather than threats, to humanity) rather than being a true adaptation of his 1950 story collection of the same title. The Laws of Robotics have in fact influenced numerous subsequent robot narratives: the programming of **Robby the Robot**, a key figure in the 1956 sf classic *Forbidden Planet* seems to have been influenced by them, and the laws are referred to in such diverse films as the cult movie *Repo Man* (1984), *Aliens* (1986), and the Japanese **anime** film *Ghost in the Shell 2: Innocence* (2004). Indeed, Asimov's ideas in general have exercised a huge influence on subsequent science fiction, including film.

ATTACK OF THE 50 FOOT WOMAN. (Dir. **Nathan Juran**, 1958.) Though a film with a reputation for being hilariously awful, *Attack of the 50 Foot Woman* remains one of the best remembered cult science fiction films of the 1950s. In the film, unhappy heiress Nancy Fowler Archer (Allison Hayes) meets up with a giant from outer space, who accidentally inflicts radioactive scratches on her neck while stealing her diamond necklace. The scratches then turn Nancy into a giant as well, after which she lumbers into town, menaces the locals (especially her unfaithful husband), and has to be shot down by the local sheriff. *Attack of the 50 Foot Woman* thus joins the shrinking-and-growing subgenre that was particularly popular in the late 1950s, including such entries as ***The Incredible Shrinking Man*** (1957), *The Amazing Colossal Man* (1957), and *Attack of the Puppet People* (1958), though this group had a forerunner as early as 1940 in *Dr. Cyclops.*

Meanwhile, *Attack of the 50 Foot Woman* is actually more interesting than a brief plot summary makes it sound, especially in its treatment of gender issues. Actually, this treatment is complex (or perhaps confused) enough that the film has been read as both pro-feminist and antifeminist. In any case, though her wealth sets her apart from the mainstream, Nancy suffers from a range of typical 1950s feminine problems. A former mental patient with a drinking problem and a philandering husband, she becomes an object of mockery in the local press when she first reports her alien encounter. Among other things, she is an image of the suffering wife, who, in the context of the 1950s, can strike back against her unfaithful husband only by making a spectacle of herself, thereby becoming a threat to the safety and security of the entire community. She is thus an image both of justified feminine revenge and terrifying feminine threat. *See also* FEMINISM AND GENDER.

AVATAR. (Dir. **James Cameron**, 2009.) *Avatar* is a 3-D science fiction epic that went on to become the biggest commercial hit of all time, easily surpassing the two billion dollar mark in global box-office receipts. The film deals with a number of topical issues, though both its plot and its treatment of these issues are ultimately predictable. It is also fairly weak on characterization, lacking the memorable iconic characters who have populated many of the greatest sf films.

Avatar is, however, an impressive visual spectacle that employs groundbreaking technologies to present audiences with an unprecedented filmgoing experience.

Costarring Cameron favorite **Sigourney Weaver** and relative newcomer Sam Worthington, *Avatar* focuses on the efforts of colonizing forces from earth to exploit the mineral resources of the distant planet Pandora, a project that is complicated by the fact that Pandora is already inhabited by an intelligent species, the tall, blue-skinned Na'vi. Further, the Na'vi live in total harmony with their environment, which they treat with reverence, but which is threatened with large-scale destruction by the human mining efforts. The humans do attempt some communication with the Na'vi by having humans inhabit artificial Na'vi bodies (the "avatars" of the title) in order to try to negotiate with the natives on their own terms, but there is little common ground between the two sides. The insensitivity of the humans (and their tendency to resort to brute military force to achieve their objectives), inevitably leads to conflict.

The story is in many ways a familiar one, and the Na'vi rather obviously represent Native Americans, while to an extent serving as a sort of allegorical stand-in for non-Western peoples as a whole. In this case, however, the history of colonialism on earth is reversed, and the Na'vi are able to win a decisive military victory over the human invaders, with the help of a group of renegade humans and of the resources of the planet itself. *Avatar* thus provides a fairly conventional critique of colonialism, supplemented by a strong emphasis on environmentalist themes. Indeed, the environment of Pandora, represented using breakthrough techniques of 3-D photography and digital animation, may be the most important "character" in the film.

Avatar is first and foremost a technological masterpiece, a striking demonstration of the way in which the most impressive technologies in a science fiction film can sometimes be the technologies that went into the making of the film itself, which in this case include a seamless integration of live action and **computer animation**, but most importantly involve three-dimension imagery that is superior to that seen in any previous film, thanks to special cameras and processing that Cameron and his crew developed in the years-long process of planning and making the film. The enthusiastic response of audiences to the film suggests that these new technologies have a promising future in science fiction films of the coming years. *See also* ENVIRONMENTALISM.

– B –

BACK TO THE FUTURE AND SEQUELS. (Dir. Robert Zemeckis, 1985–1990.) The tongue-in-cheek **time-travel** narrative *Back to the Future* was one of the key films of the 1980s, a substantial commercial success that became an iconic work of American popular culture. Executive produced by **Steven Spielberg** and directed by **Robert Zemeckis**, the film stars **Michael J. Fox** as Marty McFly, a mid-1980s teenager who travels back to the 1950s in a time machine constructed by the seemingly **mad scientist** Dr. Emmett "Doc" Brown (Christopher Lloyd) by modifying a DeLorean DMC-12 automobile. In the past, McFly meets up with his own parents as teenagers and manages to modify their lives so that they become more successful as adults than they had been in his original timeline. Using his own knowledge of the past (and of the music of Chuck Berry), he also introduces the teenagers of the 1950s to rock 'n' roll, before returning back to his own time.

The success of the initial *Back to the Future* film led to the release of a sequel, *Back to the Future Part II,* in 1989, with Zemeckis, Spielberg, Fox, and Lloyd still involved. This time, McFly uses Brown's DeLorean to travel to the future, though what he learns there causes him to travel once again back to the 1950s to prevent disastrous changes to history that have been caused by a trip back in time by the villainous Biff Tannen (Thomas F. Wilson), who previously stole the DeLorean and traveled back there to manipulate events. All is restored, though Doc (or at last one version of him) winds up back in 1885, which sets up the scenario of *Back to the Future Part III* (1990), released only six months later, the filming of which overlapped with that of *Part II.* In the third installment of the trilogy, McFly must travel back to 1885 to save Doc from being murdered by one of Tannen's ancestors (also played by Wilson). Because of the time frame of much of the action, this third film combines its science fiction elements with elements of a Western.

BAKER, RICK (1950–). Makeup artist Richard A. "Rick" Baker is one of the leading "creature effects" artists in the history of film. Baker's first professional job was as a **special effects** assistant on *The Exorcist* (1973). He gained considerable attention with his work on *An American Werewolf in London* (1981), which won him the first Academy Award for Best Makeup. Subsequently, Baker did the special makeup effects for such films as *Videodrome* (1983), Michael Jackson's music video *Thriller* (1983), *Harry and the Hendersons* (1987), *Ed Wood* (1994), **Men in Black** (1997), the remake of **Planet of the Apes** (2001), *Hellboy* (2004), and *Enchanted* (2007). Altogether, Baker has been nominated for 10 Oscars for Best Makeup, winning six times.

BATTLE BEYOND THE STARS. (Dir. Jimmy T. Murakami, 1980.) Though a reasonably entertaining outer-space adventure with surprisingly good **special effects** (given the low budget), *Battle Beyond the Stars* is perhaps most notable for the amazing array of rising talents that came together in the making of the film. Spearheaded by executive producer **Roger Corman**, the film was written by future prominent director John Sayles, while the special effects team was headed by a young **James Cameron**. **Gale Anne Hurd**, who went on to produce such Cameron-directed films as **The Terminator**, *Terminator II,* and **The Abyss** (among many other films), also worked as an assistant production manager on the film. The plot of the film involves the (ultimately successful) attempts of the denizens of a peaceful planet to hire a colorful and diverse group of mercenaries to protect them from a rapacious space outlaw and his minions. In short, riding the wave of popularity being experienced by science fiction films at the beginning of the 1980s, Sayles's script is essentially a science fiction adaptation of Akira Kurosawa's classic *Seven Samurai* (1954), just as *The Wild Bunch* (1969) had earlier reworked that film in the form of a Western.

BAVA, MARIO (1914–1980). Though best known as a director of stylishly lurid horror films, the Italian director and cinematographer Mario Bava worked extensively in a number of genres, including science fiction. For example, in 1958 he co-directed *La morte viene dallo spazio* (*The Day the Sky Exploded*), generally considered the first **Italian science fiction film**, though he was credited only as the cinematographer on that film. His best-known effort in science fiction, however, is actually a hybrid of horror and science fiction, 1965's *Terrore nello spazio* (*Planet of the Vampires*), often cited as an influence on **Ridley Scott**'s *Alien* (1979), which similarly combines genres.

BAY, MICHAEL (1965–). The American director Michael Bay is known for making big-budget action films in which spectacular **special effects** sometimes take precedence over plot or characterization. However, Bay began his career directing two successful crime films for producer Jerry Bruckheimer, *Bad Boys* (1995) and *The Rock* (1996). It was with the science fiction **disaster** film *Armageddon* (1998, also produced by Bruckheimer) that Bay began to display his signature reliance on special effects, an approach he also used outside of science fiction in *Pearl Harbor* (2001). Bay turned to more thoughtful science fiction in *The Island* (2005), a **dystopian** film with an emphasis on **genetic engineering**; his first film without Bruckheimer, *The Island,* was not well received critically or commercially. Bay seemed to find the perfect topic for his talents as a director with *Transformers* (2007) and its sequel *Transformers: Revenge of the Fallen* (2009), **alien-invasion** films featuring high-tech **robots** that provide perfect subjects for Bay's trademark high-action special effects. Both films were huge commercial successes, even if critical reaction continued to be mixed. Bay has also produced (though not directed) a number of recent horror films, mostly within franchises such as *The Texas Chainsaw Massacre* and *Friday the 13th*.

THE BEAST FROM 20,000 FATHOMS. (Dir. **Eugène Lourié**, 1953.) One of the earliest attempts to express nuclear anxieties through the venue of the **monster movie**, *The Beast from 20,000 Fathoms* features a destructive monster that is freed by atomic testing after being frozen in ice near the North Pole for millions of years. This creature, a "rhedosaurus," immediately heads for the environs of New York City, which just happens to be the natural habitat of its species. Scientists hope to capture and study the beast, but it becomes infected with a deadly contagion that threatens to spread to the population of the city. It therefore has to be killed (with the help of the military), though it cannot simply be blasted to smithereens (which might propel its germs into the air). The rhedosaurus is thus shot down with a radioactive bullet; oddly, then, what is essentially a form of nuclear weapon is used to end the threat that was initially caused by another nuclear weapon. As a result, the film seems ambivalent about the potential of nuclear science to be either a danger or a boon to humanity.

Ultimately, though, this sepia-toned black-and-white film is perhaps most important as the first film in which the monster and other **special effects** were created under the supervision of **Ray Harryhausen**. The rhedosaurus is, indeed, a fairly effective early example of the kind of **stop-motion animation** for which Harryhausen became famous; the scene in which the beast is shot down amid the flaming wreck of a roller coaster it has been demolishing is particularly impressive. However, the beast itself is depicted essentially as a mindless killing machine; it is therefore relatively uninteresting as a movie monster, even if it does at times seem as much victim as villain.

BERNDS, EDWARD (1905–2000). Though not typically mentioned among the leading lights of the science fiction film explosion of the 1950s, the American screenwriter and director Edward Bernds was actually for a brief period one of the more productive figures who participated in that phenomenon. Having worked extensively in Hollywood as a sound engineer (frequently for Frank Capra) in a career that dated back to 1929, Bernds moved into both screenwriting and directing in 1945, quickly amassing numerous directing and writing credits for such lowbrow Hollywood fare as the *Blondie* and *Bowery Boys* films. Now known as a competent, though not brilliant, director of genre films, he moved into sf film as the writer and director of the **time-travel–postapocalyptic** film *World Without End* (1956). After that, he continued to work mainly in other genres, especially Westerns, though he did enjoy one highly productive brief period when his career was concentrated in sf film, directing *Space Master X-7* (1958), *Queen of Outer Space* (1958), *Return of the Fly* (1959), and *Valley of the Dragons* (1961). He then topped off his career in sf film with a Three Stooges sf spoof, *The Three Stooges in Orbit* (1962).

BESSON, LUC (1959–). The Paris-born Luc Besson is best known as the writer and producer of a number of stylish action movies, a number of which—including *Subway* (1985), *La Femme Nikita* (1990), and *The Professional* (1994)—he also directed. Other prominent action films written and produced by Besson include the *Taxi* series and the *Transporter* series. In the realm of science fiction film, Besson's first feature-length film (which he wrote, directed, and produced) was *Le dernier combat* (*The Last Combat,* 1983), a visually striking black-and-white **postapocalyptic** film. In addition, Besson wrote and directed ***The Fifth Element*** (1997), one of the most stylish sf films of the 1990s. He also wrote and produced the **dystopian** action film *Banlieue 13* (2004, *District 13*), while many of his other action films have something of the look and feel of a science fiction film. *See* FRENCH SCIENCE FICTION FILM.

BIEHN, MICHAEL (1956–). The American actor Michael Biehn has played some of the most memorable roles in the history of science fiction film, mostly in films directed by **James Cameron**. Most notably, the then little-known Biehn had a prominent role in *The Terminator* (1984) as Kyle Reese, a human resistance fighter from the future sent back to the 1980s to protect **Sarah Connor** from the **cyborg** terminator of the title, subsequently fathering Sarah's child, **John Connor**. Biehn followed in 1986 as the space marine Hicks in Cameron's *Alien* sequel *Aliens;* in 1989 he had a major role in Cameron's *The Abyss* as Lt. Hiram Coffey, an unhinged Navy Seal. He had a brief role in Cameron's *Terminator 2: Judgment Day* that was cut from the theatrical release but restored in the DVD special edition. In 2002, Biehn played a leading role in the sf film *Clockstoppers,* directed by **Jonathan Frakes** and co-produced by **Gale Anne Hurd**. Biehn has also played numerous other roles in a variety of genres in film and television.

BILAL, ENKI (1951–). Born in Belgrade, Yugoslavia, Enki Bilal moved to Paris at the age of nine and subsequently became a leading French comic book creator, best known for his "Nikopol Trilogy" of futuristic comics. In 1989, he moved into science fiction film as the writer and director of *Bunker Palace Hôtel*. He followed in 1996 as the writer and director of *Tykho Moon,* but gained particular attention in the world of science fiction cinema with the release of *Immortel* (*ad vitam*) in 2004. This film, based on the first two volumes of the Nikopol Trilogy, employs innovative techniques of **computer-generated imagery**: many scenes involve live actors shot in front of **green screens**, but some characters are computer generated as well. With the Japanese *Casshern*, the American *Able Edwards*, and the American-British-Italian *Sky Captain and the World of Tomorrow*, all also released in 2004, *Immortel* (*ad vitam*) is regarded as a groundbreaking step toward the generation of more and more material for sf films by computer. All of Bilal's films display an innovative aesthetic that is clearly influenced by his background in comic books.

BLADE RUNNER. (Dir. **Ridley Scott**, 1982.) Based on **Philip K. Dick**'s novel *Do Androids Dream of Electric Sheep?*, *Blade Runner* is one of the most influential sf films in cinema history. In the film, "blade runner" Rick Deckard (**Harrison Ford**) is a police operative charged with hunting down and killing rogue "replicants," artificially created humans manufactured for use as slaves in dangerous environments, especially in outer space, where the human race is rapidly relocating to escape an environmentally ravaged earth. Biological rather than mechanical, these replicants obviously blur the definition of the human. Indeed, the replicants of the film often seem more alive and more human than the natural humans of the film, who tend to seem alienated and emotionally blank. This plot thus raises a number of important issues about the nature of humanity and about the relationship between humans and their own technology.

The plot also mixes elements typical of the detective story into its basic matrix of science fictional elements, creating a multigeneric texture of the kind that is typical of postmodernist culture. Indeed, *Blade Runner* is widely regarded as a key postmodernist film, both for this generic hybridity and for the way in which it combines its futuristic setting with visual elements reminiscent of the films noirs of the 1940s. It is for its confusing, but compelling "future noir" visual representation of a 2019 Los Angeles—both teeming and desolate, both decaying and dominated by a high-tech mediascape—that the film is ultimately most important, exercising a strong influence on virtually all subsequent cinematic representations of cities of the future. Meanwhile, the postmodern hybridity of the film's visual representation of the city is enhanced by the fact that it is composed of a complex mixture of architectural styles from different periods and different cultures, sometimes even within individual buildings. The film openly calls attention to its own emphasis on the visual (this commenting on the role of the visual in film as a form) through a complex network of images involving eyes, seeing, and surveillance that runs throughout the film. Though not a big initial box-office hit, *Blade Runner* has enjoyed a growing critical reputation over the years and has now probably received more attention from academic film critics than any other science fiction film. *See also* CYBERPUNK; CYBORG; ENVIRONMENTALISM; GENETIC ENGINEERING.

THE BLOB. (Dir. **Irvin S. Yeaworth Jr.**, 1958.) A film that combines the **monster movie** with the **alien-invasion** narrative, *The Blob* is a leading example of the turn in late-1950s science fiction film toward an attempt to appeal to younger audiences of teenage moviegoers, which was fast becoming a dominant demographic in the minds of Hollywood movie marketers. The film features a jello-like blob creature that crashes to earth on a meteor, then starts to grow rapidly, ingesting everything in its path, including the inhabitants of the small town near which it lands. The blob bears certain metaphorical resemblances to cold-war visions of an all-devouring communism, though it seems mindless and has no specific political agenda. The main social issues raised directly by the film have to do with the opposition between teenage protagonist Steve Andrews (Steve McQueen, in his first starring role) and the local authorities. At first, Andrews is the lone witness to the existence of the invader, and he has trouble convincing the local authorities of the authenticity of his claims. In particular, the police suspect a hoax, because, as a teenager, Andrews is automatically considered suspect (though McQueen was 28 at the time of filming and looked at least that). The sympathies of *The Blob* are, of course, with Andrews and the town's teenagers, who manage to mobilize opposition to the monster, despite the cluelessness of their elders. Though nothing seems to be able to kill the blob, it is finally frozen and deposited at the North Pole, with an ominous final warning that it is still alive and might someday thaw.

BONESTELL, CHESLEY (1888–1986). Born in San Francisco, the painter and illustrator Chesley Bonestell produced groundbreaking "space art" that exercised a strong influence on the look of science fiction film throughout the 20th century; his meticulous attention to accurate detail earned him the title of "Father of Modern Space Art." Trained as an architect, Bonestell found it difficult to get work due to the Depression in the 1930s, so he moved to Hollywood and began to work in the film industry, where he did matte paintings for a number of important films, including *The Hunchback of Notre Dame* (1939), *Citizen Kane* (1941), and *The Magnificent Ambersons* (1942). From there, Bonestell found his true calling when he moved to a series of paintings of the planet Saturn as seen from its various moons; published in *Life* magazine in 1944, these paintings made an immediate sensation and remain some of the best-known astronomical paintings in history. These and other astronomical paintings by Bonestell were collected as illustrations for Willy Ley's influential 1949 volume *The Conquest of Space,* adapted as a science fiction film in 1955. With sf film experiencing a boom in the 1950s, Bonestell returned to Hollywood in that decade, contributing **special effects** art for **George Pal**'s *Destination Moon* (1950) and *The War of the Worlds* (1953). Bonestell's illustrations of spaceflight technology for *Collier's* magazine in the early 1950s (made at the behest of Werner von Braun) are considered to be an important inspiration for the U.S. space program.

BOYLE, DANNY (1956–). The British filmmaker Danny Boyle moved into the top echelon of Hollywood directors when his film *Slumdog Millionaire* (2008) won the Academy Award for Best Picture, at the same time gaining him the Oscar for Best Director. But Boyle had already gained considerable attention much earlier with his stylish and innovative early work on *Shallow Grave* (1994) and *Trainspotting* (1996), which won him the opportunity to direct the big-budget thriller *The Beach* (2000). That film was greeted with a lukewarm response from audiences and critics, and Boyle returned to lower-budget efforts in 2002 with the innovative **postapocalyptic** film *28 Days Later,* a stylish and violent zombie movie whose zombies are created by a **plague** caused by a virus that is developed by medical researchers, then accidentally released among the general population of London. A great critical and commercial success, the film inspired a 2007 sequel, *28 Weeks Later,* though the sequel was directed by Juan Carlos Fresnadillo. Boyle himself returned to science fiction with the stylish **space opera** *Sunshine* (2007), in which the crew of a huge spacecraft attempts (apparently successfully, though none of them survive the effort) to reignite the dying sun with a gigantic bomb.

BRAZIL. (Dir. Terry Gilliam, 1985.) *Brazil* is a parodic response to the tradition of **dystopian** film that is nevertheless in many ways an effective dystopian film in its own right, especially in its satirical critique of the bureaucratization and routinization of life in the modern world. Set in a dreary near-future London that recalls the setting of George Orwell's *Nineteen Eighty-Four, Brazil* supplements this dark setting with satire, parody, and complex ironies that open a number of rich dialogues with the traditions of both utopian and dystopian fiction and film. The protagonist of *Brazil* is Sam Lowry (Jonathan Pryce), a conscientious but unambitious bureaucrat who works in the gigantic Ministry of Information, which keeps tabs on the general populace and distributes official propaganda to encourage the ongoing obedience of that population. However, the Ministry is highly inefficient, partly because the technology available to them is decidedly backward—such as computers that employ clunky mechanical typewriters for keyboards and small black-and-white televisions for monitors. All of the technology of Gilliam's future London is similarly backward, relying on a variety of bulky mechanical devices (often driven by steam), suggesting that this dystopian society in general is inimical to scientific and technical progress.

The cumbersome technology of *Brazil* also centrally contributes to the drab atmosphere of the film, which features blighted industrial landscapes, decaying urban slums, and dark, crumbling buildings. All citizens are liable to sudden and unexpected arrest at the hands of the heavily armed troops charged with keeping security, and citizens are often arrested, tortured, and even executed through administrative errors. Lowry survives amid it all by enjoying a rich fantasy life, but his attempts to convert his fantasies into reality land him in the clutches of the Information Retrieval section of the Ministry of Information. While Lowry is being tortured, the dashing Harry Tuttle (Robert De Niro) and a band of guerrillas apparently burst in to rescue him, blowing up the Ministry building in the process. Unfortunately, this escape occurs only in Lowry's mind, his body remaining in the torture chamber. Through such motifs, the film resembles a number of other dystopian works in its central opposition between political oppression and the individual imagination. However, *Brazil* neither declares the inevitable victory of the imagination nor accepts the ultimate impossibility of resistance to tyranny.

BRITISH SCIENCE FICTION FILM. Though modern science fiction can be said to have its beginnings in the work of the British writer **H. G. Wells**, and though the modern science fiction film can be said to have its beginning in the Wells-scripted *Things to Come* (1936), the output of British films in the realm of science fiction has continually been overshadowed by the glossier (and more expensive) products of **American science fiction film**, especially after the boom in American sf film of the 1950s. British sf film experienced a minor boom in the 1950s as well, marked by such efforts as *Spaceways* (1953), *The Quatermass Xperiment* (1955), and *Quatermass 2* (1957), all from **Hammer Film Productions**. Meanwhile, one of the key phenomena in British film of the late 1950s was the emergence of Hammer as a major international force in the area of horror film, including numerous films, such as their reboot of the *Frankenstein* franchise with *The Curse of Frankenstein* (1957), that might rightly be considered science fiction as well.

The early 1960s were marked by relatively minor efforts such as *The Day the Earth Caught Fire* (1961) and *The Day of the Triffids* (1962). However, with the release of such films as *First Men in the Moon* (1964), **Stanley Kubrick**'s *Dr. Strangelove or: How I Learned to Stop Worrying and Love the Bomb* (1964), and *Fahrenheit 451* (1966), one could argue that, for a brief period in the mid-1960s, British sf film supplanted American science fiction film as the world leader. Meanwhile, by this time, the British had also developed a special emphasis on **alien-invasion** films with a strong horror emphasis, especially in the films made by director **Terence Fisher**, who had earlier directed *The Curse of Frankenstein*. Also of note in the 1950s is the rise of the television series *Dr. Who* as a cultural phenomenon, including two feature-length film adaptations, *Dr. Who and the Daleks* (1965) and *Daleks' Invasion Earth: 2150 A.D.* (1966). However, that the key British sf film of the 1960s was a British-American co-production, Kubrick's magisterial *2001: A Space Odyssey* (1968) suggests that Hollywood was never far out of the picture. To some extent, British sf film of the first half of the 1970s mirrored U.S. film in its focus on the **dystopian** film, including Kubrick's U.S.-UK co-production of *A Clockwork Orange* (1971); *Z.P.G.* (1972), which focuses on the dangers of overpopulation; and *Rollerball* (1975), a British production with a Canadian director, Norman Jewison. Nicolas Roeg's *The Man Who Fell to Earth* (1976) was another highlight of British sf film in the 1970s.

The period 1977–1984, which saw a major boom in American sf film, was relatively quiet in British sf film, though it should be noted that *Moonraker* (1979), a British-French co-production released during this period, was the most science fictional of all the James Bond films, which frequently feature some sort of sf motif. Meanwhile, one major work of that boom, *The Terminator* (1984), was a British co-production. Other highlights of the 1980s included *1984* (1984), a film adaptation of George Orwell's classic dystopian novel, and Terry Gilliam's *Brazil* (1985), a film that both parodies and extends the tradition of dystopian film. Many of the most important British sf films since that time have been international co-productions, indicating the globalization of the film industry as a whole. For example, two of the highlights of the 1990s were *Event Horizon* (1997, a joint U.S.-UK production) and **David Cronenberg**'s *eXistenZ* (1999, a joint British-Canadian production).

Co-productions in the new millennium have included *The Hitchhiker's Guide to the Galaxy* (2005, U.S.-UK), **Children of Men** (2006, U.S.-UK-Japan), and **Danny Boyle**'s *Sunshine* (2007, U.S.-UK). Among strictly British productions of the new millennium, dark, **postapocalyptic** films have been dominant, including Boyle's *28 Days Later* (2002), its sequel *28 Weeks Later* (2007), and the somewhat self-parodic *Doomsday* (2008). *See also* GUEST, VAL; SCOTT, RIDLEY.

BURTON, TIM (1958–). Known as one of the most visually inventive directors in contemporary Hollywood film, Tim Burton moved from his beginnings as an animator for **Disney** to become the director of such quirky tours-de-force as *Pee-wee's Big Adventure* (1985) and *Beetle Juice* (1988), then moved into the Hollywood mainstream with his noirish big-budget comic-book adaptation *Batman* (1989) and its sequel *Batman Returns* (1992). Both of these films feature Batman's high-tech gadgets and thus have strong sf elements, as does *Edward Scissorhands* (1990), which is essentially a fairy-tale version of the Frankenstein story. Burton's *Ed Wood* (1994) tells the story of the infamously bad director of its title, concentrating especially on his making of the horrific sf film *Plan 9 from Outer Space* (1959). Burton then moved further into sf territory with the making of *Mars Attacks!* (1996), a spoof that refers back to the **alien-invasion** films of the 1990s, but also responds to the then-recent *Independence Day* (1996). Burton's first "straight" science fiction film was the 2001 "re-imagining" of *Planet of the Apes,* a visually stunning film that nevertheless lacks the satirical punch of the original. By this time, Burton seemed to have become something of a specialist in visually inventive remakes, following with *Charley and the Chocolate Factory* (2005), a remake of the children's classic *Willy Wonka and the Chocolate Factory* (1971). In 2010 Burton directed the remake of Disney's *Alice in Wonderland;* he is currently at work on a **stop-motion animation** version (also for Disney) of *Frankenweenie,* a remake of a live-action short he wrote and directed in his early days at Disney. Burton has produced most of the films he has directed, though he has not written the screenplays for any of his major films.

– C –

C-3PO. C-3PO is a humanoid **robot,** or "droid," that is one of only four characters to appear in all six films of the two *Star Wars* trilogies. C-3PO is a "protocol" droid that is fluent in millions of languages and other forms of communication. Designed for diplomatic purposes and to help further communication among the various intelligent species that populate the *Star Wars* universe, it is also an expert on the etiquette and customs of a number of societies within this universe. Fussy and officious, C-3PO often provides comic relief, finding itself in dangerous situations for which it is ill prepared, though it often provides important help to the major characters as well. Typically accompanied by the small astromech droic **R2-D2**, C-3PO is voiced in all six *Star Wars* films by actor Anthony Daniels. For *Episodes III–VI* of the *Star Wars* sequence, the principal photography of C-3PO was shot with Daniels wearing a special costume. For the principal photography in *Episodes I* and *II,* C-3PO was represented by a puppet.

CAHN, EDWARD L. (1889–1963). Though best known as the director of a series of "Our Gang" comedies from 1939 to 1943, Edward L. Cahn had a long and prolific career as a director of B movies in a variety of genres, including horror, science fiction, and teen exploitation. Indeed, films such as *Creature with the Atom Brain* (1955) and *Invisible Invaders* (1959) attempt to combine horror with science fiction, while *Invasion of the Saucer Men* (1957) combines science fiction with the teen exploitation genre. Ultimately, Cahn's most important film is probably *It! The Terror from Beyond Space* (1958), which also combines horror and science fiction. Not only one of Cahn's best films, this particular movie is also important because it apparently exercised an important influence on the later *Alien* sequence of films.

CAMERON, JAMES (1954–). The Canadian-born director James Cameron has the distinction of having directed the two largest box-office hits of all time with *Avatar* (2009) and *Titanic* (1997). However, it is for his contributions to science fiction film that Cameron is likely to be most remembered. After writing, producing, and directing the sf short *Xenogenesis* in 1978, Cameron began his feature-film career working in the shop of **Roger Corman**, supervising the **special effects** for Corman's *Battle Beyond the Stars* (1980). Cameron made his directorial debut the next year with *Piranha Part Two: The Spawning,* also produced by Corman. However, Cameron's first major directorial effort came with the landmark sf film *The Terminator* (1984), which was followed by the equally important sequel *Terminator II: Judgment Day* (1991). In between, Cameron helmed two other major science fiction films, *Aliens* (1986, the second entry in the *Alien* franchise) and *The Abyss* (1989). All of his major sf films were written or co-written by Cameron as well. They are marked by excellent special effects, engaging storytelling, and the development of compelling characters. Much of Cameron's time after *Titanic* was devoted to making documentaries and to developing new 3-D camera technologies, the latter of which ultimately came to be used in another major sf film, *Avatar* (2009), composed mostly of **computer-generated images**. Another 3-D sf film, *Battle Angel,* is currently scheduled for release in 2011.

CARLSON, RICHARD (1912–1977). The American actor Richard Carlson played prominent roles in a number of the science fiction films of the 1950s, often as a sympathetic scientist figure. His most important role, however, might have been as the free-spirited writer John Putnam in *It Came from Outer Space* (1953), the only local who realizes that a shipload of "invading" aliens are actually harmless. Carlson's scientist roles included turns in *The Magnetic Monster* (1953), *Riders to the Stars* (1954), and *Creature from the Black Lagoon* (1954), another particularly important film within the context of 1950s sf. After that film, however, Carlson's appearances were mostly restricted to television, where he played a variety of guest roles until the mid-1970s. He did, however, play an important role in *The Valley of Gwangi* (1969), a sort of science fiction Western that features cowboys battling a **dinosaur**, with **special effects** by **Ray Harryhausen**. Carlson also had a brief and undistinguished career as a director; he directed only one science fiction film, the aforementioned *Riders to the Stars.*

CARPENTER, JOHN (1948–). Though perhaps best known as a master of the horror genre, thanks to the success of such efforts as *Halloween* (1978), John Carpenter has actually worked as much in science fiction as in horror. For example, the first major film directed by Carpenter was the sf comedy *Dark Star* (1974), though he did not return to science fiction until the 1981 **postapocalyptic** film *Escape from New York*. He followed in 1982 with *The Thing*, a slickly produced remake of *The Thing from Another World* (1951). *Starman* (1984) is a much-praised **alien-invasion** narrative with a more benevolent alien, while *They Live* (1988) is a low-budget sf satire that is highly effective in its critique of modern consumer capitalism. *Big Trouble in Little China* (1986) was a box-office flop that combines elements of numerous genres, including science fiction. It has since become something of a cult favorite on home video. *Escape from L.A.* (1996) is a sequel to *Escape from New York,* relocated to the West Coast, while the high-action thriller *Ghosts of Mars* (2001) combines the horror and science fiction genres. Carpenter has written both the scripts and the music for most of the films he has directed. Many of Carpenter's films have stood the test of time: sometimes regarded as a maker of low-budget exploitation films, Carpenter now has a growing critical reputation as a genre-film *auteur.*

CASSHERN. (Dir. Kazuaki Kiriya, 2004.) Based on the 1970s **anime** television series *Neo-Human Casshern, Casshern* is a groundbreaking Japanese film that employs live actors shot almost entirely against a **green screen**, with backgrounds added in digitally in the finished film, much like the British-Italian-American *Sky Captain and the World of Tomorrow,* released in the same year. The result is a mixture of live action and animation that sometimes seems more concerned with the way it looks than with telling a story or developing characters. Still, *Casshern,* which has gained a cult following over the years, is a fairly effective **postapocalyptic** film in its evocation of a world in which the environment has been devastated by global warfare with nuclear, biological, and chemical weapons. It is also a **dystopian** film in its depiction of an oppressive postwar regime that rules the Eastern Federation in the wake of its victory over Europa and its robot army.

The plot revolves around the discovery of "neo cells" (something like super stem cells), which can be injected into recipients and used to regrow damaged or lost body parts. This research, secretly supported by sinister government officials who hope to use the neo cells to ensure their own immortality, predictably gets out of control, leading to the formation of a race of "neo-sapiens," superhumans formed when the neo cells joined together body parts harvested from the victims of a genocidal attack on the people of "Zone Seven." Most of the neo-sapiens are quickly slaughtered by the government; some, however, escape, and eventually return, backed by an army of leftover Europan combat **robots**. Meanwhile, Tetsuya (Yûsuke Iseya), the son of the scientist who discovered the neo cells, is resurrected by the cells as a superhuman who takes on the identity of "Casshern," a local deity, and eventually saves humanity from the advanced neo-humans. This extremely interesting-looking film is punctuated by numerous violent battle scenes, but the ultimate message is that violence only breeds more violence and that war is a pointless exercise in devastation. *See also* COMPUTER-GENERATED IMAGERY (CGI); ENVIRONMENTALISM; JAPANESE SCIENCE FICTION FILM.

CHAMBERS, JOHN (1923–2001). John Chambers was an American make-up artist, best known for creating the "ape" make-up used in *Planet of the Apes* (1968) and its sequels, for which he won a special Academy Award. Chambers is also known in science fiction circles for his make-up work on the original *Star Trek* television series (1966–1969), including the design of **Spock**'s pointed Vulcan ears. Chambers did make-up for *Slaughterhouse-Five* (1972) and *The Island of Dr. Moreau* (1977), as well as a number of horror films. Though uncredited, he also helped to create prosthetic make-up effects for *Blade Runner* (1982).

CHIANG, DOUG (1962–). Born in Taipei, Taiwan, Doug Chiang went on to become a central figure in the development of **special effects** technologies, especially **computer-generated imagery**, that changed sf film so dramatically in the late 20th century. As a creative director for **George Lucas**'s **Industrial Light & Magic (ILM)**, Chiang won a Best Visual Effects Oscar for *Death Becomes Her* (1992). Also at ILM, he helped to produce the special effects for such sf films as *Terminator 2: Judgment Day* (1992) and the first film of the *Star Wars* "prequel" trilogy, *Star Wars Episode I: The Phantom Menace* (1999); he was concept-design director for *Star Wars Episode II: Attack of the Clones* (2002). After leaving ILM, Chiang co-founded Ice Blink Studios in 2004. There, he worked as a concept artist on **Steven Spielberg**'s remake of *War of the Worlds* (2005). He also helped to create the innovative "motion capture" animation technique used in **Robert Zemeckis**'s *The Polar Express* (2004) and *Beowulf* (2007).

CHILDREN OF MEN. (Dir. Alfonso Cuarón, 2006.) A critically praised **postapocalyptic** narrative set in 2027 Great Britain, based on the similarly titled 1992 novel by P. D. James. In the world of the film, no new baby has been born to the human race since 2009, which has combined with a series of environmental and political disasters to produce a future in which the human race simply waits to age and die, with no hope for a next generation. Despair and suicide run rampant. The Great Britain of the narrative seems to have maintained order and living conditions somewhat better than those in the rest of the world, but at the expense of a xenophobia that has seen the country close its borders and become a virtual police state, obsessed with keeping out illegal immigrants.

When a young woman turns up pregnant, the film becomes a race to get her and the fetus to safety from the forces (both government and antigovernment) that might seek to conscript the baby for their own purposes. Theo Faron (Clive Owen) gets the principal responsibility for getting the young woman out of a Great Britain that looks suspiciously like an extension of the Bush Administration's Patriot Act–era United States. Brutal government discrimination against immigrants is obviously meant to recall Nazi Germany; the fact that it also recalls the early 21st-century United States is one of the film's central statements. The cynical Faron often seems ill-suited to the task of hero, but has apparently succeeded by the end of the film in getting both mother and infant (born along the way) to safety. The end, however, is left uncertain, as is the status of Faron, who has been shot and might be either dead or unconscious.

The plot of *Children of Men* helps to hold together the film's visual depiction of a future world in decay and on the brink of collapse, but it is definitely the visuals that lie at the center of the film. Through these visuals, Cuarón produces an entirely believable future world that is all too similar to our own. *See also* ENVIRONMENTALISM; FEMINISM AND GENDER.

CHILDREN'S SCIENCE FICTION. A number of science fiction films have been aimed at young audiences, especially from the 1990s onward, though the **Disney** company has been making films for such audiences since the 1950s. For example, Disney's *20,000 Leagues Under the Sea* (1954), while addressing a number of serious concerns of the time, was clearly designed as family entertainment. Still, science fiction films aimed specifically at children were rare in the 1950s, and films such as *20,000 Leagues Under the Sea* or *Tobor* *the Great* (1954) were definitely exceptions. However, as the decade proceeded, teen audiences became more and more important to Hollywood in general, and science fiction films (like horror films) came to be aimed more and more at teen audiences.

Disney reaffirmed their interest in making sf films that were accessible to children with the 1961 release of *The Absent-Minded Professor,* a sort of **mad-scientist** film toned down for family viewing to make the scientist ultimately quite sane and essentially an embodiment of good-ole American knowhow, if a bit distracted by the high-level thought going on inside his head. This film was quite successful and spawned a 1963 sequel, *Son of Flubber.* In 1969, a young **Kurt Russell** starred in Disney's *The Computer Wore Tennis Shoes,* something of a forerunner of cyberpunk science fiction in which the data and computing abilities of a computer are accidentally downloaded into a college student's brain. This film was possibly inspired by the budding comeback of science fiction film that began with *2001: A Space Odyssey* and *Planet of the Apes* in 1968, after the genre had lagged during most of the 1960s. *The Computer Wore Tennis Shoes* became the first film in a trilogy that also included *Now You See Him, Now You Don't* (1972) and *The Strongest Man in the World* (1975). Disney's *Escape to Witch Mountain* was also released in 1975, an **alien-invasion** film of sorts that is quite clearly aimed at children and that founded a franchise that was still alive as late as 2009 with the release of *Race to Witch Mountain.*

The phenomenal success of ***Star Wars*** in 1977 marked the founding of one of the key franchises in American film history, and one that has proved extremely popular with children, so that, from that point onward it becomes increasingly difficult to differentiate between science fiction films for children and science fiction films in general. The period 1977–1984 was one of the richest in sf film history, though, of the key films of this period, only **Steven Spielberg**'s ***E.T. the Extra-Terrestrial*** (1982) seemed aimed largely at children. However, Disney also labored to get on the sf bandwagon during this period, beginning with *The Cat from Outer Space* (1978), another alien-invasion film that was aimed at children. Disney's move into adult science fiction with *The Black Hole* (1979) and *Tron* (1982) was mostly ill fated, though the latter has become something of a cult classic, partly because of the way it presaged the coming of

computer-generated imagery, something the Disney company remained highly skeptical of through the decade of the 1980s.

By the 1990s, the Disney Renaissance had made children's film one of the most profitable enterprises in American popular culture, while the rise of Pixar in the second half of the 1990s made children's film itself a sort of science fictional undertaking, in which the technology of the films is almost more important than the films themselves. Little surprise, then, that the explosion of Pixar onto the American cultural landscape was concomitant with an explosion in the production of science fiction films for children, which, by the first decade of the new millennium, had become one of the central genres of children's film. Virtually every subgenre of science fiction film has been explored in the format of children's film in the last two decades or so, from science-gone-awry films like *Honey, I Shrunk the Kids* (1989) and *Honey, I Blew Up the Kid* (1992) to time-travel films like *Meet the Robinsons* (2007), all from Disney. In 2002, Disney even remade one of its classic films from the 1950s, the pirate adventure *Treasure Island* as a **space opera** in *Treasure Planet.*

However, with *E.T.* still standing as the prototype, the alien-invasion film has remained far and away the most prominent subgenre of sf film for children, perhaps because children, living in a world of adults, feel very much like aliens much of the time themselves. Indeed, children's alien-invasion films consistently feature benevolent aliens who are typically misunderstood and mistreated by the earthly authorities, whether these aliens be the children of Disney's *Witch Mountain* sequence or the cuddly creatures of *The Cat from Outer Space* and *E.T.* Even the vicious and deadly Stitch of Disney's **animated science fiction film** *Lilo & Stitch* (2002), genetically engineered to be vicious, ultimately becomes a cuddly pet of sorts, though still an extremely formidable one. Even when the aliens of a film arrive on earth with a show of overwhelming force, as in Disney's rewriting of the Chicken Little parable as an alien-invasion narrative in the computer animated *Chicken Little* (2005), they do so only as the result of a misunderstanding, thinking they are saving a cute baby alien from abduction by earthlings.

Studios other than Disney have begun to produce sf films for children as well. Nickelodeon's 2001 animated film *Jimmy Neutron:*

Boy Genius, based on the Nickelodeon television series, is a virtual compendium of science fiction motifs (modified for very young audiences), though it remains, at its core, an alien-invasion narrative. The alien invaders here are sinister, but comically so, and are rather easily defeated by the boy genius protagonist. Among the alien-invasion films of recent years, one of the best, most interesting, and most serious is ***The Iron Giant*** (1999), an animated film distributed by Warner Brothers and directed by Brad Bird, who went on to direct *The Incredibles* and *Ratatouille* for Pixar. *The Iron Giant* is ostensibly a children's film, but deals with a number of serious issues and engages in an extensive dialogue with science fiction films from the 1950s. Set in 1957, *The Iron Giant* is a variation on the 1950s alien-invasion film, but with a benevolent invader, who draws the ire of xenophobic townspeople and (particularly) of a U.S. government driven by cold-war paranoia.

Dreamworks' *Monsters vs. Aliens* (2009) combines the **monster movie** with the alien-invasion narrative, as the title suggests—and includes significant dialogue with earlier sf films, from which most of its "monsters" are directly derived. *Planet 51* (2009) is another children's animated film based on the alien-invasion motif, though here it is an astronaut from earth who lands on a distant planet—with comic and chaotic results. Even the classic children's book, *Cloudy with a Chance of Meatballs,* was adapted to animated film in 2009 in a version that converts the tale into science fiction. The spate of children's science fiction films to appear in 2009 might well have been partly inspired by the success of perhaps the most notable recent entry into the field of children's sf film, Pixar's *WALL-E* (2008), which combines the basic plot of a **postapocalyptic** film (with the earth having been rendered uninhabitable by excessive consumerism) with elements of space opera and a heavy reliance on **robots**. Indeed, robots seem particularly popular in children's sf film, from Tobor, to **C-3PO** and **R2-D2** of the original *Star Wars* trilogy, to the lumbering giant of *The Iron Giant,* to the recent *Robots* (2005), whose characters are, in fact, exclusively robots. Even the classic Pinocchio story has been converted into a robot narrative, in *Pinocchio 3000* (2004), though it should be noted that this versatile story had been converted to science fiction as early as 1965, with *Pinocchio in Outer Space.*

CHRISTENSEN, HAYDEN (1981–). The Canadian-born Hayden Christensen had already made numerous appearances in movies and on both Canadian and U.S. television when he was nominated, at age 20, for his role in the film *Life as a House* (2001). However, it was not until he was tapped to play **Anakin Skywalker** (on his way to becoming **Darth Vader**) in the second and third installments of the second *Star Wars* trilogy that he emerged as an international star, even though his performances in those films met with a decidedly mixed critical reaction. Christensen returned to science fiction film in 2008, playing a young man with the ability to teleport in *Jumper*. He had a central voiceover role in the NASA-inspired animated science fiction adventure *Quantum Quest: A Cassini Space Odyssey* (2010). He has been rumored to be slated to star in a film adaptation of **William Gibson**'s **cyberpunk** novel *Neuromancer,* but that casting has not been confirmed as of this writing.

CLARKE, ARTHUR C. (1917–2008). Considered (along with **Robert A. Heinlein** and **Isaac Asimov**) to be one of the three great figures of the Golden Age of science fiction, the British science fiction master remains one of the towering figures in the history of science fiction. Clarke's importance among British writers of science fiction is rivaled only by that of **H. G. Wells**; the annual award for the best science fiction novel published in Great Britain is called the Arthur C. Clarke Award, acknowledging Clarke's importance, though Clarke also helped to fund the award with an initial grant. In science fiction film, Clarke is best known as the author of "The Sentinel," a short story on which **Stanley Kubrick**'s classic film *2001: A Space Odyssey* is loosely based; Clarke also co-authored the screenplay for that film, as well as authoring a similarly titled novel that was written during the making of the film and serves as a sort of companion to it, helping to explain some of its enigmas. The film *2010* (1985), a sequel to *2001,* directed by **Peter Hyams**, is based on Clarke's 1982 novel *2010: Odyssey Two.*

A CLOCKWORK ORANGE. (Dir. **Stanley Kubrick**, 1971). Based on Anthony Burgess's 1962 novel of the same title, the **dystopian** film *A Clockwork Orange* depicts a decadent near-future Great Britain in which violent youth gangs roam the streets, raping and killing just for the pleasure of seeing others suffer. As such, it graphically depicts the horrors of living in a society in which one might become the victim of such violence at any moment. But the film also suggests the emptiness of a society that fears its own children but is unable to offer them a more positive outlet for their energies. Meanwhile, the oppressive, but inept, ruling government attempts to deal with the problem by developing experimental methods for conditioning and pacifying violent youth, rendering them literally incapable of violence (and thereby incapable of dealing with the violent world in which they find themselves).

A Clockwork Orange focuses on Alex DeLarge (**Malcolm Mc-Dowell**), a young man who begins the film as the sadistic leader of a youth gang who also happens to have a love for classical music, especially Beethoven's Ninth Symphony. Convicted of murder, he is sentenced to prison, then volunteers for the experimental conditioning program so that he can secure his early release. After the conditioning, he is unable to commit violent acts (or, for that matter, to listen to the Ninth Symphony). All in all, he is unable to cope with the society into which he is released, himself becoming the object of violence from some of his former victims. After he becomes the focus of press attention on the controversial conditioning program, Alex is deconditioned, becoming a pampered poster boy for the government's new policy of rejecting the conditioning program.

The first movie to use the now-standard Dolby sound system, A Clockwork Orange is a technically accomplished film whose music and set designs very effectively reinforce its plot to create a frightening dystopian world that is uncomfortably similar to the real world in which it was produced. The film has become a classic, though a controversial one, and many viewers have argued that it glorifies violence, rather than critiquing it.

CLOSE ENCOUNTERS OF THE THIRD KIND. (Dir. **Steven Spielberg**, 1977.) Along with *Star Wars* (released in the same year), *Close Encounters of the Third Kind* is one of two films that are typically credited as ushering in the science fiction film renaissance of 1977–1984. The first major science fiction film from director Steven Spielberg, *Close Encounters* is a highly thoughtful **alien-invasion** narrative that departs significantly from the paranoid alien-invasion films typical of the 1950s, looking back to predecessors such as *The Day the Earth Stood Still* (1951). In *Close Encounters,* benevolent aliens land their ship in a remote locale, to which a variety of people from around the world find themselves mysteriously drawn. The point seems to be to try to communicate rather than to conquer, and when the alien mothership takes off with a number of humans aboard, they are clearly invitees, rather than abductees. Meanwhile, this elegant film addresses a variety of other issues as well, especially in the way it contrasts the adventure of alien encounter with the banality of daily American life both through its depiction of the day-to-day consumer culture of the United States and through the depiction of the travails of family man Roy Neary (Richard Dreyfuss), one of those drawn to the alien landing site.

Close Encounters became, on its initial release, the largest grossing film in the history of Columbia Pictures, a success that bailed the company out of financial difficulty and propelled director Spielberg to superstar status. The film also won eight Academy Award nominations, including a Best Director nomination for Spielberg and a Best Special Visual Effects nomination for **Douglas Trumbull** and his effects crew. Of these nominations, the film won only for the cinematography of Vilmos Zsigmond, though it also won a special Oscar given to Frank Warner for sound effects editing. The film remains one of the most beloved and respected American science fiction films more than three decades after its first release.

COMEDY. The very first feature-length American sf film, *Just Imagine* (1930), was a romantic comedy that took neither itself nor sf in general very seriously. Similarly, even before the science fiction film boom of the 1950s, Universal Pictures was producing a series of films starring comedians Lou Abbott and Bud Costello that involved spoofs of science fiction or of the company's own classic **monster movies** of the 1930s, including *Abbott and Costello Meet Frankenstein* (1948), *Abbott and Costello Meet the Invisible Man* (1951), and *Abbott and Costello Go to Mars* (1953). Meanwhile, many of the sf films of the 1950s were tongue-in-cheek efforts that made campy fun of their own low-budget silliness, while others were so poorly made as to be unintentionally funny—later providing fodder for such comic science fiction as the *Mystery Science Theater 3000* television series. By the time of *The Absent-Minded Professor* (1961), comic science fiction films were being made for children and families; subsequently, virtually all **children's science fiction** films have been made in a comic mode. **Stanley Kubrick**'s *Dr. Strangelove or: How I Learned to Stop Worrying and Love the Bomb* (1964) is a masterpiece of satirical cinema that highlights the insanity of the cold-war arms race—proving at the same time that science fiction and humor can work well together. Meanwhile, moments of twinkle-in-the-eye, self-conscious humor punctuate many of the very best sf films (such as the *Terminator* sequence), while intentionally over-the-top action and dialogue add humor to numerous otherwise-serious sf films such as *Robocop* (1987) and *The Fifth Element* (1997).

Still, while numerous science fiction comedies have been produced, few pure sf comedies have been truly successful. For example, John Carpenter's first film, *Dark Star* (1974), a science fiction comedy, is not widely known. Similarly, John Sayles's low-budget *The Brother from Another Planet* (1984) is a comedy that effectively satirizes racism, but was not a commercial hit. Most of the best and most popular sf comedies have been spoofs of specific earlier sf films or other sf phenomena, as when Mel Brooks's *Spaceballs* (1987) hilariously lampooned the *Star Wars* franchise (among other well-known sf films) or when *Galaxy Quest* (1999) had fun with the *Star Trek* fan culture. The low-budget sf films of the 1950s have provided rich material for parody, as when specific films were sarcastically mocked by onlookers in the *Mystery Science Theater 3000* television series and feature film or when **mad-scientist** films of the 1950s (and even earlier) were lampooned in the Steve Martin vehicle *The Man with Two Brains* (1983). One of the finest sf comedies is **Tim Burton**'s *Mars Attacks!* (1996), which draws most of its energy from a parodic dialogue with the **alien-invasion** films of the 1950s, but also works as a spoof of *Independence Day* (1996), which had been released only a few months earlier.

Following quickly in the wake of the boom in "straight" science fiction films of the period, the 1980s were a particularly fertile period for sf comedy; several teen-oriented comedies were released in 1985 alone, including *Weird Science, Real Genius,* and *My Science Project.* Among the notable teen-oriented sf comedies of the late 1980s were the first two *Back to the Future* films in 1985 and 1989, with the third appearing in 1990. In 1989, *Bill & Ted's Excellent Adventure* (1989) was another time-travel comedy, with more of a teen-oriented edge to its humor. More recently, the most commercially successful sf comedies of all time have been the alien-invasion (and UFO paranoia) parodies **Men in Black** (1997) and *Men in Black II* (2002), which also parody the alien-invasion subgenre. Ivan Reitman's *Evolution* (2001), another alien-invasion spoof, has some of the zany energy of Reitman's earlier *Ghost Busters* films, while also generating considerable humor from a dialogue with the *X-Files* television series, aided especially by the presence in the film of former *X-Files* star David Duchovny. On the other hand, the 2009 alien-invasion spoof *Alien Trespass* (which presents itself as a lost "masterpiece" of 1950s film, newly discovered and finally released) had no luck at all at the box office, perhaps because its over-the-top parody of silly 1950s alien-invasion films provides little that cannot be derived from those films themselves. All in all, in fact, sf comedies have proved a difficult sell, especially with American audiences, and films such as the **Lost World** spoof *Land of the Lost* (2009) have generally not been successful at the box office. *See also* UNIVERSAL STUDIOS.

COMPUTER ANIMATION. *See* ANIMATED SCIENCE FICTION FILMS; COMPUTER-GENERATED IMAGERY (CGI); SPECIAL EFFECTS.

COMPUTER-GENERATED IMAGERY (CGI). Computer-generated imagery (CGI) involves the use of computer graphics to produce special visual effects for film, television, and video games. Such images have become increasingly important in science fiction film over the past several decades because they can be used to produce effects that are far more convincing and elaborate than those that could be created by physical techniques (such as the use of sets and models) on the same budget. As a result, science fiction films have long been on the forefront of the development of CGI, though the technique is now widely used in other films (especially action films) as well.

CGI was first used in the **dystopian** film *Westworld* in 1973; they were then used more extensively in that film's sequel, *Futureworld* (1976). However, the real breakthrough in the use of CGI came in

1977 with the release of *Star Wars,* which employed far more elaborate CGI than had ever been used before. From that point forward, CGI was used more and more in sf film, often generated by special companies devoted to the generation of such images, such as **George Lucas's Industrial Light & Magic**, which created the effects for his *Star Wars* sequence but branched out to create effects for numerous other films as well.

Steven Spielberg's *Jurassic Park* (1993) was the next major milestone in the development of CGI for sf film, employing the technique to create highly believable dinosaurs—and to generate huge profits at the box office. Two years later, **Pixar** (formerly a subsidiary of **Lucasfilm**, but now an independent studio) released *Toy Story,* the first animated film to be generated entirely by computer graphics—though the voices of the characters were supplied by live actors. Since that time, computer animation has become entirely dominant in the world of animated film, including **animated science fiction films**. Meanwhile, increasingly elaborate computer-generated **special effects** have been used to enhance live-action films as well, including more and more use of **green-screen** technologies, in which live actors are filmed in front of a blank screen, with the background images filled in later by computer. This tendency culminated in 2004 with the release of several films that were shot essentially entirely in front of green screens and even included some computer-generated characters, including **Enki Bilal's** *Immortel (ad vitam)*, the Japanese film *Casshern,* the low-budget U.S. film *Able Edwards,* and the relatively big-budget *Sky Captain and the World of Tomorrow.*

Increases in the power of computer hardware and the sophistication of computer software continue to enable steady improvement in the quality and complexity of computer-generated images. The generation of attractive and believable human characters by computer has thus far proved elusive, however, and audiences have tended to find computer-generated characters such as those in the film *Final Fantasy: The Spirits Within* (2001) subtly disturbing. Thus, a film such as Pixar's *WALL-E* (2008), which employs some of the most impressive computer-generated machinery and backgrounds ever put on film, employs human characters that are mere caricatures, far removed from realistic depiction, the only realistic human character being portrayed by a live actor.

COMPUTERS AND ARTIFICIAL INTELLIGENCE. Computers played a relatively small role in science fiction film before the 1960s, when advances in real-world computer technology brought that technology more into the public consciousness. Reflecting this phenomenon, computers came more and more to be a standard part of the landscape of sf film. Meanwhile, contemporary fears that computers might displace humans in a variety of ways made advanced computers perfect candidates to be villains in sf film. Thus, in Jean-Luc Godard's **dystopian** film *Alphaville* (1965), a computer rules a human society, governing with a cold logic that threatens to dehumanize its subjects. The previous year, humans prove unable to override computerized defense systems in both the United States and the USSR in **Stanley Kubrick's** *Dr. Strangelove or: How I Learned to Stop Worrying and Love the Bomb,* apparently leading to the destruction of both societies. Then, in Kubrick's *2001: A Space Odyssey* (1968), the intelligent **HAL 9000** computer becomes one of the most frightening sf villains of all time when it decides to eliminate the human crew aboard an important mission into deep space, lest their fallibility threaten to undermine the mission HAL has been programmed to protect. By 1969, even **Disney** was exploring the plot potential of computer malfunctions, as the memory and computational abilities of a computer are accidentally downloaded into the brain of a college student in *The Computer Wore Tennis Shoes* (1969).

Dangerous computers—or at least computers with minds of their own—continued to appear in the 1970s as well. *Colossus: The Forbin Project* (1970) looks back to *Dr. Strangelove* as an advanced computer is given control of all U.S. defense systems, then develops a mind of its own, links with a similar system in the Soviet Union, and announces that it is now the ruler of the world, promising a new era of peace and prosperity. The film implies, however, that this new era will be oppressive and dehumanizing. In *Westworld* (1973) and *Futureworld* (1976), the computer systems in highly automated theme parks get out of control, with deadly results. In *The Terminal Man* (1974) computer-controlled electrodes are implanted in the brain of a man to control his epilepsy, both indicating some of the medical potential of computer technology and reflecting fears that computers are intruding into humans' lives in ways that might get out of control. In this case, the man is also paranoid about the possibility that computers are beginning to replace humans as the rulers of earth, so that he predictably reacts badly to the surgery. Finally, an advanced computer seeks to "save" the human race in *Demon Seed* (1977), which introduces a theme of **environmentalism** when the computer attempts to breed with a human woman to produce an advanced new hybrid who can lead humanity into a new era in which the ravaging of the natural environment will come to an end.

Disney's *Tron* (1982) was an early milestone in computer-generated **special effects**, while at the same time making the interior of a computer the setting for much of the film's action. *Brainstorm* (1983) involves interfaces between computers and the human brain, a motif that is crucial to the **cyberpunk** fiction, which became a leading current in science fiction the next year with the publication of **William Gibson**'s novel *Neuromancer*. Cyberpunk subsequently became a major force in sf film as well. The boundary between humans and computers was also explored in the *Terminator* sequence of films, which also began in 1984. These films feature advanced computer-brained **cyborgs** that are virtually indistinguishable from humans; they also look back to films such as *Colossus: The Forbin Project* in their vision of advanced computerized defense systems that decide to seize control from their human masters. This time, however, the computers intend not to help humanity, but to destroy it.

As science fiction moved further into the cyberpunk era, motifs such as **virtual reality** became central to the portrayal of computer technology in sf film, with the difficulty of distinguishing between real and computer-generated memories and perceptions becoming a central plot point in such films as *Total Recall* (1990). In *Johnny Mnemonic* (1995) a human courier becomes a repository for computer memory, while the blurring between fiction and reality in computer-generated video game environments is central to such films as *eXistenZ* (1999) and *Avalon* (2001). Finally, in *The Matrix* (1999) and its two sequels (both released in 2003), the motif of advanced computer systems taking over the world reached a new level of sophistication as computers not only take over the world, but maintain enslaved humans in a virtual-reality environment that makes them unaware of the takeover. In *I, Robot* (2004), intelligent robots exist to serve humans, but an artificially intelligent computer triggers a revolt.

Bicentennial Man (1999) and ***Artificial Intelligence: AI*** (2001) both deal with artificially intelligent robotic systems that begin to take on increasingly human characteristics, sometimes making humans, feeling threatened, react with intolerance and prejudice. Both films give their **robots** a softer side, the second focusing on a robot child that wishes, Pinocchio-like, to be a real boy. Such humanized robots then moved firmly into the realm of children's culture with the 2005 animated film *Robots*. In the 2008 Pixar animated children's film *WALL-E,* however, the human captain of a huge spacecraft bearing the remnants of a human race that has fled the earth due to environmental destruction there must wrestle for control of the ship with AUTO, the ship's computer. Transparently modeled on the HAL 9000 computer of *2001: A Space Odyssey,* AUTO believes it is simply doing its job when it tries to prevent the captain from returning to earth. Significantly, though, the captain is aided in his successful bid to override AUTO by sympathetic robots, including the title character, who are themselves artificially intelligent machines with strongly human characteristics. Of course, the sinister characteristics often attributed to computers in science fiction films are somewhat ironic given the increasing use of computers to generate the special effects for those films. *See also* COMPUTER-GENERATED IMAGERY (CGI); GREEN SCREEN.

CONNERY, SEAN (1930–). The distinguished Scottish actor Sir Thomas Sean Connery, made a Knight Bachelor of the Order of the British Empire in 2000, is one of the leading British film stars of all time. His fame, of course, rests first and foremost on his starring role in the first James Bond films, espionage thrillers that in fact typically contain a liberal dose of science fiction. But Connery has played numerous other roles as well, including starring roles in science fiction films. In 1974, he played in *Zardoz* (1974), a film that has become something of a cult favorite purely on the basis of its strangeness and incomprehensibility. He also starred in *Meteor* (1979), a widely panned **disaster** film in which a large asteroid threatens earth—thus anticipating **Michael Bay**'s *Armageddon* (1998). In 1981 Connery starred as an outer-space lawman in *Outland* (1981), a sort of science fiction Western vaguely based on the classic Western film *High Noon* (1952). None of these films were particularly successful at the time, though Connery was a hit in a small role as Agamemnon in Terry Gilliam's *Time Bandits,* also in 1981. Connery has not since returned to science fiction proper, though some of his supporting roles—in films such as *Highlander* (1986), *The Avengers* (1998), and *The League of Extraordinary Gentlemen* (2003)—contain elements that verge on science fiction. Connery played the father of the title character in *Indiana Jones and the Last Crusade* (1989), which, like all of the *Indiana Jones* films, has much in common with the sf **adventure** genre.

CONNOR, JOHN. John Connor is a key character in the mythology of the *Terminator* series of films. The son of **Sarah Connor** and Kyle Reese, who meet in *The Terminator* (1984), John Connor first appears as a young boy, being trained by his mother for his fated future as the leader of a human resistance to the rule of human-killing machines of the future. John (Edward Furlong) first appears on screen in *Terminator 2: Judgment Day* (1991), in which he evades the attempts made on his life by a killer **cyborg**, thanks to the help of his mother and of a benevolent cyborg (played by **Arnold Schwarzenegger**) that his future self sent back to protect him. A young adult John (Nick Stahl) is similarly protected in *Terminator 3: Rise of the Machines* (2003). A teenage John (Thomas Dekker) is also featured in the television series *Terminator: The Sarah Connor Chronicles* (2008–2009). The adult John (now played by Christian Bale) replaces Schwarzenegger's terminator as the central figure of the *Terminator* film sequence in *Terminator Salvation* (2009), a **postapocalyptic** film that focuses on the Connor-led resistance movement in the years after machines have destroyed human civilization and most of the human race.

CONNOR, SARAH. Sarah Connor is a crucial character in the *Terminator* film sequence, the mother of **John Connor,** the eventual leader of the remaining human resistance against machines who have virtually destroyed the race in the **postapocalyptic** future. In *The Terminator* (1984), Sarah (**Linda Hamilton**) is a conventional young woman, mainly just interested in having a good time, until her life is interrupted by the arrival of a deadly **cyborg** "terminator" (**Arnold Schwarzenegger**), sent back from the future to kill her before she can give birth to John. In the course of that film, she is impregnated by Kyle Reese (**Michael Biehn**), a resistance fighter from the future sent back by the adult John to protect his mother. In *Terminator 2: Judgment Day* (1991), Sarah (still played by Hamilton) has become a tough, muscular resistance fighter in her own right, determined to protect her son so that he can live to lead the humans of the future in their desperate fight to survive. Sarah does not appear in the third and fourth *Terminator* films, it being stipulated that she has died of cancer. However, the wonders of time travel allowed her to be resurrected to become the central figure (now played by Lena Headey) in the television series *Terminator: The Sarah Connor Chronicles,* which ran on the Fox network from 2008 to 2009. *See also* FEMINISM AND GENDER.

CONQUEST OF SPACE. (Dir. **Byron Haskin**, 1955.) A full-color **George Pal** production, *Conquest of Space* employs some of the most ambitious **special effects** in all of 1950s science fiction film to produce one of the decade's most extensive depictions of life in space. Some of the film's scenes of life in and around an orbiting space station are particularly impressive, even if neither the available budget nor the available technology were quite up to the ambition of the film. *Conquest of Space* involves a mission that is initially intended to go to the moon but is changed at the last minute (by order of the authorities back on earth) to a trip to Mars. Subsequently, a multicultural international crew (it includes a Japanese, an Austrian, and a Jewish American, but no Russians, African Americans, or women) flies to Mars under the command of General Samuel T. Merritt (Walter Brooke), the original builder of the space station, who also brings along his own son, Captain Barney Merritt (Eric Fleming), who really does not want to go. They encounter difficulties and are stranded on Mars for a year, but manage to return safely to earth, having determined that Mars is, in fact, able to support life and thus is a good candidate for future colonization.

Aside from its ahead-of-their-time visuals, the most interesting aspect of *Conquest of Space* is the depiction of General Merritt, who becomes a deranged religious fanatic in the course of the journey, convinced that the trip to Mars is a blasphemous invasion of God's territory by arrogant humans, who were created by God to rule the earth but were never intended to go beyond it. Eventually, the Bible-toting Merritt attempts to sabotage the mission, resulting in his accidental death in a scuffle with his son. The mission is thus saved, and the surviving crew members agree to protect Gen. Merritt's memory by reporting that he died heroically working to save his crew. General Merritt's attitude may reflect genuine concerns about space flight shared by certain fringe religious groups in the 1950s, but he is clearly depicted as insane in the film, which thus becomes one of the few science fiction films of the 1950s that at least suggests a criticism of religion by presenting it as an irrational alternative to scientific rationality.

CORMAN, ROGER (1926–). Educated as an industrial engineer at Stanford University, Roger Corman has put that training to use to produce entertaining films quickly, cheaply, and efficiently, almost in assembly-line fashion. Corman got his big start in the film business directing a series of science fiction films (many in the **monster movie** subgenre) for **American International Pictures (AIP)**, beginning in 1955. These films included such efforts as *It Conquered the World* (1956), *Attack of the Crab Monsters* (1957), *Teenage Cave Man* (1958), and *The Wasp Woman* (1959). They were largely aimed at youthful audiences, and Corman quickly showed an ability to put together formulaic films that appealed to teenage moviegoers. He also quickly showed that he was more talented as a producer than as a director, and most of his work beyond the 1960s has been as the producer or executive producer of what is now a total of almost 400 films.

Of all of these, Corman is perhaps best known for the series of horror film adaptations of the work of Edgar Allan Poe that he directed and produced for AIP in the early 1960s, largely based on scripts written by **Richard Matheson**. After that, most of Corman's films were made by his own production companies, of which there have been several, beginning with New World Pictures in 1970. Despite their perceived status as B movies and exploitation films, Corman's films often deal with important topical issues. Though he has increasingly specialized in horror films in the latter part of his career, among the more notable science fiction films produced by Corman over the years are *Death Race 2000* (1975), *Deathsport* (1978), *Battle Beyond the Stars* (1980), *Space Raiders* (1983), *Dead Space* (1991), and *Not of This Earth* (1995). The latter was a campy remake of the film of the same title that Corman directed in 1957. Indeed, several of Corman's later productions have been remakes of his early films, playing up the campy aspects of those films.

The low-budget nature of most of Corman's films has often made it possible (or even necessary) for him to hire young, unknown talent to work on them. His judgment of the potential of young talent has been impressive. Thus, in addition to his numerous films, Corman has been an important force in the American film industry because of the number of prominent actors, writers, and (especially) directors who have gotten started in the industry working on his films. Directors Peter Bogdanovich, **James Cameron**, Francis Ford Coppola, Jonathan Demme, Ron Howard, John Sayles, and Martin Scorsese all worked for Corman at the beginnings of their careers, as did actors David Carradine, Robert De Niro, Bruce Dern, Peter Fonda, Dennis Hopper, and Jack Nicholson.

CORPORATION. Corporations frequently play prominent roles in science fiction film, usually as corrupt and manipulative villains, willing to go to any extreme in their quest for greater profits. Often, these evil corporations have replaced governments as the ruling powers of future societies—or at least exert considerable influence over governments, usually by corrupt means. A classic case is the **Weyland-Yutani Corporation** of the *Alien* films, which is willing to sacrifice its own employees and even endanger the entire earth in order to investigate the possibility of breeding dangerous aliens for use as weapons. Similarly ruthless is the Omni Consumer Products Corporation of the *Robocop* films, again presented satirically as willing to endanger the general population (and to brutally exploit specific individuals) in its efforts to develop better and more profitable killer **cyborgs** for police and military applications.

A similar motif operates in the representation of numerous science fiction corporations, as excessive greed leads to research programs that attempt to develop dangerous new products with a lack of reasonable caution in the pursuit of that development. Thus, the research of the Umbrella Corporation in the *Resident Evil* films leads to the growth of a zombie army that ultimately sweeps across the planet. Similarly apocalyptic results issue from the unrestrained computer research of the Cyberdyne Systems Corporation in the *Terminator* films, which ultimately leads to the development of intelligent machines that turn on their human creators and attempt to assert their dominion over the earth. One of the most sinister science fiction corporations is the Soylent Corporation of *Soylent Green* (1973), which resorts to corruption and even murder to further its profit-making goals, which include secretly recycling human beings for use as food in a dangerously overpopulated world. In *WALL-E* (2008), meanwhile, rampant consumerism fueled by the global dominance of the "Buy N Large" Corporation renders the earth uninhabitable, sending the remnants of the human race into space.

Though it adds a campy, comic twist to the motif, *The Adventures of Buckaroo Banzai Across the Eighth Dimension* (1984) makes effective satirical points about the manipulation of the general population by corporations. Here, the powerful Yoyodyne Propulsion Systems turns out to be a front for an **alien invasion**. In a similar way, the movers and shakers of corporate culture in **John Carpenter**'s *They Live* (1988) are aliens who have secretly enslaved mankind. Thus, even when individual corporations are not singled out as villains, the entire culture of corporate capitalism has often been critiqued in sf film. *See also* DYSTOPIAN FILM; ENVIRONMENTALISM; *GATTACA*; *ROLLERBALL*.

CREATURE FROM THE BLACK LAGOON. (Dir. **Jack Arnold**, 1954.) Much like *King Kong* (1933), *Creature from the Black Lagoon* is a **monster movie** that features a central monster that is an evolutionary throwback just minding its own business in a remote locale until disturbed by invading humans. Though clearly reptilian, the Creature (referred to in the films as the "Gill Man") takes on an almost human personality. Indeed, the Gill Man grows more and more sympathetic as a character through a sequence of films that also includes two sequels: *Revenge of the Creature* (1955) and *The Creature Walks Among Us* (1956).

The first film in the sequence, directed by Jack Arnold, centers on the discovery of the Gill Man (described as an evolutionary missing link between reptiles and mammals) in the remote jungles of the Amazon by a team of scientific investigators who are doing research there. The sympathies of this film are with the scientists, and the Creature remains a frightening and alien presence, though it is clear that it meant no harm until its life was disturbed by the arrival of the humans. The Creature even has its romantic moments, as in its attraction to Kay Lawrence (Julie Adams), the film's obligatory beautiful young woman scientist. Thus, when it first looks up from its underwater lair to spot Kay swimming on the surface of the lagoon (in a scene referenced in 1975 by **Steven Spielberg** in the famous signature opening shot of *Jaws*), it is immediately struck by her beauty. Later, when it plucks her off the boat on which the scientists are traveling and takes her to its secret grotto, it carries her tenderly, in a mode reminiscent of King Kong holding Fay Wray. The real villain of the film is not the monster, but a "bad" scientist, Mark Williams (Richard Denning), contrasted in the film with "good" scientist David Reed (**Richard Carlson**). Reed is interested only in learning about the world, which he regards with wonder, while Williams is interested in exploiting it for profit via his scientific knowledge.

In the first sequel, also directed by Arnold, scientists return to the Amazon, this time managing to capture the Gill Man (seemingly killed at the end of the first film) and return him to captivity in a public aquarium, where scientists study the creature, while crowds of tourists look on. Sympathy for the creature increases as he experiences considerable abuse; he is shown chained to the bottom of a tank, repeatedly shocked by a cattle prod as scientists seek to train him. His status as a lone individual, surrounded by strangers who do not understand him is emphasized, particularly when Helen Dobson (Lori Nelson), this film's beautiful young woman scientist, tells her professor boyfriend, scientist Clete Ferguson (**John Agar** again), "I pity him sometimes. He's so alone. The only one of his kind in the world." In addition, the scientists discover that the Gill Man is far closer, biologically, to humans than they originally suspected. All in all, the Gill Man thus becomes a metaphor for the alienated individual in the modern world, held in chains and regarded as a curiosity by all those around him. Eventually, the Gill Man, always with an eye for the ladies, develops a yen for Helen. He manages to escape from captivity, then to make off with Helen pursued by a massive police search. This motif clearly goes beyond cliché, however, and the Gill Man's kidnapping of Helen becomes a metaphor for the dangers that lurk in the workplace for women who wander out of the domestic sphere, while this motif also addresses the converse anxieties of women over the impact on their careers if they try to have a family life.

In the end, the Gill Man is once again apparently killed, but he returns for still another sequel, this time directed by John Sherwood. This film revolves around noted scientist Dr. William Barton (**Jeff Morrow**) and his beautiful young wife, Marcia (Leigh Snowden), whom Barton dominates and even terrorizes, helping to identify the scientist as the villain of the piece. Meanwhile, this "bad" scientist is again opposed by a "good" scientist, this time in the person of Dr. Thomas Morgan (Rex Reason). Morgan, in an expression of a central perception of the 1950s, believes that the human race is at a crucial crossroads, and he hopes, through his work, to help humanity move forward, rather than backward. Meanwhile, Barton becomes something of a **mad scientist**, conducting diabolical experiments on the hapless Gill Man, who has now been recaptured after being spotted in the Everglades. The creature is badly burned in the process; his gills are destroyed and his scales fall off, revealing that he has human skin underneath the scales and a set of lungs that begin to work once the gills are lost.

Thus, now more human than ever, the Gill Man becomes the object of increased sympathy in this film. As the film proceeds, the opposition between Barton and Morgan is supplemented by the opposition between Barton and the creature, with suggestions that Barton is actually the more savage (and the Gill Man the more human) of the two. Eventually, enraged by Barton's abusive behavior, the creature breaks out of his pen, ransacks the Barton house and kills Barton, though leaving Morgan and Marcia untouched. The creature, now clearly an object of pathos, lumbers back to the beach, looks longingly at the water, his former home, then starts forward again, presumably to go into the water, where he will be drowned due to his lack of gills.

CRICHTON, MICHAEL (1942–2008). The American writer Michael Crichton may ultimately be best known as the creator of the television medical drama *E.R.,* which aired from 1994 to 2009. However, Crichton's novels, many of them science fiction, have proved a rich source of material for the film industry since 1971, when his science fiction novel *The Andromeda Strain* was made into a successful film, directed by **Robert Wise**. Other science fiction films based on Crichton novels include *The Terminal Man* (1974), *Congo* (1995), *The Lost World: Jurassic Park* (1997), *Sphere* (1998), and *Timeline* (2003). Crichton himself wrote the screen adaptation of his own novel in *Jurassic Park* (1993). Crichton also wrote original screenplays for several other science fiction films, including *Westworld* (1973), *Looker* (1981), and *Runaway* (1984), all three of which he also directed.

CROMWELL, JAMES (1940–). The versatile actor James Cromwell has played a wide variety of roles in both film and television. He moved into science fiction films (of a sort) with a role in the **mad-scientist** spoof *The Man with Two Brains* (1983). His most important performance thus far in a science fiction film was as scientist Dr. Zefram Cochrane (inventor of the earth's version of the warp drive) in *Star Trek: First Contact* (1996). Himself known for his (leftist) political activism, Cromwell followed with supporting roles as prominent politicians in the erotic **alien-invasion** film *Species II* (1997), in which he played a U.S. senator, and in the sf **disaster** film *Deep Impact* (1998), in which he played Secretary of the Treasury Alan Rittenhouse. Cromwell also played an important role in the aging-astronaut film *Space Cowboys* (2000). In 2004, he once again played a prominent scientist as Dr. Alfred Lanning in the **robot** thriller *I, Robot* (2004), a role he in some ways reprised as the inventor of the robotic technology that lies at the heart of *Surrogates* (2009), though in that film he turns against his own technology, whereas in *I, Robot* the technology turned against him.

CRONENBERG, DAVID (1943–). Though he has recently gained mainstream recognition for films such as *A History of Violence* (2005) and *Eastern Promises* (2007), the Canadian director built his reputation on offbeat, independent horror and science fiction films, often featuring images of abject violence to the human body. The largely forgotten *Crimes of the Future* (1970) is something of a **postapocaylptic** film, set in a world in which contaminated cosmetics have killed off the entire population of sexually mature women. *Scanners* (1981) combines sf and horror in its depiction of a sinister

corporation that attempts to exploit individuals with psychic abilities. *Videodrome* (1983) is a satirical exploration of the manipulation of individuals by the media that has become a cult classic. Cronenberg's 1986 remake of *The Fly* dramatically improves the visual imagery of the 1958 original, though it is probably a less effective film. Meanwhile, *eXistenZ* (1999) was one of a flurry of films at the century's end that explored a growing public fascination with **virtual reality**. Finally, Cronenberg has attempted two of the most difficult film adaptations in history with his film versions of two experimental novels with strong science fiction elements: *Naked Lunch* (1991, based on the 1959 novel by William S. Burroughs) and *Crash* (1996, based on the 1973 novel by J. G. Ballard).

CRUISE, TOM (1962–). The American movie star Tom Cruise has made a name for himself in action thrillers such as the *Mission Impossible* sequence of films, though he has also played extremely colorful and interesting character roles in films such as *Magnolia* (1999) and *Tropic Thunder* (2008). His first foray into science fiction was as the lead character in *Vanilla Sky* (2001), an undistinguished remake of the Spanish film *Abre los ojos* (*Open Your Eyes,* 1997). However, he followed that role with the lead in **Steven Spielberg's** excellent futuristic thriller *Minority Report* in 2002. Cruise returned to work with Spielberg in his 2005 remake of *War of the Worlds,* a commercial success that was not a big hit with the critics.

CUSHING, PETER (1913–1994). The British actor Peter Cushing may have had a fairly limited range as a thespian, but he made the most of it, appearing in a wide array of films in a long and successful career that made him one of the icons of the horror film genre, where he became the best-known face of the numerous horror films made by **Hammer Film Productions**. Beginning with his role as Victor Frankenstein in *The Curse of Frankenstein* (1957), he quickly followed as the vampire hunter Lawrence Van Helsing in *Dracula* (1958), establishing himself as a major presence in both of Hammer's flagship horror franchises. He remained a major figure in horror films for decades to come, though he also moved into science fiction as Dr. Who in *Dr. Who and the Daleks* (1965), adapted from the popular British sf television series. He returned the next year in the sequel,

Daleks' Invasion Earth: 2150 A.D., but after that he appeared primarily in horror films until 1976, when he had a major role in the sf **adventure** *At the Earth's Core.* He is best known to science fiction fans, however, for his iconic role as the sinister Grand Moff Tarkin in *Star Wars* (1977), though he had no subsequent sf roles until 1986, when he had an important supporting role in the family-oriented **time-travel** narrative *Biggles* (1986), his last film.

CYBERPUNK. Cyberpunk was an important movement within written science fiction that flourished in the 1980s and that is often said to have initiated with **William Gibson**'s 1984 novel *Neuromancer,* though Gibson had several important predecessors, including **Philip K. Dick**. Cyberpunk is typically set in a near future world that differs relatively little from the world of the 1980s. If anything, the social, economic, and political problems of the 1980s tend to have gotten worse in this future, though it may involve significant advances in technology, especially in technology of **computers** and **virtual reality**. Meanwhile, cyberpunk features biomedical and electronic body modifications, direct interfaces between human brains and computers, artificial intelligences equipped with "human" qualities, and the electronic transcendence provided by new technological spaces, thus calling into question what it means to be human. Indeed, much of the action of cyberpunk typically occurs in the virtual-reality world of *cyberspace* (a term coined by Gibson).

Because of the growing prevalence of **computer-generated imagery** in science fiction film, the medium appears to be ideal for the representation of cyberpunk narratives, and the film *Blade Runner* (1982) has often been cited as one of the crucial influences on the cyberpunk movement. However, cyberpunk has proved notoriously difficult to adapt convincingly to film. The most direct early attempt at such adaptation was *Johnny Mnemonic* (1995), but this attempt, starring **Keanu Reeves**, was not well received. Other early American films with virtual-reality themes—including *The Lawnmower Man* (1992), *Strange Days* (1995), and *Virtuosity* (1995)—departed even more from the feel of cyberpunk. Japanese **anime**, especially beginning with *Kôkaku kidôtai* (1995, *Ghost in the Shell*), was actually more successful in capturing the style and themes of cyberpunk, though later American films, including **Alex Proyas**'s *Dark City* (1998), **David Cronenberg**'s *eXistenZ* (1999), and Josef Rusnak's *The Thirteenth Floor* (1999) were a bit more successful. The Japanese-Polish co-production *Avalon* (2001) also makes important use of virtual reality, this time following *eXistenZ* in drawing upon the important theme of video gaming as a form of virtual reality.

By most accounts the first truly successful adaptation of cyberpunk to film was **Andy and Larry Wachowski**'s **dystopian** film *The Matrix* (1999), again starring Reeves. *The Matrix* was followed by two sequels in 2003, *The Matrix Reloaded* and *The Matrix Revolutions*. Here, most human beings live their lives in a virtual-reality environment, unaware that, in the physical world, they are entrapped in small pods where the machines that now rule the world use them as a power source.

Numerous films have involved **robots**, **cyborgs**, or **artificial intelligence**, including some very successful ones, such as the *Terminator* sequence or **Steven Spielberg**'s *Artificial Intelligence: AI* (2001), but these films have generally lacked the countercultural spirit that tends to characterize cyberpunk.

CYBORG. The term *cyborg* is short for *cybernetic organism,* an entity that combines organic (biological) components with artificial (electro-mechanical) components. Cyborgs frequently appear in science fiction, in which the biological components are typically human. The relative percentage of human and electro-mechanical parts within a cyborg can vary widely, though the cyborgs of science fiction are most often composed primarily of electro-mechanical parts, with the addition of a small human component. For example, the most famous cyborg in science fiction film is probably the title character of *The Terminator* (1984), which is almost entirely robotic except for a covering of human tissue that allows it to travel via the film's time machines, which are able to transport only humans. Another typical variant of the cyborg involves a robotic body controlled by a human brain, as is the case with the title character in *Robocop* (1987), a former policeman whose original body was virtually destroyed in a shootout with criminals.

One of the key elements of the *Robocop* sequence is the struggle of Murphy, its protagonist, to maintain his humanity despite his artificial body. Meanwhile, one of the most famous villains in all of science fiction film, **Darth Vader** from the *Star Wars* sequence, is a cyborg whose loss of humanity through his turn to the dark side of **the Force** is symbolized by the fact that his body is almost entirely robotic. Such motifs indicate the way in which the hybrid character of the cyborg makes it an ideal figure for the exploration of the relationship between human beings and their technological creations. As in *Robocop* and *Star Wars,* the image is often a menacing one, as mechanical parts gradually encroach on the human body until they threaten to take it over altogether. It should be noted, however, that the influential theorist Donna Haraway has envisioned the cyborg as a liberating image, especially for women, one whose fluid identity helps to serve as a counter to the rigid expectations thrust upon individuals by patriarchal capitalism.

The success of the *Terminator* and *Robocop* films helped to inspire a flurry of subsequent films featuring cyborgs, including the sequels to those films themselves. Many of these are simply action films featuring stars who seek to duplicate the success of **Arnold Schwarzenegger** in the *Terminator* sequence. In this category are the Jean-Claude Van Damme vehicles *Cyborg* (1989) and *Universal Soldier* (1992) and the cyborg films starring French kickboxer Olivier Gruner, including *Nemesis* (1993) and *Automatic* (1995), the first of which directly alludes to *Terminator* several times, as when its chief cyborg villain occasionally lapses into Schwarzenegger impressions. In *Death Machine* (1994) the excesses of this film cycle begin to turn to self-parody, a phenomenon that becomes fully developed in Stuart Gordon's *Space Truckers* (1996), whose numerous campy elements include a turn by Charles Dance as a former corporate scientist turned rapacious—but hilariously dysfunctional—cyborg.

Cyborgs are particularly prevalent in Japanese manga and **anime**. Thus, the future world of the *Ghost in the Shell* sequence involves a population composed primarily of cyborgs who have had one or another forms of artificial implants or modifications to their original human bodies. Here, however, one of the most common modifications reverses the usual sf tradition, involving the replacement of the human brain by a computerized substitute.

– D –

DANTE, JOE (1946–). The American director Joe Dante has enjoyed a successful career in Hollywood film, much of it on the margins of science fiction and horror. For example, in 1984 and 1990 he directed the two *Gremlins* movies, which are essentially lighthearted horror films aimed especially at young audiences, even children. In 1985, Dante directed *Explorers,* a space fantasy adventure for children, then moved into sf **comedy** in 1987 by directing *Innerspace,* as well as several segments of the skit compilation *Amazon Women on the Moon,* a spoof of science fiction B movies. *Matinee* (1993) is another spoofy salute to B movies, featuring a scholcky filmmaker who attempts to cash in on the Cuban missile crisis. In 1998, Dante directed *Small Soldiers,* a kid-oriented science fiction action film about a toy company that inadvertently produces deadly high-tech toy soldiers.

DARK CITY. (Dir. **Alex Proyas**, 1998.) The stylish *Dark City* was one of the visual high points of sf film in the 1990s. Its theme of reality modification was very much in line with an increased interest in **virtual reality** at the end of the 1990s, but its approach to the motif is unique. As the title suggests, the film takes place in a dark urban setting that looks like it could have come straight out of film noir. Much of the plot resembles film noir as well, as protagonist John Murdoch (Rufus Sewell) awakes to find that he has lost his memory—and also to find the body of a dead woman the police (and, initially, he himself) suspect him of murdering. As this basic plot unfolds, we gradually learn that the city of the film is a sort of experimental laboratory where a race of aliens, "The Strangers" (gruesomely inhabiting the bodies of dead humans), conduct experiments in an attempt to find the secret to the human "soul"—in particular the secret to what makes humans who they are as individuals. The Strangers constantly manipulate, or "tune" reality, adjusting the memories of their human subjects accordingly, just to see how humans react to the changed conditions. In so doing, they hope to find the key to saving their own dying race, which they believe may lie in the vitality of human individualism. Murdoch, however, has unaccountably developed the ability not only to resist their manipulations but also to tune reality on his own, which makes him extremely dangerous to the aliens. Pursued by both the police and the aliens, Murdoch attempts to learn the truth about conditions in the dark city and about his own life, including his relationship with his wife, Emma (Jennifer Connelly). Eventually, Murdoch, who has been given enhanced tuning abilities by one Dr. Daniel P. Schreber (Kiefer Sutherland), a human psychiatrist who had been working for the aliens, triumphs over the Strangers; as the film ends, Murdoch prepares to start his life with Emma (now reprogrammed as a woman named Anna) anew, now free of outside manipulation. *Dark City* is not only visually stunning; it is also a thoughtful philosophical film that asks us to consider how much of what we consider to be reality is actually being manipulated by others.

THE DAY THE EARTH STOOD STILL. (Dir. **Robert Wise**, 1951.) One of the first demonstrations of the true potential of science fiction film to address serious issues in a thoughtful way, *The Day the Earth Stood Still* is an early cold-war film that includes a plea for global peace and understanding rather than paranoid warnings against sinister enemies. In particular, the film features an alien "invader," Klaatu (**Michael Rennie**), who comes to earth not to conquer it but to issue, as the representative of a sort of interstellar peacekeeping organization, a stern warning against the dangerous path along which the cold-war arms race is taking the earth. Klaatu is repeatedly identified in the film not only as superhuman, but as a figure of Christ, helping to reinforce the notion that he is here for the earth's own good. Unfortunately, his peaceful mission is met with violence by the xenophobic military forces that greet him, and Klaatu, having landed his spacecraft on the Mall in Washington, DC, is immediately shot down. His towering robot, Gort, revives him and later has to revive him again when he is again shot down. These incidents confirm the reason for Klaatu's mission: earthlings are so violent and so thoughtless in their use of weaponry that they might soon become a threat not only to themselves, but to the rest of the galaxy. Backed by Gort, Klaatu issues an ultimatum: stop the arms race or Gort and others like him may be forced to destroy the earth. The warning concerning the destructive potential of the arms race is clear. Meanwhile, the film also conveys an internationalist and prointellectual message. Klaatu refuses to negotiate with the

United States alone or with politicians in general; instead, he insists on dealing with an international conference of leading scientists, here presented as the world's proper leaders.

The film was remade with the same title in 2008, with the cold-war arms race now replaced by environmental destruction as the reason for an alien intervention. Here, Klaatu arrives to prevent humans from rendering the earth uninhabitable, habitable planets being rare treasures in the galaxy. Despite this seemingly useful emphasis on **environmentalism**, the lackluster remake fails to engage contemporary issues in the compelling way of the original. *See also* ENVIRONMENTALISM.

DE LAURENTIIS, DINO (1919–). The Italian film producer Augustino "Dino" de Laurentiis has had a long and prolific career on both sides of the Atlantic. Beginning his career immediately after World War II, de Laurentiis was always something of a cinematic entrepreneur, establishing his own production company early on. Within the next decade, this company, Dino de Laurentiis Cinematografica, produced such "art" films as Federico Fellini's *La Strada* (1954) and *Nights at Cabiria* (1957). In the 1960s, de Laurentiis even built his own studio facilities, in which a number of films were made, included the campy 1968 science fiction classic *Barbarella.* In the 1970s, de Laurentiis moved his studio facilities to the United States, establishing the De Laurentiis Entertainment Group (DEG) studios in Wilmington, North Carolina. Here, de Laurentiis and his company produced a number of acclaimed films, including Ingmar Bergman's *The Serpent's Egg* (1977). However, the company began to gain something of a reputation for sensationalism and for a willingness to take on difficult projects (such as adaptations of beloved books), sometimes treating this material with what many perceived as a lack of high seriousness.

The company's 1976 remake of *King Kong* was a much-hyped commercial success, though critical reception was mixed. However, a 1986 sequel, *King Kong Lives,* did not fare well with critics or at the box office. *Flash Gordon* (1980), de Laurentiis's extremely campy feature-film adaptation of the classic 1930s sf serials has highly entertaining moments (often recalling *Barbarella*) and was a big hit in Great Britain; it did not do well at the box office in the United States, though it has nevertheless subsequently become a cult favorite there, a status for which it seems almost to have been custom designed. De Laurentiis's most controversial sf film was the much-maligned 1984 adaptation of Frank Herbert's *Dune,* directed by **David Lynch**. From that time on, de Laurentiis and DEG have specialized in horror and crime films, some quite high profile. De Laurentiis and his production companies have also contributed to science fiction film by boosting the careers of such future sf stars as **Arnold Schwarzenegger**, with the DEG production of *Conan the Barbarian* (1982). In addition, the first feature film of writer-directors **Larry and Andy Wachowski**, *Bound* (1996), was co-produced by the De Laurentiis Company. In 2001, de Laurentiis received the Irving G. Thalberg Memorial Award, a lifetime achievement award, from the Academy of Motion Picture Arts and Sciences.

DESTINATION MOON. (Dir. Irving Pichel, 1950.) Widely regarded as the first major American feature-length science fiction film, *Destination Moon,* produced by **George Pal**, set the stage for the explosion in production of science fiction films that marked the American film industry in the 1950s. The film was scripted by science fiction master **Robert A. Heinlein**, nominally based on his 1947 juvenile science fiction novel *Rocket Ship Galileo.* As such, it takes its role as science fiction quite seriously, and seems designed not merely to entertain audiences with a compelling story of space adventure, but also to educate audiences not only about the technology of space flight but also about its practical, real-world implications. It even includes an embedded education film (a cartoon featuring Woody the Woodpecker) designed to teach characters in the film about space flight, but clearly designed to educate the film's audience as well. Subsequently, the film presents details about the technology of space flight in an almost documentary fashion, even if its vision of thermonuclear-powered space flight did not become reality.

The film centers on the first manned mission to the moon, mounted by a private consortium of American businesses. In keeping with the film's cold-war context, the mission is propelled by the perceived urgency of getting Americans to the moon before any other nation (clearly the Soviet Union, though the Soviets are not mentioned by name in the film and the villains of the original novel were actually Nazis) can get there. In particular, the film stipulates that a base on the moon would give any nation unquestioned military superiority, with the ability to launch missile attacks against which targets on earth would be utterly defenseless. On the other hand, the mission is financed and carried out by a private consortium, stipulating that bureaucratic red-tape would delay a government-sponsored program far too long.

The success of *Destination Moon,* a relatively high-budget Technicolor production, ushered in the 1950s craze for science fiction films, many of which seemed to go out of their way to reproduce various elements of *Destination Moon.* Indeed, by the time the highly publicized film had opened in August 1950, it had already been beaten to the screen by a similar but lower-budget film, **Rocketship X-M,** which had been rushed into production (and released in June) to take advantage of the hype over *Destination Moon* and the growing popular interest in spaceflight in general.

DICK, PHILIP K. (1928–1982). One of the most critically respected authors in the history of science fiction, Dick has become one of the favorite authors of science fiction filmmakers as well. The first, and still most important, film based on Dick's work was **Blade Runner** (1982), which was based on *Do Androids Dream of Electric Sheep?* (his 1968 novel). Dick's thoughtful and inventive work is quite often concerned with fundamental philosophical issues (such as the nature of reality and the difficulty of distinguishing between reality and simulation in the postmodern world) and as such is difficult to adapt well to film. Even *Blade Runner* is a rather loose adaptation of its source material, and the appropriate credit line for most Dick adaptations is probably that used in **Total Recall** (1990), which is designated as having been "inspired by" (rather than "based on") Dick's short story, "We Can Remember It for You Wholesale." Subsequent films inspired by Dick's writings include *Screamers* (1995), *Impostor* (2001), *Paycheck* (2003), *A Scanner Darkly* (2006), *Next* (2007), and *Radio Free Albemuth* (2009). **Steven Spielberg**'s *Minority Report* (2002) joins *Blade Runner* and *Total Recall* as the most interesting films based on Dick's work thus far.

DIESEL, VIN (1967–). The American actor Vin Diesel seems to have found a niche for himself in B-grade action movies, including ultraviolent science fiction films. However, one of Diesel's first roles in film was as the voice of the title character in *The Iron Giant* (1999). Meanwhile, his most successful role has probably been that of tough guy Richard B. Riddick in **David Twohy**'s action-packed *Pitch Black* (2000). Diesel returned as Riddick in Twohy's sequel, *The Chronicles of Riddick* (2004), the title of which highlights the importance of his character. The sequel, however, lacked the appeal of the original. Diesel also played the lead role as the mercenary Toorop in the much-maligned *Babylon A.D.* (2008).

DINOSAUR. *Dinosaur* is the collective name given to the various reptiles (some of them gigantic in size) who roamed and ruled the earth for millions of years before the advent of human beings, from about 230 million to about 65 million years ago. Wiped out by some cataclysmic series of events (perhaps triggered by a collision of the earth with an asteroid), dinosaurs have long been an object of fascination to observers from professional scientists to imaginative children. Given their size and power, combined with their exoticism, dinosaurs are ideal creatures to be featured in **monster movies**. Dinosaurs figured in science fiction films as early as the 1925 silent-film adaptation of Sir Arthur Conan Doyle's *The Lost World,* and were portrayed particularly effectively in *King Kong* (1933), in which the eponymous giant ape is first discovered on a remote island that is also inhabited by dinosaurs, created through the stop-motion **special effects** of **Willis O'Brien**.

This motif of the discovery of a remote locale in which dinosaurs still exist has been a favorite one in sf **adventure** films, including **Irwin Allen**'s 1960 remake of *The Lost World.* Similarly, *The Land that Time Forgot* (1975), based on a 1918 novel by Edgar Rice Burroughs and set during World War I, takes the survivors of a sinking British ship in World War I to an island inhabited by dinosaurs and other prehistoric animals. That film spawned a direct sequel, *The People that Time Forgot* (1977), in which dinosaurs and primitive people coexist, another common motif in film, though humans and dinosaurs never inhabited the earth at the same time. This subgenre, which also included such entries as the Western-inflected *The Valley* *of Gwangi* (1969), in which cowboys battle a dinosaur, descended into self-parody by the time of *Land of the Lost* (2009). In a variation on this theme, space travelers have sometimes discovered dinosaurs on other planets, as in *King Dinosaur* (1955), *Voyage to the Prehistoric Planet* (1965), and *Planet of Dinosaurs* (1978).

The monsters of 1950s sf film were often dinosaurs, or dinosaur-like, often awakened from millions of years of slumber (or even created to begin with) by the effects of radiation. Thus, the "rhedosaurus" of **The Beast from 20,000 Fathoms** (1953) is essentially a dinosaur, freed by nuclear testing after being frozen in Arctic ice millions of years earlier—and animated in the film by the **stop-motion animation** of **Ray Harryhausen**. Japan's **Godzilla**, another byproduct of nuclear testing, also has much in common with dinosaurs, though he has numerous dragon-like characteristics as well.

In more recent times, dinosaurs have often been represented as cute and cuddly animals in works for children, rather than as mere monsters. Particularly important here is Don Bluth's animated film *The Land Before Time* (1988), which became the foundation of an entire franchise consisting of 12 straight-to-video sequels, a television series, and extensive merchandising. *The Land Before Time,* which features talking dinosaur "children" as its protagonists, was executive produced by **Steven Spielberg**, who soon afterward returned dinosaurs to the realm of monsters, but with a dramatic increase in the technical sophistication of their representation in *Jurassic Park* (1993), a huge hit that used a **genetic engineering** motif to provide a reasonably believable scientific basis for the presence of dinosaurs in the contemporary world. It also employed the latest advances in **computer-generated imagery** to produce extremely realistic dinosaurs that often move very quickly, as opposed to their consistent (and inaccurate) representation as plodding behemoths in previous films. *Jurassic Park* spawned two sequels, *The Lost World: Jurassic Park* (1997, also directed by Spielberg) and *Jurassic Park III* (2001, directed by Joe Johnston). Impressive and realistic-looking dinosaurs are also produced by computer animation in Disney's *Dinosaur* (2000), a children's film in which the dinosaurs, however realistic looking, can talk and have human personalities as they attempt to deal with the asteroid collision that will ultimately spell the end of their reign on earth.

DISASTER. Films relating natural disasters such as floods, fires, earthquakes, or volcano eruptions have formed a major genre of American film since the early 1970s, when films such as *The Towering Inferno* (1974, produced by **Irwin Allen**, the "Master of Disaster") and *Earthquake* (1974) were major box-office hits. Sometimes, these disasters involve the failure of manmade systems, such as the sinking of an ocean liner or the crash of an airliner. Thus, *Airport* (1970) is sometimes considered to be the beginning of the 1970s cycle of disaster films, while *The Poseidon Adventure* (1972, also produced by Allen) is one of the best-known of these films. In this sense, **James Cameron**'s *Titanic* (1997), the largest-grossing film of all time (until his *Avatar* surpassed it in early 2010), can be considered a disaster film. Such films employ a classic disaster film structure in which a large cast of characters is introduced at the beginning of the film, followed by the announcement of a looming disaster, followed by a narration of the various ways in which the characters we have come to know deal with the disaster. In most cases, these films cannot really be considered to be science fiction, even though the high stakes involved in disaster films are similar to those that are often found in science fiction film.

Many disaster films, however, clearly move into the realm of science fiction. For example, the 1970s cycle of disaster films was topped off in 1979 with the much-maligned *Meteor* (1979), about a giant asteroid that threatens to collide with the earth, and thus a film that is rightly considered science fiction. The **postapocalyptic** film cycle of the 1950s, as well as the **monster movie** boom of that decade, are both heavily informed by science fictional conceits, such as the destruction of society by advanced technologies, or the production of monsters by unrestrained scientific inquiry. Meanwhile, a classic case of the science fiction disaster film can be found as early as 1951 with **When Worlds Collide**, in which the earth is destroyed in a collision with another planet—though a few humans manage to survive by rocketing to still another planet that conveniently happens to be passing by as well. **Val Guest**'s *The Day the Earth Caught Fire* (1961) is also a good example of the early sf disaster film, this time involving a perturbation in the earth's orbit (caused by nuclear testing) that sends the planet hurtling toward the sun.

Such cosmic catastrophes are typical of the science fiction disaster film, which came to particular prominence in the 1990s, as advances in **computer-generated imagery** made it possible to produce convincing **special effects** for the depiction of such disasters. One of the first films of this disaster film renaissance was **Roland Emmerich's** *Independence Day* (1996), an **alien-invasion** drama that employs the classic structure of the disaster film. A cycle of more conventional cosmic disaster films followed, including *Deep Impact* and *Armageddon,* both released in 1998, in which the earth is threatened by impending collision with a comet and an asteroid, respectively, while scientists and astronauts scramble to avert the collisions. In *The Core* (2003), sf disaster turns inward as scientists tunnel into the earth to try to restart the rotation of the earth's core. Meanwhile, **Danny Boyle's** *Sunshine* (2007) is more typical of sf disaster films, as scientists travel into space to prevent disaster, this time to try to restart the dying sun. Meanwhile, *Knowing* (2009) looks back to *When Worlds Collide* as a solar event wipes out life on earth, but a small group of humans manage to escape (this time with the help of advanced aliens) to another planet.

Emmerich has become perhaps the central figure in this latest cycle of sf disaster films, though **Michael Bay**, the director of *Armageddon,* has employed many elements of the disaster film structure in his two *Transformers* films (2007, 2009). Emmerich followed *Independence Day* by resurrecting the classic Japanese movie monster **Godzilla** and setting it upon New York City, but his 1998 film *Godzilla* was not a big success. Emmerich had better success in 2004 with *The Day After Tomorrow,* a work with a theme of **environmentalism**, as global warming causes catastrophic weather events across the United States. Finally, Emmerich's *2012* (2009) deals with the ultimate global catastrophe; based on ancient Mayan predictions of the end of the world in 2012, Emmerich's film deals with the realization of those predictions—and with human attempts to preserve the race nonetheless.

DISNEY. The Walt Disney Company is typically associated in the popular mind with fantasy and magic, an association that the company has encouraged through its own marketing strategies. And it is certainly the case that Disney's best-known films, from *Snow White and the Seven Dwarfs* (1937) to later efforts such as *Beauty and the Beast* (1991), have tended to be of the fairy-tale fantasy variety. However, the Disney Company is, as of this writing, the world's largest media conglomerate; it currently produces numerous films in a variety of genres under a number of different "brand" labels, in addition to the Walt Disney Pictures label. A number of these productions are science fiction films; it is also the case, however, that Disney has long had an interest in producing science fiction films, even in the days when it was a relatively small enterprise producing a relatively small number of products.

Disney's first foray into science fiction film came in 1954, with the release of **20,000 Leagues Under the Sea**, a relatively big-budget, high-gloss adaptation of **Jules Verne**'s similarly titled 1870 novel. The film was a success, though the company did not return to science fiction film until 1961 with the release of *The Absent-Minded Professor,* another success that triggered a 1963 sequel, *Son of Flubber.* In the meantime, they released *Moon Pilot* (1962), a comedy that gently satirizes the U.S. government and the budding space program. Disney moved more firmly into science-fictional territory with *The Computer Wore Tennis Shoes* (1969), which eventually became the first entry in a trilogy of sf films starring a young **Kurt Russell**. Other films in the sequence include *Now You See Him, Now You Don't* (1972) and *The Strongest Man in the World* (1975). *The Island at the Top of the World* (1974) is an entry in the sf **adventure** subgenre in which a modern-day arctic expedition discovers a lost island still inhabited by Vikings. *Escape to Witch Mountain* (1975) is an unusual **alien-invasion** film that has much of the texture of Disney's fantasy films. Its central conceit of human-looking children who turn out to be aliens with magical powers was a hit with audiences and triggered an entire franchise that includes two direct sequels *Return from Witch Mountain* (1978) and *Beyond Witch Mountain* (1982), followed by a 2009 reboot in *Race to Witch Mountain. The Cat from Outer Space,* a narrative concerning a benevolent alien invader who looks exactly like an ordinary house cat, was also released in 1978; this film contains a surprising amount of satire in its depiction of the paranoid reaction of the authorities to the arrival of the newcomer. In 1979, Disney released *Identified Flying Oddball* (aka *The Space-*

man and King Arthur), a lighthearted science fictional adaptation of Mark Twain's 1889 **time-travel** novel *A Connecticut Yankee in King Arthur's Court.*

With the release of *The Black Hole*, a **space opera**, in 1979, Disney sought to get in on the science fiction film boom that was then underway by making a big-budget, effects-driven science fiction drama for adult audiences. The endeavor was a notorious failure, though that did not prevent Disney from producing another adult sf film, *Tron*, in 1982, which has since become something of a cult hit. *Flight of the Navigator* (1986), however, is a return to more youth-oriented sf. By the time of *Honey, I Shrunk the Kids* (1989) and its sequel, *Honey, I Blew Up the Kid* (1992), the Disney renaissance was underway and the company had firmly returned to its roots in children's films. Disney continued to make lighthearted, live-action science fiction films with the comedies *Rocketman* (1997) and *My Favorite Martian* (1999), but moved into animated sf films primarily for children with such fare as the sf adventure *Atlantis: The Lost Empire* (2001) and the alien-invasion narrative *Lilo & Stitch* (2002). The release of an animated sf adaptation of the company's classic film version of *Treasure Island* (1950), moved into outer space as *Treasure Planet*, occurred in 2002. *Meet the Robinsons* (2007) is a particularly child-oriented animated time-travel narrative.

Disney's **Pixar** unit has shown a continuing interest in science fiction throughout its history, producing high-tech films that are themselves virtually examples of science-fictional technologies. Disney's adult-oriented Touchstone Pictures unit has also been actively involved in sf film, producing or co-producing such films as the somewhat spoofy alien-invasion narrative *Spaced Invaders* (1990), the ultraviolent *Starship Troopers* (1997), the sf disaster film *Armageddon* (1998), the **robot** film *Bicentennial Man* (1999), the space exploration drama *Mission to Mars* (2000), the **postapocalyptic** film *Reign of Fire* (2002), the alien-invasion film *Signs* (2002), the satirical *The Hitchhiker's Guide to the Galaxy* (2005), and the robot crime drama *Surrogates* (2009).

DOMERGUE, FAITH (1924–1999). For a brief moment in the mid-1950s, the American actress Faith Domergue was a prominent figure in science fiction film. She broke into sf film in 1955 with major woman-scientist roles in **This Island Earth** and *It Came from Beneath the Sea.* However, already in her thirties, Domergue was not able to parlay this auspicious beginning into a successful subsequent career. In 1956 she appeared in the minor sf film *The Atomic Man* (aka *Timeslip*), but most of her roles after 1955 were in low-budget horror movies and in foreign films, especially in Italy. Domergue's final role in sf film was in 1965, when she joined Basil Rathbone to star in the add-on footage that was shot in converting the 1962 Soviet monsters-on-Venus film *Planeta Bur* to the English-language *Voyage to the Prehistoric Planet* (1965).

DONNIE DARKO. (Dir. Richard Kelly, 2001.) Part **time-travel** narrative, part teen drama, and part social satire, *Donnie Darko* was a box-office disaster that nevertheless drew critical acclaim that helped to make it one of the most talked-about films of the beginning years of the 21st century, becoming an almost instant cult favorite. In the film, the eponymous Darko (Jake Gyllenhaal) is a troubled teenager in an affluent suburb who narrowly escapes death when a commercial jet engine falls from a plane in the sky, landing on and demolishing his bedroom. Though the engine falls in the middle of the night, Donnie is saved because he is out sleepwalking, in the course of which he meets a man named Frank (James Duval) who is dressed as a large (and murderous-looking) bunny. This encounter initiates a series of visions in which Donnie receives apparent warnings of the impending end of the world, though the film, through most of its run-time, leaves open the possibility that he is simply insane. In the meantime, the film includes some scathing commentary concerning the pretentious denizens of the Darko suburb and some of the faculty of Donnie's high school, especially the overbearing (but entirely incompetent) health teacher, Kitty Farmer (Beth Grant), who has developed a fascination with local self-help guru Jim Cunningham (Patrick Swayze). Cunningham is an obvious charlatan who turns out to be obsessed with kiddie porn; in the film he becomes a virtual walking embodiment of all that is wrong with contemporary American society: dishonesty, crass commercialism, superficiality, and the quest for quick fixes to complex problems. Ultimately, events in the film lead to disastrous consequences, including the death of young Gretchen Ross (Jena Malone), Donnie's new girlfriend. Meanwhile, however, Donnie has been pursuing the secret of time travel, which seems to have been discovered by a local old woman widely regarded as a senile crackpot. Donnie then travels back in time and places himself in the way of the falling plane engine, thus averting the events that lead to the death of Gretchen—while also preventing the impending end of the world. A 2009 sequel, *S. Darko,* directed by Chris Fisher, did not involve Kelly and drew little attention from critics or from fans of the original film.

DOURIF, BRAD (1950–). While the American character actor Brad Dourif has never had a starring role in a major science fiction film, he has played several memorable characters in the genre, often as a **mad-scientist** figure. However, he has acted in a wide variety of films (including numerous horror films) and has never specialized in sf. Dourif burst onto the Hollywood scene with his Oscar-nominated role as Billy Bibbit, one of the mental patients in Miklos Forman's *One Flew Over the Cuckoo's Nest* (1975), and he went on to play numerous deranged or offbeat characters. His first major sf role was as the Mentat Piter de Vries in **David Lynch's** *Dune* (1984). Dourif did have a lead role as mad scientist Jack Dante in the campy sf-horror blend *Death Machine* (1994) and also played a key scientist role in *Alien: Resurrection* (1997), in which he helped to produce a hybrid clone of **Ellen Ripley** and the alien of the title. He continued the scientist theme as a professor who works with alien abductees in *Progeny* (1999), in which he attempts to help a woman who has been impregnated by aliens. In Werner Herzog's *The Wild Blue Yonder* (2005), Dourif plays an alien who has spent several decades on earth. He also played a key role in the sf television miniseries *Wild Palms* (1993) and has made guest appearances on a number of sf TV series, including *The X-Files, Babylon 5,* and *Star Trek: Voyager.*

DR. STRANGELOVE OR: HOW I LEARNED TO STOP WORRYING AND LOVE THE BOMB. (Dir. **Stanley Kubrick,** 1964.) Though it deals with the deadly serious topic of nuclear war, Stanley Kubrick's *Dr. Strangelove* is widely acknowledged as one of the funniest films ever made—even if its satirical depiction of the insanity of the cold-war arms race is uncomfortably accurate. Loosely based on Peter George's much more serious novel *Red Alert* (1958), *Dr.*

Strangelove became a cult favorite of the 1960s youth movement and was one of the classics of American culture of the 1960s, even though it was a British-American co-production and was actually made at London's Hawk Studios.

The film depicts both the United States and the Soviet Union as so caught up in the arms race that they pursue insane courses that make nuclear holocaust almost inevitable. In the film, this holocaust is triggered by the literal insanity of American General Jack D. Ripper (Sterling Hayden), unhinged by his extreme anticommunist paranoia. Ripper sets off the main events of the film when he orders a bomber attack on the Soviet Union, thereby activating automatic response systems that ensure the mutual destruction of both sides.

Much of the film is set in the memorable war room, where President Merkin Muffley (Peter Sellers) convenes a meeting of his chief strategic advisors in an inept attempt to deal with the crisis. The most important of these advisors is the eponymous Strangelove (also played by Sellers, in a bravura performance), a former Nazi who has clearly not overcome his fascist inclinations, signaled by the fact that he becomes increasingly involved in a comic wrestling match with his bionic right arm, which wants to shoot upward in a Nazi salute. Actually, the bombers are nearly recalled, averting the crisis, but one bomber has been damaged and fails to receive the abort message. Then, in one of the iconic scenes of American film, the plane drops its deadly nuclear bomb, with the plane's commander, Major J. T. "King" Kong (Slim Pickens), astride it bronco-style, waving his cowboy hat and whooping it up as the bomb falls to earth, triggering the destruction of modern civilization.

The screen then goes white as the bomb hits, signaling the beginning of the end of human civilization, and perhaps human life, on earth. However, the film itself continues with a sort of coda in which Strangelove suggests a plan to preserve civilization by founding colonies at the bottom of mine shafts, which are safe from the radioactive cloud. In a burlesque of virtually all of the **postapocalyptic** fictions of the long 1950s that reveals the fantasy elements that lie behind so many of them, Strangelove suggests that, in order to repopulate the earth, the new colonies should include 10 women for every man and that, in order to encourage reproductive activity, these women should be chosen for their "stimulating sexual characteristics." The men will, of course, be those gathered in the war room and their ilk.

Other than its suggestion that the madness of the cold war is an extension of the madness of the German Nazis, *Dr. Strangelove* does little to examine the cold war in historical and political terms. Instead, it depicts the Soviet-American confrontation as an ego contest between American madmen and Russian madmen. In the kind of association between violence and sexuality that is central to much of Kubrick's work, the film characterizes the cold war as a phallic competition driven by erotic energies, with macho generals on both sides trying to establish their greater manhood by proving that they have the bigger and more effective weapons. It did, however, serve as such an effective sendup of the mentality of the nuclear arms race that some have argued that the film actually played a role in cooling cold-war hysteria.

DUNE. (Dir. **David Lynch**, 1984.) The film adaptation of Frank Herbert's classic 1965 sf novel *Dune* had a long and troubled history even before it was finally brought to the screen by David Lynch in 1984. Subsequently, that adaptation was widely panned by critics, fans of the novel, and even Lynch himself. Indeed, in one of several subsequent DVD releases of the film, the director is listed not as Lynch but as "Alan Smithee," a pseudonym frequently used by directors who want to distance themselves from films over which they had been denied creative control. It is certainly true that the **special effects** of the film look cheap, despite the film's $40 million production budget, which was quite high for the time—more than six times the budget of *The Terminator,* released in the same year. It is also true that the costumes border on campiness, that the narrative is disjointed and almost incoherent, and that the film fails to capture the sense of grandeur that made the novel such a success. This is especially apparent in Kyle MacLachlan's portrayal of Paul Atreides, the film's central character, a figure of great magnitude in the book, but one who in the film seems by comparison slight and insignificant. It is also the case that the film omits some of the book's most important themes, especially Herbert's focus on **environmentalism** in his portrayal of the desert planet of Arrakis.

Nevertheless, Lynch's film has gained something of a cult follow-ing over the years, especially among those who are willing to view it as an independent work and not simply an adaptation of the novel. The film has a large and impressive cast of now-recognizable actors, even in fairly minor roles (such as **Patrick Stewart** as the warrior Gurney Halleck), even if many of them seem uncomfortable in their roles (and in their costumes). Despite always being on the verge of spilling over into unintentional campiness, *Dune* is in fact one of the most interesting-looking sf films of the 1980s. Numerous individual shots show something of Lynch's particular painterly vision, even if the film as a whole fails in its (apparently sincere) attempt to capture the grand scale of Herbert's epic novel. In addition, there is a way in which the film's tendency to seem silly at times gives it an element of political satire that is not really present in Herbert's novel. In particu-lar, the scheming and back-biting with which the various characters maneuver to further their own power seems especially cheap and tawdry within the visual context of the film, suggesting the cheapness of such self-serving maneuvers in general.

DYKSTRA, JOHN (1947–). When top **special effects** man **Douglas Trumbull** was approached by **George Lucas** about doing the special effects for the first *Star Wars* movie, Trumbull declined but recom-mended a young John Dykstra, who had recently assisted Trumbull on the effects for *Silent Running* (1972). Dykstra then spearheaded the groundbreaking special effects for *Star Wars,* thereby helping to launch a revolution in special effects technologies, especially those involving **computer-generated imagery (CGI)**. Indeed, the spe-cial camera used for many of that film's effects came to be known as a *Dystraflex* because of Dykstra's lead role in its development. Dykstra soon left Lucas's **Industrial Light & Magic**, however, and subsequently worked on both the original *Battlestar Galactica* televi-sion series (1978–1979) and *Star Trek: The Motion Picture* (1979). Dykstra's special effects work on *Firefox* (1982) was particularly impressive, pushing the CGI envelope considerably forward. Sub-sequently, Dykstra has worked on the effects for such sf films as *Lifeforce* (1985), *Invaders from Mars* (1986), and *My Stepmother Is an Alien* (1988). However, his most impressive later work has been for superhero films, including *Batman Forever* (1995), *Batman &*

Robin (1997), *Spider-Man* (2002), and *Spider-Man 2* (2004). He won Visual Effects Oscars for *Star Wars* and *Spider-Man 2* and was nominated for *Star Trek, Stuart Little* (1999), and *Spider-Man.*

DYNAMATION. Dynamation, touted as "the miracle of the screen," was a technique developed by **special-effects** artist **Ray Harryhausen** in the 1950s to combine **stop-motion animation** with live-action footage. The process essentially involved filming a combination of live actors and stop-action models against previously filmed rear-projected background action. Harryhausen used the technique to great effect in such films as *Jason and the Argonauts* (1963) and *Clash of the Titans* (1981). Notable science fiction films in which Harryhausen used the process include *It Came from Beneath the Sea* (1955), **20 Million Miles to Earth** (1957), and **First Men in the Moon** (1964).

DYSTOPIAN. Dystopian narratives turn the optimistic visions of utopian narratives on their heads, depicting societies in which the dream of an ideal society becomes a nightmare, often in ways that provide a satirical commentary on the real-world society in which the narrative was produced. Dystopian narratives in film have proved far more popular than utopian narratives, probably because they present more opportunities for narrative-generating conflicts, especially between the desires of specific individuals and the demands of the oppressive society that surrounds them. The category of dystopian film is closely related to that of **postapocalyptic** film, and dystopian societies often arise in the wake of natural or manmade disasters that have led to the destruction of the societies that came before them. However, dystopian societies can also arise as a natural consequence of the direct historical extension of certain flaws in current-day society, with no intervening catastrophe.

    Fritz Lang's *Metropolis* (1927), often regarded as the founding work of modern science fiction film, is a dystopian film that extends current conditions under capitalism to depict a future society in which workers have virtually become machines, enslaved by their rich masters. The line between utopia and dystopia is not always simple or clear, and conditions that one person might regard as utopian could easily be regarded as dystopian by another person. This complexity can be seen in science fiction film as early as *Things to Come*

(1936), a film (based on a novel by **H. G. Wells**, who also wrote the screenplay) that is largely designed to portray the utopian potential of humanity's future, but in which the utopian society portrayed has strong dystopian components as well. Few actual depictions of either utopian or dystopian societies can be found in science fiction film prior to Jean-Luc Godard's *Alphaville* (1965), which depicts a harsh, machine-ruled society that strips its citizens of spiritual and creative sustenance. Godard's fellow French New Waver François Truffaut directed *Fahrenheit 451*, which depicts a future dystopia in which books have been banned (in favor of television) as a means of helping to prevent independent thought. The ape-ruled future earth of *Planet of the Apes* (1968) can also be regarded as a dystopia.

In the United States, science fiction film took a decidedly dystopian turn in the early 1970s, mirroring a more pessimistic turn in American society itself. In 1971, the joint U.S./UK production *A Clockwork Orange,* directed by **Stanley Kubrick**, showed some of the complexities of dystopian thought. Here, a nightmarish future in which violent youth gangs terrorize the general population is opposed to an even more nightmarish attempt at official mind control in an effort to quell this violence. In the same year, *THX 1138,* the first film from future *Star Wars* creator **George Lucas**, is a classic dystopia in which a white-dominated mise-en-scène reinforces the sterile and oppressive nature of the society being depicted. Much of the plot of this film revolves around an attempted escape from the dystopia, which became a classic motif in dystopian film. **Richard Fleischer**'s *Soylent Green* (1973) indicates a dystopian future made so by official attempts to deal with overpopulation and environmental decay, while Norman Jewison's *Rollerball* (1975) shows a corporate- and media-dominated dystopian future in which corporations exploit a popular fascination with violent media spectacles to help control the general population. Finally, Michael Anderson's *Logan's Run* (1976), like *THX 1138,* features an enclosed dystopia from which the protagonists escape into a formerly devastated world that turns out, once again to be inhabitable. In contrast to these serious dystopias of the 1970s, Woody Allen's *Sleeper* (1973) is a farcical parody that spoofs many of the conventions of the dystopian genre.

Particularly influential in the visual development of dystopian imagery was **Ridley Scott**'s *Blade Runner* (1982), with its compelling images of a teeming future city, dominated by media images and struggling to survive as the human race decays while machines advance. Virtually all subsequent future cities in science fiction film were heavily influenced by this imagery, with *Dark City* (1998) and *Natural City* (2003) serving as particularly prominent examples. *Blade Runner* was followed in 1984 by a British film adaptation of George Orwell's *Nineteen Eighty-Four,* bringing perhaps the single most important dystopian novel to film in the year in which the novel is set. That year also saw the release of the first film in the *Terminator* franchise, which projects a dystopian future in which machines rule the earth and are determined to wipe out humans altogether. On the other hand, Terry Gilliam's *Brazil* followed the next year with what was essentially a spoof of the dystopian tradition, though its vision of an excessively bureaucratic future contained many legitimate dystopian images in its own right. Also notable in the 1980s was **John Carpenter**'s *They Live* (1988), in which a campy style only slightly veils a rather bitter critique of contemporary American consumer capitalism as a dystopian system that is already in place rather than projected into the future.

By the end of the 20th century, visions of a dark dystopian future had become a virtual convention of science fiction film. The films of the *Matrix* franchise followed the *Terminator* films in projecting a machine-ruled future, this time with humans preserved in individual pods where they are used as power sources for the machines, kept docile by immersion in a **virtual-reality** fantasy world. Notable recent films with dystopian inclinations include *Gattaca* (1997), *Equilibrium* (2002), *Minority Report* (2002), *Banlieue 13* (*District 13,* 2004), *Casshern* (2004), *V for Vendetta* (2005), and *Children of Men* (2006). These more recent dystopian films have become particularly clear in the way their dystopian futures are not predictions so much as satirical commentaries on the present world of consumer capitalism. *See also* ENVIRONMENTALISM; UTOPIAN FILMS.

– E –

E.T. THE EXTRA-TERRESTRIAL. (Dir. **Steven Spielberg**, 1982.) Conceived largely as a science fiction film for children, *E.T.* was a huge critical and commercial success and is now regarded as a classic of both science fiction film and children's film. Like *Close Encounters of the Third Kind* (1977), its predecessor in Spielberg's oeuvre, *E.T.* is an **alien-invasion** narrative that features benevolent aliens who have come to earth on a peaceful mission. Indeed, one could almost describe *E.T.* as a children's version of *Close Encounters* in that it emphasizes the same general themes, but for a younger audience. In the case of *E.T.*, the aliens, presented as vulnerable and harmless, seem simply to be gathering scientific data. Interrupted by a sinister-seeming group of humans, the aliens flee back to their ship, taking off in such haste that they leave one of their number behind. This alien, the film's title character, then spends the rest of the film struggling both to survive on earth and to find a way to get back home, despite the efforts of certain humans to capture it, presumably for study. Indeed, this film quite consistently reverses the terms of the classic alien-invasion narrative, making the alien sympathetic, while making most humans (especially those in positions of authority) seem villainous.

Children, however, are treated more sympathetically, and eventually E.T. takes refuge with the children of a middle-class suburban family (sans the father who is missing via divorce), forming an especially close bond with 10-year-old Elliott (Henry Thomas). Though sentimentally presented almost as a sort of cuddly pet, E.T. is in fact a highly advanced alien who manages (after a number of close calls and one moment when he even appears to be dead) to cannibalize available earth devices to build a communication device that calls a ship from his home planet back to earth to pick him up. As the film ends, E.T. flies away after a tearful farewell.

This relatively simple narrative is punctuated by a number of memorable scenes that help to make *E.T.* probably the most beloved of all of Spielberg's films. In addition to its tremendous box-office success, it won Oscars for Best Original Musical Score, Best Sound, Best Sound Effects Editing, and Best Visual Effects (especially for Carlo Rambaldi's design of the mechanical figure used to represent E.T., who is very much the star of the film). Indeed, the lovability of the central alien is one of the secrets of the success of the film, which centrally depends on sympathy for E.T. in delivering its message of tolerance toward the Other. Meanwhile, the film delivers a considerable amount of commentary on American society, though this aspect of the film is considerably muted relative to the sometimes sharp critique in *Close Encounters*. Moreover, *E.T.* includes, among other things, a number of allusions to films (such as **Star Wars**), making it a tribute to the power of the movies and to the central role played by movies in shaping the popular American imagination. *See also* CHILDREN'S SCIENCE FICTION.

EMMERICH, ROLAND (1955–). Roland Emmerich is a German director, producer, and screenwriter, known primarily for his big-budget action and disaster films, made in Hollywood. Even Emmerich's early German films were made in English (with mostly American actors) in the hope of reaching a wider audience, though that hope was not realized. Of these, *Moon 44* (1990) was an outer-space action film that showed a clear visual flair (especially for **special-effects** scenes), but it was otherwise unremarkable and went straight to video in the United States without a theatrical release. *Universal Soldier* (1992) was Emmerich's first Hollywood science fiction film. A **cyborg** action film clearly influenced by the **Terminator** franchise, *Universal Soldier* again features effective action scenes, but lacks substance. Emmerich's *Stargate* (1994) was much more successful, and its central premise involving a series of "stargates" that allow instantaneous travel between various points around the galaxy spawned an extensive television franchise.

Following *Stargate,* Emmerich had the Hollywood clout to make truly big-budget pictures, which he did to great effect as the producer and director of **Independence Day** (1996), one of the highlights of 1990s science fiction film. An **alien-invasion** film with the structure of a disaster film, *Independence Day* was a huge box-office hit with scenes of large-scale destruction that remain effective more than a decade later. Emmerich's subsequent big-budget remake of **Godzilla** (1998) applied many of the same strategies to the **monster movie**, but was much less successful and was particularly disliked by devoted fans of the Japanese movie franchise. In 1999, Emmerich produced (but did not direct) the **virtual-reality** film *The Thirteenth Floor*. Emmerich's next effort in science fiction was as director and producer of *The Day After Tomorrow* (2004), which addresses the important theme of global warming, but again puts more emphasis on spectacular action sequences than on thoughtful examination of complex issues. The film was nevertheless a major commercial success. In 2009, Emmerich directed and produced *2012,* a **postapocalyptic** film built on the ancient Mayan prediction of the end of the world in the year of the title.

ENEMY MINE. (Dir. Wolfgang Petersen, 1985.) Based on the Hugo Award–winning novella by Barry Longyear, *Enemy Mine* is essentially a science fiction remake of John Boorman's *Hell in the Pacific* (1968). *Enemy Mine* is set late in the 21st century, when humans have begun the colonization of outer space, bringing them into conflict with the Dracs, an alien species that claims dominion over some of the same territory. After a battle in space, human pilot Willis Davidge (**Dennis Quaid**) and Drac pilot Jeriba Shigan (Louis Gossett Jr.) both crash on a deserted planet, just as an American and a Japanese soldier had been stranded on a desert island in Boorman's film. Though the human-Drac conflict is obviously informed by considerable mutual racial hatred, Willis and Jeriba (who Willis comes to call "Jerry") eventually reach a grudging agreement to cooperate in order to survive on the grim and dangerous planet. They learn each other's languages and eventually become genuine friends. Dracs, as it turns out, reproduce asexually, and Jeriba is soon discovered to be pregnant. When the Drac dies in childbirth, Willis cares for the newborn Drac, which Jeriba had named Zammis (Bumper Robinson), trying his best to acquaint the child with its Drac heritage. Eventually, human slavers come to the planet and capture Zammis, leaving Willis for dead after he is shot attempting to defend the young Drac. Ultimately, however, Willis is rescued and then (in a rather farfetched sequence of events) manages to rescue Zammis and take the youngster (along with a group of other freed Drac slaves) back to the Drac home planet.

That *Enemy Mine* is meant to be a parable about the evils of racism is abundantly clear. In particular, partly because Jeriba is played by an African American actor, the Dracs clearly stand in for African Americans, especially in the sequences in which they are taken into slavery. *See also* MULTICULTURAL SCIENCE FICTION FILM.

ENVIRONMENTALISM. Environmentalism was a prominent theme in science fiction even before Rachel Carson's *Silent Spring* (1962), a book often credited with founding the modern environmentalist movement. For example, the satirical novel *The Space Merchants* (1952), by Frederik Pohl and Cyril Kornbluth, features an earth so ravaged by pollution and overpopulation that the human race is contemplating a migration to Venus. Blighted landscapes were often featured in the science fiction films of the 1950s, though they were typically caused by nuclear war or some other specific catastrophe, rather than the logical consequences of ongoing industrial development and population growth. Films in which specific catastrophes devastate the environment have continued to be produced ever since, as when the Japanese film *Casshern* (2004) evokes a world in which the environment has been devastated by global warfare with nuclear, biological, and chemical weapons.

Partly because of the rise of the environmentalist movement in the 1960s, by the early 1970s it was becoming increasingly common in science fiction film to depict a future earth in the throes of serious environmental decay that is the result of a direct extension of current abuses of the environment, with no specific intervening catastrophe. In *Silent Running* (1972), the degradation of the earth's environment has made it impossible for forests (and most plants, apparently) to survive there, so the remnants of the forests are removed to habitats in space, where they are tended toward the day when they can be returned to earth. That same year, *Z.P.G.* explored the potential future impact of overpopulation, a motif that would become a major theme in *Soylent Green* (1973), in which a combination of gross overpopulation and environmental decay has made it impossible to grow enough food to support the human race by ordinary means, so new means (such as processing the remains of recently deceased humans into cubes of innocuous-looking food) have to be explored. Finally, in *Demon Seed* (1977), an intelligent organic computer attempts to prevent humans from "raping" the earth, but itself becomes obsessed with essentially raping its creator's wife, hoping to produce a child that will save the world.

In **Ridley Scott's** *Blade Runner* (1982), the human race is in the process of relocating to outer space to escape an earth that has been environmentally devastated by unspecified causes (though, in the

Philip K. Dick novel on which the film is based, the cause is identified as nuclear war). Soon afterward, **Hayao Miyazaki's** *Kaze no tani no Naushika* (1984, *Nausicaä of the Valley of the Wind*) used the format of the animated film to explore a blighted landscape in the wake of an environmental catastrophe. In *Millennium* (1989) agents from a future so polluted that humans have all become sterile travel to the past to retrieve fertile humans in the hope of repopulating the planet in some far future time when the pollution has abated. Occasional other films explored such themes as well, as when *Waterworld* (1995) envisions a future earth almost entirely covered by water thanks to the melting of the polar ice caps.

By the 21st century, environmentalism moved very much to the fore in science fiction as more and more films took it as a virtual given that earth's future will be troubled by environmental calamities. **Steven Spielberg's** *Artificial Intelligence: AI* (2001) is set in a postapocalyptic world in which the natural human population has been decimated by the effects of environmental catastrophe, necessitating the production of humanoid **robots** to perform tasks for which there are no longer a sufficient number of human workers. In **Roland Emmerich's** *The Day After Tomorrow* (2004), global warming causes a catastrophic melting of the polar ice caps, providing a warning of similar catastrophes that could occur in the real world in the relatively near future, as the film's title indicates. Unfortunately, the scene puts more emphasis on spectacular **special effects** than on a thoughtful exploration of the issues it addresses.

In the same year, the experimental film *Able Edwards* is set in a future in which environmental catastrophe has forced the surviving members of the human race to abandon the earth and take up residence in an orbiting habitat called the "Civipod." A similar motif also occurs in **Pixar's** *WALL-E* (2008), in which the excesses of consumerism on an earth dominated by the gigantic "Buy N Large" (BNL) megacorporation lead to an uninhabitable environment covered by garbage. As a result, the remnants of the human race have to be removed to outer space habitats for a period of 700 years, at which time the earth is beginning to be livable again, as signaled by the return of plant life to the planet's surface. Also in 2008, the classic **alien-invasion** film *The Day the Earth Stood Still* was remade, this time shifting its warnings about the possible consequences of an unrestrained arms race to ones about the consequences of continued environmental irresponsibility. 2008 also saw the release of *The Happening*, by **M. Night Shyamalan**, in which the earth itself issues that humans must stop mistreating it. **James Cameron**'s environmentalist adventure *Avatar*, released in 2009, went on to become the top-grossing film of all time.

– F –

FAHRENHEIT 451. (Dir. François Truffaut, 1966.) Based on the 1953 novel by Ray Bradbury and directed by leading French New Wave director François Truffaut, the British-produced *Fahrenheit 451* is a **dystopian** film that was one of the highlights of science fiction film in the 1960s, a relatively slow decade for the genre. It features the Austrian-born actor Oskar Werner as Guy Montag, a "fireman," who begins to doubt his role in the future dystopian society of the film. That role involves hunting down and burning books, which have been banned in this future society because they might tend to encourage independent thought, shaking people out of the emotionless tranquility that is the hallmark of life in this world. Instead of books, this society employs mind-numbing television programming in order to entertain and pacify the population. Montag's disillusionment with his profession grows as he himself begins to be attracted to the books he is supposed to destroy, and is further encouraged by his encounter with Clarisse (Julie Christie), a free-spirited young woman who believes in the power of books to enrich the mind. As the film ends, Montag's indiscretions with books have been discovered and he has gone on the run, ending up, along with Clarisse, in a community of "book people," who memorize books, thus preserving their content, even though the physical books may no longer exist.

The film is typical of the dystopian form in its delineation of mindless and passive conformity as a key to the stability of its future society, while the identification of books as the key to challenging this conformity borders on cliché. Nevertheless, it is an effective film that has held up well over time, even if its visual imagination of the future has a definite 1960s feel.

FEMINISM AND GENDER. Science fiction as a whole has a mostly deserved reputation as a male-dominated genre, and science fiction film is generally no exception. Science fiction films have tended to be dominated by masculine heroes, with women characters serving as helpers and love interests for the male protagonists. In many cases, scantily clad female characters have served largely as eye candy, as in Roger Vadim's *Barbarella* (1968), which begins with a notorious striptease scene featuring the director's then-wife, Jane Fonda. Much of this traditional treatment of women in science fiction film comes from the perception that young men are the principal audience for the genre, though it is also the case that the directors of science fiction film have virtually all been men as well.

Nevertheless, there have been a number of important exceptions to masculine domination of sf film. Crucial here are the appearances of **Sigourney Weaver** as **Ellen Ripley** in the four *Alien* films, all of which feature Ripley as a strong female protagonist able to take on formidable alien monsters through use of brains, courage, and muscle. Also extremely important is **Linda Hamilton**'s portrayal of **Sarah Connor** in the first two *Terminator* films, in which she evolves from a relatively conventional young woman into a muscular and deadly guerrilla fighter. These two figures provide crucial inspiration for the appearance of numerous tough, strong, action-oriented female heroes in film and television of the 1990s and 2000s.

Among science fiction films directed by women, the most politically overt is *Born in Flames* (1983), a near-future sf film featuring radical feminist revolutionaries, made by radical-feminist director Lizzie Borden. Perhaps the best-known science fiction film directed by a woman is Kathryn Bigelow's **virtual-reality** thriller *Strange Days* (1995). Otherwise, sf films directed by women have been few and far between, including such efforts as Katt Shea's low-budget *Last Exit to Earth* (1996, made for TV—and for **Roger Corman**), Mimi Leder's sf **disaster** film *Deep Impact* (1998), and Lynn Hershman-Leeson's cloning **comedy** *Teknolust* (2002). *See also ATTACK OF THE 50 FOOT WOMAN; CHILDREN OF MEN;* JOVOVICH, MILLA.

THE FIFTH ELEMENT. (Dir. **Luc Besson**, 1997.) A gorgeous film that combines stunning visuals with a plot that is part **alien invasion**

and part **space opera**, *The Fifth Element* is a highly entertaining film
that includes both campy comedy and compelling action. In the film,
action star **Bruce Willis** plays Korben Dallas, a retired military operative who returns to duty from his job as a cab driver (in a futuristic
hovercraft cab) in order to save the earth from total destruction from
an alien attack. To save the earth, Dallas must locate and retrieve the
five "elements" of an ancient high-tech weapon, the fifth of which is
Leeloo (**Milla Jovovich**), a "supreme being" sent to earth by benevolent aliens to save the planet from the evil aliens. Leeloo is brilliant,
beautiful, and deadly, but entirely innocent. Her physical perfection
becomes a running joke throughout the film. In the end, the weapon
is assembled and the aliens defeated, while Dallas and Leeloo end up
in love (she is literally the "perfect woman" he has long sought) in
conventional Hollywood fashion.

However, *The Fifth Element* is a highly unconventional film. In
fact, though the action plot works well and though Willis and Jovovich perform well in the lead roles, the slightly excessive visuals
and the outrageous performances of Gary Oldman as a key villain
and Chris Tucker as a glitzy media personality lend the entire film a
campy air. *The Fifth Element* contains a number of elements that are
familiar from other sf films, but uses those elements in playful and
surprising ways, making the film both a successful sf action film and
a running commentary on the entire genre of sf film.

FIRST MEN IN THE MOON. (Dir. **Nathan Juran**, 1964.) Based
on the 1901 novel by **H. G. Wells**, *First Men in the Moon* is an
entertaining effort (with then state-of-the-art **special effects** by **Ray
Harryhausen**) that places its Victorian main plot within the frame
of a modern-day trip to the moon. The film begins as a United Nations–sponsored crew makes what they think is the first manned lunar
landing, only to discover evidence that English explorers had landed
on the moon as early as 1899. The bulk of the film tells the story
of those explorers, as had Wells's original novel. In this tale, eccentric scientist Joseph Cavor (Lionel Jeffries) discovers a substance
("Cavorite") that can be used to block the effects of gravity; coating
their ship with this substance allows Cavor and his investor, Arnold
Bedford (Edward Judd), to fly to the moon, with Bedford's fiancée,
Katherine Callender (Martha Hyer) aboard as a stowaway. There,

they are shocked to discover an underground civilization of insect people ("Selenites"), with whom the idealistic Cavor hopes to establish friendly relations, though Bedford realizes that the Selenites may be up to no good and that their curiosity about Cavorite might suggest an ambition to invade the earth. Bedford and Callender escape the Selenites and return to earth (where no one, of course, believes their story of having been to the moon), while Cavor voluntarily stays behind. Back in the frame narrative, the modern-day astronauts discover that the Selenites have been wiped out, apparently through their lack of resistance to the cold germs with which Cavor inadvertently infected them. In the novel the Selenites are not wiped out, though they apparently kill Cavor, hoping to eradicate the knowledge that might allow earth to invade the moon. The filmmakers thus tack on an ending taken almost directly from Wells's *The War of the Worlds* and its 1953 film adaptation.

FISHBURNE, LAURENCE (1961–). After a major role in *Apocalypse Now* (1979) while still a teenager, Laurence Fishburne has gone on to become one of the most respected American film actors of his generation, playing a variety of roles in a number of different genres. In the realm of sf, his most importance appearances have been as the human rebel leader, Morpheus, in *The Matrix* (1999) and its two sequels. Before that, Fishburne had an important role in the **postapocalyptic** film *Cherry 2000* (1987) and the lead role in the ambitious UK-U.S. co-produced **space opera**–horror hybrid *Event Horizon* (1997).

FISHER, TERENCE (1904–1980). The British director Terence Fisher was perhaps the most important figure in the surge in production of horror and science fiction films by England's **Hammer Films** in the 1950s and 1960s. Fisher's *Spaceways* (1953) was the studio's first science fiction film. Fisher's big breakthrough, though, came with *The Curse of Frankenstein* (1957), a **monster movie** in which the monster is produced by the unrestrained pursuit of scientific inquiry; this film was a major hit that propelled the studio to new international prominence. Fisher followed with a barrage of monster movies featuring Frankenstein's monster, Dracula, werewolves, mummies, and other classic movie monsters. Fisher also made several science fiction-horror hybrids that essentially employed the monster-movie format, including the **alien-invasion** films *The Earth Dies Screaming* (1964) and *Night of the Big Heat* (1967), and the science-gone-awry film *Island of Terror* (1966).

FIVE. (Dir. **Arch Oboler**, 1951.) Shot on a shoestring budget (largely in the director's own home), *Five* is nevertheless an interesting **postapocalyptic** film that addresses the cold-war fear of nuclear holocaust in thoughtful ways. It also appears to be the first film to have dramatized the effects of a nuclear holocaust, managing at the same time to identify and critique certain elements of the preholocaust society that might have contributed to the conditions that made nuclear war a possibility. In particular, *Five* suggests that certain aspects of American society, such as racism and egoism, might have been key factors in the drift toward nuclear war, thus going well beyond the simple anti-Soviet cold-war hysteria that informed many nuclear holocaust films of the 1950s. *Five* is an unusually enlightened film, more in the spirit of the contemporaneous ***The Day the Earth Stood Still*** (also 1951) than of the fellow nuclear holocaust films of the coming decade. *Five* seems a bit pessimistic in its vision of the virtual destruction of the entire human race by nuclear war, though it ends hopefully, with one man and one woman left standing, prepared to repopulate the earth.

FLEISCHER, RICHARD (1916–2006). The Brooklyn-born Richard Fleischer began his career as a director working on animated shorts (including Betty Boop and Popeye cartoons) produced by his father. He worked on a variety of projects for RKO Studio during World War II and won an Academy Award as producer of the 1947 documentary *Design for Death,* which examines the historical forces that propelled the Japanese into their participation in the war. In the late 1940s and early 1950s, Fleischer directed a series of films noirs, but burst onto the sf scene as the director of the high-profile ***20,000 Leagues Under the Sea*** for **Disney** in 1954. Fleischer remained prolific as the director of films in a variety of genres through the 1980s, including thrillers and war pictures, as well as fantasy films such as *Doctor Dolittle* (1967) and *Conan the Destroyer* (1984). During this period, he directed such prominent sf films as *Fantastic*

Voyage (1966) and ***Soylent Green*** (1973). Fleischer was the highly competent director of numerous successful mainstream commercial projects, and his work in sf helped to move that genre more into the Hollywood mainstream.

FORBIDDEN PLANET. (Dir. Fred Wilcox, 1956.) Filmed in brilliant color and widescreen Cinemascope, *Forbidden Planet* provides some of the most memorable science fiction images of the 1950s, from the dazzling green sky of the planet Altaira IV to the marvelous high-tech residence of the **mad scientist** Morbius (played by distinguished actor **Walter Pidgeon**) to the lovable but formidable **Robby the Robot**. It is an ambitious film that features a broad collection of key science fiction motifs from the decade, including space travel, an alien planet, a mad scientist, numerous high-tech devices (including the remarkable **robot** and Morbius's house of the future), and an advanced (but extinct) alien race. The film's groundbreaking all-electronic soundtrack is also notable, and the futuristic look of *Forbidden Planet* is greatly supplemented by its high-tech sound. Created by Bebe and Louis Barron, this soundtrack does a great deal to create an otherworldly aura for the film. In addition to being one of the most technically impressive science fiction films of the 1950s (thanks partly to the largest budget of any science fiction film that had yet been made), *Forbidden Planet* also has considerable artistic ambitions, beginning with the fact that it takes its basic plot from Shakespeare's *The Tempest,* moved from Prospero's island into outer space.

It is also, however, very much a film of its time that addresses many of the key concerns of the 1950s. For example, the film centers on the destruction of the alien Krel through the development of technologies that were ultimately beyond their control, a motif that obviously resonates with concerns about nuclear holocaust at the height of the cold war. At the same time, in its representation of Robby the Robot and Morbius's marvelous house (both built using advanced Krel technology), it also shows a typical 1950s American fascination with technology, and especially with the promise of technology to produce devices that make day-to-day life easier and more convenient. *Forbidden Planet* has remained an important film for more than half a century, and the release of its 50th-anniversary DVD in 2006 was greeted with much fanfare.

THE FORCE. A crucial element of the *Star Wars* film sequence, the "Force" is a somewhat enigmatic power drawn upon by the **Jedi** Knights of that sequence to help them battle against evil, though the Force also has a dark side that is drawn upon by the **Sith** order (including the iconic **Darth Vader**) within *Star Wars* in the pursuit of evil. *Star Wars* creator **George Lucas** has said that the origin of the Force lies in the 1964 experimental film *21-87*. At times the Force seems to be mystical in nature, allowing both the Jedi and the Sith orders not only to enhance their natural abilities (including physical abilities such as speed, agility, and strength, as well as mental abilities such as telekinesis and precognition) but seemingly to violate the laws of physics. At other points in the sequence, the Force seems to have a (somewhat farfetched) physical explanation as a sort of ever-present field that interacts with microorganisms called *midi-chlorians* that reside within the cells of all living things. Those who are trained to use the Force are thus learning to communicate and use the powers of the midi-chlorians, though some individuals (such as **Anakin Sky-walker,** who later becomes the sinister Vader) have a higher natural ability to do this than others because they have a higher-than-normal concentration of midi-chlorians within their cells.

FORD, HARRISON (1942–). When he was cast as **Han Solo** in *Star Wars* (1977), Harrison Ford was a virtual unknown who had labored in Hollywood obscurity for more than a decade. The role, re-enacted by Ford in the next two *Star Wars* films as well, propelled Ford to stardom, though between the second and third *Star Wars* films he had also starred as Indiana Jones in *Raiders of the Lost Ark* (1981), probably his best-known role. He also starred as android hunter Rick Deckard in *Blade Runner* (1982), perhaps his most important role in a science fiction film. After *Star Wars Episode VI: Return of the Jedi* (1983), Ford moved away from science fiction, concentrating on big-budget action thrillers (including several more Indiana Jones films) to become one of Hollywood's most bankable leading men. It should be noted, however, that the latest Indiana Jones film, *Indiana Jones* *and the Kingdom of the Crystal Skull* (2008), includes a prominent **alien-invasion** motif and thus might rightly be considered a work of science fiction.

FOX, MICHAEL J. (1961–). The Canadian-born actor Michael J. Fox first became known to American audiences as Young Republican Alex P. Keaton in the *Family Ties* television series (1981–1989). While still appearing in that series, he also played the lead role of Marty McFly in the **time-travel** film *Back to the Future* (1985), an extremely successful **comedy** that spawned sequels (also starring Fox) in 1989 and 1990. Fox continued to have moderate success in film roles over the next several years, returning to science fiction comedy with a key role in **Tim Burton**'s *Mars Attacks!* (1996). Fox also had the key voiceover role in the animated **children's science fiction** adventure *Atlantis: The Lost Empire* (2001). Fox was diagnosed with Parkinson's disease in 1991, a fact that he concealed from the public for some time; since 1998 he has been prominent as an advocate for research into the treatment and cure of the disease.

FRAKES, JONATHAN (1952–). Jonathan Frakes will probably always be best known among sf fans for his role as Commander William T. Riker in the television series *Star Trek: The Next Generation*, a role he reprised as a guest star in three subsequent *Star Trek* television series and in four subsequent *Star Trek* feature films as well. However, Frakes has also had an extensive career as the director not only of episodes of several different *Star Trek* television series but of two feature films, *Star Trek: First Contact* (1996) and *Star Trek: Insurrection* (1998). Frakes also directed *Clockstoppers* (2002), an sf film for young audiences, and *Thunderbirds* (2004), an sf adventure (with live actors) based on the 1960s British television series (featuring marionettes) from **Gerry and Sylvia Anderson.**

FRANKENSTEIN. (Dir. **James Whale**, 1931.) *Frankenstein* is one of the founding films of the modern **monster-movie** genre and one of the most important films in the history of American cinema. It provided some of the best-known images of American popular culture in the 20th century and served as the prototype not only for the dozens of Frankenstein movies made in subsequent years, but of the **mad-**

scientist horror film in general. Based loosely on Mary Shelley's 1818 novel (but more directly on a 1930 stage adaptation of Shelley's novel by Peggy Webling), this story of the pitfalls of unbridled scientific inquiry expressed some of American society's anxieties over the rapid scientific and technological advances that had occurred in the first three decades of the 20th century. Constructed from the spare parts of dead bodies and brought to life with a jolt of electricity by scientist Henry Frankenstein (Colin Clive) and his hunchback assistant, Fritz (Dwight Frye), the monster turns out accidentally to have been given the brain of a hardened criminal, with predictably disastrous results. Still, though dangerous, the film's shambling monster (Boris Karloff) is mostly just confused and misunderstood.

As the film ends, the monster, having committed a series of killings, is pursued by an angry mob and apparently driven to a fiery death, though in Whale's 1935 sequel, *The Bride of Frankenstein* (considered by many the greatest of the *Frankenstein* movies), it is revealed that the monster actually escaped death by taking refuge from the flames in a water-filled cellar. Meanwhile, the shots of the sinister, deranged townspeople who constitute the mob are among the most interesting in the film. These shots clearly contribute to the audience's potential sympathy for the monster, despite his malevolent appearance and grisly origins. A lone, one-of-a-kind individual whose only crimes have been either accidental or in self-defense, the monster becomes an odd sort of Byronic hero.

FRENCH SCIENCE FICTION FILM. Via the 19th-century writings of **Jules Verne**, French science fiction was on the cutting edge of the evolution of the new genre of science fiction. And, thanks to the innovative turn-of-the-century work of filmmaker-magician **Georges Méliès** (much of it based on the writings of Verne), French cinema was at the forefront of the development of science fiction film as well. Subsequently, French cinema made little in the way of contributions to the early evolution of science fiction film. Abel Gance's *La fin du monde* (*End of the World*, 1931) was one of the first sf **disaster** films; it features a comet that hurtles toward the earth, threatening to destroy the planet and thus anticipating later cosmic disaster films such as *When Worlds Collide* (1951), *Armageddon* (1998), and *Deep Impact* (1998)—the latter of which, in fact, again features a threat from a comet. Unfortunately, *La fin du monde* was very poorly received, and Gance did not return to science fiction, though he continued to make films for decades. French cinema, in fact, placed little emphasis on science fiction in the coming troubled decades of Depression and war, focusing instead on more realistic themes.

Chris Marker's haunting *La jetée* (1962) was perhaps the next real highlight in French sf film. Jean-Luc Godard's French-Italian co-production *Alphaville* (1965, a somewhat tongue-in-cheek **dystopian** film) brought the French New Wave into sf film, and Godard's fellow New Waver François Truffaut followed as the director of the British-produced *Fahrenheit 451* (1966). Another important contribution of French culture to sf film came in 1968, when Pierre Boulle's novel *Planet of the Apes* was effectively adapted to a U.S. film of the same title. That same year saw the release of Roger Vadim's *Barbarella,* a French-Italian co-production that became a cult classic. Alain Resnais's *Je t'aime, je t'aime*, a French-Spanish co-production dealing with **time travel**, was also released in 1968.

The impressive output of 1968 did not, however, signal an overall boom in French science fiction film, and the 1970s were a relatively sparse decade, punctuated by such highlights as the Czech-French animated film *La planète sauvage (Fantastic Planet,* 1973) and Louis Malle's *Black Moon* (1975), both of which featured surrealistic elements rarely seen in Anglophone science fiction film. *Moonraker* (1979), a British-French co-production, was the most science fictional of all the James Bond films. The 1980s were sparse as well, though they began with an interesting French-British-German co-production in Bertrand Tavernier's *La mort en direct (Death Watch,* 1980). This decade also saw the arrival of **Luc Besson**, whose *Le dernier combat (The Last Combat,* 1983) engages in a wry dialogue with the **postapocalyptic** film boom of the 1980s. In 1989 comics artist **Enki Bilal** released the dystopian film *Bunker Palace Hôtel.* In 1991 famed German director Wim Wenders was at the helm of the French-German-Australian co-production *Bis ans Ende der Welt (Until the End of the World)*, a **cyberpunk** thriller that is built around a disaster scenario. That same year, *Terminator 2: Judgment Day* was a joint U.S.-French production, as was **Roland Emmerich**'s *Stargate* (1994). In 1996, Bilal directed the futuristic thriller *Tykho Moon,* a joint French-German production. The highlight of the 1990s in French sf film, however, was surely Besson's *The Fifth Element* (1997), a campy English-language effort that remains a highly effective thriller as well as providing a self-conscious commentary on virtually the entire tradition of sf film.

In recent years, science fiction has enjoyed a new prominence in French cinema, with the production of a number of action-oriented thrillers, often featuring fast-cut, MTV-style editing. In 2004, for example, releases included the frenetic dystopian action film *Banlieue 13 (District 13)*, written and produced by Besson, and *Immortel (ad vitam)* (a French-Italian-British co-production), written and directed by Bilal and featuring groundbreaking use of **green-screen** technologies. In 2007, *Chrysalis* was a futuristic crime thriller that reminded many of the American *X-Files* television series; that same year, *Eden Log* was a visually inventive dystopian-postapocalyptic film featuring a number of cyberpunk elements. *Babylon A.D.* (2008) was a high-action joint U.S.-French production featuring American actor **Vin Diesel**; it was, however, poorly received by critics. *See also* ITALIAN SCIENCE FICTION FILM.

– G –

GATTACA (Dir. **Andrew Niccol**, 1997). *Gattaca* is a **dystopian** film that explores the consequences of **genetic engineering** in a future society divided into the "Valids" (those who have been engineered) and the "In-Valids" (those who have not). The film focuses on In-Valid Vincent Freeman (Ethan Hawke) who discovers that he is cursed not only with a faulty physical body but also with a psychological stigma that keeps most desirable social and professional areas closed to him. Since childhood, Freeman has dreamed of being an astronaut, but finds that such careers are, in practice, available only to the Valid, despite the existence of genetic antidiscrimination laws. Freeman then concocts a plan to assume the identity of Jerome Morrow (**Jude Law**), a highly engineered Valid with impeccable genetic credentials who has been rendered unable to pursue such a career due to paralysis from a broken back incurred in an apparent suicide attempt. Freeman goes through a variety of elaborate procedures to pull off the imposture, landing a job with the Gattaca Aerospace **Corporation**, whose sparkling, sterile headquarters serves as a symbol of the advanced but soulless nature of this future society. After a number of close calls (including the near revelation of his true identity as the result of a murder investigation subplot), Freeman realizes his dream of going into space on a key mission, blasting off as the film ends, while the real Morrow commits suicide, leaving behind DNA samples so that Freeman can continue to impersonate him after his return to earth. Human achievement, the film suggests, depends not just on DNA but also on the human spirit.

GENDER. *See* FEMINISM AND GENDER.

GENETIC ENGINEERING. Genetic engineering involves the manipulation of DNA in order to produce an organism with certain specific desired characteristics. It is closely related to the notion of cloning, or the production of an exact genetic replica of a particular parent organism. Genetic engineering is a relatively recent concept, and the scientific understanding of the fundamental nature and structure of DNA only began to become clear in the 1950s. However, science fiction concepts often anticipate those of science, and a form of genetic engineering appears in sf film as early as the German silent film *Alraune* (1928), as well as the sound version (1930) of the same film, in which a **mad scientist** artificially impregnates a prostitute with the semen of a hanged murderer, producing a sexually obsessed and murderous offspring with an inability to feel love. The central themes of the **Frankenstein** story, which dates back to Mary Shelley's 1818 novel and of which the most important of several film versions was made by **James Whale** in 1931, also border on genetic engineering with their focus on the creation of an artificial human being.

These examples show that the tendency for science fiction films to treat genetic engineering negatively as a dangerous and potentially sinister activity was developed early. It should come as no surprise, then, that one of the first modern films featuring genetic engineering, *The Boys from Brazil* (1978) involves a plot by Nazi scientists to try to clone Adolf Hitler. One of the best-known examples of such negative treatment of genetic engineering in science fiction originates in the original *Star Trek* television series in the episode "Space Seed" (1967), in which the crew of the *Enterprise* discovers a craft from earth dating back to the 1990s. In it, frozen in stasis, are a number of exiles from earth's "eugenics wars," which led to the banning of human genetic engineering on earth. These exiles include the formidable Khan Noonien Singh (Ricardo Montalban), a genetically engineered superman who, once awakened, plans a program of conquest to recover the extensive political power he once held on earth. Captain Kirk and his crew are able to thwart Khan's efforts and to exile him and his followers to a barren, uninhabited planet, though he uses his considerable abilities to mount another plan of conquest from there, resulting in the action that will eventually lead to his death in the second *Star Trek* theatrical film, *The Wrath of Khan* (1982).

The Soviet film *Per Aspera ad Astra* (1981, later dubbed in English as *Humanoid Woman*) is a **space opera** involving the genetic engineering of a humanoid clone with supernatural abilities. It is far less silly than it appears in the English version, known to Western viewers primarily as an object of mockery in *Mystery Science Theater 3000*.

Harold Ramis's *Multiplicity* (1996) is a humorous look at the theme of cloning in which an overworked man creates multiple clones of himself to share the load, with considerable comic consequences. Lynn Hershman-Leeson's *Teknolust* (2002) is also a **comedy** based on cloning. Meanwhile, the replicants of *Blade Runner* (1982), one of the most influential sf films of all time, are the products of genetic engineering, even if they are designed not to be fully human. They have both superhuman abilities and very limited lifespans; they are intended for use essentially as slave labor in hazardous environments in outer space. Among other things, their representation points toward the way in which genetic engineering potentially redefines the boundaries of what it means to be human.

Andrew Niccol's *Gattaca* (1997) explores the potential social consequences of genetic engineering though its depiction of a future society in which genetic engineering has advanced to the stage that virtually all defects can be eliminated through genetic manipulation of human embryos. As a result, humans born without such manipulation (known as In-Valids) are immediately suspected of being defective and are therefore the objects of considerable discrimination. Renny Harlin's *Deep Blue Sea* (1999) then topped off the 1990s with what is essentially an underwater **monster movie**, with the added sf twist that the monsters in question are sharks made more dangerous by a genetic experiment gone wrong.

As human genetic engineering (and even human cloning) moved closer to scientific possibility in the early 21st century, science fiction film responded with an increased interest in the motif, still usually treating it as dangerous and open to abuse. For example, the classic sf film *Planet of the Apes* was remade by **Tim Burton** in 2001 with big-budget **special effects** and with a thematic shift for the cause of the supplementation of the human race by apes from nuclear holocaust to genetic engineering. In 2002 in the Korean thriller *Yesterday* (set in a unified Korea in the year 2020) a series of murders of aging scientists gradually leads the Korean police into a complex investigation that ultimately reveals the killer to be a man who had been involved as a young boy in a series of illicit genetic experiments 30 years earlier. **Michael Bay**'s big-budget thriller *The Island* (2005), is a **dystopian** film in which clones of wealthy clients are reared in an enclosed facility toward the day when their bodies might be needed as spare parts for the clients. The film acknowledges the possible positive medical implications of the technologies it examines, but nevertheless seems to have little sympathy for those technologies. Meanwhile, if this film seemed particularly topical given some of the advances in genetics-based medical research then underway in the real world, it is also the case that the basic scenario of *The Island* so closely resembled that of the 1979 film *Parts: The Clonus Horror* that the makers of *The Island* were forced to pay a settlement after the creators of *Clonus* filed a lawsuit. In the video-game adaptation *Doom* (2005), genetic experiments seek to recreate a former Martian species of superhumans, but produce monsters instead. Kurt Wimmer's action-packed **dystopian** film *Ultraviolet* (2006) also explores the negative implications of genetic engineering, but here it has a positive side in that a young woman is given superhuman abilities by genetic engineering that allow her to battle the forces of an oppressive government. *See also* FEMINISM AND GENDER.

GERMAN SCIENCE FICTION FILM. German filmmakers were at the very forefront of the early evolution of science fiction film, producing such important silent films as *Das Kabinett des Doktor Caligari* (1920, *The Cabinet of Dr. Caligari*), which features a sort of **mad**

scientist and employs a German expressionist style that influenced numerous later sf films. *Alraune* (1928) also spans the boundary between sf and horror and anticipates a later sf interest in genetics. Meanwhile, **Fritz Lang**'s *Frau im Mond* (*Woman in the Moon*) is a serious sf film about a trip to the moon that introduces a number of future conventions for the cinematic representation of rocket launches. The most important work of German silent sf film, however, was undoubtedly Lang's *Metropolis* (1927), which exercised an incalculable influence on the subsequent development of sf film.

In 1930, German sf film entered the sound era with the remaking of *Alraune*, with sound and with the same star (**Brigitte Helm**). (It was remade again in 1952 in West Germany.) The pro-Nazi film *Der Tunnel* (1933) focuses on the building of a transatlantic tunnel; it was simultaneously made in parallel German- and French-language versions—then later remade in an English version in 1935, but without the pro-Nazi propaganda. In 1934, *Gold* anticipated many later sf films in its focus on the attempt of an evil tycoon to hijack a major scientific discovery for profit.

During the era of the divided Germany, East Germany's Deutsche Film-Aktiengesellschaft (DEFA) Studios produced a number of notable sf films, including the East German–Polish co-production of *Der schweigende Stern* (1960, *The Silent Star*), an adaptation of **Stanisław Lem**'s novel of that title. An expurgated version of this film was released in the United States in 1962 as *First Spaceship on Venus*. In 1972, DEFA released *Eolomea,* a science fiction thriller, and in 1976 they released *Im Staub der Sterne* (*In the Dust of the Stars*), a **space opera** in a hip style that shows a clear influence of the Western counterculture of the 1960s and early 1970s.

In West Germany, *Die Herrin der Welt* (*Mistress of the World*) was released in two parts in 1960, involving a plot that combines the development of a new high-tech weapon with international intrigue. *Space Men* (1960), directed by **Antonio Margheriti**, was a joint Italian–West German production. In 1964, the spooky **alien-invasion** drama *Der Chef wünscht keine Zeugen* (*No Survivors, Please*) was a joint West German–U.S. production. *Der große Verhau* (1971, *The Big Mess*) was a **dystopian** film that was also a **comedy**. *Alien Contamination* (1980, aka *Contamination*) was a joint West German–Italian production that was clearly influenced by the success of *Alien* the year before. Also in 1980, *La mort en direct* (*Death Watch*) was a joint West German–French production. In 1982, *Kamikaze 1989* was a dystopian thriller. **Roland Emmerich**'s *Moon 44* (1990) was a joint West German–U.S. production released shortly before German reunification. Emmerich went on to make a number of major sf films in the United States. Indeed, he might be considered the most important figure in contemporary German sf film, though his subsequent sf films have been U.S. productions or international co-productions without German involvement.

Since reunification, most sf films with German involvement have been international co-productions. Renowned German director Wim Wenders helmed the French-German-Australian co-production *Bis ans Ende der Welt* (1991, *Until the End of the World*), a **cyberpunk** thriller that is built around a **disaster** scenario. In 1996, comics artist **Enki Bilal** directed *Tykho Moon,* a joint French-German production. The new millennium, however, has seen little activity in German sf film, the most visible example being the video-game adaptation *Doom* (2005), a Czech-German-British co-production. Also in 2005, the well-known German filmmaker Werner Herzog directed *The Wild Blue Yonder* (2005), a German-French-Austrian-British co-production.

GHOST IN THE SHELL. (Dir. **Mamoru Oshii**, 1995.) An adaptation of the manga of the same title by Masamune Shirow, *Ghost in the Shell* (Japanese title *Kôkaku kidôtai*) was particularly popular in the United States, where it brought new attention to the Japanese genre of **anime** film. This particular film can be considered an entry in the Japanese **mecha** genre because of its heavy reliance on sophisticated technological devices. It also features an elaborate array of **cyborg** characters who have undergone a variety of electromechanical brain and body augmentations. *Ghost in the Shell* was also one of the first successful adaptations of the central themes and motifs of **cyberpunk**. Though featuring spectacular violence and substantial animated female nudity, *Ghost in the Shell* is far from an exploitation film. Instead, it uses beautiful animation to produce a powerful meditation on the relationship between humans and their technology that challenges the boundaries of what we define as *human*. In particular, it asks whether technological devices can become so sophisticated that they should be considered human, whether humans can become so augmented with technological devices that they become machines, and whether, in an increasingly sophisticated technological age, it even makes sense to try to distinguish between humans and machines in the absolute mode of the past.

The plot revolves around the attempts of special police agents, led by Major Motoko Kusanagi (voiced in English by Mimi Woods) and her partner Bateau (Richard George), to track down a rogue hacker known as the Puppet Master (Abe Lasser) in an unnamed futuristic cityscape (identified by the film's makers as modeled on Hong Kong). Kusanagi has a cyborg body into which a human mind has been uploaded, while Bateau's body is mostly human, but with certain augmentations. The Puppet Master, they discover, is essentially an artificial intelligence (though he insists that he is a living being and should not be regarded as "artificial"). In the end, the Puppet Master and Kusanagi merge, and their combined consciousness is uploaded into a new (female) cyborg body. As the film ends, the new hybrid being sets out to encounter the world.

A sequel, *Innocence* (*Ghost in the Shell 2: Innocence*), also directed by Oshii, was released in 2004, featuring many of the same characters and motifs as the original film. The *Ghost in the Shell* manga was also the basis for an anime television series that began broadcasting in 2002, while the original film and the television series have both been adapted into video games. *See also* ANIMATED SCIENCE FICTION FILMS.

GIBSON, MEL (1956–). Though born in Peekskill, New York, the actor and director Mel Gibson grew up in Australia, where he also started his acting career, getting his big break when he was cast in the lead role of the **postapocalyptic** film *Mad Max* (1979). Gibson's voice was actually dubbed in the United States release of that film, but he gained considerable attention with *Mad Max 2*, released in the United States as *The Road Warrior* (1981). By the time Gibson returned to the role for *Mad Max Beyond Thunderdome* (1985), he had starred in several more mainstream films in both Australia and the United States and was rapidly becoming an important film star in the world. The *Lethal Weapon* films subsequently made him a top box-office draw. He has done relatively little work in science fiction since the *Mad Max* films, though he did star in *Forever Young* (1992), a **time-travel** narrative of sorts, and in **M. Night Shyamalan's alien-invasion** film *Signs* (2002). By the time he directed and starred in the Academy Award–winning *Braveheart* in 1995, Gibson had reached the absolute pinnacle of the film industry, where he stayed through the box-office success of *The Passion of the Christ* (2004), which he directed but did not star in. Controversy over the potentially antisemitic implications of that film and subsequent troubles in Gibson's private life have tarnished his image in recent years, however.

GIBSON, WILLIAM (1948–). William Gibson is the single writer most identified with the **cyperpunk** movement in science fiction. Though born in Conway, South Carolina, and still a U.S. citizen, William Gibson has spent most of his life as a resident of Canada (he now lives in Vancouver), where he fled in 1967 to avoid the Vietnam-era draft. Though he had already published a number of short stories with themes related to what later became known as cyberpunk (many later reprinted in the 1986 collection *Burning Chrome*), Gibson burst into prominence with the publication of *Neuromancer* (1984), his first novel and the book that is generally taken to have announced the arrival of cyberpunk as a full-blown literary phenomenon. *Neuromancer* remains the signature work of the movement and was quickly followed by other volumes in the same vein, solidifying Gibson's reputation as the most important writer of cyberpunk. By the time of *Pattern Recognition* (2003), however, Gibson shifted to a somewhat different mode, moving his setting entirely from the future to the present.

The film industry has shown considerable interest in cyberpunk and in Gibson's work in particular. Gibson's writing has clearly influenced successful films such as *The Matrix* (1999), though his work has thus far proved difficult to adapt directly. *Johnny Mnemonic* (1995), scripted by Gibson, himself, based on one of his short stories, was widely considered to be unsuccessful. *New Rose Hotel* (1998) is a relatively obscure adaptation of another short story by Gibson. The 1993 television miniseries *Wild Palms* was also heavily influenced by Gibson's fiction, and featured Gibson in a cameo role. A film adaptation of *Neuromancer* has been discussed since the 1990s, but has yet to appear, though ***Star Wars*** star **Hayden Christensen** has been cast in the starring role. A film adaptation of *Pattern Recognition* is also reportedly in development.

GODZILLA. The huge, fire-breathing prehistoric reptile Godzilla (aka *Gojira*) first appeared in **Ishirō Honda**'s low-budget **monster movie** of the same title in 1954. The monster, seemingly part **dinosaur** and part dragon, is the result of genetic mutations caused by radiation from nuclear weapons. Though heavily influenced by previous movie monsters, especially the title figure of *King Kong* (1933), Godzilla has had a unique attraction for movie audiences ever since. He was introduced to widespread American audiences in 1956 in an English-dubbed adaptation of the original film called *Godzilla: King of the Monsters!* That film contains additional scenes directed by Terry Morse, featuring American actor Raymond Burr, to give American audiences a character with whom to identify. Burr also supplied voiceover narration to some scenes to make them more intelligible to audiences in the United States. Burr plays American reporter Steve Martin, who just happens to have stopped over in Tokyo on his way to another assignment when the giant prehistoric reptile Godzilla, a monster apparently produced by nuclear testing, attacks. This theme of the dangers of nuclear weapons obviously had special resonance for Japanese audiences, as did the outcome, in which Godzilla is killed by a Japanese-developed superweapon, thus giving the Japanese a sort of fantasy victory over nuclear weaponry.

American audiences could also appreciate the theme of nuclear threat, which was already prominent in American sf films of the time, and the adapted film was a hit in the United States in theaters, and eventually became a long-term staple on American television as well as the first in a series of English-language adaptations of Japanese Godzilla movies. Some of the attraction of the film has to do with the unintentional campiness of its low-budget **special effects**, but the film clearly entertains audiences on other levels as well. Among other things, the long life of the Godzilla franchise suggests that the monster itself has a special appeal. Godzilla went on to become the center of a long-lived film franchise in Japan and has, to date, starred in a total of 28 Japanese films, some of which feature the famous monster as a defender of humanity, battling against other monsters. A big-budget American remake of *Godzilla,* directed by **Roland Emmerich**, was released in 1998, with state-of-the-art special effects. The remake, however, lacked the charm of the original and was not a great success.

GOLDBLUM, JEFF (1952–). The American actor Jeff Goldblum has played a number of roles, but roles as nerdy scientist types have become something of a specialty, giving him a number of opportunities in science fiction film. Indeed, he began to be cast in such films early in his career. One of his first major roles was in the 1978 remake of *Invasion of the Body Snatchers,* and he followed with a role as an eccentric scientist in *Threshold* (1981). Goldblum's performance in the cult sf film *The Adventures of Buckaroo Banzai Across the Eighth Dimension* (1984), was rather forgettable, but he burst into sf stardom as a **mad scientist**–turned–insect in **David Cronenberg**'s 1986 remake of *The Fly*. Now almost type-cast as a scientist, Goldblum was subsequently cast as geneticist Jim Watson in *Life Story* (1987), a made-for-television drama about the real-life discovery of DNA. Goldblum's appearance in the sf **comedy** *Earth Girls Are Easy* (1988) drew little attention, but he moved back into a prominent position in sf film with his role as Ian Malcolm, still another scientist (this one a chaos theorist who is much hipper than Goldberg's usual) in **Steven Spielberg**'s *Jurassic Park* (1993). Goldberg maintained his stardom as computer geek David Levinson in *Independence Day* (1996), then returned as Malcolm in *The Lost World: Jurassic Park* (1997). His work since then has been outside of science fiction.

GOLDMAN, GARY. The American screenwriter got his start as the co-writer of **John Carpenter**'s *Big Trouble in Little China* (1986). He also co-wrote the 1990 action film *Navy Seals* (1990). But Goldman has become something of a specialist in adapting the works of science fiction master **Philip K. Dick** to film. He and **Ronald Shusett** wrote the screenplay for **Paul Verhoeven**'s *Total Recall* (1990); they then wrote a script for a screen adaptation of Dick's short story "The Minority Report." That script was never used, but the story was eventually adapted to film by **Steven Spielberg** as *Minority Report* in 2002, with Goldman and Shusett credited as executive producers. Goldman also co-wrote the script for *Next* (2007), based on Dick's short story "The Golden Man." He served as an executive producer for that film as well.

GOLDSMITH, JERRY (1929–2004). The American composer Jerry Goldsmith was one of the most prominent writers of scores in the history of American film. He was nominated for a total of eighteen Academy Awards, though his only win for Best Score was for the horror film *The Omen* (1976). Goldsmith, in fact, was a prolific composer who worked in a number of genres, but much of his most memorable work was for science fiction films, beginning with his classic score for **Planet of the Apes** (1968). After *Logan's Run* (1976) and *Capricorn One* (1978), Goldsmith wrote the score for **Alien** (1979) and for **Star Trek: The Motion Picture** (1979), firmly establishing himself in the world of sf film as a composer exceeded only by **John Williams** in prominence. Goldsmith went on to provide the scores for a total of five *Star Trek* films, while his rousing theme from the first *Star Trek* film also became the theme for the television series *Star Trek: The Next Generation* and remains the music most widely associated with the franchise. Goldsmith's later scores for sf film include *Innerspace* (1987), *Leviathan* (1989), **Total Recall** (1990), and *Forever Young* (1992).

GORDON, BERT I. (1922–). A key figure in the low-budget science fiction explosion of the 1950s, the American director, writer, and producer Bert I. Gordon seems to have been especially fascinated with the notion of small humans being menaced by large monsters. Famous for what now look like particularly unconvincing rear-projection techniques to create his effects, Gordon nevertheless had a knack for constructing oddly compelling narratives. His *Beginning of the End* (1957) is one of the more effective giant-bugs-created-by-radiation films of the 1950s, and *The Amazing Colossal Man* (1957) is a highly entertaining reversal of **Jack Arnold**'s **The Incredible Shrinking Man** from that same year, here with a protagonist who grows huge and thus inadvertently becomes a threat to humanity. Gordon also directed and produced *War of the Colossal Beast,* a sequel to *The Amazing Colossal Man* released in 1958, the year Gordon also made *Earth vs. the Spider,* another big-bug film, and *Attack of* *the Puppet People,* in which a lonely dollmaker (and part-time mad inventor) develops a device to shrink real people to the size of dolls. After the two prolific years of 1957 and 1958, Gordon produced relatively little of note. *Village of the Giants* (1965) and *The Food of the Gods* (1976) were both rather unsuccessful adaptations of **H. G. Wells's** 1904 novel *The Food of the Gods,* despite the fact that the premise of Wells's novel (about an experimental food that spurs fantastic growth) should have been perfect for Gordon's talents. Gordon's giant-ant film *Empire of the Ants* (1977), however, was something of a return to his form of 20 years earlier, with slightly better **special effects**.

GORDON, FLASH. *See* SERIALS.

GRAVES, PETER (1926–2010). Prior to his iconic role as team leader Jim Phelps in the television series *Mission Impossible* (1967), the American actor Peter Graves had an extensive career in a variety of film roles, including a number of science fiction films. In the 1950s, for example, he appeared in such forgettable movies as *Red Planet Mars* (1952), *Killers from Space* (1954), and *It Conquered the World* (1956), though his competent performance in **Bert I. Gordon's** *Beginning of the End* (1957) helped to make that particular film reasonably successful. After his turn in *Mission Impossible,* Graves returned to sf film as the star of the made-for-TV **postapocalyptic** film *Where Have All the People Gone?* (1974). He played an ambitious politician who has himself cloned in order to use the clone for spare parts in *Parts: The Clonus Horror* (1979). He also had a small cameo role playing himself in *Men in Black II* (2002).

GREEN SCREEN. Using a process also known as the *chroma key* technique, many of the **special effects** for science fiction movies are produced by filming actors in front of a blank screen (usually green, but sometimes blue) and then filling in the background later through the use of separate images, often composed using **computer-generated imagery (CGI)**. A similar technique had been used as early as the 1930s to allow separate filming of foreground and background action, but the modern-day use of the technique to implement CGI effects was pioneered in the early *Star Wars* films and reached its zenith in 2004 when four different sf films were released in which all of the live action was shot in front of green screens with background action composed using CGI. These films included France's *Immortel* (*ad vitam*), Japan's **Casshern,** and the U.S. films *Able Edwards* and *Sky Captain and the World of Tomorrow* (the latter actually a joint British-Italian-American production). Virtually all sf films of the 21st century include at least some use of the green-screen technique for composing computer-generated special effects, though it is becoming more and more common to generate entire scenes (foreground and background) by computer.

GUEST, VAL (1911–2006). After an early career in film that dated back to the mid-1930s, the British director, writer, and producer Val Guest became a prominent figure in **British science fiction film** as the writer and director of *The Quatermass Xperiment* (1955) and then *Quatermass 2* (1957), for **Hammer Films**. Guest continued to work in a variety of genres (especially crime dramas), but stayed active in science fiction as well, writing and directing an eclectic collection of sf films, including *The Day the Earth Caught Fire* (1961, which he also produced, in which nuclear testing inadvertently sends the earth hurtling toward the sun, with disastrous consequences), *When Dinosaurs Ruled the Earth* (1970, featuring cavemen struggling with **dinosaurs**), and *Toomorrow* (1970, an sf musical featuring Olivia Newton-John). Guest also directed three episodes of the television series *Space: 1999* in 1976 and 1977.

GUINNESS, SIR ALEC (1914–2000). Among the numerous performances of the distinguished British actor, the ones for which he will likely be best remembered by the most people are his performances as the aging **Obi-Wan Kenobi** in all three films of the original *Star Wars* trilogy. A particularly important character in the first *Star Wars* film, Kenobi was killed off (in a memorable light saber battle with **Darth Vader**) in that film, only to return as a posthumous presence in *The Empire Strikes Back* (1980) and *Return of the Jedi* (1983). Guinness had also starred in *The Man in the White Suit* (1951), a thoughtful exploration of the ramifications of the scientific discovery (by Guinness's character) of a cloth that never wears out, thus threatening the textile industry.

– H –

HAL 9000. The HAL 9000 is the advanced **computer** that is charged with overseeing the automated operations of the spaceship *Discovery* as it travels into deep space in response to an apparent signal from advanced aliens in **Stanley Kubrick**'s *2001: A Space Odyssey* (1968). Programmed to ensure the success of the mission at all costs, HAL concludes that the human crew aboard the ship are actually a threat to the mission due to their fallibility. The computer therefore sets about to eliminate the troublesome humans in order to safeguard the mission—and nearly succeeds in doing so. One of the first computers to figure prominently in science fiction film, the coldly logical HAL 9000 is also one of sf film's most frightening and compelling villains. In 2003, the American Film Institute listed HAL as the 13th greatest movie villain of all time, just ahead of the deadly creature from *Alien* (1979). *See also* COMPUTERS AND ARTIFICIAL INTELLIGENCE.

HAMILTON, LINDA (1956–). Though she has appeared in numerous films and television series (including a starring role in the 1987–1990 fantasy series *Beauty and the Beast*) the American actress Linda Hamilton will always be best remembered for her portrayal of **Sarah Connor** in *The Terminator* (1984) and *Terminator 2: Judgment Day* (1991). In the first of these films, she was effective as a relatively ordinary young woman whose somewhat superficial existence is interrupted by the discovery that she is fated to become the mother of the potential savior of the human race—but only if she can avoid first being killed by a deadly **cyborg** assassin sent back from the future to prevent her son, **John Connor**, from ever being born. Hamilton also had a lead role in the horror film *Children of the Corn* for a second major appearance in 1984. Those roles helped her to land the starring role in **Dino de Laurentiis**'s *King Kong Lives* (1986), a much-hyped sequel to de Laurentiis's 1976 commercially successful remake of the original *King Kong,* but the sequel was not a success, critically or commercially.

It was in *Terminator 2*, however, that Hamilton made her big splash. After having given birth to John and having spent years training him for his future as a guerrilla leader in the coming human war against machines, Sarah has herself become a skilled and seasoned fighter—tough, muscular, and ruthless in her devotion to helping her son fulfill his destiny. Portraying her character as a strong, determined, and formidable woman hero, Hamilton made Sarah a feminist icon, somewhat in the vein of *Alien's* **Ellen Ripley**, though some feminists were troubled by the fact that Sarah seems on the verge of hysteria throughout *Terminator 2* and that her central function in the film is as a protective mother. Hamilton made numerous subsequent appearances, especially in crime dramas, but was unable to repeat her success in *Terminator 2* or to achieve major subsequent stardom. *See also* FEMINISM AND GENDER.

HAMMER FILM PRODUCTIONS. Great Britain's Hammer Film Productions was founded in 1934, but rose to international prominence in the mid-1950s with the release of a series of horror films that were largely extensions of American horror film franchises established in the 1930s. Particularly important among these was their resurrection of the *Frankenstein* franchise with *The Curse of Frankenstein* (1957), a film with strong sf elements as well. Indeed, Hammer was at the forefront of **British science fiction film** during the 1950s, producing such films as *Spaceways* (1953), *The Quatermass Xperiment* (1955), and *Quatermass 2* (1957), of which the latter two include strong horror elements as well. Hammer also rebooted the Dracula and Mummy franchises in the 1950s.

Hammer's horror and science films of this era generally had rather low budgets and were regarded as entertainment films only, though they were often marked by distinctive Gothic visual styles. Through the 1960s and 1970s, the company shifted more and more into pure horror and away from science fiction. For example, the sequence of horror-sf hybrids directed by **Terence Fisher** (who had been Hammer's leading director in the late 1950s) in the 1960s was produced by other companies. Hammer has been virtually dormant in recent years, having released no films since their production of two short-lived television series in the early 1980s. However, the company (now owned by Dutch producer John De Mol and his Cyrte Investments firm) remains in operation and has several horror projects in the making.

HARRYHAUSEN, RAY (1920–). The legendary special-effects wizard Ray Harryhausen, inspired by watching the original *King Kong* (1933), devoted most of his long and productive career to the creation of compelling **monster-movie** effects. His first professional work in the industry was as an assistant to **Willis O'Brien** on the *Mighty Joe Young* (1949), something of a clone of *King Kong,* though it is widely believed that Harryhausen actually did most of the **stop-motion animation** on that film. Harryhausen's first work as a lead special-effects animator came in *The Beast from 20,000 Fathoms* (1953), at which time he had already gone a long way toward perfecting the **Dynamation** animation technique for which he became famous. He subsequently directed the visual effects for such science fiction films as *It Came from Beneath the Sea* (1955), *20 Million Miles to Earth* (1957), *First Men in the Moon* (1964), and *The Valley of Gwangi* (1969), though he was ultimately best known for the effects in fantasy-adventure films such as *Jason and the Argonauts* (1963) and *Clash of the Titans* (1981). His work has been immensely influential on other special-effects artists, making him arguably the most important special-effects artist in the film industry.

HASKIN, BYRON (1899–1984). Having done a significant amount of **special effects** work for Hollywood films in the 1930s and 1940s, Byron Haskin was a natural choice to direct science fiction films when they became popular in the 1950s. Indeed, especially in his work with producer **George Pal**, Haskin became one of the most successful sf directors of the decade, though he had several previous directorial credits as well, including the 1950 **Disney** adaptation of the classic pirate tale *Treasure Island.* But it was when Haskin directed *The War of the Worlds* (1953) for Pal that he found the form that suited him best as a director. He directed *The Naked Jungle* (1954) and *Conquest of Space* (1955) for Pal as well, and ended his directorial career with still another collaboration with Pal in the 1968 sf thriller *The Power.* In between, Haskin had also directed *From the Earth to the Moon* (1958) and the much-admired *Robinson Crusoe on Mars* (1964). Haskin also directed six episodes of the sf-themed television anthology *The Outer Limits* in 1963 and 1964, including "The Architects of Fear," one of the series' best-remembered episodes and one of the inspirations for Alan Moore's classic graphic novel *The Watchmen* (1986). All of Haskin's work is marked by technical competence and by an ability to tell convincing stories, even on a minimal budget.

HEINLEIN, ROBERT A. (1907–1988). Considered (along with **Isaac Asimov** and **Arthur C. Clarke**) to be one of the three great figures of the Golden Age of science fiction, Robert A. Heinlein is still one of the most discussed figures in the history of science fiction. The political implications of Heinlein's work are still hotly debated, partly because his own perspective shifted over time, from the straightforward liberalism of his early juvenile novels to the virulent anticommunism (which some feel bordered on fascism) of his middle period to the more clearly libertarian orientation of his later work. Heinlein got involved in science fiction film when the form was still in its infancy, adapting his own 1947 novel *Rocket Ship Galileo* to the screen as **Destination Moon** in 1950. Heinlein also adapted one of his stories to film, as *Project Moon Base* (1953). That was the end of Heinlein's direct work in the film industry, and most of his novels and stories have proved difficult to adapt to the screen. However, *The Brain Eaters* (1958) seems to have been based, without acknowledgment, on Heinlein's *The Puppet Masters* (1951), which prompted a lawsuit from Heinlein that was settled out of court. That novel was adapted with acknowledgment under the same title in 1994. The most notable screen adaptation of a Heinlein novel was **Paul Verhoeven**'s *Starship Troopers* in 1997, based on the 1959 novel of the same title. *Starship Troopers* and Heinlein's novels *Space Cadets* (1948) and *Red Planet* (1949) have also been adapted to television.

HELM, BRIGITTE (1906–1996). The first film role of the German actress Brigitte Helm was as Maria in **Fritz Lang**'s *Metropolis* (1927), one of the founding works of the modern genre of science fiction film. Propelled to stardom, she had lead roles in a number of films (including science fiction films) during the next several years. She played the title character in the silent version of *Alraune* (1928), as well as the sound version (1930) of the same film, a **mad-scientist** narrative that involves an early version of **genetic engineering**. Helm also played the female lead in *Gold* (1934), an alchemical thriller in which a sinister tycoon attempts to appropriate a scientific breakthrough for his own nefarious ends. Though still a major star in Germany, Helm retired to Switzerland in 1935 to avoid working in a Nazi-dominated German film industry.

HESTON, CHARLTON (1923–2008). The American actor Charlton Heston rose to major stardom when he played Moses in the 1956 Biblical epic *The Ten Commandments,* a performance that he followed by playing the title character in *Ben-Hur* (1959). He remained best known for these two roles for the rest of his life, though he played many roles in many genres in a long and prolific career. He also garnered considerable attention as the pro-gun president of and spokesman for the National Rifle Association from 1998 to 2003, and he was involved in a number of conservative political causes from the 1980s forward, following earlier activist participation in liberal causes in the 1950s and 1960s. Heston starred in **Byron Haskin**'s 1954 film *The Naked Jungle,* which borders on science fiction, but he became a particularly prominent sf star with his lead role in *Planet of the Apes* (1968). Lead roles in *The Omega Man* (1971) and *Soylent Green* (1973) quickly followed, solidifying his sf credentials. Ironically, one of Heston's last roles was a small (uncredited) part as an aging ape who warns against the dangers of guns in **Tim Burton**'s 2001 remake of *Planet of the Apes.*

HOLM, IAN (1931–). The prolific British character actor Sir Ian Holm (knighted in 1998) has appeared in more than 100 films, some of the most memorable of which were science fiction. His lone Academy Award nomination (for Best Supporting Actor) was for *Chariots of Fire* (1981), although his best-known role is probably that of Bilbo Baggins in *Lord of the Rings: The Fellowship of the Ring* (2001) and *Lord of the Rings: The Return of the King* (2003). He made a big impression on science fiction audiences with his role as Ash (a **robot** sent by the **Weyland-Yutani Corporation** to act as their spy aboard the *Nostromo*) in **Ridley Scott**'s *Alien* (1979). He followed with important roles in two sf films directed by Terry Gilliam: *Time Bandits* (1981) and *Brazil* (1985). Other notable science fiction credits include appearances in several films by leading sf directors, including **Luc Besson**'s *The Fifth Element* (1997), **David**

Cronenberg's *eXistenZ* (1999), and **Roland Emmerich**'s *The Day After Tomorrow* (2004).

HONDA, ISHIRŌ (1911–1993). After an early career that included working as an assistant to the legendary Akira Kurosawa, the Japanese filmmaker Ishirō Honda was propelled to worldwide fame as the director of *Godzilla* (1954) and *Godzilla, King of the Monsters* (1956). Other films in the *tokusatsu* (**special effects**) genre followed, including the **monster movie** *Rodan! The Flying Monster* (1956), the technically innovative **alien-invasion** film *Chikyû Bôeigun* (1957, *The Mysterians*), and *Bijo to Ekitainingen* (1958, *The H-Man*), a rather good-natured warning against the potential effects of radiation on humans. A string of monster movies (some of them featuring alien invasions) followed in the 1960s and 1970s, including some that pitted classic Western movie monsters against Japanese monsters, such as *Kingu Kongu tai Gojira* (1962, *King Kong vs. Godzilla*) and *Furankenshutain tai chitei kaijû Baragon* (1965, *Frankenstein vs. Baragon*). Indeed, Honda came to specialize in "monster versus monster" movies, the best of which is perhaps *San daikaijû: Chikyû saidai no kessen* (1964, *Ghidora, The Three-Headed Monster*), in which Honda's own Godzilla, Rodan, and Mothra team up to battle an invading monster from outer space. His last feature film was *Mekagojira no gyakushu* (1975, *Terror of Mechagodzilla*), in which Godzilla must battle against a giant **robot**, or **mecha** version of himself. Honda directed numerous science fiction and superhero programs for Japanese television in the 1970s, but ended his career as it began, working as an assistant to Kurosawa on the latter's last films, including *Ran* (1985) and *Dreams* (1990). *See also* JAPANESE SCIENCE FICTION FILM.

HORNER, JAMES (1953–). James Horner is one of his generation's leading composers of music for film. A prolific composer with numerous film scores to his credit, Horner has worked widely in science fiction film, for which his dramatic style is often well suited. He began his career working for **Roger Corman**, leading to his first screen credit as a composer for the Corman-produced *Battle Beyond the Stars* (1980). **James Cameron** worked on the visual effects for that film, and Horner subsequently wrote the well-known score for

Cameron's *Aliens* (1986), a score that has been widely excerpted in film trailers for other movies. Horner also wrote the score for Cameron's science fiction film *Avatar* (2009). Other science fiction films scored by Horner include *Star Trek II: The Wrath of Khan* (1982), *Krull* (1983), *Star Trek III: The Search for Spock* (1984), *Cocoon* (1985), *Honey, I Shrunk the Kids* (1989), *Deep Impact* (1998), and *Bicentennial Man* (1999). Horner has also composed widely for television and for non-science fiction films. In fact, his best-known work of all is probably the Academy Award–winning score for Cameron's *Titanic* (1997). Horner has had six other Oscar nominations for Best Score, including that for *Aliens*. Though sometimes criticized for sampling heavily from his own previous scores and from the works of classical composers (such as Sergei Prokofiev and Dmitri Shostakovich), Horner has produced some of the most dramatically effective music in recent film history.

HURD, GALE ANNE (1955–). After beginning her career as a production assistant for **Roger Corman**, Gale Anne Hurd immediately became an important figure in sf film when she served as the producer of *The Terminator* (1984), which she co-wrote with director **James Cameron**, whom she married in 1985. Hurd has gone on to have an important career as the producer of a number of big-budget, highly commercial sf films. Cameron and Hurd also worked together as director and producer of *Aliens* (1986), the second film in the *Alien* franchise. The pair teamed again for *The Abyss* (1989), after Hurd had separately served as the producer of *Alien Nation* (1988). Hurd and Cameron divorced in 1989, but she served as the executive producer for his *Terminator 2: Judgment Day* in 1991. Hurd subsequently produced a number of sf films not directed by Cameron, including *Armageddon* (1998), *Virus* (1999), *Clockstoppers* (2002), and *Æon Flux* (2005). She also served as an executive producer for *Terminator 3: Rise of the Machines* (2003) and has produced a number of non-sf films as well.

HYAMS, PETER (1943–). Though never involved in a major science fiction hit, the writer and director Peter Hyams has nevertheless had an extensive career in science fiction film. He both wrote and directed *Capricorn One* (1978), about a hoax involving a manned landing on Mars after a planned real mission to Mars has to be aborted. Hyams also wrote and directed *Outland* (1981), a competent sf thriller featuring **Sean Connery** as a federal marshal investigating mysterious deaths in a mining outpost on a moon of Jupiter. In 1984, Hyams wrote and directed *2010,* the sequel to the classic sf film *2001: A Space Odyssey* (1968). Hyams also directed *Timecop* (1994), a **time-travel** action film starring Jean-Claude Van Damme.

– I –

THE INCREDIBLE SHRINKING MAN. (Dir. **Jack Arnold**, 1957.) Based on **Richard Matheson**'s 1956 novel, *The Shrinking Man,* and scripted by Matheson, *The Incredible Shrinking Man* is one of the most memorable science fiction films of the 1950s. It tells the story of one Robert Scott Carey (Grant Williams), a typical 1950s man, who is accidentally exposed first to a strange, floating, radioactive cloud, then to pesticides, causing him to start to shrink. Eventually, he reaches such a small size that he is nearly eaten by the family cat, then gets lost in the basement of his home and is unable to make himself known to his normal-sized wife Louise (Randy Stuart). Louise, believing her husband to have been eaten, prepares for life as a widow, leaving Carey to fend for himself in the basement, which now functions as a vast wilderness, given his small size. In a sort of retelling of the Robinson Crusoe story, Carey resourcefully begins to build a life for himself in this new environment from whatever tiny materials are at hand. Ultimately, he kills what to him is a giant spider to become the unrivaled master of this new domain. The film then ends with a somewhat unconvincing philosophical twist in which Carey literally shrinks to nothingness—though at the same time he becomes one with the cosmos.

The Incredible Shrinking Man contains some of the most effective **special effects** of the 1950s as, through the use of huge prop furniture and other items, it convincingly conveys Carey's diminishing size. More significantly, the film dramatizes important phenomena at work in American society in the late 1950s. For example, Carey, who feels more and more isolated from those around him as he grows smaller, embodies the sense of alienation felt by so many Americans at the time. This sense of being freakishly different from all other humans is, in fact, captured in a number of "size-change" films produced at about the same time. For example, *The Amazing Colossal Man,* released six months later, takes the size change in the opposite direction, while ***Attack of the 50 Foot Woman*** (1958) looks at such changes from a feminine perspective. *The Incredible Shrinking Man* is, however, the best of these films, partly because of the effectiveness with which it captures the embattled state of American manhood in the late 1950s. Thus, much of Carey's growing bitterness comes from the way he experiences his shrinkage as a loss of manhood, as he grows smaller and less powerful, while his wife, relatively speaking, grows larger and more powerful. Moreover, as he gets smaller and smaller, Carey is increasingly unable to fulfill his conjugal obligations, becoming more a son to Louise than a husband. *See also* FEMINISM AND GENDER.

INDEPENDENCE DAY. (Dir. **Roland Emmerich**, 1996.) *Independence Day*, which skillfully applies the **disaster** film formula to the **alien-invasion** narrative, was one of the biggest blockbuster hits of the 1990s. It made its director the new "master of disaster" and set one of its stars, **Will Smith**, on the road to becoming the top actor in science fiction film. The premise of the film is simple: a giant mothership containing what is apparently the entire population of an advanced alien race comes to earth bent on conquest. They send attack ships (protected by seemingly impenetrable energy shields) to various cities across the globe, wreaking havoc and destroying several key sites, including one memorable scene in which they blow up the White House. Heroic Americans led by President Thomas J. Whitmore (Bill Pullman) respond, concocting a plan to disable the alien shields and then destroy the alien ships. Thanks to the expertise of electronics genius David Levinson (**Jeff Goldblum**) and the valor of fighter pilot Captain Steven Hiller (Smith), the plan works, and the aliens are defeated.

Independence Day is very much a feel-good film in which the aliens are presented as unequivocally evil and their ultimate destruction as an unequivocal human triumph. More specifically, it is very much an American triumph, and the film (despite having a German director) is something of a paean to American ingenuity, know-how, and bravery. Whitmore is a sort of fantasy president—courageous, bold, and unflinchingly honest—while the other characters tend to embody positive American traits as well. Most obviously, the title of the film associates it with the American Independence Day holiday (July 4th), an association that is emphasized both because the events of the film take place in early July and because the film itself opened in the United States on July 3rd, bringing in huge crowds over the holiday weekend. Nevertheless, the film was extremely popular worldwide, and well over half of its $817 million box-office take came from outside the United States.

Independence Day looks back to the paranoid alien-invasion films of the 1950s in its vision of rapacious aliens with no redeeming positive features. It also looks back to the disaster films of the 1970s in its basic structure, which was employed so successfully that it helped to usher in a new cycle of science fiction–oriented disaster films over the next several years, including Emmerich's own *Godzilla* (1998), *The Day After Tomorrow* (2004), and *2012* (2009).

INDUSTRIAL LIGHT & MAGIC (ILM). Founded by **George Lucas** in 1975 specifically to make the **special effects** for the upcoming *Star Wars* (1977) movie, ILM has gone on to become one of Hollywood's preeminent special-effects design and production studios, remaining on the cutting edge of new developments in special-effects technology. Still a subsidiary of **Lucasfilm** Limited, the company has been especially important in the development of techniques for the **computer-generated imagery (CGI)** in science fiction films—and in films in general. In recent years, in fact, they have focused almost exclusively on CGI effects. In addition to creating the special effects for Lucas's own productions—including the *Star Wars* films and the Indiana Jones films—the company has now produced special effects for more than 200 other films and has won more than three dozen Academy Awards in the Best Visual Effects and other technical categories. In addition to their work on the *Star Wars* sequence, some of ILM's most notable achievements in effects for sf films include the genesis effect in *Star Trek: The Wrath of Khan* (1982), the aqueous pseudopod for *The Abyss* (1989), the liquid metal effects for the T-1000 terminator in *Terminator 2: Judgment Day* (1991), the computer-generated dinosaurs for *Jurassic Park* (1993), and the urban destruction effects for the

disaster film *The Day After Tomorrow* (2004). *See also* COMPUTER-GENERATED IMAGERY (CGI).

INVADERS FROM MARS. (Dir. **William Cameron Menzies**, 1953.) *Invaders from Mars* features sneaky alien invaders who hide their ship underground and then use nefarious techniques to take over and control the minds of humans in positions of authority, using these minions to move secretly toward taking over the United States and, by implication, the world. It is the first film, in short, to use the **alien-invasion** format to provide an all-out dramatization of contemporary fears of a subtle communist takeover of the United States. Among other things, the plot of the film responds directly to contemporary concerns over reports that American POWs in Korea had been brainwashed by their communist captors. Meanwhile, the film secures our antipathy toward the invaders by telling its story from the perspective of young David Maclean (Jimmy Hunt), whose youthful innocence helps to identify the earthlings as the good guys, opposed to the ultra-sophisticated (and thus evil) Martians. In opposition to the simple David, the Martians are led by a commander who is essentially a brain in a jar, waving its weird tentacles, and controlling, through telepathy, a troop of dronelike mutant slaves who do all of its physical work. Described as the ultimate product of evolution, this Martian thus becomes a figure of the era's anxieties over intellectuals, suggesting that excessive intellectual development might produce individuals who lose touch with their true humanity, then heartlessly take over and control the rest of us.

Fortunately, David (with surprising ease) finds two adult authority figures who are willing to listen to his story, in the persons of medical doctor Pat Blake (Helena Carter) and astronomer Stuart Kelston (Arthur Franz). As a scientist, Kelston has particularly high credibility, and he seems to have no trouble getting the military to accept his warnings, even though General Mayberry (William Forrest), the highest ranking officer in the area, has been taken over by the Martians. From this point on, *Invaders from Mars* is a relatively straightforward combat film, with the earthlings employing direct, honest tactics as opposed to the sneaky tactics of the aliens. The film includes a great deal of stock footage of the American military in action (columns of tanks figure especially prominently), and one clear message of the film is that the military is a formidable force, up to any task. In this sense, the film departs dramatically from Senator Joseph McCarthy's notorious alarmist depiction (in hearings that began in 1953, the year *Invaders from Mars* was released) of the military as dangerously compromised by communist infiltration.

INVASION OF THE BODY SNATCHERS. (Dir. Don Siegel, 1956.) One of the definitive science fiction films of the 1950s (and one of the definitive *American* films of the decade), *Invasion of the Body Snatchers* well captures the paranoid American sense of threat from communists and other external enemies, while at the same time responding to anxieties from more domestic threats, including *anti*-communism. Based on Jack Finney's 1954 novel, *The Body Snatchers,* the film stars Kevin McCarthy as Miles Bennell, a small-town doctor in Santa Mira, California, who seems to be the only person able to realize that the inhabitants of the town (especially authority figures such as police) are gradually being replaced by replicants grown from alien seed pods that have somehow drifted in from outer space. As the film ends, Bennell has finally been able to get out of the town and get the attention of authorities who initiate action to stop the proliferation of the pod people. However, though this "optimistic" ending was insisted on by the studio, the pod people have also spread beyond Santa Mira, and it is not at all clear that the attempt to stop them will be successful.

Though *Invasion of the Body Snatchers* was very much a film of the 1950s, its basic scenario has proved compelling enough that the film has been remade several times. The 1978 version, directed by Philip Kaufman, is the most direct remake of the original, though it does move the action to San Francisco and makes its protagonist, played by **Donald Sutherland**, a city health inspector rather than a small-town doctor. That film also has a more pessimistic ending than the original, while introducing a significant amount of satire relevant to the late 1970s. A 1993 remake, entitled *Body Snatchers,* moves the action to the small-town South, with rather unfortunate results. The big-budget film *The Invasion* (2007) makes its protagonist a woman (played by megastar Nicole Kidman), but this film was not a critical or commercial success, though it was important enough to trigger a **mockbuster** version entitled *Invasion of the*

Pod People, also released in 2007. *Invasion of the Body Snatchers* has been parodied in films such as *Strange Invaders* (1983) and *Invasion of the Body Squeezers* (1998).

THE IRON GIANT. (Dir. Brad Bird, 1999.) *The Iron Giant* is an animated film ostensibly aimed at children, though it deals with a number of complex themes and engages in some fairly sophisticated dialogue with earlier science fiction films, especially the paranoid **alien-invasion** films of the 1950s. Here, a giant, metal-eating **robot** from outer space lands on earth (near the small, aptly named town of Rockwell, Maine—as in Norman Rockwell, the official artist of small-town Americana, with perhaps a side reference to Roswell, New Mexico, as well). The mission of this robot is never made entirely clear in the film, and it is clear that the robot is potentially dangerous (and heavily armed) whatever its mission. Even the robot, however, loses all memory of this mission after it is zapped with electricity while trying to eat a power plant early in the film. It is then saved and befriended by a young boy, Hogarth Hughes (voiced by Eli Marienthal), who subsequently tries to teach it about life on earth, with the help of local hipster sculptor Dean McCoppin (voiced by Harry Connick Jr.), who just happens to own a junkyard that serves as a source of materials for his art but that also provides food for the metal-eating robot. Ultimately, sinister governmental investigator Kent Mansley (voiced by Christopher McDonald) is dispatched to the area to check out reports of sightings of the robot. The paranoid and cowardly Mansley serves as a strong critique of U.S. government attitudes during the cold war, and his actions ultimately almost destroy the entire town when he panics and calls in a nuclear strike on the robot, which is at that moment in the center of the town. The robot then heroically sacrifices itself to save the town, though there are hints at the end of the film that the robot, seemingly obliterated in a high-altitude collision with the nuclear missile, is beginning to reassemble itself from parts scattered around the globe. *See also* ANIMATED SCIENCE FICTION FILMS; CHILDREN'S SCIENCE FICTION.

IT CAME FROM OUTER SPACE. (Dir. **Jack Arnold**, 1953.) One of the most thoughtful (and least paranoid) of the **alien-invasion** films of the 1950s, *It Came from Outer Space* features aliens that are dangerous to humans only because we are too primitive and xenophobic to understand them. The aliens crash-land on earth purely by accident, with no intention of conquest or colonization; they then quickly set out to repair their ship and get on with their travels. Their landing is spotted by writer John Putnam (**Richard Carlson**), a free spirit who lives alone out in the desert; Putnam then tries to warn the nearby small town of Sand Rock, Arizona, that the aliens have landed. The conservative townspeople already don't trust the unconventional Putnam, so they ignore his warnings, until townspeople begin to disappear only to reappear as zombie-like replicas. Despite the alien-possession motif, Putnam learns that the aliens mean no harm, that they intend to restore the original earthlings once they are finished with the repairs on their ship, and that they have only assumed human form out of fear that their strange appearance (which is only hinted at in fleeting shots) will frighten the narrow-minded earthlings.

Ignoring Putnam's protestations that the aliens are harmless, the locals quickly become a murderous mob and head out to attack the aliens, though Putnam is able to delay the mob just long enough to allow the aliens to complete their repairs and blast off back into space. Putnam, however, warns (or maybe promises) the townspeople that the aliens will no doubt return some day, but only after earthlings have evolved far enough to be able to greet them properly.

ITALIAN SCIENCE FICTION FILM. While not exactly a major player in the evolution of international science fiction film, Italian cinema has made important contributions to the genre, especially in relatively low-budget formats that have combined science fiction and horror. The Italian film industry has also been involved in a number of international co-productions, especially in French-Italian co-productions. For example, the Italians attempted to join in the science fiction film boom of the 1950s with Paul Heutsch's *La morte viene dallo spazio* (*The Day the Sky Exploded*), which is often regarded as the first Italian sf film although in fact it was an Italian-French co-production. In this **disaster** film, an atomic-powered rocket crashes into the sun, causing massive solar explosions that threaten to engulf the earth in flames. (Oddly enough, these solar events were removed entirely from the English-language version and replaced with a vague threat from the asteroid belt.) Even purely Italian productions in science fiction film have often imported British or American stars in an attempt to reach the lucrative Anglophone market. Thus, *Il pianeta degli uomini spenti* (1961, *Battle of the Worlds*), an unusual **alien-invasion** narrative in which aliens approach the earth using a traveling asteroid as their base, features British-born American transplant Claude Rains, who starred in a number of distinguished films, including numerous roles in horror films in the 1930s, beginning with his role as the title character in **James Whale**'s adaptation of **H. G. Wells**'s *The Invisible Man* (1933).

In 1964, the first of three screen adaptations of **Richard Matheson**'s 1954 novel *I Am Legend* was released as an American-Italian co-production, with Vincent Price in the lead role. In 1965 Jean-Luc Godard's *Alphaville* was a French-Italian co-production, while **Mario Bava**'s *Terrore nello spazio* (a Spanish-Italian co-production released in the United States with the nicely descriptive title *Planet of the Vampires*) starred American actor Barry Sullivan in a film that effectively combines horror and **space opera**, influencing such later films as *Alien* (1979). That same year, Elio Petri's *La decima vittima* (*The 10th Victim,* based on a short story by American author Robert Sheckley) starred Marcello Mastroianni and Ursula Andress in a satire of violence in entertainment that became a cult classic. Roger Vadim's campily erotic *Barbarella* (1968), starring American actress Jane Fonda, was also a French-Italian co-production.

The 1970s were a slow decade in Italian sf film, though Italian cinema did attempt to join the post–*Star Wars* boom by re-releasing *2+5: Missione Hydra,* a low-budget effort from 1965, as *Star Pilot* in 1977. Similarly, Luigi Cozzi's *Starcrash* (1979, a joint U.S.-Italian production) clearly attempted to cash in on the success of *Star Wars*. Meanwhile, Cozzi's *Alien Contamination* (1980, a joint Italian–West German production) was clearly derivative of *Alien*. In the early 1980s, Italian sf cinema found a new niche for itself with a sequence of campily ultraviolent **postapocalyptic** films. In 1982 *1990: I guerrieri del Bronx* (*1990: The Bronx Warriors*) and *I nuovi barbari* (*The New Barbarians*) were released, followed in 1983 by the release of *2019—Dopo la caduta di New York* (*2019: After the Fall of New York*) and *Fuga dal Bronx* (*Escape from the Bronx*). Subsequently, Italian contributions to sf film have been fairly sparse, including the 1989 U.S.-Italian co-productions *Arena* and *Leviathan,* the 1997 **virtual-reality** thriller *Nirvana* (a French-Italian co-production), and the innovative *Immortel* (*ad vitam*) (2004, a British-French-Italian co-production) and *Sky Captain and the World of Tomorrow* (2004, a British-American-Italian co-production). *See also* FRENCH SCIENCE FICTION FILM.

– J –

JACKSON, SAMUEL L. (1948–). The African American actor Samuel L. Jackson first gained extensive critical attention for his role in Spike Lee's *Jungle Fever* (1991) and made his first appearance in science fiction film as a computer analyst in **Steven Spielberg's** *Jurassic Park* (1993). Jackson was then propelled to stardom via his performance as Jules Winnfield in Quentin Tarantino's *Pulp Fiction* (1994). Since that time, he has appeared in dozens of films, including several high-profile science fiction films. In 1998, he joined a cast of Hollywood heavyweights (including Dustin Hoffman and Sharon Stone) in the **undersea adventure** *Sphere,* which he quickly followed with a major role in another undersea adventure, *Deep Blue Sea* (1999). In that same year he (briefly) played Mace Windu in *Star Wars: Episode I—The Phantom Menace,* thus gaining his greatest exposure to science fiction fans. He reprised that role in *Star Wars: Episode II—Attack of the Clones* (2002) and *Star Wars: Episode III—Revenge of the Sith* (2005). Jackson had a central role in the teleportation drama *Jumper* (2008). He also provided the voice of Windu in the animated *Star Wars: The Clone Wars* (2008) and has done additional voiceover work in *The Incredibles* (2004), *Astro Boy* (2009), and *Quantum Quest: A Cassini Space Odyssey* (2010).

JAPANESE SCIENCE FICTION FILM. Japanese science fiction film has long been associated primarily with the **monster-movie** genre, particularly with the low-budget monster movies produced by **Toho Studios** beginning in the 1950s. Of the Toho monsters, **Godzilla** (with the original Japanese name of Gojira) is clearly the most notable, though others, such as Rodan and Mothra, have made multiple appearances as well, often sharing the screen with Godzilla. Godzilla first appeared in a self-titled film (directed by **Ishirō Honda**) in 1954, gaining enough attention that the film was rereleased in an English-dubbed version in 1956 as *Godzilla: King of the Monsters!* with additional scenes directed by Terry Morse and featuring American actor Raymond Burr to give American audiences a character with whom to identify. Since that time, Toho has released more than 20 Godzilla movies, as well as numerous other *kaiju* monster movies, some combining well-known Western movie monsters with their own creations, as in *Kingu Kongu tai Gojira* (1962, *King Kong vs. Godzilla*).

The same inexpensive (but often highly effective) **special effects** technologies used in the *kaiju* film have also been used by Toho in a number of effects-driven *tokusatsu* science fiction movies. Toho soon moved into other genres of science fiction film as well, as in the **alien-invasion** drama *Chikyû Bôeigun* (1957, *The Mysterians*) and its sequel *Uchu daisenso* (1959, *Battle in Outer Space*), both of which also found Western audiences in dubbed versions. Toho's output in the 1960s was dominated by monster movies, though some of these, such as *Kaijû daisenso* (1965, *Invasion of Astro-Monster*) had especially strong science fictional elements. In addition, their ongoing output of monster movies has often been spiced up with the addition of new science fictional elements. For example, in *Mekagojira no gyakushu* (1975, *Terror of Mechagodzilla*), Godzilla must defend the earth from an alien-built robotic **mecha** version of himself. Other Toho films of the 1970s included the **disaster** film *Nihon chinbotsu* (1973, *Japan Sinks*, remade with the same title in 2006) and the alien-invasion film *Wakusei daisenso* (1977, *The War in Space*).

In 1980, the plague film *Virus* (made by producer Haruki Kadokawa's own company, but distributed in Japan by Toho) was the most expensive Japanese film to date; however, it was an international box-office failure that curbed the growth of the science film industry in Japan. In the following decade, Toho and other Japanese studios turned toward the production of **anime** science fiction movies, often as spinoffs of anime television series. This phenomenon has led to a decline in Toho's dominance of Japanese sf film, with several different studios, such as Bandai Visual Company, making contributions to anime science fiction. Internationally, the best-known producer of anime films is probably **Hayao Miyazaki**'s Studio Ghibli, many of whose films—including the **postapocalyptic** film *Kaze no tani no Naushika* (1984, ***Nausicaä of the Valley of the Wind***)—can be considered science fiction. Many Studio Ghibli films have been distributed in Japan by Toho, however.

Of special note are the films of **Mamoru Oshii**, who began his work as an anime director in the early 1980s with the *Urusei Yatsura* animated television series, which led him to direct two spinoff films of this alien-invasion story, *Urusei yatsura 1: Onri yû* (1983, *Urusei Yatsura: Only You*) and *Urusei Yatsura: Byûtifuru dorîmâ* (1984, *Urusei Yatsura: Beautiful Dreamer*). In 1989, Oshii directed another anime science fiction film, *Kidô keisatsu patorebâ: Gekijô-ban* (*Patlabor: The Movie*), as part of an extensive franchise involving manga, serial television, and straight-to-video films, as well as this theatrical film and its eventual theatrical sequel, *Kidô keisatsu patorebâ: The Movie 2* (1993, *Patlabor 2: The Movie*). In the West, Oshii is probably best known as the director of the Bandai-produced anime **cyberpunk** film *Kôkaku kidôtai* (1995, ***Ghost in the Shell***), as well as its sequel, *Innocence* (2004, *Ghost in the Shell 2: Innocence*), which became the first animated film to be nominated for the Palme d'Or at the Cannes Film Festival.

Among the anime science fiction films produced or co-produced by Toho are the groundbreaking *Akira* (1988), an animated remake of the classic science fiction film ***Metropolis*** (2001), and the big-budget animated steampunk film *Steamboy* (2004). Toho also co-produced the 2004 version of *Appurushîdo* (*Appleseed*, which had been filmed in a straight-to-video version in 1988), though it was not involved in the making of the sequel, *Ekusu makina* (2007, *Appleseed: Ex Machina*). Other leading anime science fiction films produced by other companies include *Kaubôi bibappu: Tengoku no tobira* (2001, *Cowboy Bebop: The Movie*) and *Toki o kakeru shôjo* (2006, *The Girl Who Leapt through Time*). While anime films are typically animated mostly by hand, some (such as the *Appleseed* films) rely primarily on computer animation. Japan has also made other contributions to the development of computer animation, especially in such films as ***Casshern*** (2004), which employs live actors filmed entirely in front of **green screens**, with backgrounds later filled in with **computer-generated imagery**. Such imagery is also used extensively in the 2001 live-action Japanese-Polish co-production *Avalon*, directed by Oshii. Meanwhile, the Japanese-U.S. production *Final Fantasy: The Spirits Within* was also released in 2001. Rather than employing the anime style, this film (loosely based on a popular Japanese role-playing video game) was the first attempt to make a photorealistic animated sf film. The film had a large budget and employed an impressive cast of well-known American voice actors, but was a failure at the box office. *Final Fantasy VII: Advent Children* (2005), was not really a sequel, but simply another film based on the same video game series, this time specifically on the game *Final Fantasy VII,* thus the title. This all-Japanese production had a much lower budget, but was able to achieve a similar animation style, thanks to advances in technology between 2001 and 2005. The 2006 **postapocalyptic-dystopian** film ***Children of Men*** was another international co-production, involving Japan, Great Britain, and the United States. Finally, the cyberpunk themes that have been so popular in anime films have sometimes appeared in live-action films as well, as in the 1998 crime thriller *Andromedia. See also* TSUBURAYA, EIJI.

JEDI. The order of Jedi Knights are among the crucial presences in the entire *Star Wars* sequence of films. A quasimonastic order, they draw upon the power of the **Force** in their attempt to keep peace and fight evil in the *Star Wars* universe, employing weapons that include their signature light sabers. Among the important Jedi in the *Star Wars* sequence are the wise old master **Yoda** (a member of an unknown alien species) and such humans as **Obi-Wan Kenobi** and **Luke Skywalker**. Another prominent Jedi is the young **Anakin Skywalker**, who is eventually drawn to the dark side of the force, becoming the sinister **Darth Vader**, a member of the **Sith** order, essentially the evil counterparts of the Jedi.

JEUNET, JEAN-PIERRE (1953–). Though his body of work is still small, the French actor, writer, and director Jean-Pierre Jeunet has developed a substantial reputation for the quirkiness and visual inventiveness of his work, much of which has been in science fiction. After making a series of short films (mostly animated), he gained considerable attention with his first feature-length film, *Delicatessen* (1991), which he co-directed with his friend comic-book artist Marc Caro. This film is a decidedly unusual dark comedy in which a butcher/landlord in a **postapocalyptic** world serves up human flesh in order to feed his tenants amid a widespread famine. Jeunet's next film, *The City of Lost Children* (1995), is a visually striking fantasy that includes science fiction elements, such as a **mad scientist** who serves as the central villain of the film. Jeanet moved into mainstream Hollywood science fiction with *Alien: Resurrection* (1997), a film on which he still placed his distinctive stamp, despite its status as a member of a well-known franchise. That film met with the most mixed reviews of any of the *Alien* films, however, and Jeunet has not since returned to science fiction film.

JOURNEY TO THE FAR SIDE OF THE SUN. (Dir. Robert Parrish, 1969.) Also known as *Doppelgänger,* this film was written and produced by **Gerry and Sylvia Anderson**, best known for sf television series such as *Thunderbirds* (1965–1966), *UFO* (1970–1971), and especially *Space: 1999* (1975–1978). The unlikely premise (more *Twilight Zone* than hard sf) of *Journey to the Far Side of the Sun* revolves around the discovery of a new planet about the size of the earth and the same distance from the sun, but synchronized in its orbit so that it is always on the opposite side of the sun from the earth, which is why it has not been previously discovered. After some political intrigue and personal drama, a mission is launched to explore the new planet, leading to confusing results, until it is finally realized that the other planet is an exact duplicate of earth, inhabited by the same individuals, except that it is a mirror image. In fact, a mission from the parallel earth was launched to explore earth at exactly the same time, with the same crew aboard. Unfortunately, when the one surviving astronaut (played by Roy Thinnes) attempts to return to our earth, he crashes into the space center on the other earth, destroying it in a series of fiery explosions. Presumably, the space center on our earth is destroyed in the same way, though the film leaves this possibility open to conjecture. The film ends as mission director Jason Webb (Patrick Wymark), the lone survivor of the project, lives out his life in an asylum (on which earth is not clear, but probably both), unable to convince anyone of the existence of the other earth that mirrors his own.

JOVOVICH, MILLA (1975–). The Ukrainian-born Milla Jovovich moved to the United States at a young age and grew up in the Los Angeles area, subsequently becoming a successful model, actress, and singer. Though she previously had several important film roles, Jovovich's breakthrough in the realm of science fiction came in 1997, when she played the physically perfect super being Leeloo in **Luc Besson**'s *The Fifth Element*. Jovovich's principal claim to fame in the science fiction world is as the tough, zombie-killing Alice in *Resident Evil* (2002), *Resident Evil: Apocalypse* (2004), and *Resident Evil: Extinction* (2007), with a fourth *Resident Evil* film reportedly in the works as of this writing. Jovovich played a similar role in *Ultraviolet* (2006), something of a **dystopian** film that relies mostly on hyperkinetic action scenes for its entertainment value. Here, Jovovich plays the role of Violet, a young woman given superhuman abilities by **genetic engineering** that allow her to battle the forces of an oppressive government, though she ends up running afoul of the resistance as well. In the alien abduction narrative *The Fourth Kind* (2009), Jovovich plays a psychiatrist researching the experiences of alien abductees. *See also* FEMINISM AND GENDER.

JURAN, NATHAN (1907–2002). Born in a part of Austria-Hungary that is now Romania, Nathan Hertz Juran immigrated with his family to the United States at the age of five and went on to become one of the most prominent directors of the **American science fiction film** boom of the 1950s. Trained as an architect (with a master's degree in architecture from the Massachusetts Institute of Technology), Juran began his film career as an art director on such films as the *How Green Was My Valley* (1941), which won a Best Picture Oscar and for which Juran won the Best Art Direction Oscar. It is, however, as the director of science fiction films that he is best remembered, even if some of his directorial efforts, such as *The Brain from Planet Arous* (1957) and *Attack of the 50 Foot Woman* (1958) are perhaps best remembered for their camp value as ostentatiously bad films— so much so that Juran directed them under the pseudonym Nathan Hertz. Films, such as *The Deadly Mantis* (1957), that Juran directed under his own name were a bit better in quality, especially those in which he worked with **special-effects** artist **Ray Harryhausen**, including *20 Million Miles to Earth* (1957) and *First Men in the Moon* (1964). Juran also directed the fantasy classic *The 7th Voyage of Sinbad* (1958), for which Harryhausen did the special effects. Most of Juran's work after *First Men in the Moon* was for television, including episodes of the classic **Irwin Allen**–produced sf series *Voyage to the Bottom of the Sea, The Time Tunnel, Lost in Space,* and *Land of the Giants.*

JURASSIC PARK. (Dir. **Steven Spielberg**, 1993.) Based on a 1990 novel of the same title by **Michael Crichton**, *Jurassic Park* deals with a wild-animal park that is established on a remote island. The park is special because the animals in it include **dinosaurs** and other extinct prehistoric species, specimens of which have been produced through **genetic engineering**, based on DNA samples extracted from the blood contained in amberized mosquitos that fed on the animals tens of millions of years earlier. The film involves an inspection tour of the park prior to its opening in which a team of independent scientists is brought in to verify that the park is safe before it is opened to the public. These scientists include paleontologist Alan Grant (Sam Neill), paleobotanist Ellie Sattler (Laura Dern), and chaos theorist Ian Malcolm (**Jeff Goldblum**). Predictably, the park is not safe. Things go badly wrong during the inspection tour, and many of the dinosaurs, including an especially deadly pack of small, quick velociraptors, break free of their restraints (largely because of human sabotage) and begin to wreak havoc. Meanwhile, things threaten to get even more out of control when it is discovered that the dinosaurs are breeding, even though all of them were supposed to be female. An extra dimension of suspense is added by the fact that two young children are present on the tour, but, after a number of close calls (and casualties among the secondary characters), the major characters (and the children) manage to escape the island by helicopter. Nevertheless, the film's lessons about the dangers of tampering with nature remain clear.

Jurassic Park was a breakthrough film that employed a combination of advanced animatronics (electromechanical models) and state-of-the-art **computer-generated imagery** to produce creatures that were far more realistic and believable than those featured in previous dinosaur films. Indeed, the film itself was a technological marvel that was marketed largely on the basis of its astounding **special effects**, and to a large extent the film is not really about genetically engineered dinosaurs but about computer-generated ones. In any case, audiences paid to see these dinosaurs in droves, making

Jurassic Park the highest-grossing film in history at that time. It remains Spielberg's most commercially successful film as of this writing. Spielberg also directed a sequel, *The Lost World: Jurassic Park* (1997), while a second sequel, *Jurassic Park III* (2001) was directed by Joe Johnston.

JUST IMAGINE. (Dir. David Butler, 1930.) Sometimes considered the first feature-length **American science fiction film**, *Just Imagine* is a musical romantic **comedy** that uses its futuristic sf setting (in 1980) primarily as an opportunity for jokes, many of which can be highly entertaining. The film is typical of its time in that it assumes the future will bring dramatic advances in technology. Indeed, many of its science fictional technologies (such as flying cars) are essentially sf clichés of the day. Meanwhile, this future technological utopia is accompanied by a number of **dystopian** social practices. For example, in this future society, people have numbers rather than names, and all marriages must be approved by a government panel, which seems to place a great deal of weight on how "distinguished" a man is. Denied permission to marry the woman he loves (LN-18, played by Maureen O'Sullivan), a young man (J-21, played by John Garrick) sets out on a journey to Mars so that he can return with enough distinction to get his choice of marriage partner. Comic hijinks ensue, highlighted by the performances of former vaudevillians El Brendel and Marjorie White. All, of course, works out well in the end.

– K –

KELLEY, DEFOREST (1920–1999). The American actor DeForest Kelley made over 100 appearances in film and television, but he will always be remembered for one role, that of the grumpy-but-loveable Dr. **Leonard McCoy**, the ship's doctor aboard the starship *Enterprise* in the original *Star Trek* television series and in the first six *Star Trek* feature films. Kelley appeared widely in film and (especially) television before *Star Trek* came along, often playing villains. He first entered the realm of science fiction with guest spots on three episodes of television's *Science Fiction Theatre* (1955–1956), in which he also played a doctor. He made several other appearances as doctors as well, leading up to his casting as McCoy. From that time onward, Kelley's career was dominated by the role of McCoy, with which he became intimately identified in the popular imagination, supplemented only by the occasional one-shot guest appearance on television.

KENOBI, OBI-WAN. Obi-Wan Kenobi (played by distinguished British actor **Sir Alec Guinness**) is the aging **Jedi** master who helps **Luke Skywalker** to realize his own destiny as a Jedi in *Star Wars: Episode IV—A New Hope,* the initial film in the *Star Wars* franchise. Though killed in a light-saber battle with the villainous **Darth Vader** in that film, Kenobi is so strongly linked to the **Force** that he remains an important spiritual influence on Luke in the next two films, long after his own physical death. A younger Kenobi (now played by **Ewan McGregor**) returns as an important character in the second *Star Wars* trilogy, making him one of the few characters to appear in all six films of the main *Star Wars* sequence. In the second trilogy, Kenobi is a mentor and eventual partner to the young Jedi **Anakin Skywalker** (played as an adult by **Hayden Christensen**), but is unable to prevent the younger Jedi from going over to the dark side and becoming Darth Vader. In 2003, the American Film Institute listed Kenobi as the 37th greatest movie hero of all time, placing him third among sf film heroes.

KING KONG. (Dir. Merian C. Cooper and Ernest B. Schoedsack, 1933.) One of the founding films of the American **monster-movie** genre, *King Kong* made its title figure an American cultural icon. The film established a formula for the genre that was imitated in countless other films, including a number of direct sequels. It also established female lead Ann Darrow (Fay Wray) as the paradigm of the threatened victim, while setting a standard for **special effects** and visual trickery, thanks to the **stop-motion** special effects of **Willis O'Brien** that was unsurpassed for decades. Perhaps most important, however, is the film's treatment of the giant ape Kong, however alien and dangerous he may be, as a sympathetic figure, thus making him a sort of tragic hero. Indeed, he is treated even more sympathetically than the monster in ***Frankenstein*** (1931), who, though constructed of human parts, ultimately lacks the humanity with which Kong is endowed in the 1933 film.

In *King Kong,* daredevil filmmaker Carl Denham (Robert Armstrong) travels to the remote island where the giant ape lives among **dinosaurs**; the filmmaker then manages to capture the ape, but only after some harrowing moments, including the capture of Darrow by Kong. Denham then brings the captive ape back to civilization, where he attempts to use him for profit as an exhibit and as the "star" of one of his films, playing opposite the down-on-her-luck actress Darrow. Famously, Kong breaks free and again makes off with the actress, with whom he has become infatuated. He then climbs the Empire State Building and, in one of the truly iconic moments in American film, is attacked by planes and eventually shot from the building, falling to his death.

The film's opposition between Kong as an emblem of primitive power who is ultimately no match for the forces of modern technology makes the film a sort of parable of the power (and danger) of modernity. In addition, the film is enriched by its open acknowledgment of its background in Depression-era America, and much of the action is motivated by hardship-driven economic necessity. The film can also be read as a cautionary tale about Hollywood, Denham's unfettered ambition to produce an exciting film having created a dangerous monster much in the way that Dr. Frankenstein's unfettered scientific curiosity did. Finally, the sympathetic portrayal of Kong can be taken as an enactment of the American admiration for the outlaw hero. In the end, he becomes a sort of paradigm of the lone individual, the only creature of his kind, meaning well but misunderstood by all.

King Kong was remade in 1976, with Jessica Lange in the role that had been played by Fay Wray. The film was not a big success. It was remade again in 2005 in a mega-budget version directed by Peter Jackson, then coming off the huge success of his *Lord of the Rings* trilogy. Though this latest version received a tremendous amount of fanfare, many felt that this version, which runs for more than three hours, was a bit too slow-moving. The film barely made back its $207 million production budget at the U.S. box office, but receipts of over $300 million outside the United States still made it a commercial success.

KING, STEPHEN (1947–). A writer whose prolific output and vast commercial success in horror and science fiction has sometimes led many to believe that his work must lack literary merit, King is gradually beginning to receive more serious attention from critics. In 2003, for example, he was awarded the Medal for Distinguished Contribution to American Letters by the U.S. National Book Foundation. King has long, however, had the attention of the film industry, which has adapted a substantial portion of his vast literary output to the screen. Though horror films such as *Carrie* (1976) and *The Shining* (1980) are probably the best-known film adaptations of King's work, numerous science fiction films have been based on his work as well. The **dystopian** film *The Running Man* (1987) presents a violent, materialistic, media-saturated future society that is uncomfortably similar to our own. *Dreamcatcher* (2003) is an **alien-invasion** narrative in which the authorities meeting the threat seem as sinister as the aliens themselves. The **virtual-reality** thriller *The Lawnmower Man* (1992) is nominally based on one of King's short stories, though he has disavowed the film as having nothing to do with his work. In addition, films such as *The Mist* (2007), probably best categorized as horror, contain extensive science fiction elements, in this case an invasion of monsters from another dimension. Of King's work that has been adapted to television, probably the most significant from the point of view of science fiction is the mini-series *The Stand* (1994), a postapocalyptic film based on King's 1978 novel of the same title.

KIRK, JAMES T. Captain James Tiberius Kirk (played by **William Shatner**) was the commander of the starship *Enterprise* in the original *Star Trek* television series, a role he continued to play in the first seven *Star Trek* feature films. At one point the character rose to the rank of Admiral, only to be busted (to his own great pleasure) back to the rank of starship captain. The courageous, lusty, sometimes impetuous Kirk, given extra life by Shatner's over-the-top acting style, went on to become one of the iconic figures of American popular culture, joining with his half-Vulcan science officer/first mate **Spock (Leonard Nimoy)** and the irascible ship's doctor **Leonard McCoy (DeForest Kelley)** to form one of the most effective trios in the history of science fiction. Kirk is a brilliant and charismatic leader, but his sometimes excessive zeal often needs to be tempered by Spock's cold logic or McCoy's old-fashioned common sense, and the three are very much a team in leading the *Enterprise* crew into action. A young Kirk is also a central character in the 2009 *Star Trek* franchise reboot/prequel, in which he is played by Chris Pine.

KOREAN SCIENCE FICTION FILM. Once obscure, Korean cinema in general has gained increasing international attention in the first decade of the 21st century. Science fiction film has been included in this phenomenon, especially beginning in 2002 with the release of *2009: Lost Memories,* one of the most elaborate **alternate-history** films ever made, and *Yesterday,* a slick, violent, big-budget (by Korean standards) sf thriller. When the visually impressive *Natural City* followed in 2003, the arrival of the South Korean film industry as an important player in international science fiction cinema seemed beyond doubt. The big-budget 2006 **monster movie** *The Host* gained considerable positive critical attention worldwide, though it saw only limited release outside of Korea. The 2007 monster movie *D-War* (aka *Dragon Wars*), containing strong fantasy and action elements, was another of the most expensive productions in Korean history, indicating the prominence that sf-related film had gained in the South Korean film industry; though the film received a largely negative critical response, it was a box-office success in Korea and was, in the United States, the highest-grossing Korean-made film ever.

KUBRICK, STANLEY (1928–1999). An American filmmaker who often worked in Great Britain (where he lived during most of the last 40 years of his life), Stanley Kubrick was one of the most respected film directors of his generation. He also holds an important position in the history of science fiction film, having directed three films in the genre, all of which are classics of their kind. *Dr. Strangelove or: How I Learned to Stop Worrying and Love the Bomb* (1964) is a masterpiece of satirical cinema that lampoons the paranoid mentality of cold-war America, at the same time making serious points about the madness of the cold-war arms race. Kubrick's next film was *2001: A Space Odyssey* (1968), a philosophical **space opera** in a much more serious mode that has been widely credited as the first film to demonstrate that a science fiction film could be a true work of art. It also helped to revitalize science fiction cinema after several relatively slow years and has exercised an immense influence on subsequent sf films. Kubrick followed in 1971 with his third straight work of science fiction, the stylish and disturbing **dystopian** film, *A Clockwork Orange.* Kubrick produced no more works of science fiction in his lifetime. However, one of the projects that was in the planning stage at his death was the film that became *Artificial Intelligence: AI,* directed by **Steven Spielberg** and released in 2001.

– L –

LANG, FRITZ (1890–1976). Born in Vienna, the screenwriter and director Fritz Lang was one of the pioneers of German cinema during the important period in which the influential expressionist style was being developed. This style was especially influential on the later American film noir movement, in which Lang became an important director. But it has also exercised an influence in science fiction. Indeed, one of the great works of German expressionist cinema was Lang's own *Metropolis* (1927), one of the founding works of modern science fiction film. Lang also wrote and directed *Frau im Mond* (1929, U.S. titles *By Rocket to the Moon* and *Woman in the Moon*), a forward-looking film that is known for inventing the countdown to the launch of a rocket as a dramatic device, among other innovations. In 1934 Lang fled Nazi Germany for Paris, subsequently moving on to the United States. His work in the United States was primarily as a director, mostly as one of the architects of film noir, though he never reached the level of prominence in the United States that he had enjoyed in Germany. *See also* GERMAN SCIENCE FICTION FILM.

LAW, JUDE (1972–). The British actor Jude Law has enjoyed a rich career in Hollywood film, including a number of appearances in prominent science fiction films. His turn as the genetically gifted (but accidentally crippled) Jerome Eugene Morrow in **Andrew Niccol**'s *Gattaca* (1997) was one of the roles that initially introduced him to American audiences. Two years later, Law had an important role in **David Cronenberg**'s *eXistenZ*. He followed in **Steven Spielberg**'s *Artificial Intelligence: AI* (2001), in which he played a **robot** gigolo. Finally, he played the title role in the innovative *Sky*

Captain and the World of Tomorrow (2004), as of this writing his latest science fiction role.

LEM, STANISŁAW (1921–2006). The Polish science fiction writer Stanisław Lem is widely recognized as one of the giants of the genre. The author of thoughtful, meditative works that often have substantial satirical content, Lem worked in a number of genres, but is best known as a writer of philosophical science fiction that challenges the imagination in the way that only the best science fiction can. His science fiction is marked by a certain formal experimentation as well, which, combined with the philosophical bent of his work, might suggest that his writing is difficult to adapt to film. It also sets his work apart from most American science fiction, of which Lem was notoriously critical, citing only the work of **Philip K. Dick** for praise. It is thus not surprising that Lem's work has been seldom adapted to film in the West, with the 2002 adaptation of his 1961 novel *Solaris* being the only real example—and even that was as much a remake of the 1972 Soviet film adaptation as a direct adaptation of the book.

On the other hand, in addition to that Soviet classic, Lem's work has been adapted several times to film and (especially) television in Eastern Europe, beginning with the East German–Polish production *Der schweigende Stern* (1960), an adaptation of Lem's first book-length work, *The Astronauts,* a juvenile science fiction novel published in 1951. This film, incidentally, did make its way into the U.S. market in an expurgated and modified version, dubbed in English as *First Spaceship on Venus* (1962), a film that Lem denounced and disowned. Lem himself wrote the script for the Polish animated short *Bezludna planeta* (1962), and several of his stories were adapted for Polish television in the 1960s and 1970s. Meanwhile, the Soviet-Polish film *Test pilota Pirxa* (1979), a low-budget, but thoughtful, meditation on the possible replacement of humans by androids (somewhat reminiscent of the work of Dick), is based on a story by Lem. *Szpital przemienienia* (1979, *Hospital of the Transfiguration*) is based on Lem's partly autobiographical novel of that title (published in 1955, but mostly written in 1948); it is not science fiction, however. Between then and the 2002 U.S. remake of *Solaris,* only a few relatively obscure adaptations were made of Lem's work, including two West German shorts based on his satirical Ijon Tichy stories in

1999 and 2000. The Hungarian film *1* (2009), based on a review of an imaginary book contained in Lem's collection *One Human Minute* (1986), is as much philosophical speculation as science fiction.

THE LOST WORLD. (Dir. **Irwin Allen**, 1960.) This version of *The Lost World* is probably the best of several film adaptations of Sir Arthur Conan Doyle's 1912 novel of the same name, a founding work in what is sometimes referred to as the "lost world" genre of **adventure** narratives. Allen's film features a relatively well-known cast in this story of an expedition to the deepest jungles of the Amazon in search of an isolated plateau where **dinosaurs** still roam. Professor George Edward Challenger (Claude Rains) heads the expedition, which also includes noted explorer Lord John Roxton (**Michael Rennie**), newspaper reporter Ed Malone (David Hedison), local pilot Manuel Gomez (Fernando Lamas), and wealthy socialite Jennifer Holmes (Jill St. John), among others. They do, of course, find dinosaurs (made for the film by gluing extra protuberances onto ordinary lizards and then filming them to make them look huge). They are also stranded on the plateau and nearly killed by the members of a primitive local tribe. However, they survive and escape, bearing with them a baby dinosaur as proof of what they have observed, not to mention several large and valuable diamonds recovered on the plateau.

In addition to its problematic representation of the "savage" natives, the film is particularly dated in its treatment of gender. Holmes is described as wanting to join the expedition in the hope of landing Roxton, so that she can "marry a title." When love instead blooms between her and Malone, Roxton wishes them well, noting that "Mrs. is still the best title for a woman." This same story was adapted to silent film in 1925 and was again made into theatrical films in 1992 and 1998. The BBC produced a made-for-television version in 2001. *See also* FEMINISM AND GENDER.

LOURIÉ, EUGÈNE (1903–1991). The Russian-born director, art director, and set designer Eugène Lourié moved to France at an early age. He later began a successful career in French film, then moved on to the United States, where he also had a successful career, especially in the science fiction films of the 1950s. His directorial efforts—including ***The Beast from 20,000 Fathoms*** (1953), *The Colossus of*

New York (1958), *The Giant Behemoth* (1959), and *Gorgo* (1961)—show an unusual visual flair that is indicative of his art and design background, even when they are otherwise uninteresting. Lourié's work as a designer and art director was generally outside of science fiction, though he did serve as the art director for the 1976 made-for-TV film *Time Travelers*.

LUCAS, GEORGE (1944–). George Lucas is one of the leading figures of the American film industry, based largely on the immense success of the **Star Wars** franchise, which Lucas created and most of whose films he directed. Lucas's first feature (as writer and director) was the **dystopian** film *THX 1138* (1971), a film that already shows an excellent grasp of storytelling and visual design. Lucas moved outside of science fiction as the writer and director of *American Graffiti* (1973), his first commercial success, but then returned to science fiction with a flourish in 1977 with the first *Star Wars* film. In 1981, Lucas was the executive producer of *Raiders of the Lost Ark* and has remained a driving force behind the important Indiana Jones sequence ever since, though the films have been directed by Lucas's close friend **Steven Spielberg**.

In addition to his role as the principal creative force behind the actual films, Lucas's work on the *Star Wars* sequence has also placed him in a key position as one of the leading innovators in the development of **special-effects** technology for science fiction film in general, especially in the realm of **computer-generated imagery**. The success of *Star Wars* helped to make Lucas's own studio, **Lucasfilm**, originally founded in 1971, a major player in the film industry, whose respective visual effects and sound effects divisions, **Industrial Light & Magic** and Skywalker Sound, have become leaders in their field, producing effects not only for Lucasfilm's own films but for a wide variety of other films as well.

LUCASFILM. Lucasfilm is the film studio founded by **George Lucas** in 1971 after the making of his first theatrical film, the **dystopian** film *THX 1138* (1971), based on a student film-school project. Lucas's next film, *American Graffiti* (1973) was the first film produced by Lucasfilm, which then co-produced *Star Wars* (1977) with **20th Century Fox**. The *Star Wars* films (distributed by Fox) and

MAD MAX AND SEQUELS • 175

the Indiana Jones films (distributed by Paramount), all produced by Lucas himself, have remained the heart of the company's efforts in film production ever since. Lucasfilm has also been a leader in the development of innovative filmmaking technologies, especially in the area of **special effects**, in which their subsidiary **Industrial Light & Magic** is an industry leader, especially in the realm of **computer-generated imagery**. Their Skywalker Sound subsidiary is an innovator in sound technology for film, and the company was responsible for the development of the industry-standard THX sound reproduction system. Lucasfilm's computer graphics group was sold to Steve Jobs in 1986, subsequently evolving into the film production company **Pixar**, now a subsidiary of **Disney**.

LYNCH, DAVID (1946–). Known as the writer and director of complex, surreal, and often indecipherable art films, David Lynch has also often veered into science fiction territory in his work. His first major film, *Eraserhead* (1977), is set in a strange landscape that takes it into the realm of **postapocalyptic** film and **dystopian** films. He returned to similar atmospheric territory much later in *Inland Empire* (2006), though the latter is more dystopian and less postapocalyptic than the former. Lynch's only pure sf film has been *Dune* (1984), an adaptation of Frank Herbert's classic 1965 science fiction novel. The film's budget was inadequate to do justice either to Herbert's novel or to Lynch's vision, and the film was especially disliked by fans of the book. It is, however, an interesting effort. *Mulholland Drive* (2001) is probably Lynch's most commercial film, though it still contains a number of strange elements that take it well outside the range of realism. Such elements led the film to be nominated for four **Saturn Awards**. Lynch's near-legendary television series *Twin Peaks* (1990–1991) also includes a number of science fictional elements, including hints of a possible **alien invasion**.

– M –

MAD MAX **AND SEQUELS.** (Dir. George Miller, 1979–1985.) The first *Mad Max* film, released in 1979, is a combination **postapocalyptic** film and revenge fantasy in which a young (and then unknown)

Mel Gibson plays Max Rockatansky, a young highway patrolman whose wife and young child are brutally killed by a biker gang that has a grudge against Max. Unhinged, Max sets out on a violent quest for revenge, traveling the roads of a postapocalyptic Australia with a murderous determination. A low-budget film with lots of rough spots, *Mad Max* was nevertheless a hit, especially in Australia, leading to a much more elaborate and expensive sequel, *Mad Max 2* (1981), released in the United States as *The Road Warrior.* This film extends the themes of the first, as Max continues to be a loner, traveling the outback with only his faithful dog for a companion. Nevertheless, he is drawn into a conflict between a vicious gang of killers and a basically good group who happen to have possession of a large amount of gasoline, the most valued possession in this blighted world. Indeed, one of the central themes of the entire *Mad Max* series is our obsession with gasoline-driven vehicles; not only does the collapse of reliable oil supplies play a central role in the apocalyptic downfall of civilization, but the survivors in the postapocalyptic world seem to have learned nothing, maintaining their quest for petroleum-based fuels at all costs. Max helps the good guys win, escaping the desert (with their fuel) to Australia's northern coast, where conditions are a bit less dismal. Max himself, however, remains in the outback, still a lonely and tormented soul.

Mad Max 2 was a major hit that propelled Gibson to Hollywood stardom. It also helped to trigger an important cycle of violent postapocalyptic films that became one of the key cinematic phenomena of the 1980s. Still another sequel, *Mad Max: Beyond Thunderdome,* was released in 1985, featuring the same basic scenario but filling in additional details about the original apocalypse, which now seems to have involved a nuclear war triggered by an energy crisis. Max again helps others escape the desert (this time to a ruined Sydney) while himself remaining behind. This third film was also a hit. Plans for still another sequel, also to be directed by Miller, have not come to fruition as of this writing. Nevertheless, they remain in development, with the latest discussions involving a possible **anime**-style animated version.

MAD SCIENTIST. Though often more associated in the popular imagination with the genre of horror, the mad scientist (if only by virtue of his occupation) also resides within the realm of science fiction. Indeed, numerous science fictional narratives involve mad scientists, or at least scientists who have gone beyond the bounds of propriety in one way or another, typically in an unrestrained quest for scientific knowledge, without proper regard for the potential consequences. In this sense, the prototype of the figure is Victor Frankenstein, the title character of Mary Shelley's 1818 novel *Frankenstein,* though Frankenstein was renamed Henry Frankenstein in **James Whale**'s 1931 film of that title, still the best-known adaptation of the novel. Meanwhile, the Frankenstein story has influenced any number of future mad-scientist films, many of which—such as **Tim Burton**'s *Edward Scissorhands* (1990)—take the tale in interesting new directions. Other 19th-century versions of the mad scientist include Robert Louis Stevenson's Dr. Jeckyll and **H. G. Wells**'s Dr. Moreau, both of whom later figured in film adaptations such as *Dr. Jeckyll and Mr. Hyde* (1931) and *The Island of Dr. Moreau* (1977 and 1996).

Partly because of the legacy of such 19th-century works, the mad-scientist motif became prominent very early in the development of science fiction film. For example, the title character in *Das Kabinett des Doktor Caligari (The Cabinet of Dr. Caligari)*, an early German expressionist film, is a sort of mad scientist. Similarly, the scientist Rotwang (Rudolf Klein-Rogge) in **Fritz Lang**'s *Metropolis* (1927) is a mad-scientist figure. The classic mad-scientist motif of inappropriate tinkering with nature is crucial to the German silent film *Alraune* (1928), as well as the sound version (1930) of the same film; here, a mad scientist artificially impregnates a prostitute with the semen of a hanged murderer, producing a sexually obsessed and murderous offspring with an inability to feel love.

In addition to the horror films of the 1930s, the mad-scientist motif appears in such early U.S. science fiction films as *Dr. Cyclops* (1940). The development of nuclear weapons in World War II provided ample evidence of the destructive potential of scientific research, and it comes as no surprise that mad scientists were particularly prominent in **American science fiction films** of the 1950s, though scientists were often heroes as well. Throughout the *Creature from the Black Lagoon* sequence, for example, scientists play sinister roles, culminating in the depiction of Dr. William Barton (**Jeff Morrow**) as insanely vicious in *The Creature Walks Among*

Us (1956), the third and last of these films. **Irvin S. Yeaworth Jr.**'s
4D Man (1959) is a particularly interesting example of the 1950s
film in which a scientist's research leads him into sinister territory;
another particularly well-known example of the mad-scientist film of
the 1950s is **Kurt Neumann**'s *The Fly* (1958), in which the attempts
of scientist Andre Delambre (David Hedison) to create a teleportation device cause him to become a horrifying human-fly hybrid. The
mad-scientist aspect of this film, incidentally, is more thoroughly
developed in **David Cronenberg**'s 1986 remake of the film, which
pays particular attention to the mental deterioration of scientist
Seth Brundle (**Jeff Goldblum**) as he gradually loses his humanity
in the process of becoming more and more flylike. Still, the most
prominent early example of a mad scientist in an American sf film
is probably *Forbidden Planet* (1956). Here, the scientific curiosity
of Dr. Morbius (**Walter Pidgeon**) unleashes monstrous forces from
his unconscious mind; perhaps more importantly, an entire advanced
civilization is destroyed because of its collective inability to curb its
hunger for more and more scientific and technological progress.

By the 1960s, the mad-scientist motif had been seen so widely
used that it spread beyond its origins into other genres, as when the
villains of the James Bond espionage thrillers tend to be mad scientists, beginning with the title character of *Dr. No* (1962). Meanwhile,
the mad-scientist motif was well enough known that it could become
an object of gentle parody in the **Disney** family film *The Absent-
Minded Professor* (1961), in which Professor Ned Brainard (Fred
MacMurray), as the title implies, is more absent-minded than mad,
though the line between the two tends to be a narrow one in science
fiction. The title figure of **Stanley Kubrick**'s *Dr. Strangelove or:
How I Learned to Stop Worrying and Love the Bomb* (1964) is a
lampoon of the mad Nazi scientist and is thus a comic representation
with decidedly dark undertones. A later example of a more benevolent comic mad scientist is Dr. Emmett "Doc" Brown (Christopher
Lloyd), who invents the crucial time machine in the *Back to the
Future* sequence of films (1985–1990). Brown is clearly depicted as
mad, but comically and benevolently so; he is also extremely brilliant, illustrating the way in which the entire mad-scientist motif in
science fiction tends to rely on the popular notion that there is a fine
line between madness and brilliance.

By the 1990s, the rise of personal computing and the Internet had not only created a whole new subculture of geeks and hackers in the real world, but had also inspired a new kind of mad-scientist figure in science fiction film. Actor **Brad Dourif**'s turn as mad scientist Jack Dante in the campy sf-horror blend *Death Machine* (1994) is typical of the way these figures have often tended to spill over into self-parody, though it should be noted that Dourif (having first risen to prominence playing a mental patient in *One Flew Over the Cuckoo's Nest* in 1975) has had a number of mad-scientist roles, including a turn as a scientist in *Alien: Resurrection* (1997). Among numerous campy elements in Stuart Gordon's *Space Truckers* (1996) is the over-the-top performance by Charles Dance as a former corporate scientist turned **cyborg**, looking back on the ways in which mad scientists (beginning with the mechanical right hand of Rotwang in *Metropolis*) have often found technology encroaching on their bodies.

THE MAN WHO FELL TO EARTH. (Dir. Nicolas Roeg, 1976.) Loosely based on a 1963 novel of the same title by Walter Tevis, *The Man Who Fell to Earth* tells the story of an alien (played by David Bowie) who comes to earth seeking a way to ship water back to his own desiccated and dying planet. The alien (adopting the name "Thomas Jerome Newton") draws upon his knowledge of advanced alien technology to build a business empire in an effort to gather the resources necessary to carry out his water transportation project. This aspect of the film allows for considerable commentary on the workings of capitalism. In addition, Newton establishes a romantic connection with a simple earth girl named Mary-Lou (Candy Clark), who attempts to introduce the foreigner (he claims to be from England) to various aspects of American culture. His estranged view of earth customs thus provides a point of view that defamiliarizes these customs and asks us to consider them from a fresh perspective. Ultimately, however, Newton finds that two aspects of American culture, television and alcohol, are so alluring to him that he becomes addicted, derailing his relationship with Mary-Lou. His water recovery mission fails as well, mostly because of U.S. government intervention, which produces a substantial political commentary on government xenophobia, short-sightedness, and ruthlessness.

A film with considerable artistic ambitions, *The Man Who Fell to Earth* is known for its surreal imagery as well as its serious subject matter. It has become a cult hit over the years, though many of its specifics place it very firmly in the 1970s. However, an update/remake is reportedly in production at the time of this writing.

MARGHERITI, ANTONIO (1930–2002). Antonio Margheriti was an Italian director who worked in a number of genres, including science fiction, horror, and spaghetti Westerns, typically under the pseudonym "Anthony M. Dawson." He was particularly prolific in the 1960s, when he directed such sf films as *Space Men* (1960), *Battle of the Worlds* (1961), and *Wild, Wild Planet* (1965). The latter was the first in a quadrilogy of films known as the Gamma I Quadrilogy; that sequence also includes *The War of the Planets* (1966), *War Between the Planets* (1966), and *The Blue Devils* (1967). Like many Italian films of the 1960s, Margheriti's films of that period were often made with an eye toward distribution in the United States; his films often found major U.S. distributors, a situation that was presumably furthered by his Anglophone pseudonym. All of the films of the *Gamma I* sequence, for example, were distributed in the United States by M-G-M. Margheriti's best-known work from the 1970s was *Flesh for Frankenstein* (1973, aka *Andy Warhol's Frankenstein*), a cult classic of horror film. He remained active in the 1980s, when he directed such films as *Yor, the Hunter from the Future* (1983), a sort of hybrid of science fiction and sword-and-sorcery adventure. In 1987 he directed the Italian–West German television miniseries *Treasure Island in Outer Space,* which anticipates the **Disney animated science fiction film** *Treasure Planet* (2002) in moving Robert Louis Stevenson's classic pirate tale *Treasure Island* to an outer-space setting. *See also* ITALIAN SCIENCE FICTION FILM.

MARLOWE, HUGH (1911–1982). Though he had already appeared in such important films as *Meet Me in St. Louis* (1944), *Twelve O'Clock High* (1949), and *All About Eve* (1950), the actor Hugh Marlowe became especially familiar to American audiences with his appearances in science fiction films of the 1950s. In 1951, he had an important role in the classic *The Day the Earth Stood Still* as Tom Stevens, a self-serving insurance salesman who epitomizes the wrongheadedness of earthlings. In *Earth vs. the Flying Saucers* (1956), however, he graduated to a lead role as Dr. Russell Marvin, a heroic scientist whose invention helps to ward off an **alien invasion**. That same year, he also had a lead role as astronaut John Borden in the **time-travel–postapocalyptic** film *World Without End*. From that point forward, most of his appearances were on television, and he probably reached his zenith as a face recognizable to American audiences with his long-running role as a regular on the television soap opera *Another World* from 1969 to 1982.

MARS. As the closest planet to earth, Mars has understandably long been the object of science fiction speculation. Beginning with **H. G. Wells**'s 1898 novel *The War of the Worlds,* which has itself been the source of major film adaptations in 1953 and 2005, visions of Mars as a potential source of **alien invasion** has been a favorite science fiction motif. *Red Planet Mars* (1952), one of the most bizarre sf films ever made, features an alien invasion of sorts from Mars, when contact with Mars (and subsequent messages that seemingly come from Jesus Christ, who now apparently has a base on Mars) lead to large-scale disruptions on earth. In addition to the first adaptation of *The War of the Worlds,* 1953 also saw the release of another major Martian invasion film, *Invaders from Mars* (which was remade in 1986). As we have learned more and more about Mars, the prospect of intelligent life there has seemed more and more remote, leading to a rapid decline in the number of films featuring invasions of the earth from Mars. Indeed, the most effective Martian invasion film after the 1950s has probably been **Tim Burton**'s retrospective lampoon of and homage to such films in *Mars Attacks!* (1996).

Because it is likely to be the first planet visited by explorers from earth, numerous films have also involved trips from earth to Mars, beginning with the early Soviet silent film *Aelita* (1924), in which Soviet explorers help to engineer a proletarian revolt on Mars. The first **American science fiction film,** *Just Imagine* (1930), also involves a journey to Mars, as do two of the central space exploration films of the 1950s, *Rocketship X-M* (1950) and *Conquest of Space* (1955). Lesser films from that decade, such as *Flight to Mars* (1951) and *The Angry Red Planet* (1959), also feature trips to Mars, as does the much-admired *Robinson Crusoe on Mars* (1964), in which a lone astronaut is stranded on the red planet. *Capricorn One* (1978) is a conspiracy film in which an apparent trip to Mars turns out to be a hoax. **Paul Verhoeven**'s *Total Recall* (1990) is a particularly effective film that revolves around a mining colony on Mars. The turn of the millennium, meanwhile, saw the release of a spate of films involving trips to Mars, including Brian De Palma's ambitious *Mission to Mars* (2000), Antony Hoffman's *Red Planet* (2000), and **John Carpenter**'s *Ghosts of Mars* (2001). The latter, with its monster-on-Mars theme, is something of a throwback to the Martian exploration films of the 1950s, as is the ultraviolent *Doom* (2005), a video-game adaptation. *See also* VENUS.

MARS ATTACKS! (Dir. **Tim Burton**, 1996.) *Mars Attacks!* is a parodic **alien-invasion** narrative that both lampoons and pays homage to the paranoid alien-invasion films of the 1950s, though it was most directly based on a trading card series released in 1962. On the other hand, released only five months after the blockbuster alien-invasion hit *Independence Day,* the film was inevitably seen by many as a direct response to that film. Indeed, like *Independence Day, Mars Attacks!* employs the narrative structure of the **disaster** film to tell its story, except that now the sinister alien invaders look ridiculous and are defeated by ridiculous means. (It turns out that their heads explode when they are exposed to the singing and yodeling of country singer Slim Whitman.)

Though often mimicking the hokey, low-budget **special effects** of 1950s sf films, *Mars Attacks!* had a relatively big budget and employs a number of state-of-the-art effects. It also had an A-list cast and director; Burton's visual flair and an over-the-top performance by megastar Jack Nicholson in dual roles helped to make it not only one of the most expensive science fiction spoofs of all time, but also one of the most effective. *See also* COMEDY; MARS.

MATHESON, RICHARD (1926–). The American writer Richard Matheson has long been an important presence in sf film, as both a screenwriter and an author writer of novels that have served as source material for films. Sometimes, the two careers merged, as when his first sf screenplay, for the classic 1957 film *The Incredible Shrinking Man,* was based on his own 1956 novel, *The Shrinking Man.*

This same novel was the basis for *The Incredible Shrinking Woman* (1981), a more comic version, while still another adaptation of this novel is in the works for release in 2010. The romantic **time-travel** film *Somewhere in Time* (1980) was also written by Matheson based on his own novel, *Bid Time Return* (1975). Writing under the name "Logan Swanson," Matheson also co-wrote the **postapocalyptic** film *The Last Man on Earth* (1964), based on his novel *I Am Legend* (1954). This same novel was later adapted to film twice more (with different screenwriters), as *The Omega Man* (1971) and *I Am Legend* (2007). Matheson also wrote the screenplays or provided the source material for a number of horror films. Much of his best-known work, however, was for television, especially as the writer of 16 episodes of *The Twilight Zone* (1959–1964). He also wrote the script for "The Enemy Within" (1966), one of the best remembered episodes of the original *Star Trek* series.

THE MATRIX AND SEQUELS. (Dir. **Larry and Andy Wachowski,** 1999–2003.) *The Matrix,* released in 1999, is a **postapocalyptic** film that presents a world in which humans have been enslaved by their own machines and are kept in catatonic captivity (for use as power sources), their minds occupied by **virtual-reality** visions of the world as it once was, which the humans mistake for reality. This notion of a world of simulations resonates in some ways with the descriptions of the postmodern world by French philosopher Jean Baudrillard, whose work is, in fact, referenced in the film. As such, *The Matrix* includes a certain amount of potential social and political commentary, and it is probably the first fully successful cinematic exploration of virtual reality and of the associated themes of **cyberpunk** science fiction. It is thoughtful enough that it has spawned a considerable critical literature. Ultimately, though, *The Matrix* is first and foremost an action film, memorable more than anything for its numerous ultraviolent fight scenes, which involve both hand-to-hand combat reminiscent of Hong Kong martial arts films and considerable gunplay, including super-slow-motion camerawork that allows the tracking of individual (computer-generated) bullets to their targets. All of this action, of course, is made more spectacular by the fact that it takes place in cyberspace, so that the conventional laws of physics need not apply.

The central figure in these scenes is one Neo (**Keanu Reeves**), a sort of Chosen One who has been anointed to lead the humans from their machine-imposed servitude, but who is initially unaware of his fated role, living a simulated life like most other humans. Almost as important in the fight scenes, however, is Trinity (Carrie-Anne Moss), a woman resistance fighter who helps lead Neo to his destiny, battling computer-generated "agents" in her black, skin-tight latex suit. These fighters, meanwhile, are guided by Morpheus (**Laurence Fishburne**), a sort of guru figure. *The Matrix* was clearly one of the highlights of 1990s science fiction film, and its technical achievements were truly groundbreaking. It won the **Saturn Award** for both best director and best science fiction film, beating out *Star Wars: Episode I—The Phantom Menace*, which won the award for best **special effects** of 1999. However, *The Matrix* trounced its *Star Wars* rival in the effects categories of the Oscars; it was nominated for four Oscars and won all four in the categories of best editing, best sound effects editing, best visual effects, and best sound.

The Matrix inspired two sequels, *The Matrix Reloaded* and *The Matrix Revolutions*, both released in 2003, but these subsequent films failed to live up to the promise of the original and broke little new ground. The mythology surrounding the increasingly superpowered Neo becomes more and more religious in these films, while the reliance on special-effects action sequences in the battles between the machines and the human resistance movement grows greater. The *Matrix* franchise also includes a fourth film, *The Animatrix* (2003), a collection of nine short animated films (commissioned by the Wachowski Brothers) set in the world of the *Matrix* trilogy and done primarily in the style of Japanese **anime**, though they employ a variety of animation techniques. *See also* ANIMATED SCIENCE FICTION FILMS.

McCOY, LEONARD. Dr. Leonard "Bones" McCoy (played by **De-Forest Kelley**) was the cantankerous, but highly competent ship's doctor aboard the starship *Enterprise* in the original **Star Trek** television series and in the first six *Star Trek* feature films. McCoy teamed with Captain **James T. Kirk (William Shatner)** and the science officer/first mate **Spock (Leonard Nimoy)** to form one of the most effective (and popular) character groupings in science fiction history. Though always irritable and irascible (and quick to remind anyone who will listen that he is a doctor, and not anything else), McCoy serves as something of the conscience of the series, tempering Spock's quest for logic with his own highly emotional views and moderating Kirk's sometimes excessive zeal for action with his own common sense. Though a respecter of tradition who is often wary of technology, McCoy is also consistently horrified by reminders of the primitive ways in which medicine was practiced in previous centuries. A younger version of McCoy (played by Karl Urban) appears in the 2009 *Star Trek* reboot/prequel film.

McDOWALL, RODDY (1928–1998). The British actor Roddy McDowall began his career as a child star in Great Britain, a career he continued after coming to America to escape the bombing of Britain in World War II. In the United States, he distinguished himself in such films as the Academy Award–winning *How Green Was My Valley* (1941). He subsequently worked widely in film and television, though never quite achieving the stardom his early success (and obvious talent) seemed to suggest might be his. He did, however, achieve a prominent place in the history of science fiction film for his performance as the chimpanzee scientist Cornelius in the *Planet of the Apes* franchise. McDowall ultimately became a central figure who held that franchise together, playing the role of Cornelius in the original 1968 film as well as in the second sequel, *Escape from the Planet of the Apes* (1971), then playing the role of Caesar, Cornelius's son, in *Conquest of the Planet of the Apes* (1972) and *Battle for the Planet of the Apes* (1973). McDowall also played the role of the ape administrator Galen in the short-lived 1974 television series that was spun off from the films. McDowall also had many other roles in science fiction film and television, though he generally played more and more minor roles in increasingly obscure works as his career proceeded. Some highlights of his later career included appearances in three episodes of *The Martian Chronicles* on television in 1980 and a lead role in the 1995 made-for-TV **undersea adventure** *The Alien Within*. McDowall also did a considerable amount of voiceover work, including supplying the voice for the **robot** V.I.N.CENT in *The Black Hole* (1979).

McDOWELL, MALCOLM (1943–). Among the many roles played by the prolific British film actor Malcolm McDowell are a number of prominent appearances in science fiction films, especially as villains, beginning with his much acclaimed performance as Alex DeLarge, the sadistic central character in **Stanley Kubrick**'s *A Clockwork Orange* (1971). McDowell then stayed away from sf film for many years, though he did appear in some horror and fantasy films. In 1990, he returned as Major Lee in **Roland Emmerich**'s relatively obscure *Moon 44* (1990); he also played the evil Lord Talon in *Cyborg 3: The Recycler* (1995). McDowell returned to the sf film mainstream the previous year as Dr. Tolian Soran, the villain who kills **James T. Kirk** in *Star Trek: Generations*. He followed as Kesslee, the villainous CEO of the global Water and Power Company in the campy **postapocalyptic** film *Tank Girl* (1995). McDowell provided the voice of the evil inventor Scamboli in *Pinocchio 3000* (2004); in *Doomsday* (2008), he played genetic scientist Dr. Marcus Kane, who becomes a sort of feudal lord in the postapocalyptic world of that film.

McGREGOR, EWAN (1971–). The Scottish actor Ewan McGregor gained the attention of Hollywood and of worldwide film audiences with his performance in **Danny Boyle**'s 1996 film *Trainspotting*, beginning a rise that saw him become a major movie star with his appearance as **Obi-Wan Kenobi** in the *Star Wars* prequel, beginning with *Star Wars: Episode I—The Phantom Menace* in 1999. He followed with another starring role in a high-profile science fiction film in **Michael Bay**'s *The Island* (2005). McGregor also provided the voice for the **robot** Rodney Copperbottom, the central character in the animated **children's science fiction** film *Robots* (2005).

MECHA. In Japanese popular culture, the term *mecha* is used to indicate both any of a wide variety of **robot**-like mobile vehicles and the genre of film that features such vehicles (though in Japan that genre is widely known as "robot anime"). Mecha are often heavily armed war machines, but they may also be used in a variety of dangerous or arduous civilian applications. Mecha are generally controlled by a pilot, and are typically (but not necessarily) bipedal, modeled in form on the human body. Sometimes mecha blur the boundary between the animate and the inanimate, as in films in which the mecha acquire the ability to think and act autonomously, frequently with destructive results. For example, the boundary between the mecha film and the **monster movie** is blurred as when a robotic version of the classic movie monster **Godzilla** (known as "Mechagodzilla") threatens humanity—and the "real" Godzilla— in several films. Besides being featured in numerous Japanese **anime** science fiction films, mecha can be found in many Western science fiction films, from the Martian war machines of the various film adaptations of *The War of the Worlds* to the walkers of the *Star Wars* sequence. A classic case is the war machines of Stuart Gordon's *Robot Jox* (1990). *See also* JAPANESE SCIENCE FICTION FILM.

MELCHIOR, IB (1917–). The Danish-born Ib Melchior was a novelist and short-story writer who also saw extensive work as a screenwriter and film director, often in low-budget science fiction films made by **American International Pictures**. He both wrote and directed *The Angry Red Planet* (1959), in which a manned mission to Mars encounters a variety of horrific creatures there. He also wrote and directed *The Time Travelers* (1964) and was the co-author of the English-language script for *Planet of the Vampires* (1965). Melchior wrote such minor films as *Reptilicus* (1961) and *Journey to the Seventh Planet* (1962), and his short story "The Racer" formed the basis of the 1975 film *Death Race 2000* and its 2008 remake *Death Race*. Melchior's most important sf film credit was as the co-writer of the script for **Byron Haskin's** *Robinson Crusoe on Mars* (1964). Though he never received formal credit, Melchior claims to have come up with the original idea that became **Irwin Allen's** television series *Lost in Space* (1965–1968). In 1976, the Academy of Science Fiction, Fantasy and Horror Films awarded Melchior the Golden Scroll Award of Merit for Outstanding Achievement.

MÉLIÈS, GEORGES (1861–1938). The pioneering French filmmaker Georges Méliès used his background as a stage magician to help him formulate some of the first **special effects** in the history of film. As the father of cinematic special effects, Méliès enjoys a special position in the history of science fiction film, which has depended so heavily on such effects for the creation of settings and events outside the range of contemporary reality. Indeed, Méliès himself recognized early on the potential of his techniques for making science fiction films, drawing particularly upon the work of the pioneering French science fiction writer Jules Verne as a source in his work. Méliès's best-known film, *Le voyage dans la lune* (*A Trip to the Moon,* 1902), inspired by **Jules Verne**'s 1865 novel *De la terre à la lune,* is a charming fantasy that features a number of whimsical effects, including a famous shot in which a bullet-shaped spaceship, fired from a space cannon on earth, strikes the man in the moon in the eye. *Le voyage à travers l'impossible* (*The Impossible Voyage,* 1904), loosely based on a play by Verne, similarly uses special effects to depict a fantastic voyage in which some world travelers accidentally ascend from the earth (in a train) and crash into the sun, subsequently returning to the earth in a submarine. Méliès's *20,000 lieues sous les mers* (*20,000 Leagues Under the Sea,* 1907) is also based on a novel by Verne. Hand-tinted frame-by-frame, this became one of the first color films. In order to provide facilities for the production of the impressive special effects in his films, Méliès constructed what is generally considered to be the fist motion picture studio. *See also* FRENCH SCIENCE FICTION FILM.

MEN IN BLACK **AND** *MEN IN BLACK II.* (Dir. Barry Sonnenfeld, 1997 and 2002.) *Men in Black* and its sequel, *Men in Black II,* are the two most commercially successful science fiction **comedy** films in movie history. The films are based on the similarly titled comic books by Lowell Cunningham, which themselves actually give fairly serious treatment to the UFO conspiracy theory that government-employed agents (or at least someone claiming to be government agents), dressed in black, were systematically attempting to squelch evidence that alien visitors were present on planet earth. The films, however, treat this **alien-invasion** scenario as an opportunity for farcical comedy, with mock-serious Men in Black working to control what turns out to be a numerous and varied collection of wacky (and mostly harmless) aliens on earth. As such, the film was also a sort of spoof of more serious alien-invasion films, such as **Roland Emmerich**'s *Independence Day,* which had been a major hit the year before the first *Men in Black* film was released. Indeed, both *Men in Black* films star **Will Smith**, who had been one of the stars of *Independence Day.* Meanwhile, the films were made primarily by **Steven Spielberg**'s Amblin Entertainment production company and executive produced by Spielberg, who had been responsible for two of the best and most successful alien-invasion films of all time, *Close Encounters of the Third Kind* (1977) and *E.T. the Extra-Terrestrial* (1982).

In both *Men in Black* films, Smith and Tommy Lee Jones are the two key government agents who are assigned to control earth's alien infestation. They work for the ultra-secret Men in Black agency, headed by the hilariously deadpan Chief Zed (Rip Torn) and featuring a large collection of seemingly interchangeable black-suited human agents, as well as a panoply of comic aliens who work with and for them. There is much work to be done, because in these films the earth is teeming with aliens, most of whom mean no harm and who are here with official permission, the main restrictions being that they must register with the Men in Black agency and must promise to keep their presence a secret from the general human population. One of the most common ways they do so is by disguising themselves as humans; one of the key jokes that runs through both films is that numerous prominent humans (such as Michael Jackson, Martha Stewart, and Elvis Presley—who didn't die, we discover, but merely returned to his home planet) are among these disguised aliens. However, aliens do sometimes pose a threat to humanity, presenting the opportunity for some (still comical) action sequences as the Men in Black step in to save the day, defending the earth with an arsenal of high-tech weaponry, much of it obtained from alien sources.

Both *Men in Black* films openly engage in dialogue with both their predecessors in sf film and with the entire tradition of UFO conspiracy theories, gaining considerable comic mileage from the sometimes extreme nature of both of these traditions. Especially in their engagement with previous films, they have a great deal in common with their most recent predecessor, **Tim Burton**'s *Mars Attacks!* (1996), which draws much of its energy from dialogue with the alien-invasion films of the 1950s. However, the *Men in Black* films, employing state-of-the-art **special effects**, refer more directly to the big-budget films of the 1990s. Still, the most direct predecessors of the *Men in Black* films, in tone and spirit, are probably the *Ghostbuster* films of the 1980s, with the farcical ghosts of those films replaced by farcical alien invaders. Meanwhile, the use of expensive special effects in the *Men in Black* films primarily for the production of sight gags rather than thrilling action sequences demonstrates the comic potential of **computer-generated imagery**, while at the same time serving as a potential parodic commentary on the reliance of contemporary science fiction films on special-effects technology.

MENZIES, WILLIAM CAMERON (1896–1957). In 1936, the American film director and producer William Cameron Menzies was tapped to direct *Things to Come* (1936), the first major science fiction film of the sound era, even though he had relatively little directorial experience at that time. However, Menzies was already well known as a set designer and art director for films such as *The Thief of Baghdad* (1924) and had won two Academy Awards for Best Art Design. He put his production design talents to good use in *Things to Come,* which seeks to create a believable world of the future. Menzies also directed the sf film *Invaders from Mars* (1953), but will probably always be best remembered for his production designs, especially of *Gone With the Wind* (1939).

METROPOLIS. (Dir. **Fritz Lang**, 1927.) Often considered the first truly important science fiction film, *Metropolis* certainly exercised a strong influence on the films that came after it. Itself influenced heavily by German expressionism, this silent film is striking in its presentation of a futuristic city in which the dehumanized urban population is enslaved both by the tyrants who rule them and by the machines they tend. Though set in the year 2000, *Metropolis* is in many ways very much a film of its own time, reflecting a growing sense of crisis that was felt throughout the Western world in the late 1920s, and that was especially strong in interwar Germany, where it was made.

In the future city of the film, the class structure of capitalist society has become particularly overt, with the population separated into "Masters" (who rule the city while leading lives of great luxury and hedonistic pleasure) and workers, who live dark and dreary lives, laboring away beneath the city to tend the machines that create the high-tech paradise in which the Masters revel. As the film opens, the workers seem on the verge of revolution, but they are dissuaded from violence by the gentle Maria (**Brigitte Helm**), a worker's daughter and a charismatic leader who preaches a doctrine of moderation and compassion. Meanwhile, the male protagonist Freder (Gustav Fröhlich), son of Metropolis's ruler Joh Fredersen (Alfred Abel), becomes sympathetic to the plight of the workers after he visits the subterranean machine rooms and views the conditions there. He also becomes fascinated with Maria. Meanwhile, the elder Fredersen enlists one Rotwang (Rudolf Klein-Rogge), a sort of **mad scientist**, to aid him in repressing the budding rebellion. Rotwang kidnaps Maria and replaces her with a **robot** double, then instructs the robot to instigate a self-defeating workers' rebellion. The workers respond with a violent attack on the machines that also leads to the flooding of their underground city. Blaming the ersatz Maria, they turn on her and burn her at the stake, thereby discovering that she is in fact a robot. Freder, meanwhile, rescues the real Maria from Rotwang and convinces his father to make peace with Grot (Heinrich George), leader of the workers, to cooperate in rebuilding Metropolis, thus joining, as the film puts it, the "head and the hand" of the city.

Though numerous aspects of *Metropolis* appear sentimental, simplistic, or just plain confused, it should also be pointed out that all prints of the original German version were long thought to be lost and that existing American versions have been patched together in ways that led Lang himself to refer to the American version as his film's "mutilated surrogate." (An apparently authentic, but badly damaged, print of the original was discovered in 2008 and is being restored as of this writing.) Nevertheless, the film's striking visual images remain largely intact, and it is for these images—and the way they reflect modern anxieties over technology and urbanization—that the film is important. The film's images of advanced technologies have been an important inspiration for any number of subsequent science-fiction films, while its vision of dispirited and downtrodden workers, trudging mechanically to and from their workplaces, remain a central part of the dystopian imagination, even in the 21st century. *See also* DYSTOPIAN FILM; GERMAN SCIENCE FICTION FILM.

MEYER, NICHOLAS (1945–). The American director, writer, and producer Nicholas Meyer is best known for his involvement in the *Star Trek* film franchise, especially as the director of *Star Trek II: The Wrath of Khan* (1982), a film the success of which is widely

credited as having saved the *Star Trek* film franchise after the disappointment of the first *Star Trek* feature film. In 1979, Meyer had
directed the **time-travel** film *Time After Time* (1979), and in 1983 he
followed the success of *Khan* by directing the acclaimed made-for-
TV **postapocalyptic** film *The Day After*. Meyer resumed his work
with the *Star Trek* franchise as the co-writer of *Star Trek IV: The
Voyage Home* (1986); in 1991 he directed and co-wrote *Star Trek VI:
The Undiscovered Country*.

MINORITY REPORT. (Dir. **Steven Spielberg**, 2002.) Loosely based
on a short story by **Philip K. Dick** and set in the year 2054, *Minority
Report* details a future Washington, D.C., in which a group of three
"pre-cognitives," or "pre-cogs" have an ability to envision murders
before they happen, thanks to a mutation induced by a specific drug
taken by their mothers during pregnancy. The pre-cogs are being
used in a government-sponsored pilot program to foresee murders,
so that the killers-to-be can be arrested and incarcerated, thereby
saving the victims. The program, although controversial for obvious reasons, has had a stellar track record and seems on the verge
of going national, when Chief John Anderton (**Tom Cruise**), the
head cop assigned to the program, is suddenly identified as a future
killer. Most of the plot involves Anderton's subsequent efforts to
evade capture long enough to prove that he has somehow been set up
and that the program is corrupt. Eventually, it turns out that Lamar
Burgess (Max von Sydow), the chief administrator in charge of the
entire "pre-crime" program, once committed a murder to protect the
program and that he has arranged for Anderton to be framed in order
to prevent him from looking into that murder and into the possibility
that the visions of the pre-cogs are not entirely reliable, given that
one of them sometimes sees the future differently from the other two,
thus issuing the "minority report" of the title. Eventually, Burgess's
crimes are revealed and the Precrime program is shut down. The
pre-cogs are released from what had essentially been slavery so that
they can pursue a quiet life together, while Anderton seems poised to
recover his normal life as well.

Minority Report is a stylish thriller that uses an unusual blue-
tinted, slightly grainy look throughout to create a sense of unfamiliarity that suggests being in the future. In addition, despite its effective

action sequences, it explores a number of important ideas, many of them common to **dystopian** film, though in this case they are treated in a complex way that suggests multiple possible viewpoints on the issues. Thus, the pre-crime program, though based on a particularly questionable form of surveillance, really has succeeded in dramatically decreasing the murder rate in Washington. Meanwhile, numerous striking images reinforce this surveillance theme, including the nimble **robot** "spiders" that invade homes, scanning the irises of the inhabitants in search of criminals, or the heavy use of eye imagery throughout, suggesting (as in *Blade Runner*) the crucial importance of surveillance as a theme in the movie.

MITCHELL, CAMERON (1918–1994). The American actor Cameron Mitchell worked widely in film, television, and stage productions and was one of the founding members of The Actor's Studio in New York City. After a number of early performances, Mitchell gained considerable attention in 1951 with his performances as Happy Loman in the film adaptation of *Death of a Salesman.* That same year, he also starred in *Flight to Mars,* thus beginning his career as an actor in science fiction films. He worked widely outside of science fiction for the remainder of the decade. In the 1960s, he starred in a number of Italian horror films, some of which were directed by **Mario Bava**. He subsequently became a well-known face on American television, including a lead role in the made-for-TV alternate-earth film *The Stranger* (1973, aka *Stranded in Space*). In 1974 he starred in another made-for-TV sf film, *Death in Space,* and in 1988 he returned to theatrical film (albeit in a low-budget production) in *Space Mutiny.*

MIYAZAKI, HAYAO (1941–). The Japanese animator and filmmaker Hayao Miyazaki is one of the towering figures of modern Japanese culture. The maker of a number of animated films aimed at audiences from very young children to adults, Miyazaki is often compared with Walt **Disney** in the United States. To an extent, the comparison is apt. For example, as the founder of Studio Ghibli, Miyazaki long spearheaded his nation's most important children's film company. However, whatever his talents, Disney was not an artist and never directed a film, whereas Miyazaki is a talented artist and film director in his own right. Much of Miyazaki's work can be considered science fiction, and even his most magical and fantastical films typically contain science fictional elements and advanced technological devices, especially a variety of flying machines.

Miyazaki first began to gain attention for his work on *Gulliver's Travels Beyond the Moon* (1965), a science fictional adaptation of a major work of Western literature. On that film, he was employed as an ordinary animator, but ended up making major creative contributions to the script. In 1968, Miyazaki was the chief animator on Isao Takahata's *Prince of the Sea: The Great Adventure of Horus* (aka *Little Norse Prince*), often considered the first work of modern **anime** in its use of a distinctive new style that broke away from the Disney-influenced styles of earlier Japanese animated films. Miyazaki and Takahata often worked together over the next three decades. He worked extensively on the television series *Future Boy Conan* (1978), in which a young protagonist attempts to rediscover lost technologies in a city of the future. His reputation as an animator and writer growing, Miyazaki directed his first feature film in 1979 in *The Castle of Cagliostro,* an animated heist thriller based on the *Lupin III* television series, on which he had previously worked. Miyazaki's second film is considered by many to be his finest and one of anime's greatest classics: *Kaze no tani no Naushika* (1984, **Nausicaä of the Valley of the Wind**). Though it contains important elements of the fantasy-adventure genre, *Nausicaä* is in fact a **postapocalyptic** film that resides firmly within the territory of science fiction and that is best suited for fairly mature audiences.

Miyazaki continued to build a reputation in Japan with a series of subsequent fantasy films, including *Laputa: Castle in the Sky* (1986), *My Neighbor Totoro* (1988, aimed at younger children than most of his films), and *Kiki's Delivery Service* (1989). With *Princess Mononoke* (1997), another of his most respected films, Miyazaki returns to many of the themes of *Nausicaä,* depicting a postapocalyptic world ravaged by militarism and environmental irresponsibility. **Environmentalism**, in fact, is a theme in many of Miyazaki's films, as is antimilitarism. Some have also seen **feminism** as an issue in his tendency to employ female protagonists. The fantasy film *Spirited Away* (2001) was another major hit, which went on to win the first

Academy Award for Best Animated Feature Film. *Howl's Moving Castle* (2004) is another fantasy film, but one that contains an especially large amount of science fictional hardware.

All of Miyazaki's films have been produced primarily with traditional hand-drawn animation, though computer animation has been used in a supplementary fashion since *Princess Mononoke*. On the other hand, Miyazaki's latest film, *Ponyo* (2009, again aimed at smaller children), was produced entirely by hand-drawn animation. Though relatively little known outside of Japan through most of his career, Miyazaki is now internationally renowned, partly because his films have been embraced by the powerful Disney company, which, since 1999, has been producing and distributing English-language DVD versions of his films (in some cases first released in theaters), beginning with *Princess Mononoke,* but moving back to include earlier films as well. *See also* FEMINISM AND GENDER; JAPANESE SCIENCE FICTION FILM.

MOCKBUSTER. The term *mockbuster* refers to a low-budget, quickly made knockoff of a major theatrical film that is expected to achieve blockbuster status. Mockbusters are typically released straight-to-video, with the expectation that the popularity of the films on which they are based will lead to peripheral business for these knockoffs. Despite the suggestion of mockery in the term, mockbusters do not usually parody or lampoon their originals. As a result, some prefer the term "knockbuster," indicating the knockoff status of the films, which are typically B-movie versions of the basic premises of the originals, often with extra violence and nudity thrown in for good measure. The increasing quality of fairly inexpensive **computer-generated imagery** has made science fiction a particularly viable genre for the mockbuster in recent years. Science fiction mockbusters have been a particular specialty of The Asylum, a small, independent studio that has produced several knockoffs of specific sf blockbusters, usually with motifs or plot elements from other well-known sf films thrown in as well. Their films include *H. G. Wells' War of the Worlds,* linked to **Steven Spielberg**'s 2005 *War of the Worlds* remake; *Transmorphers* (2007) and *Transmorphers: Fall of Man* (2009), based on the two *Transformers* movies of **Michael Bay;** *I Am Omega*, linked to *I Am Legend* (2007); *Monster*, based on *Cloverfield*

(2008); *The Day the Earth Stopped,* keyed to the 2008 remake of *The Day the Earth Stood Still;* and *Terminators,* linked to *Terminator Salvation* (2009).

MONSTER MOVIES. Though sometimes fitting more comfortably into the horror genre than into science fiction, numerous monster movies are rightly considered science fiction, especially when their monsters are produced by science itself. The prototype of all such science-created monsters, of course, was the creature made by scientist Victor Frankenstein in Mary Shelley's 1818 novel *Frankenstein,* which was brought successfully to the screen in **James Whale**'s classic 1931 film adaptation with Boris Karloff as the lumbering monster. While the other movie monsters of the 1930s (such as Dracula) tended to be more supernatural in origin, perhaps the greatest of all 1930s monster movies, *King Kong* (1933) featured a monster with a natural origin, a giant ape who lived among **dinosaurs** who had survived (by natural means) to the present day on a remote island. Captured and brought back to civilization by human profit-seekers, Kong escapes and wreaks havoc, but remains more victim than villain, making him a powerful prototype for numerous later films that treat their monsters sympathetically. Among the films directly inspired by *King Kong* was *Mighty Joe Young* (1949), another giant-ape film, whose **special-effects** crew included **Ray Harryhausen**, who went on to produce special effects for some of the best movie monsters of the 1950s.

Monsters created by scientific experiments or technological devices gone awry became particularly popular in the 1950s. Frankenstein's monster itself enjoyed something of a renaissance in the decade, especially after **Hammer Film Productions'** *The Curse of Frankenstein* (1957) became an international hit that spawned several sequels and numerous imitations. The 1950s are also notable for the numerous **alien-invasion** films produced during the decade, many of which depicted the invading aliens as monsters, as in the giant Venusian reptile of *20 Million Miles to Earth* (1957), with monster effects by Harryhausen, or in *The Blob* (1958). The most important movie monsters of the 1950s, however, were giant creatures (usually either insects or reptiles) produced (or, in some cases, merely freed from long entrapment) by the effects of radiation or weapons testing.

Among the giant reptiles unleashed by radiation or weapons testing during the decade was the giant "rhedosaurus" of *The Beast from 20,000 Fathoms* (1953), a dinosaur long frozen in the polar ice cap but freed by atomic weapons testing in the Arctic. *The Giant Behemoth* (1959), a joint American-British production, was essentially a remake of *The Beast from 20,000 Fathoms,* and even featured the same writer and director (**Eugène Lourié**). Of course, the most famous of the radiation-induced giant reptiles of the 1950s was the Japanese **Godzilla**, first introduced in the **Toho Studios** film of the same title in 1954, then made popular in the West with the release, in 1956, of *Godzilla: King of the Monsters,* dubbed in English and with American actor Raymond Burr playing an added point-of-view character. Godzilla, of course, inspired an entire film subindustry in Japan and had numerous imitators elsewhere as well.

In a variant of the giant reptile movie, adventurers in films such as *The Lost Continent* (1951) and *The Lost World* (1960) sometimes stumbled on isolated prehistoric enclaves where (as in the original *King Kong*) dinosaurs had survived until the present day. The voyagers of *Journey to the Center of the Earth* (1959) discover that giant dinosaur-like lizards still inhabit the subterranean world, where evolution has presumably stood still. The best of the evolutionary-throwback movies of the 1950s, however, were probably those in the sequence that began with *Creature from the Black Lagoon* (1954), which features a somewhat sympathetic monster (retrieved, like Kong, from a remote third-world locale), who is described as an evolutionary "missing link" between dinosaurs and humans.

Perhaps the best of the giant insect films of the 1950s is *Them!* (1954), in which radiation produces a swarm of gigantic ants that threatens the American Southwest, eventually to be destroyed (with flamethrowers) in the sewers of Los Angeles. In **Jack Arnold**'s *Tarantula* (1955), a scientist develops a radiation-charged nutrient that produces a giant killer spider. In *Beginning of the End* (1957), grasshoppers also dine on experimental irradiated food, then grow huge and invade Chicago. The giant insect of *The Deadly Mantis* (1957) was unusual in the 1950s in that it was a prehistoric remnant released (from the polar ice cap) by a natural geological disturbance. Meanwhile, other films of the 1950s seemed fascinated with the monstrous possibilities offered by combining humans with insects, as in *The Fly* (1958) and *The Wasp Woman* (1959), the latter directed by **Roger Corman**, who became one of the kings of B-grade monster movies during this period.

Science fictional monster movies fell somewhat out of favor from the 1960s to the 1980s, though Japanese production of the Godzilla sequence and other films in the same vein (featuring not only the original Godzilla, but other monsters such as Rodan and Mothra) remained strong. The most important monster movies from this period involved the sequence of zombie films made by George Romero, beginning with *Night of the Living Dead* (1968) and extending through *Diary of the Dead* (2007). These films produced thoughtful political and social commentary of a kind that many have associated more with science fiction than horror and had something of the texture of **postapocalyptic** films, though they had no obvious science fictional explanation for the zombies. They did, however, inspire numerous other zombie films, including a pair of British films, *28 Days Later* (2002) and *28 Weeks Later* (2007), that eventually did supply a science-experiment-gone-wrong origin for the zombies, while maintaining the postapocalyptic atmosphere of the Romero films.

A 1976 remake of *King Kong* was one of the highlights of the genre in the 1970s, but was far less compelling than the original. Probably the most successful sf monster of the 1970s and 1980s was the "xenomorph" of the *Alien* films, though the killer **cyborg** of the *Terminator* films (which began to appear in 1984) is something of a monster as well. Increasing technological capabilities, especially in the realm of **computer-generated imagery** opened new possibilities for monster movies by the end of the 1980s, though the monster movies from the 1990s onward have often relied so heavily on special effects that they have suffered in terms of plot and characterization. **Roland Emmerich**'s 1998 big-budget remake of *Godzilla,* for example, was not well received. Peter Jackson's megabudget remake of *King Kong* (2005) was more successful, though many still felt that it lacked the heart of the original.

The invading Decepticons of *Transformers* (2007) might also be considered monsters, though, as **robots**, they lack the personality that made monsters such as Kong so successful. Executive produced by **Steven Spielberg**, *Transformers* was in many ways reminiscent of Spielberg's own remake of *War of the Worlds* (2005), which employed state-of-the-art special effects to make **H. G. Wells**'s invading Martians into implements of urban obliteration (in New York) that looked back to Godzilla but that also reminded many viewers of the destruction of the World Trade Center on September 11, 2001. The innovative *Cloverfield* (2008) was also widely taken as referring to the 9/11 bombings, though that film was perhaps more notable for its use of images from a shaky handheld camera and for its effective deployment of a monster that was barely even seen on the screen. On the other hand, both *The Zombie Diaries* (2006) and *Diary of the Dead* (2007), which might be considered monster movies, came before *Cloverfield* in that respect, while all of these films owe an obvious debt to *The Blair Witch Project* (1999).

MORROW, JEFF (1907–1993). The journeyman actor Jeff Morrow had a long and varied career that stretched from 1950 to 1986 and included dozens of appearances, even though he turned to professional acting rather late, having first pursued a career as a commercial artist. Most of his appearances were guest spots on various television series, though he appeared in a variety of films as well. He is particularly associated with the science fiction boom of the 1950s, on the basis of four key appearances within a three-year span. In *This Island Earth* (1955), he played the alien envoy Exeter, who comes to earth seeking scientific brain power to import back to his home planet. He then followed as the violent and unstable scientist Dr. William Barton in *The Creature Walks Among Us* (1956), the final installment of the **Creature from the Black Lagoon** trilogy. In 1957, he made two important appearances in sf film. He played test pilot Mitch MacAfee in *The Giant Claw* (a forgettable **monster movie** about a giant killer bird); in *Kronos* (a much more interesting **alien-invasion** film), he played Dr. Leslie Gaskell, who helps lead the fight against an invading planet killer bent on draining earth of all its energy. After these four films, he appeared mostly on television, though he did reprise his standard role as a scientist fighting monsters in the obscure 1971 film *Octaman*.

MULTICULTURAL SCIENCE FICTION FILM. Science fiction film is inherently multicultural, to the extent that science fiction film is a global phenomenon, with films being produced all over the world. Indeed, many sf films are international co-productions involving contributions from companies or individuals from multiple nations or continents. However, science fiction in general, especially in the United States, has a reputation of being primarily the domain of young, white, males. And even science fiction films produced in other parts of the world do not necessarily make an issue of their multiculturalism. For example, Japanese **anime** films, while typically set in Japan, are drawn in a sort of cross-cultural style in which the ethnicity of the characters is indistinct—with all characters in a given film usually having the same ethnicity. There have been, however, a number of important science fiction films that have specifically made racial, ethnic, national, or cultural differences a key part of their subject matter.

As early as the 1950s, some sf films gestured toward the importance of understanding and appreciating other cultures, as when the alien visitor Klaatu in *The Day the Earth Stood Still* (1951) insists on delivering his message from the galactic powers that be to a gathering of scientists from all over the world. Also in 1951, the **postapocalyptic** film *Five* comments on the folly of racism through its depiction of a fascistic white survivor whose racial prejudices survive a nuclear war, with tragic results. Other early examples of films that make a point of multiculturalism include *Conquest of Space* (1955), in which a multicultural international crew (including a Japanese, an Austrian, and a Jewish American, but no Russians, African Americans, or women) travels to Mars. In *Robinson Crusoe on Mars* (1964), a white American astronaut stranded on Mars befriends a slave (with clear Native American ethnic characteristics) who escapes from an interplanetary mining operation that comes to the red planet.

Even as the original *Star Trek* television series (1966–1969) was making a point of the multiculturalism of the crew of the starship *Enterprise*, *Planet of the Apes* (1968) brought multiculturalism in sf film to a new level of prominence with its depiction of a postapocalyptic world in which apes brutally oppress humans as their racial Others. Meanwhile, the sudden reversal in perspective that makes humans the object of race hatred on the part of animals (and, by extension, whites the despised Others of blacks) provides precisely the sort of cognitive jolt that provides all the best science fiction with its principal power. This change in perspective asks audiences to see the senselessness of racism with fresh eyes, and the effect is only enhanced by the fact that the rhetoric of modern racism, as first developed in the 19th century, has long employed the strategy of suggesting that supposedly inferior races are in fact more similar to apes than to genuine human beings.

Meanwhile, racist thinking seems to be a habit among the apes, who also maintain strong, often racist, distinctions between different species of apes as well, suggesting the ways in which racial prejudice can spread beyond its origins to contaminate other social attitudes as well. This focus on racism extends into the sequels to *Planet of the Apes* as well. Particularly clear in this sense is *Conquest of the Planet of the Apes* (1972) set in 1991, eight years after a worldwide plague (caused by a virus brought back from outer space) has killed every dog and cat on earth, leaving humans unaffected. In response, humans have adopted apes (immune to the virus) as pets, but over the years, the apes have gradually become slaves, making the film an overt allegory about slavery and racism.

Science fiction, which so often involves encounters with the Other (including extraterrestrial Others), is partly well suited for the constructions of such allegorical commentaries on racism. The prototype of such commentaries in science fiction is **H. G. Wells**'s *The War of the Worlds* (1898), an **alien-invasion** narrative that was the source of major film adaptations in 1953 and 2005. In Wells's novel (though the motif is less clear in the films) Martian invaders rapaciously overwhelm Great Britain in a mode that is quite transparently meant as a commentary on British colonial conquests in the late 19th century. Indeed, the xenophobia with which humans greet extraterrestrial visitors in any number of sf films can be taken as a commentary on racism, one of the clearest examples of which is the recent alien-invasion film *District 9* (2009), in which a crippled alien ship arrives at the earth, its damaged state depriving the aliens of the technological superiority that they generally enjoy over humans in alien-invasion films. Subsequently, the aliens are brought to earth and consigned to a ghetto (the "District 9" of the title), where they suffer considerable racist abuse in a motif that is further reinforced by the fact that they land in South Africa, a nation whose history is almost synonymous with racist oppression.

Particularly effective as an allegory about racism is Wolfgang Petersen's *Enemy Mine* (1985), in which a human (played by white actor **Dennis Quaid**) and an alien "Drac" (played by African American actor Louis Gossett Jr.) are stranded together on a desolate planet, learning to overcome their mutual racial animosity when they are forced to cooperate in order to survive. In *Alien Nation* (1988), a film successful enough that it triggered a followup TV series and five made-for-TV sequels, a shipload of alien slaves crash lands on earth; the aliens, or "Newcomers," then attempt to assimilate into earth society, but encounter considerable racial prejudice as they attempt to do so. Meanwhile, aliens are not the only Others who have figured in science fiction film. In *Gattaca* (1997), for example, **genetic engineering** has become so prevalent that the unengineered are discriminated against as inherently deficient. And, in **Steven Spielberg's** *Artificial Intelligence: AI* (2001), human suspicion of and animosity toward **robots** serves as a commentary on racism, in a motif that dates back at least to the robot stories and novels of **Isaac Asimov**, in which "racist" prejudices against robots play a central role.

In addition to providing such critiques of racism, science fiction film has been on the forefront of multiculturalism in American society in the sense that the casts of science fiction films, from the eclectic crew of *Star Trek's* original *Enterprise* onward, have been interracial or international, among other providing important opportunities for actors of varied ethnicities. Indeed, beginning with his appearance in *Independence Day* (1996), the African American actor **Will Smith** has probably been the biggest star in science fiction film.

MYSTERY SCIENCE THEATER 3000. *Mystery Science Theater 3000* (*MST3K*) is a comic cable television program in which a hapless janitor (originally played by the show's creator Joel Hodgson, then by writer Mike Nelson) is launched into space and forced to watch bad B movies (generally science fiction) by a pair of **mad scientists**. Accompanied by intelligent **robots** that he builds himself, the janitor wisecracks his way through the films, providing sarcastic commentary that is generally more entertaining than the films themselves. Numerous bad sf films, especially from the 1950s, are probably now best known through their appearance on *MST3K*. However, the 1996 feature-film version of the series centered on the rather good 1955 film *This Island Earth,* because producers felt that the kind of bad films usually seen in the series would not attract theatergoers. *MST3K* got its start on local Minneapolis–St. Paul television station KTMA in 1988, then moved to the national Comedy Channel cable network in 1989 and aired there until 1996, by which time The Comedy Channel had become Comedy Central. It then aired on the Sci Fi cable channel until 1999. A cult hit, the series was ranked 11th in *TV Guide's* 2004 list of the "25 Top Cult Shows Ever."

– N –

NATURAL CITY. (Dir. Min Byung-chun, 2003.) Widely touted as the "Korean *Blade Runner,*" *Natural City* is a stylish action thriller that does, in fact, have a great deal in common with **Ridley Scott's** 1982 classic, especially in its effective visual representation of a future megacity. Set in the year 2080, *Natural City* is a gorgeous film that envisions a world of flying cars and floating billboards where humans intermingle with **cyborgs**, though the latter definitely represent an oppressed group. As in *Blade Runner,* for example, they are manufactured with life-specific expiration dates that presumably give them lifespans short enough to prevent them from becoming bitter and rebellious in response to their subjugation. Also like *Blade Runner, Natural City* features special police who are charged with tracking down and terminating any cyborgs who nevertheless do rebel. Two of these police, R (Yu Ji-tae) and Noma (Yun Chang), stumble upon a secret plot to develop the technology to transfer the consciousness of a cyborg into a human body, thus allowing the cyborg to live out a normal human lifespan. Meanwhile, their investigation is complicated by the fact that R has fallen in love with Ria (Rin Seo), his companion cyborg, or "doll," whose expiration date is nearing. As a result, R is tempted to try to use the illicit technology to transfer Ria's consciousness into the body of Cyon (Lee Jae-un), a young, orphan streetwalker. The plot thickens as it becomes clear that this technology is part of a larger plan for a largescale cyborg uprising, led by Cyper (Jung Doo-hong), a sort of supercyborg. After a number of extended high-action battle scenes typical of **Korean science**

fiction film, Ria is allowed to expire, the rebellion is thwarted, and life returns to normal in the city.

NAUSICAÄ OF THE VALLEY OF THE WIND. (Dir. **Hayao Miyazaki,** 1984.) *Nausicaä of the Valley of the Wind* (Japanese title *Kaze no tani no Naushika*) is an **anime** film that includes numerous elements of the fantasy-adventure genre, but that resides primarily within the realm of science fiction. In particular, it is a **postapocalyptic** film set 1000 years after wars ravaged the face of the earth, leaving civilization in ruins and the earth in a state of environmental collapse. The film thus embodies in a particularly clear way the themes of antimilitarism and **environmentalism** that have been central to much of director Miyazaki's career. It is also typical of Miyazaki's films in employing a female protagonist, the young and heroic *Nausicaä* (voiced in the **Disney**-produced English-language version by Alison Lohman), Princess of the Valley of the Wind, one of several enclaves in which human settlements still persist. Most of the planet, however, is covered by a toxic forest ("Sea of Decay" in the Japanese original) inhabited by giant, deadly insects, a forest that is gradually advancing, covering more and more of the earth's surface.

As it turns out, this forest, though it is deadly to humans, is actually cleansing the earth of toxins put there by earlier human activity, including the cataclysmic war. It thus represents a sort of revenge by the earth on the humans who ravaged it, though it is primarily simply a self-healing strategy on the part of the earth. Meanwhile, most of the plot of the film involves the efforts of two rival city-states, Pejite and Tolmekia, to gain control of a surviving "warrior," one of the gigantic, living war machines that were central to the earlier war. Each state hopes to use the warrior not only to gain dominance over the other, but to destroy the advancing forest and reassert human dominion over the earth. Nausicaä, however, realizes that the consequences of these plans could be the destruction of the earth's environment once and for all and manages to lead a successful effort to destroy the warrior and thwart these plans, allowing the earth to continue the process of healing itself, but perhaps more in harmony with the surviving humans who now understand the value of the forest.

The success of *Nausicaä* enabled Miyazaki to found his own studio (Studio Ghibli), which subsequently became the most important force in Japanese children's animated film, comparable in some ways to the role played in the United States by the Walt Disney Company, which now produces and distributes English-language versions of Miyazaki's films in the United States and elsewhere. Winner of the Animage Anime Grand Prix in 1984, *Nausicaä* put Miyazaki's much-heralded career into high gear. Miyazaki himself also produced an accompanied **manga** version of the story, which appeared in serial form from 1982 to 1994. *See also* JAPANESE SCIENCE FICTION FILM.

NEUMANN, KURT (1908–1958). The German-born director Kurt Neumann came to the United States upon the advent of the "talkie," when he was brought in to direct German-language versions of Hollywood films for distribution in his home country. Having mastered English, he quickly moved into directing original films of his own, though generally of the low-budget variety. He is now best known for the science fiction films that he directed late in his career, including *Rocketship X-M* (1950), one of the first films of the science fiction explosion of the 1950s. He followed that film with some undistinguished efforts in other genres, but returned to sf with *Kronos* (1957), an **alien-invasion** narrative that foreshadows later real-world energy crises. *She Devil,* released in the same year, is a hybrid of horror and science fiction. He followed with what is probably his best-known film, the cheesy but strikingly effective horror-sf hybrid *The Fly* (1958). He died, however, shortly before that film was released.

NICCOL, ANDREW (1964–). The New Zealand–born screenwriter and director Andrew Niccol first came to prominence in Hollywood as the writer and director of the **genetic-engineering** thriller *Gattaca* in 1997. A year later, he followed as the writer and producer of *The Truman Show,* a critique of media manipulation with strong science fictional elements. Niccol wrote, produced, and directed the virtual-reality drama *Simone* (2002), which also addresses media manipulation in its focus on a computer-generated film star. After work in other genres, Niccol returned to science fiction as the writer, producer, and director of *The Cross* (2010), an international production filmed in Australia.

NIMOY, LEONARD (1931–). The American actor, director, and photographer Leonard Nimoy will no doubt always be best remembered by science fiction fans for his role as **Spock**, the ultralogical half-Vulcan science officer and first mate aboard the USS *Enterprise* in the original *Star Trek* television series. Nimoy reenacted that role in the first six *Star Trek* theatrical films, in which Spock rose to the rank of captain (not to mention rising from the dead). Nimoy also directed the third and fourth *Star Trek* films. He returned to the role of Spock in the 2009 reboot of the *Star Trek* film franchise. Though never able to overcome audience identification of him with the character of Spock, Nimoy has played a number of other roles over the years, many of them in science fiction films. He had a prominent role in the 1978 remake of *Invasion of the Body Snatchers,* and also appeared in made-for-TV sf films such as *Brave New World* (1998) and *The Lost World* (1998). In the 2009 tongue-in-cheek sf **adventure** *Land of the Lost,* Nimoy provided the voice of the Zarn, a murdered alien who has left behind a holographic message. Nimoy also did voiceover work in the original animated film version of *The Transformers* (1986) and in *Atlantis: The Lost Empire* (2001).

– O –

O'BANNON, DAN (1946–2009). The American writer, director, and actor Dan O'Bannon got his start in science fiction film while still a student at the University of Southern California, where he worked on a short student film entitled *Dark Star* with fellow student **John Carpenter**. O'Bannon later worked as a writer, editor, and actor on Carpenter's subsequent full-length commercial version of the film, released in 1974. After working as a computer animator on the original *Star Wars,* O'Bannon was hired to supervise the **special effects** for a proposed film adaptation of Frank Herbert's classic 1965 sf novel *Dune,* to be directed by Chilean Alejandro Jodorowsky. That project fell through, leaving O'Bannon destitute, though he sprang back as the co-author (with **Ronald Shusett**) of the story that formed the basis for **Ridley Scott's** *Alien* (1979). He also helped to pull together much of the creative talent from the *Dune* project to work on *Alien.* In 1985, O'Bannon directed and wrote the script for *Return of* *the Living Dead,* a zombie film that spoofs George Romero's *Living Dead* films. That same year, O'Bannon co-wrote (with horror writer Don Jakoby) the script for *Lifeforce,* a British-produced combination **space opera** and vampire film, directed by Tobe Hooper. In 1986, O'Bannon and Jakoby wrote the script for Hooper's remake of the 1953 **alien-invasion** classic *Invaders from Mars.* O'Bannon and Shusett co-wrote the script for **Paul Verhoeven**'s *Total Recall* (1990), based on a short story by **Philip K. Dick.** In 1995, O'Bannon and Miguel Tejada-Flores co-scripted another adaptation from a Dick story, released as *Screamers.*

O'BRIEN, WILLIS (1886–1962). Though less well known than his protégé **Ray Harryhausen,** Willis O'Brien was a true pioneer in the use of models to create **stop-motion animation.** O'Brien was producing stop-motion effects for films as early as 1915, with *The Dinosaur and the Missing Link: A Prehistoric Tragedy.* In 1925, he produced the **special effects** for the original silent film version of *The Lost World,* and in 1933 he created his most famous work, the **dinosaurs** and the giant ape of *King Kong* (1933). O'Brien also did the special effects for the sequel, *The Son of Kong* (1933), and for the later Kong-inspired *Mighty Joe Young* (1949). After that, O'Brien worked only sparingly, and generally on obscure projects, though he did work as an effects technician on the 1960 version of *The Lost World.* In 1997, O'Brien was given a posthumous lifetime achievement award from the International Animated Film Society.

OBOLER, ARCH (1909–1987). Born in Chicago, the son of Latvian immigrants, Arch Oboler became a successful, but sometimes controversial, script writer for radio plays in the 1930s, specializing in horror. He moved into film in the 1940s and into science fiction film in 1951 when he wrote, produced, and directed *Five* (1951), an early **postapocalyptic** film shot largely at Oboler's own Frank Lloyd Wright–designed house. He followed with the action-adventure film *Bwana Devil* (1952), distinguished mostly by its pioneering use of 3-D **special effects.** He returned to science fiction in 1953 as the writer, producer, and director of *The Twonky* (1953), an entertaining sf satirical comedy about a professor whose new television set is possessed by an entity from the future. Oboler subsequently wrote for Broadway and television, but returned to sf film with *The Bubble* (1966), an **alien-invasion** film again notable primarily for its use of 3-D effects.

ORGANA, LEIA. Princess Leia Organa (played by Carrie Fisher) is one of the central protagonists of the first *Star Wars* trilogy. When first introduced in *Star Wars: Episode IV—A New Hope* (1977), Princess Leia, a former Senator of the Republic, is acting as a spy for the forces that are rebelling against the evil Empire that has supplanted the Republic. She is captured by **Darth Vader**, but only after she has stolen the plans for the Death Star, a powerful new planet-killing weapon being developed by the Empire. She has hidden the plans inside the Astromech droid **R2-D2**, which she has sent to the planet Tatooine in search of **Obi-Wan Kenobi**, whom Leia hopes can get the plans to the rebel forces, which can use them to design an attack against the Death Star. Leia eventually escapes, joining Kenobi, **Luke Skywalker**, and **Han Solo** to become one of the best-known hero teams in all of science fiction film. As the first trilogy proceeds, Leia eventually becomes the wife of Solo. It is also revealed that she is the twin sister of Skywalker, the two having been separated at birth and sent on separate ways in the hope of concealing them from their father, **Anakin Skywalker**, already well along the dark path that will lead him to become Darth Vader. Though less effective in this regard than characters such as **Ellen Ripley** of the *Alien* sequence or **Sarah Connor** of the *Terminator* sequence, Leia is a strong, heroic woman character with potential for delivering positive messages about feminine capability. *See also* FEMINISM AND GENDER.

OSHII, MAMORU (1951–). The Japanese filmmaker Mamoru Oshii has made important contributions to both **anime** and live-action film with his philosophically complex, visually inventive films. He has also worked extensively as a manga artist, and has based many of his films on manga. Citing Chris Marker's *La jetée* (1962) as an important early influence (along with the work of numerous other European filmmakers), Oshii broke into directing in the early 1980s with the *Urusei Yatsura* animated television series, which led him to direct two spinoff films of this **alien-invasion** story,

Urusei yatsura 1: Onri yû (1983, *Urusei Yatsura: Only You*) and *Urusei Yatsura: Byûtifuru dorîmâ* (1984, *Urusei Yatsura: Beautiful Dreamer*). In 1989, Oshii directed another anime science fiction film, *Kidô keisatsu patorebâ: Gekijô-ban* (*Patlabor: The Movie*), as part of an extensive franchise involving manga, serial television, and straight-to-video films, as well as this theatrical film and its eventual theatrical sequel, *Kidô keisatsu patorebâ: The Movie 2* (1993, *Patlabor 2: The Movie*).

In 1987, he directed the live-action **dystopian** film *Jigoku no banken: akai megane* (*The Red Spectacles*), which also went on to be part of an extensive multimedia franchise (the "Kerberos Saga"), including two feature-film sequels, the live-action *Jigoku no banken: kerubersu* (1991, *Stray Dog: Kerberos Panzer Cops*) and the animated *Tachiguishi retsuden* (2006, *Amazing Lives of the Fast Food Grifters*). In the West, however, Oshii is probably best known as the director of the anime **cyberpunk** film *Kôkaku kidôtai* (1995, ***Ghost in the Shell***), as well as its sequel, *Innocence* (2004, *Ghost in the Shell 2: Innocence*), which became the first animated film to be nominated for the Palme d'Or at the Cannes Film Festival. He also directed the Japanese-Polish live-action co-production *Avalon* (2001), a **virtual-reality** thriller that centers on a video game. *See also* JAPANESE SCIENCE FICTION FILM.

– P –

PAL, GEORGE (1908–1980). Prolific producer George Pal was one of the central movers behind the science fiction film explosion of the 1950s. Born in Cegléd in what was then Austria-Hungary, Pal had already been extremely active in the European film industry in the 1930s, directing numerous films, including many animated with his own patented "Puppetoon" process. He emigrated to the United States in 1940 to escape the Nazis and began to work for Paramount Studios, mostly as the producer and director of Puppetoon shorts. Pal hit his real stride when he moved into the production of science fiction films beginning with ***Destination Moon*** in 1950. He quickly followed with ***When Worlds Collide*** in 1951 and ***The War of the Worlds*** in 1953. The director of the latter was **Byron Haskin**, beginning a collaboration between producer Pal and director Haskin that also included *The Naked Jungle* (1954), **Conquest of Space** (1955), and *The Power* (1968). Pal both produced and directed **The Time Machine** (1960) and *Atlantis, The Lost Continent* (1961). His science fiction films are marked by an imaginative visual style that shows the influence of his background in animation and sets them apart from many of the other sf films of his era.

PIDGEON, WALTER (1897–1984). Walter Pidgeon had already had a long and distinguished career when he was cast to play the key role of Dr. Edward Morbius in *Forbidden Planet* (1956). He had received Best Actor Academy Award nominations for his roles in *Mrs. Miniver* (1942) and *Madame Curie* (1943) and had gained considerable visibility with his starring role in the Oscar-winning *How Green Was My Valley* (1941). Indeed, the casting of this distinguished British actor in *Forbidden Planet* was a sign of the desire of this science fiction film to be taken seriously as a work of art. Ironically, the role of Morbius is probably the one for which Pidgeon is now best remembered. He was similarly cast as Admiral Harriman Nelson in an effort to add gravity to **Irwin Allen**'s *Voyage to the Bottom of the Sea* (1961) and returned to the undersea world in *The Neptune Factor* (1973), playing the director of an underwater oceanographic research lab that is lost in an earthquake. In his later years he became a familiar face on American television, starring in several made-for-TV movies and guest starring in numerous series. In 1975, Pidgeon was given a Lifetime Achievement Award by the Screen Actors' Guild.

PIPER, RODDY (1954–). After a highly successful career as a professional wrestler, the Canadian-born Roddy Piper became one of a number of muscle-bound actors who attempted to emulate the success of **Arnold Schwarzenegger** in science fiction and action films. His first starring role in a science fiction film was as protagonist Sam Hell in the **postapocalyptic** film *Hell Comes to Frogtown* (1988), a campy take-off on the *Mad Max* films. This film highlighted Piper's unusual on-screen charisma, which helped to make up for a noticeable lack of talent as an actor. His unusual skill set was put to particularly effective use in **John Carpenter**'s satirical **alien-invasion** narrative *They Live* (1988), but from there it was pretty much downhill, though he managed to land numerous action-oriented roles. In science fiction, he played the lead role in the straight-to-video *Sci-fighters* (1996) and had a major supporting role in the Canadian postapocalyptic film *Shepherd* (1999).

PIXAR. Pixar Animation Studios is the industry leader in the production of state-of-the-art computer animated films for children and families. The company began as the computer graphics group of **George Lucas**'s **Lucasfilm** studio, but was then sold off to Steve Jobs in 1986. Under his leadership, they evolved from what at first was primarily a computer hardware company into an important film production company, producing a number of innovative short computer animated films before making a major breakthrough with *Toy Story* (1995), the first film to be entirely generated using computer animation. That film and its sequel, *Toy Story 2* (1999), make use of science fictional imagery; for example, one of the central characters is "Buzz Lightyear," a toy spaceman marketed in conjunction with a children's science fiction television program. Similarly, the Pixar film *Monsters, Inc.* (2001) makes use of the common science fictional conceit of parallel worlds, while building centrally upon the tradition of the **monster movie**. In some ways, though, Pixar's films themselves verge on science fiction, because each film pushes the boundaries of computer animation technology into unprecedented realms. The commercial success of Pixar's films is also unprecedented: each of their 10 theatrical releases has been a major blockbuster hit at the box office. Meanwhile, Pixar moved into science fiction proper with *WALL-E* (2008), a **postapocalyptic** film that includes important **space opera** elements and features a title character that is a **robot**. Their next film, *Up* (2009), includes a number of elements of the sf **adventure** genre and also features a villain who is something of a **mad scientist**. *See also* ANIMATED SCIENCE FICTION FILMS; CHILDREN'S SCIENCE FICTION; COMPUTER-GENERATED IMAGERY (CGI).

PLAGUE. Science fiction films often deal with the potentially catastrophic effects of plagues and contagions, or, alternatively, with efforts to prevent the outbreak of such a plague. For example, in the realm of **postapocalyptic** films, the apocalypse involved has often been some sort of plague. One of the prototypes for this sort of narrative is **Richard Matheson**'s 1954 novel *I Am Legend,* in which a mysterious plague transforms most of the world's population into vampires, except for one lone human survivor. This novel has been adapted to film three times, as *The Last Man on Earth* (1964), *The Omega Man* (1971), and *I Am Legend* (2007), with Vincent Price, **Charlton Heston,** and **Will Smith** as the respective sole survivors. In many ways, the vampires of these films (and the original novel) seem more like zombies than traditional vampires. Indeed, one of the classic forms of the postapocalyptic plague film deals with the motif of the "zombie apocalypse." After all, zombies themselves are typically carriers of contagion in that their bites are generally infectious. Moreover, the zombies are quite often created by some sort of virus or other deadly biological agent in the first place. George Romero's classic sequence of zombie films does not specify a virus or other biological agent as the original cause of the zombie outbreak, but Romero's film *The Crazies* (1973) concerns a virus that is engineered for combat by the military but gets loose and threatens to turn the entire population into rabid killing machines.

Such scientifically engineered viruses have become especially popular as causes for zombie outbreaks in more recent films, including such examples as **Danny Boyle**'s *28 Days Later* (2002), which presents graphic images of a desolate London, devastated by zombies produced by a virus that is accidentally released from an experimental laboratory, triggering a plague that spreads rapidly because those infected by zombie bites themselves turn into murderous zombies within seconds. Similarly, research conducted by the sinister Umbrella Corporation leads to the release of a virus that causes a zombie apocalypse in the *Resident Evil* sequence: *Resident Evil* (2002), *Resident Evil: Apocalypse* (2004), and *Resident Evil: Extinction* (2007). In addition, the postapocalyptic film *Doomsday* (2008) is set in a future Scotland that has been quarantined from the rest of the world due to the outbreak of a deadly virus there and has subsequently descended into a violent state somewhat reminiscent of the *Mad Max* films. The release of an experimental biological agent in *Planet Terror* (2007) also triggers a plague of zombies, though this over-the-top, tongue-in-cheek effort is as much a send-up (though a celebratory one) of the zombie genre as an example of it. Finally, in

Quarantine (2008), an American remake of the 2007 Spanish film *REC,* a virus stolen from a military research facility leads to the outbreak of a plague that turns the infected into crazed killers.

In other sf films, plagues operate more conventionally, infecting and killing their victims rather than turning them into zombies or vampires. Plagues began to figure in this way in science fiction films as early as 1936, when the British film *Things to Come,* scripted by science fiction pioneer **H. G. Wells** and based on his book *The Shape of Things to Come* (1933), looked at the future of the city of Everytown, which at one point is virtually destroyed by a deadly plague that sweeps the globe as the result of the use of biological weapons. In this case, the city is rebuilt by visionaries who make it a sort of utopia. Other post-plague scenarios are not so optimistic. In *Twelve Monkeys* (1995) a deadly virus wipes out most of the population of the earth, driving the survivors into underground refuges. Scientists in this postapocalyptic future then send an agent back in time to before the outbreak to try to recover unmutated samples of the virus so that they can try to develop a cure.

The plague in *Twelve Monkeys* decimates the human population, leaving the surface to the "cats and dogs." In a reversal of this motif, *Conquest of the Planet of the Apes* (1972) is set in 1991, eight years after a worldwide plague (caused by a virus brought back from outer space) has killed every cat and dog on earth, leaving humans unaffected. In response, humans have adopted apes (immune to the virus) as pets, but over the years, the apes have gradually become slaves, making the film an overt allegory about slavery and racism. Another key plague film, *The Andromeda Strain* (1971), also features a microorganism from outer space, but this one is immediately deadly to humans, leading scientists to race against the clock in an effort to find a way to neutralize it. They barely avoid a disaster when they nearly try to destroy the contagion with a nuclear bomb—which would only have supercharged it with energy, likely leading to a worldwide outbreak. Meanwhile, both a deadly plague and a nuclear holocaust threaten to wipe out the human race in the big-budget Japanese production *Virus* (1980). And a contagion from outer space is also the central threat in the **alien-invasion** narrative *The Invasion* (2007), which reworks *Invasion of the Body Snatchers* (1956) from the original replacement-by-alien-replicants motif to one of more straightforward infection. Then again, the motif of alien contagions from outer space in sf film goes back at least to *The Quatermass Xperiment* (1955). Meanwhile, in a reversal of this motif, the American film *Virus* (1999) features alien invaders who think that humans are a virus infecting the earth and thus attempt to eradicate the species.

If fears of contagion from outer space have often informed science fiction films, fears of germs from other parts of the world have provided numerous science fiction plots as well. Probably the best-known film of this variety is Wolfgang Petersen's *Outbreak* (1995) in which an all-star cast led by Dustin Hoffman races against time to prevent the runaway outbreak of a deadly virus brought back from Africa by a monkey. Meanwhile, in one of the many ways in which the film recalls motifs from *The Andromeda Strain*, they have to avert a plan by a sinister general to cover up the military's role in the development of the virus by bombing the town where the outbreak has started. *Outbreak,* however, responded most directly to contemporary concerns about exotic contagions from Africa, such as the Ebola virus and (especially) the human immunodeficiency virus.

PLANET OF THE APES. (Dir. Franklin Schaffner, 1968.) *Planet of the Apes* joined **Stanley Kubrick**'s *2001: A Space Odyssey* as one of two landmark sf films to be released in 1968, bringing an end to several relatively slow years in the genre. *Planet of the Apes* is an impressive bit of filmmaking that broke new technical ground, especially via the makeup, designed by **John Chambers**, with which it transformed human actors into believable simian characters. A **postapocalyptic** film that envisions a future earth dominated by apes after humans have destroyed their own civilization, it also addresses themes such as racism, the generation gap, and fundamental social injustices in ways that resonated greatly with audiences in the tumultuous year in which it was released. This film, which details the experiences of a group of American astronauts who are inadvertently propelled into the ape-ruled future of earth (thinking they have landed on a strange planet) is one of the most iconic of all sf films and includes some of sf film's most memorable scenes—as in the moment when the astronaut Taylor (**Charlton Heston**) discovers the ruins of the Statue of Liberty at the end of the film and realizes at last that he is on a postapocalyptic earth.

The success of the original *Planet of the Apes* led to the making of four sequels. *Beneath the Planet of the Apes* (1970) is a direct followup involving a mission that is sent to rescue Taylor and his crew. Taylor himself even returns, ending the film by setting off a doomsday device that will presumably destroy all life on earth. *Escape from the Planet of the Apes* (1971) reverses the scenario of the first two films by featuring a crew of apes from the future who fly a spacecraft (having escaped the conflagration of the second film) back in time to the human-ruled earth of the 1970s. Here, the apes are the sympathetic protagonists, while the humans mostly greet them in a mode of savage xenophobia. *Conquest of the Planet of the Apes* (1972) is an overt allegory about slavery and racism. It is set in 1991, eight years after a worldwide **plague** (caused by a virus brought back from outer space) has killed every cat and dog on earth. In response, humans have adopted apes (immune to the virus) as pets, but over the years, the apes have gradually become slaves. Finally, *Battle for the Planet of the Apes* (1973) is set several years later, after a nuclear holocaust has largely destroyed human civilization. The events of this film pave the way for peaceful human and ape coexistence, possibly leading to a change in the course of history that will prevent the baleful consequences outlined in the first two *Apes* films. *Planet of the Apes* also inspired two unsuccessful television series. It was remade as a big-budget feature film in 2001, with director **Tim Burton** shifting the cause of the decline of humanity from nuclear holocaust to **genetic engineering**. Visually impressive, the remake is otherwise muddled and unremarkable.

PLANET OF THE VAMPIRES. (Dir. **Mario Bava**, 1965.) Co-produced by **American International Pictures** and Italy's International Film, *Planet of the Vampires* (Italian title *Terrore nello spazio*) employs an international cast and serves as a landmark in the development of international co-productions in sf film. It also combines genres, endowing a science fictional premise with the atmosphere of a horror film, thus serving as a predecessor for later films such as the *Alien* sequence. Here, two spaceships land on the planet Aura, only to find that the denizens of this dying world have lured them there to inhabit the bodies of their crew members, subsequently to escape Aura on the ships. When the crew members resist this plan, the Aurans decide to kill them and inhabit their reanimated dead bodies. Despite the best efforts of the newcomers to resist this alien possession, this nefarious plan succeeds, and the film ends as one of the ships sails through space carrying two of the possessed and reanimated corpses, though the ship itself is damaged. As a result, the "vampires" decide to land on and colonize an obscure little world that they happen to be passing near. It is called "earth" and is the third planet from the star "Sol."

POSTAPOCALYPTIC. Tales involving cataclysmic disaster and its aftermath are among the oldest narratives in human culture. However, in the years following World War II, the combination of cold-war tensions and nuclear proliferation brought an unprecedented urgency to such stories. Accordingly, the postapocalyptic narrative was one of the central subgenres in the explosion of production in sf film that marked the 1950s, especially in the United States. Beginning with **Arch Oboler**'s *Five* (1951), one film after another envisioned the destruction of civilization (usually by nuclear war, but also by other catastrophes), followed by a depiction of the struggles of survivors in the postapocalypse world. Some of these visions of apocalyptic destruction and its aftermath, including *Invasion U.S.A.* (1952), *Red Planet Mars* (1952), and *The 27th Day* (1957), overtly promoted a paranoid fear (and hatred) of communism as a dehumanizing force, often with invading aliens standing in for invading communists. **Roger Corman** entered the fray with such films as *Day the World Ended* (1955), one of the few films of the decade to depict the imagined effects of radiation on humans. For example, one of the most popular (and expensive) postapocalyptic films of the decade was Stanley Kramer's *On the Beach* (1959), which shows no such effects. In this film, set in 1964 and based on the bestselling postholocaust novel of the 1950s, Nevil Shute's 1957 Australian novel of the same title, a global nuclear war has apparently destroyed all human life everywhere on earth, except Australia, where the characters of the film await certain death from the clouds of deadly radiation that are slowly but inexorably drifting toward their continent as well.

Ray Milland's *Panic in Year Zero* (1962) resembles *On the Beach* in its focus on the human drama of the survivors of the disaster, not the human tragedy of the victims. The film is essentially a survivalist adventure, in which a resourceful family meets the challenges of the living in the aftermath of nuclear catastrophe. A British film, **Val Guest's** *The Day the Earth Caught Fire,* released in 1961, is less romantic in its dramatization of nuclear-related destruction, but it displaces this destruction from nuclear war to nuclear testing, which inadvertently sends the earth careening off course and hurtling toward the sun. In this sense, Guest's film is something of a forerunner to **Danny Boyle's** *Sunshine* (2007), which details an attempt to reignite the sun after it begins to die, threatening the earth with extermination, though Boyle's film is more a gritty **space opera** than a postapocalyptic narration proper. The short 1962 French film, *La jetée,* captured a haunting postapocalypse world mostly through still images and ultimately provided much of the inspiration for Terry Gilliam's time-travel–postapocalyptic narrative, *Twelve Monkeys* (1995). Visions of apocalypse crept into other subgenres of sf film as early as the 1950s, as when the explorers of *Rocketship X-M* (1950) encounter the aftereffects of a nuclear war on **Mars** or when time travelers in *World without End* (1956) or **George Pal's** *The Time Machine* (1960) discover postapocalyptic futures. Meanwhile, **Richard Matheson's** thoughtful postapocalyptic last-man-on-earth–vampire tale *I Am Legend* (1954) eventually inspired a number of film adaptations over the years, including *The Last Man on Earth* (1964, starring Vincent Price), *The Omega Man* (1971, starring **Charlton Heston**), and *I Am Legend* (2007, starring **Will Smith**).

Stanley Kubrick's *Dr. Strangelove or: How I Learned to Stop Worrying and Love the Bomb* (1964) satirized the follies of the cold-war nuclear arms race so effectively that it virtually ended the production of postapocalyptic films for years to come. Still, the notion of an apocalyptic end to human civilization remained very much a part of the modern imagination and had an important impact on such films as *Planet of the Apes* (1968). The initiation of George Romero's sequence of zombie films occurred in 1968 with *Night of the Living Dead,* a sequence that brought the postapocalyptic narrative to the horror genre, where it remained with such later zombie narratives as the *Resident Evil* films (2002–2007) and Boyle's *28 Days Later*

(2002) and its sequel, *28 Weeks Later* (2007). Possible future apocalypse was also very much at the center of such early 1970s films as **Robert Wise**'s *The Andromeda Strain* (1971), **Douglas Trumbull**'s *Silent Running* (1972), **Richard Fleischer**'s *Soylent Green* (1973), and Michael Anderson's *Logan's Run* (1976). The focus of these films began to shift from visions of nuclear holocaust to a variety of environmental or biological catastrophes, though *A Boy and His Dog* (1975) again focused on a post–nuclear war world.

Science fiction film began to swing toward more positive visions with the success of *Star Wars* (1977). However, spurred by the alarmist rhetoric (and aggressive policies) of the Ronald Reagan Administration in the United States and the Margaret Thatcher Administration in Great Britain, postapocalyptic sf films experienced a worldwide resurgence in the 1980s. The most important of these was the sequence of *Mad Max* films from Australia, which had already begun with the low-budget *Mad Max* in 1979, but which came to the fore with *Mad Max 2: The Road Warrior* (1981), which made **Mel Gibson** a star and produced a violent vision of the postapocalyptic future that crucially influenced any number of subsequent films. A second sequel, *Mad Max Beyond Thunderdome,* followed in 1985. The success of the *Mad Max* films helped to inspire a sequence of ultraviolent Italian postapocalyptic films, including *1990: I guerrieri del Bronx* (1982, *1990: The Bronx Warriors*), *I nuovi barbari* (1982, *The New Barbarians*), and *2019—Dopo la caduta di New York* (1983, *2019: After the Fall of New York*). The best of the films in this vein, however, was probably **John Carpenter**'s *Escape from New York* (1981), which spawned a much-later sequel, *Escape from L.A.* (1996). In other American films, the particularly campy *Max Hell* sequence, beginning with *Hell Comes to Frogtown* (1988), was essentially a parody of the *Mad Max* movies, as can be seen from the title of the second film in the sequence, *Toad Warrior* (1996). **Luc Besson**'s *Le dernier combat* (*The Last Combat,* 1983), was a particularly interesting example of the early 1980s postapocalyptic film, marked by a number of striking black-and-white visuals. More thoughtful postapocalyptic films continued to appear in the 1980s as well, including New Zealand's *The Quiet Earth* (1985), while graphic depictions of the possible aftereffects of a nuclear war were central to such U.S. films of the 1980s as *Testament* (1983) and

Nicholas Meyer's made-for-TV film *The Day After* (1983); *Threads* (1984) is a British entry in the same vein.

The initiation of the **Terminator** sequence in 1984 ushered in an important sequence of apocalypse-related sf films that ran into the 21st century. The human versus machine scenario of the *Terminator* films is also central to the sequence of films that began with *The Matrix* (1999), involving a postapocalyptic future in which humans have been overthrown by their own machines. Meanwhile, films such as *Waterworld* (1995), *The Postman* (1997), *Six-String Samurai* (1998), *Reign of Fire* (2002), *The Day After Tomorrow* (2004), ***Children of Men*** (2006), *Doomsday* (2008), and *2012* (2009) continued to demonstrate the relevance of such narratives in the post–cold war era in Great Britain and the United States. These films were again dominated by visions of environmental or biological catastrophes, though *Reign of Fire* adds the twist that the apocalypse is caused by a worldwide attack of dragons (here with a scientific, rather than magical explanation). **Pixar**'s *WALL-E* (2008) even brought the motif of environmental apocalypse to **animated science fiction film**, though in fact **Hayao Miyazaki**'s Japanese *Kaze no tani no Naushika* (1984, *Nausicaä of the Valley of the Wind*) had done the same as early as 1984. *WALL-E* was then followed in 2009 by Shane Acker's much darker *9* (produced by **Tim Burton**), a visually inventive animated postapocalyptic film that seems much more aimed at adults, borrowing its apocalyptic scenario from machine vs. man conflicts such as those in the *Terminator* and *Matrix* films. Postapocalyptic elements are also crucial to Japan's *Nihon chinbotsu* (1973, *Japan Sinks,* remade with the same title in 2006), *Virus* (1980), and ***Casshern*** (2004), as well as a number of **anime** films, indicating the ongoing global reach of the subgenre. *See also* ENVIRONMENTALISM; ITALIAN SCIENCE FICTION FILM.

PROYAS, ALEX (1963–). Alex Proyas was born in Egypt to Greek parents who moved with him to Australia when he was three years old. After growing up there, he moved to Los Angeles to pursue a film career, which he began by directing music videos and television commercials. However, his first feature film, the science fiction thriller *Spirits of the Air, Gremlins of the Clouds* (1989) was made in Australia and garnered little attention worldwide. However, Proyas gained considerable attention for his direction of the visually striking comic-book adaptation *The Crow* (1994). Many of the same dark, urban images can also be found in *Dark City* (1998), a science fiction reality-bender that he wrote and produced, as well as directed. The success of this film gained Proyas the assignment of directing *I, Robot* (2004), a big-budget action film dominated by state-of-the-art **special effects**. In 2009, Proyas wrote, produced, and directed another big-budget science fiction film *Knowing* (2009), an end-of-the-world–**alien-invasion** drama. Though less prolific than many directors, Proyas has a growing body of solid science fiction films to his credit that seems to bode well for the future.

– Q –

QUAID, DENNIS (1954–). The journeyman American actor Dennis Quaid has had a long and prolific career in Hollywood film, typically in lead roles, without ever quite reaching the top levels of movie stardom. Beginning with Wolfgang Petersen's *Enemy Mine* (1985), a number of Quaid's most prominent roles have been in science fiction films. In 1987 he starred as a Navy pilot reduced to microscopic size in the sf action **comedy** *Innerspace*. In *Frequency* (2000) he played a firefighter who communicates across time with the future adult version of his young son; he then returned to a paternal role as a heroic climatologist who braves a global warming–induced arctic storm to save his son in *The Day After Tomorrow* (2004). He did voiceover work in the animated *Battle for Terra* (2007) and had a major role as General Hawk, commander of the elite G. I. Joe team in the sf-action film *G.I. Joe: The Rise of Cobra* (2009). He starred as an astronaut aboard a haunted spacecraft in *Pandorum* (2009).

THE QUIET EARTH. (Dir. Geoff Murphy, 1985.) An interesting **postapocalyptic** film made and set in New Zealand, *The Quiet Earth* at first focuses on scientist Zac Hobson (Bruno Lawrence) who awakens one morning to find that he is apparently the last man left alive on earth. Hobson concludes that the situation is the result of the runaway side-effects of a scientific experiment in which he had participated, though in which Americans were the primary culprits.

Hobson grapples with the situation, setting up housekeeping in a mansion home and generally taking advantage of all the resources now available to him. At times he seems on the verge of madness, partly because he feels guilty for his participation in the experiment that appears to have killed off the human race and partly out of sheer loneliness. Eventually, the latter is eased when he meets a young woman, Joanne (Alison Routledge), who has also survived the cataclysmic event. The two begin to form a bond, which is then strained when they meet still another survivor, Api (Pete Smith). Api's aborigine ancestry never really becomes much of an issue in the film, though tensions do arise between Api and Zac as they begin to compete for leadership of the group and for Joanne's attentions. When Zac realizes that the event may be about to occur again, he decides to sacrifice himself to try to stop it, but only succeeds in apparently genuinely becoming the only human to survive this second event. Thoughtful and at times haunting, *The Quiet Earth* is an excellent entry in the last-man-on-earth genre.

– R –

R2-D2. R2-D2 is a small astromech droid, or **robot**, that is one of the few characters to appear in all six films of the main *Star Wars* sequence. Appearing a bit like a washing machine on wheels, R2-D2 communicates via a series of clicks and whistles that were created by sound designer Ben Burtt. Influenced in design by the "drones" of **Douglas Trumbull**'s *Silent Running*, R2-D2 has considerable computational abilities and serves a variety of functions (such as helping ships navigate through space); it also comes equipped with a variety of gadgets and attachments to aid it in its tasks. Though it often appears alone, it is frequently seen in tandem with the protocol droid **C-3PO**, with which it makes up a duo that provides comedy relief from the often highly momentous action of the *Star Wars* films—but that also sometimes provides important support to the main protagonists in their battles against evil. R2-D2 is represented in the films via a variety of mechanical models, as well as suits worn by actor Kenny Baker. Though not humanoid, R2-D2 has a winning personality and has become a well-known figure in American popular culture.

REEVES, KEANU (1964–). Though he had made many previous appearances (mostly on television), the Lebanese-born Keanu Reeves was propelled into prominence with his appearances as the spaced-out Ted Logan in the **time-travel** spoofs *Bill & Ted's Excellent Adventure* (1989) and *Bill & Ted's Bogus Journey* (1991). Reeves then hovered on the edge of stardom, scoring numerous major roles—including the lead role in the **cyberpunk** film *Johnny Mnemonic* (1995)—but never quite making it into the Hollywood elite. He then made his breakthrough appearance as Neo, the protagonist of *The Matrix* (1999), a role he reenacted in two sequels, *The Matrix Reloaded* and *The Matrix Revolutions,* both released in 2003. Now identified as a prime science fiction leading man, Reeves subsequently starred in *A Scanner Darkly* (2006), based on a novel by **Philip K. Dick**, and in the 2008 remake of the 1951 classic *The Day the Earth Stood Still,* in which he played the role of the alien visitor Klaatu, played by **Michael Rennie** in the original.

RENNIE, MICHAEL (1909–1971). The British actor Michael Rennie never quite made it to the top level of Hollywood stardom, but he did have an extensive and successful career. In the realm of science fiction film, he will long be remembered for his role as the alien visitor Klaatu in the 1951 classic *The Day the Earth Stood Still.* He also had a major role as opportunistic explorer Lord John Roxton in *The Lost World* (1960) and played the lead role as a **cyborg** visitor from the future (thus foreshadowing the *Terminator* films) in the obscure *Cyborg 2087* (1966). Rennie made guest appearances in several sf television series in the 1960s.

RIPLEY, ELLEN. Played by **Sigourney Weaver** (in a role originally written for a man), Ellen Ripley is the star of the *Alien* sequence of movies and the leading female hero in the history of sf film. She has become something of a feminist icon because of her status as one of the first strong, independent, female action heroes. In the first *Alien* film (1979), Ripley (in this film referred to only by her last name) is a warrant officer on the *Nostromo,* a space vessel that is employed by the **Weyland-Yutani Corporation** to tow large amounts of ore back to earth from mining facilities in outer space. When the deadly alien creature of the title gets aboard the ship and starts to pick off the members of the crew, Ripley eventually becomes the last survivor, saving herself (and her cat, Jones) by entering an escape pod and jettisoning the alien into deep space when it attempts to follow, then blasting the creature with the pod's engine exhaust.

In the first sequel, *Aliens* (1986), Ripley (now given a first name) is picked up by the company after drifting in space in hypersleep (suspended animation) for 57 years. Because of her experience with the alien, she is then convinced to accompany a military mission back to the planet where the alien was picked up by the *Nostromo.* Looking a bit more muscular, she now seems a more adept alien-fighter, though she also shows a motherly side in her protectiveness toward a little girl found on the planet. (In the extended version of the film we learn that Ripley, herself, left a daughter, Amanda, when she undertook her first mission on the *Nostromo,* though Ripley has now spent so much time in space that Amanda has died at the age of 66.) Meanwhile, Ripley's hostility toward her employer grows due to her increasing realization of the destructive potential of the irresponsible and cynical quest for profit that has led the company to seek to harvest the aliens for use as weapons.

Ripley again barely escapes with her life, only to find herself, in *Alien³* (1992), stranded on a prison planet, surrounded by rapists and murderers—and again threatened by one of the aliens. Here Ripley shows a sexual side for the first time, as it becomes clear that one of the cumulative effects of the various films is to flesh out her humanity. However, that humanity is challenged in *Alien Resurrection* (1997), when, having apparently died at the end of the previous film, sacrificing herself to wipe out the alien, she is now resurrected (after a series of horribly failed experiments) as a clone with a healthy dose of alien DNA added to Ripley's original genetic makeup. Now a virtual superhero, she helps to ward off a threat that nearly takes the aliens to the earth itself, herself winding up back on the mother planet, along with her **robot** sidekick. In 2003, the American Film Institute ranked Ripley as the eighth greatest movie hero of all time, placing her higher than any other sf film hero. *See also* FEMINISM AND GENDER.

ROBBY THE ROBOT. Robby the Robot is the highly advanced **robot** constructed by Dr. Edward Morbius (**Walter Pidgeon**) in *Forbidden*

Planet (1956) using technology left behind hundreds of thousands of years earlier by the now-extinct Krel race on the planet Altair IV. Designed by Robert Kinoshita, Robby was at that time one of the most complex and (at a reported cost of $125,000 to make) expensive devices yet created for the movies. Actually, the "robot" was played by an actor-operator (officially Frankie Darrow, though prop-man Frankie Carpenter stood in for Darrow in many of the scenes) inside a costume, nearly seven feet high, made of vacuum-formed plastic. The costume included a number of high-tech flourishes, including the spinning antennae outside and the whirling mechanisms inside its see-through head, as well as a system of electrical motors that allowed various parts of the body to be manipulated from an exterior control panel, independent of the actor inside. Robby was also given a genuine personality of its own and, as voiced by announcer Marvin Miller, had some of the funniest lines in the entire film.

Robby was also a highly successful character that was a big hit with audiences in 1956. Capable of great feats of strength and speed and bearing considerable destructive capacity, Robby is also capable of performing extremely delicate tasks and even ordinary household chores, such as cooking and cleaning. Using its advanced capabilities for chemical manipulation, it can produce virtually any substance, seemingly from thin air, making it a forerunner of the wondrous replicators that are so crucial to the technology of the later *Star Trek* franchise. Though the Krel were ultimately done in by their own technology (which nearly does in the human visitors to Altair IV as well), Robby is nevertheless an extremely useful piece of hardware that is spirited away from the planet by the humans as they flee and that promises to provide a tremendous boost to earth's technological knowledge when they get back home.

The robot was so successful (and so expensive) that the costume was subsequently reused several times, making Robby something of a media star in his own right. It was brought back in 1957 to play a leading role in *The Invisible Boy* and later (played by different actors and ultimately with the original costumer replaced by a facsimile) appearing in such later films as *Gremlins* (1984), *Cherry 2000* (1987), and *Earth Girls Are Easy* (1989). It also made numerous appearances on television, including guests roles on *The Twilight Zone, Wonder Woman, Mork and Mindy,* and *Lost in Space.* In the latter case, it even demonstrated his range as an actor, playing a villainous robot that docs battle against the loveable robot of that series (a robot that was, incidentally, also designed by Kinoshita—and was basically just a low-budget version of Robby). Robby has also been the center of a successful merchandising campaign, over the years serving as the model for a variety of children's toys and even expensive, full-scale replicas designed for sale to collectors.

ROBINSON CRUSOE ON MARS. (Dir. **Byron Haskin**, 1964.) As the title indicates, this film, one of the most respected science fiction films of the early 1960s, is essentially a retelling of Daniel Defoe's well known *Robinson Crusoe,* this time featuring an astronaut who is stranded on **Mars**, rather than a sea traveler shipwrecked on a remote island. In particular, two astronauts (and a monkey) who are orbiting Mars are forced to crash land on the planet after their ship runs out of fuel in evading an object in space. One of the astronauts is killed in the crash. The other astronaut, Commander Christopher "Kit" Draper (Paul Mantee) survives, becoming the Crusoe figure of the title, accompanied by the monkey, Mona. Mars is depicted as a hellish rock-strewn place, with flames shooting up from the ground and fireballs flying through the air. On the other hand, it is surprisingly amenable to human habitation. Temperatures seem quite tolerable, and Draper is able to find sources of food, water, and even oxygen on the planet. In short, in the interest of telling its Crusoe story, the film is not much concerned with scientific accuracy in its depiction of Mars, though it is also the case that much less was known in 1964 about conditions on the planet than is known now.

The first half of the film is essentially concerned with Draper's efforts to find the necessities that he needs to survive on the planet for an extended time. As he meets the basic physical necessities, and as weeks pass, he becomes more and more concerned with the psychological problems of living in such isolation on the barren planet. Mona does provide companionship of a sort, but even more companionship is eventually provided when Draper is joined by a slave (played by Victor Lundin) who escapes from a traveling outer space mining operation that has come to Mars seeking valuable ores. Draper, explicitly comparing himself to Robinson Crusoe (he has also earlier compared himself to Christopher Columbus), dubs the newcomer (who looks suspiciously similar to a Native American) "Friday." The rest of the film is concerned with the efforts of the two to get to know each other as they gradually become friends (after Draper's initial attempts to establish his dominance), all the while having to evade the slavers, who launch periodic attacks on them from their spaceships. The film thus provides a certain amount of commentary on racism and on acceptance of the Other, though it seems primarily concerned with concocting a compelling adventure story. Ultimately, after much hardship, the film ends happily as the two greet a rescue ship that has come from earth.

ROBOCOP. (Dir. **Paul Verhoeven**, 1987.) A film that clearly shows the influence of the then-recent *Terminator, Robocop* was one of the surprise box-office hits of the late 1980s. When initially proposed, it was a film that no director wanted to direct and no actor wanted to appear in. Eventually, though, director Paul Verhoeven was imported from Holland for his first American film, and a suitable cast was assembled. A highly satirical film that does not treat its science fictional elements entirely seriously, *Robocop* nevertheless delves into a number of very serious issues, and its **cyborg** hero, a former policeman given an electromechanical body after his original human body is virtually destroyed in a shootout with criminals, became one of the iconic figures of **American science fiction film.** This hero lived on in two film sequels, two television series, and a series of comic books while also serving as a central inspiration for the spate of sf films in the 1990s that also featured **robots** or cyborgs as central characters. *Robocop* was also an effective work of political satire that produced one of the definitive film critiques of late–Reagan era America.

Set in a decaying Detroit where crime is rampant, *Robocop* centers on the policeman Murphy (**Peter Weller**) whose brain is used (without his permission) to drive a new robotic body designed for police applications in the film's violent urban world. Much of the film involves graphically violent scenes in which Murphy uses his new high-powered body to battle criminals, but the real plot involves Murphy's attempts to retain his humanity despite his new artificial body. The action is punctuated with snippets of television broadcasts within the film's fictional world, including a fictional news headlines program and a number of commercials, thus adding media satire to the texture of the film. The principal satirical target, however, is the evil **corporation** Omni Consumer Products (OCP), designers and manufacturers of the Robocop prototype as well as other robotic devices for police and military applications. They are the ultimate rapacious corporation, bent only on making a profit despite the human cost.

In *Robocop* 2 (1990), Weller's good robocop must battle against a more advanced model that has been given the brain of a drug dealer and is thus predictably evil, echoing the scenario of *Frankenstein* (1931), whose monster is plagued by a criminal brain. By *Robocop* 3 (1993) the sequence descends into total silliness as the good robocop (now played by Robert Burke and able to fly thanks to an add-on jet pack) battles a group of android ninjas built by the evil Japanese corporation, Kanemitsu, which has now taken over OCP.

ROBOT. The term "robot" refers to an artificial entity, usually electromechanical, that can carry out complex tasks, often with a considerable degree of decision-making capability. Robots are a prominent presence in science fiction, where they tend to have **artificial intelligence** and to be humanoid in shape. Indeed, it was a work of science fiction—Karel Čapek's 1921 play *R.U.R.*—that gave the word *robot* to the English language, though Čapek's robots are artificially created living creatures (somewhat like the replicants of the 1982 film *Blade Runner*), not machines. Robots are especially prominent in science fiction film, where they provide excellent opportunities for the visual representation of advanced technologies. In fact, robots are ever-present as sidekicks and simply as part of the high-tech landscape of science fictional worlds, and they sometimes assume major roles in science fiction films, becoming important characters in their own right. Čapek's original robots ultimately rebel against their human makers and assume control of the earth, initiating a strain of science fiction in which robots are treated as potentially dangerous rivals to humans. On the other hand, robots are often depicted in science fiction as cute and comical or as important allies and helpers for humans.

Robots began to play important roles, even in early science fiction films. In **Fritz Lang**'s pioneering silent science fiction film

Metropolis (1927) a sinister robot duplicate is used to impersonate the good-hearted worker, Maria, in an attempt to inspire a self-destructive rebellion among the city's discontented workers. In the 1951 classic *The Day the Earth Stood Still,* the towering robot Gort is a dangerous and menacing figure, though he is ultimately a force for good, a member of an intergalactic robotic peacekeeping force sent to try to convince the people of earth to quell their dangerous tendency toward self-destruction. The potential lovability of robots comes to the fore in *Tobor the Great* (1954), in which a powerful robot serves almost as a child's pet, meanwhile enacting the potential value of robots as surrogates for humans in dangerous tasks such as travel to outer space. Finally, one of the iconic figures of 1950s science fiction was **Robby the Robot** from *Forbidden Planet* (1956), who went on to have a significant career in film and television beyond that original film, playing a major role in *The Invisible Boy* (1957), as well as in episodes of such television series as *The Twilight Zone* and *Lost in Space.*

The best-known robots from the science fiction of the 1960s is probably the sometimes-histrionic robot of the *Lost in Space* (1965–1968) television series, remembered mostly for his frantic warnings of danger to young Will Robinson. One of the most memorable aspects of the film *Silent Running* (1972) is the group of waddling robots (referred to in the film as *drones* and dubbed "Huey, Dewey, and Louie") that help tend the remnants of earth's destroyed forests in an outer-space habitat. These drones might be regarded as the forerunners of the "droids" of the *Star Wars* films, including the especially prominent **C-3PO** and **R2-D2,** who are two of only four characters to appear in all six films of the two *Star Wars* trilogies. These two droids play key roles in the action of *Star Wars,* though they provide considerable comic relief as well.

Children seem particularly drawn to C-3PO and R2-D2, and robots in general have been particularly important characters in **children's science fiction** films, from the original Tobor to the massive, metal-eating alien robot of *The Iron Giant* (1999) to the characters of the aptly titled *Robots* (2005), all of which are, in fact, robots of various kinds. Even the classic Pinocchio story has been converted into a robot narrative in *Pinocchio 3000* (2004), in which the title character is a robot rather than a puppet.

Meanwhile, the Pinocchio narrative is one of the major influences behind **Steven Spielberg**'s *Artificial Intelligence: AI* (2001), a film originally conceived by **Stanley Kubrick**. Here, a boy robot has been programmed not merely to appear human but to experience human emotions, with the result that, like Pinocchio, he becomes centrally motivated by the desire to become a real human boy. In *Bicentennial Man* (1999), based on a short story by **Isaac Asimov** and a followup novel—*The Positronic Man* (1993)—by Asimov and Robert Silverberg, an advanced humanoid robot becomes more and more human over the many years of its own life (even adding biological components to make itself a **cyborg**, rather than a robot proper), eventually fighting to have its humanity legally recognized. Such humanlooking robots (often referred to as *androids*) obviously pose particularly strong challenges to the boundary between human beings and their machines and are therefore frequently found in science fiction, as in the world of the *Alien* films, in which protagonist **Ellen Ripley** displays a strong distrust of the androids often employed by the **Weyland-Yutani Corporation**, which often pose as humans among their fellow workers. However, in *Aliens* (1986), the second film in the sequence, Ripley is aided by the android Bishop (Lance Henriksen), who proves courageous and loyal. By the time of *Alien: Resurrection* (1997), the fourth film of the *Alien* franchise, Ripley acquires a new android sidekick, Call (Winona Ryder).

On the other hand, robots have sometimes figured as dangerous killing machines in science fiction film, often for military applications. Such robots can be very effective weapons, but they often turn on their makers or otherwise become dangerous to human protagonists. Advanced police/military robots tend to threaten the general human population in the *Robocop* sequence of films, though the title character there (like the advanced killing machines of the *Terminator* films) is actually a cyborg, part human–part machine, and therefore not, strictly speaking, a robot. In the satirical **space opera *Space Truckers*** (1996) deadly military robots that seem modeled on the extra-terrestrial monsters of the *Alien* films nearly wipe out the main human characters. In *Red Planet* (2000) a group of humans who land on **Mars** are menaced by their own military robot after it becomes damaged. In **Alex Proyas**'s *I, Robot* (2004), high-tech robots designed to serve humanity manage to get around

Isaac Asimov's Three Laws of Robotics, formulated in the short story collection from which the film takes its title, though the film is only loosely based on Asimov's stories. In any case, the film's robots rebel against their human masters under the influence of an artificial intelligence that believes it is working for the good of humanity. Finally, in the recent *Transformers* movies (directed by **Michael Bay** in 2007 and 2009), immensely powerful shape-shifting "good" robots, known as "Auto-Bots," battle against the evil Decepticons, robots who can similarly transform into the shapes of different machines and who threaten humanity.

ROCKETSHIP X-M. (Dir. **Kurt Neumann**, 1950.) Though it went into production after *Destination Moon*, *Rocketship X-M* was rushed through production and released slightly before *Destination Moon*, giving it some claim to being the first major feature-length **American science fiction film**. The attempt of *Rocketship X-M* to cash in on the extensive publicity campaign for *Destination Moon* was so overt that *Rocketship X-M*, originally conceived as a story about a trip to the moon, was reformulated as the story of a trip to **Mars** after a threatened lawsuit from *Destination Moon* producer **George Pal**.

In the film, a rocket is launched for the moon, bearing a professional crew of scientists and military men. Perhaps the most interesting aspect of the crew is that it includes a woman, Dr. Lisa Van Horn (Osa Massen), who is a legitimate scientist, though she is there largely as the assistant to Dr. Karl Eckstrom (John Emery), the ship's designer and the expedition's principal scientist. Unfortunately, the ship veers off course and toward Mars after it encounters a meteor shower in space. When they subsequently approach the red planet, the crew decides to land there to take advantage of this tremendous accidental opportunity to advance scientific knowledge. While exploring the barren landscape, the earthlings find evidence of a once-advanced civilization, now in ruins, apparently due to a nuclear holocaust. The film was thus perhaps the first to dramatize the potential destruction of an entire civilization by nuclear weaponry, predating the postapocalyptic film *Five* by a year. The only remaining Martians are a race of hostile, caveman-like primitives who have literally been bombed back into the stone age. Indeed, they look pretty much like primitive humans, helping to make the point that the human race might be headed for the same fate on earth. The savage Martians attack the earthlings, killing two, but the others, led by Graham, manage to take off and fly back to earth. Then, in a rather shocking finish, their rocket runs out of fuel and crashes on earth, killing everyone on board. The crash, however, does not deter the scientists on earth from immediately starting construction of Rocketship X-M II.

RODDENBERRY, GENE (1921–1991). The American writer and producer Gene Roddenberry was the principal creative force behind the original *Star Trek* television series (1966–1969), possibly the most important and influential single work in science fiction history. He endowed that series with his own secular humanist point of view, marked by an optimism that advances in technology would be able to solve humanity's social and economic problems in an essentially utopian future. Roddenberry continued to oversee the *Star Trek* franchise after the original series went off the air and eventually reappeared in syndication, where it achieved its greatest popularity. This popularity put the franchise in a perfect position to take advantage of the boom in science fiction film that started in 1977, and in 1979 *Star Trek: The Motion Picture* was released with Roddenberry as the producer. That film was a disappointment to many, but the franchise had enough staying power to warrant a sequel, and the 1982 film *Star Trek: The Wrath of Khan*, on which Roddenberry served as an "executive consultant," was much better received. He maintained the consultant title for the next three *Star Trek* films as well, though he was also the executive producer for *Star Trek V: The Final Frontier* (1989). Meanwhile, in 1987 he spearheaded the return of *Star Trek* to episodic television in the new series *Star Trek: The Next Generation,* which was a major success that helped to propel the franchise through three additional spin-off television series, as well as what now stands at a total of six additional feature films.

Though not directly involved in those projects, Roddenberry has been posthumously credited as creator of the original *Star Trek* in all of the official *Star Trek* films and television series, and he remains indelibly associated with the entire franchise. After his death, a portion of his ashes was carried into space on the Space Shuttle Columbia, and another portion was placed in orbit aboard a private rocket launched by Space Services International.

ROGERS, BUCK. *See* SERIALS.

ROLLERBALL. (Dir. Norman Jewison, 1975.) Based on a short story by William Harrison, who also wrote the screenplay, *Rollerball* is a **dystopian** film that portrays a future society in which countries have collapsed, leaving all power in the hands of a few global megacorporations. These **corporations** have built a world of seemingly universal affluence, but one that also seems bereft of spirit or true individualism. Indeed, the corporations employ a number of strategies to squelch individualism, thus assuring the obedience of the general population to their corporate dictates. One of their chief strategies involves official sponsorship of the sport of rollerball, a game so violent that few players can survive for very long, thus demonstrating the futility of individual effort. *Rollerball* is an effective film that, by focusing on a single character, Jonathan E. (James Caan), clearly promotes individualism in opposition to the corporatism of this future world. Jonathan is the only superstar ever produced by the game, the one man whose individual achievements seem to undermine the very purpose of the sport. The main plot of the film thus involves the efforts of the corporations to do him in; he of course emerges as the victor within the limits of the action of the film, though we are left to speculate on his future after his triumph in the final rollerball game depicted in the film. In addition to its critique of corporate power, *Rollerball* seems designed to criticize our culture's fascination with violence, a critique that is made problematic by the film's own heavy emphasis on violent spectacles.

RUSSELL, KURT (1951–). The American actor Kurt Russell began his career as a child actor, mostly on television, in the 1950s. He rose to prominence at age 18 when he starred in **Disney**'s youth-oriented science fiction film *The Computer Wore Tennis Shoes* (1969) as a college student who has the memory and computational abilities of a computer downloaded into his brain. This film was successful enough that he subsequently starred in two sequels, *Now You See Him, Now You Don't* (1972) and *The Strongest Man in the World* (1975). After that, his clean-cut image received a radical makeover in his next appearance in a science fiction film, **John Carpenter**'s *Escape from New York* (1981), in which he played rough-edged adventurer Snake

Plissken. He reprised the role of Plissken in a sequel, *Escape from L.A.* (1996). In the meantime, he solidified his credentials as a science fiction star with lead roles in Carpenter's *The Thing* (1982) and *Big Trouble in Little China* (1986), as well as **Roland Emmerich**'s *Stargate* (1994). Russell subsequently starred in the ultraviolent *Soldier* (1998) and had a major supporting role as the psychiatrist in *Vanilla Sky* (2001). In 2005, his career in sf-related film came full circle when he had a central role in Disney's teen-oriented superhero film *Sky High*.

RUSSIAN SCIENCE FICTION FILM. *See* SOVIET/RUSSIAN SCIENCE FICTION FILM.

– S –

SATURN AWARDS. Saturn Awards are given annually by the Academy of Science Fiction, Fantasy and Horror Films in the United States. The award honors the year's finest achievements in theatrical film, television, and home video in the categories covered by the academy. The award is given in a variety of categories, though the one for Best Science Fiction film is probably the most prestigious of the Saturn Awards. It was first given in 1972 for *Slaughterhouse-Five* and has subsequently gone to such respected sf films as *Star Wars* (1977), *Alien* (1979), *E.T. the Extra-Terrestrial* (1982), *The Terminator* (1984), *Total Recall* (1990), *Terminator 2: Judgment Day* (1991), and *The Matrix* (1999). On the other hand, it has sometimes gone to films that are only marginally science fictional, such as *X-Men* (2000) and *X2: X-Men United* (2003).

SCHALLERT, WILLIAM (1922–). Though probably best known to American audiences for his regular roles in several successful television series, the character actor William Schallert also made numerous guest appearances on television, including a role in one of the most fondly remembered episodes of the original *Star Trek* television series, "The Trouble with Tribbles" (1967). He also made a number of film appearances, including several in science fiction film. As early as 1951, he had an important supporting role as Dr. Mears in **Edgar**

G. Ulmer's *The Man from Planet X.* He had minor (uncredited) roles as a newscaster in the paranoid **alien-invasion** drama *Invasion USA* (1952) and as an ambulance attendant in *Them!* (1954). Though he never became a major figure in the sf boom of the 1950s, he had a credited role as a reporter in *Tobor the Great* (1954) and he played a doctor in *The Incredible Shrinking Man* (1957). After becoming a familiar face on American television through the 1960s, he had important supporting roles in *The Computer Wore Tennis Shoes* (1969) and *Colossus: The Forbin Project* (1970). Schallert has appeared almost exclusively on television through the rest of his career, though he did appear in the sf action **comedy** *Innerspace* in 1987.

SCHWARZENEGGER, ARNOLD (1947–). The Austrian-born Arnold Schwarzenegger first came to prominence as a competitive bodybuilder, winning the Mr. Universe title at age 22, after a move to the United States the year earlier in order to further his competitive career. He ultimately won seven prestigious Mr. Olympia titles; his success as a superstar bodybuilder also helped him to get into films, when (as "Arnold Strong") he played the role of Hercules in the 1970 film *Hercules in New York,* though his German accent was still so strong that his speaking part was dubbed by another actor. In 1973, still credited as Arnold Strong, he had a small part as a gangster's strongman in Robert Altman's *The Long Goodbye,* in which his character was a deaf-mute, thus solving the problem of his strong accent. Schwarzenegger gained additional attention with his central presence in the 1977 bodybuilding documentary *Pumping Iron.* In 1982, he had the starring role in the sword-and-sorcery epic *Conan the Barbarian,* in which he used his actual speaking voice. The film was a major step forward in his career. However, lest the role of the laconic, muscle-bound barbarian seem to be the part of a lifetime for a bodybuilder who was still struggling with English, Schwarzenegger found an even better fit for his skill set in **James Cameron**'s *The Terminator* (1984), in which he played the virtually unstoppable killer **cyborg** of the title. That role, which he reprised in *Terminator 2: Judgment Day* (1991) and *Terminator 3: Rise of the Machines* (2003), made him a major Hollywood star—so much so that the scenario of the two latter films was modified to make him a hero, rather than a villain, in the latter two films.

In the meantime, he became Hollywood's most bankable action star, appearing in such action-oriented science fiction films as the futuristic satire *The Running Man* (1986) and the violent **alien-invasion** drama *Predator* (1987). In such films, Schwarzenegger managed to overcome his limited acting skills and lack of facility with English through his commanding physical presence and a surprising on-screen charisma that reflected his sharp intelligence and sense of irony. He also starred in **Paul Verhoeven's** *Total Recall* (1990), though here playing a somewhat more vulnerable protagonist than his usual virtual superhumans. His career was punctuated by occasional changes of pace such as the comedy *Twins* (1988), and Schwarzenegger continued to be an important action star into the 1990s (and into his 50s), though both the action comedy *Last Action Hero* (1993) and the spy drama *True Lies* (1994, again directed by Cameron) can be taken as spoofs of precisely the sorts of films that made Schwarzenegger a superstar in the 1980s, suggesting that his career might have passed its peak. That perception was surely reinforced by his turn as Mr. Freeze in the disastrous 1997 superhero flick *Batman & Robin*. Action films such as the supernatural thriller *End of Days* (1999) and the cloning drama *The 6th Day* (2000) failed to return Schwarzenegger to his former glory, and even his third *Terminator* film was generally judged to be far inferior to the first two.

By the time of the release of the spoofy **adventure** *Around the World in Eighty Days* (2004), in which he had a minor cameo role, Schwarzenegger seemed a farcical parody of his former self as an actor, but he had by this time emerged elsewhere as someone to be taken seriously indeed when he was elected governor of California in the recall election of late 2003. A moderate Republican in a typically Democratic state, he was easily re-elected in 2006.

SCOTT, RIDLEY (1937–). The British director Ridley Scott first drew the attention of Hollywood as the director of the Napoleonic war drama *The Duellists* (1977), released the same year that *Star Wars* initiated a craze for science fiction films among Hollywood producers and studios. Scott was then tapped to direct one of the science fiction films that the studios were then scrambling to produce, and the result was *Alien* (1979), a film whose visual inventiveness and meticulous attention to detail displayed precisely the cinematic virtues that made Scott a major star in Hollywood. Scott followed as the director of *Blade Runner* (1982), a film that was even more visually impressive—and one that seemed firmly to establish Scott's credentials as a director of science fiction film, then still Hollywood's hottest genre. Instead of pursuing further sf films, however, Scott followed with the fantasy/adventure *Legend* (1985), then with a string of crime dramas and historical dramas. He remains a major director of big-budget Hollywood films, but has not, as of this writing, returned to science fiction.

SEARS, FRED F. (1913–1957). Before his untimely death (due to a heart attack) at the age of 44, the American director Fred F. Sears, known for working quickly, managed to direct more than 50 films, the majority of them during one brief prolific period from 1953 to his death in 1957. Though something of a specialist in the Western, he worked in a number of genres. In fact, his best-remembered films (both released in 1956) are probably the rock 'n' roll film *Rock Around the Clock* and the **alien-invasion** narrative *Earth vs. the Flying Saucers.* His sf-**monster movie**, *The Werewolf,* was also released in 1956. Among five Sears-directed films released in 1957 were another (notoriously bad) monster movie, *The Giant Claw,* and the sf-disaster movie, *The Night the World Exploded.*

SERENITY. (Dir. **Joss Whedon**, 2005.) More a wrap-up than a follow-up, *Serenity* took the television series *Firefly* (which ran briefly on Fox in the fall of 2002) into the realm of theatrical film, giving fans a bit of closure to the much-admired but short-lived series. Featuring the same characters and scenario as the series, *Serenity* combines **space opera** with many of the typical tropes of the Western as its colorful crew of space outlaws aboard the cargo ship *Serenity* ventures into the frontiers of settled space more than 500 years in the future, mostly just trying to get by but on the way doing battle against an array of villains. The most powerful of these is the Alliance, an oppressive interplanetary state of the "central planets" that also extends its tendrils into the frontier planets of the "Outer Rim," having earlier won a war against rebel forces for hegemony in the region. Indeed, *Serenity* is captained by one Malcolm Reynolds (Nathan Fillion), a veteran of the rebel "Browncoat" forces and still very much an enemy of the Alliance, as are, for various reasons, his crew. The presence of the Alliance gives the film something of the texture of a **dystopian** narrative, though the film in fact partakes of numerous genres, including horror—via the cannibalistic "Reavers," vicious monsters created as the byproduct of a secret Alliance experiment in mass mind control that went awry and killed 30 million people on a remote planet. Most of the film's plot revolves around the discovery of this secret by Reynolds and his crew and the attempts of the Alliance to prevent the secret from getting out.

Ultimately, the film's narrative veers well into **cyberpunk** territory as well, especially through the introduction of the character known as Mr. Universe (David Krumholtz), a sort of super-geek who monitors electronic signals from around the galaxy from his high-tech headquarters and is killed by a deadly Alliance Operative pursuing *Serenity*. Nevertheless, Mr. Universe posthumously helps the crew of *Serenity* broadcast the truth about the experiment that created the Reavers. *Serenity* was not a box-office success, but it has gained something of a cult following, especially among loyal Whedon fans, and has sold unusually well on DVD. It won a number of awards, including recognition from the British sf magazine *SFX* as the greatest science fiction film of all time, via a 2007 online fan poll.

SERIALS. Serial films were episodic sequences in which a continuous narrative unfolded over several short "chapters," typically shown one per week as a way of attracting viewers to movie theaters on an ongoing basis. Serials, with Westerns as the most popular genre, date back to the silent-film era, but remained highly popular in the early sound era of the 1930s and 1940s. However, they were almost entirely supplanted first by radio serials then by television programming, of which they were an important forerunner, beginning in the 1950s. Several popular science fiction serials were produced as well, especially in the 1930s, especially in the genre of **space opera**. Particularly popular were the three Flash Gordon serials and the Buck Rogers serial of that decade, all based on popular syndicated comic strips and all featuring actor Buster Crabbe in the central roles. These plot-driven serials featured **special effects** that were extremely crude by today's standards, but that presented thrilling alternatives to the gray Depression-ridden world of the 1930s.

The Flash Gordon and Buck Rogers serials were produced in episodes of 15–20 minutes in length, with each serial running for 12–15 episodes, each typically ending with a cliffhanger designed to bring viewers back the next week. The first Flash Gordon serial, *Flash Gordon: Space Soldiers* (1936), is an **alien-invasion** story in which Flash and his attractive, rather skimpily clad sidekick, Dale Arden (Jean Rogers), battle the evil Emperor Ming of the planet Mongo who intends to colonize earth. In *Flash Gordon's Trip to Mars* (1938), Ming the Merciless resumes his assault on earth, this time in an alliance with the queen of **Mars**. But Flash and Dale take the battle to Mars, winning another victory. In *Flash Gordon Conquers the Universe* (1940), Ming showers the earth with a purple powder that causes a deadly planetwide **plague**. However, Flash and Dale (now played by Carol Hughes) manage to find an antidote and foil Ming once again. The 1939 Buck Rogers serial is something of a **dystopian** film the title character of which is a 1930s test pilot who has been placed in suspended animation and has awakened several hundred years in the future. It also involves alien invaders, but this time they are benevolent, helping Buck and the rebel forces of the Hidden City defeat 25th-century dictator and criminal kingpin Killer Kane.

Both Flash Gordon and Buck Rogers have become iconic figures in American popular culture. They went on to be featured in a variety of other media, including the campy 1980 feature-film *Flash Gordon*.

SHATNER, WILLIAM (1931–). Trained as a Shakespearean actor, the Canadian-born William Shatner got off to a relatively slow start in Hollywood, appearing mostly in guest spots on television before he was cast to play Captain **James T. Kirk** in the original *Star Trek* television series in 1966. He had, however, already forayed into the margins of science fiction when he starred in two episodes of *The Twilight Zone,* including the classic episode "Nightmare at 20,000 Feet" (1963). Shatner also starred in an episode of *The Outer Limits* in 1964. However, he will forever be best remembered for his performance as Kirk throughout the original series, which ran for only three years but had a dramatically successful second life in syndication. Meanwhile, Shatner reprised the role of Kirk in the first seven *Star Trek* theatrical films. His unusual on-screen charisma and distinctive, haltingly histrionic acting style helped to make Kirk one of the iconic characters of science fiction on both film and television, while Shatner himself became one of sf's iconic actors. He has also had important starring roles in two other television series, *T. J. Hooker* (1982–1986) and *Boston Legal* (2004–2008), though neither was science fiction. He has appeared in numerous films and has used his trademark vocal style in voiceover work for several films, including the sf film *Quantum Quest: A Cassini Space Odyssey* (2010). Shatner has also parlayed his success as Kirk into a successful career as a science fiction novelist, including co-authoring several novels set in the *Star Trek* universe, as well as authoring the *TekWar* series of novels.

SHUSETT, RONALD. The American writer and producer Ronald Shusett made his first impact on science fiction film by co-writing (with **Dan O'Bannon**) the story for the film that became **Ridley Scott**'s *Alien* (1979), launching one of the most important sf franchises in film history. He also served as an executive producer for *Alien* and for the unsuccessful *King Kong Lives* (1986). His next major contribution to sf film, however, as the co-writer (with **Gary Goldman**) and producer of **Paul Verhoeven**'s *Total Recall* (1990), based on a short story by **Philip K. Dick** that Shusett had originally optioned back in 1974. He and Goldman also wrote a screen adaptation of Dick's short story "The Minority Report." That script was never produced, but the story was adapted to film in **Steven Spielberg**'s *Minority Report* (2002), with Shusett and Goldman as executive producers. Shusett also co-wrote and co-produced the combination **time-travel** and **dystopian** film *Freejack* (1992).

SHYAMALAN, M. NIGHT (1970–). Born in Pondicherry, India, the son of two Indian medical doctors, M. Night Shyamalan grew up in Penn Valley, Pennsylvania, a suburb of Philadelphia. He had written and directed two small, independent films when he finally made his way into the Hollywood spotlight in 1999 as the co-writer of *Stuart Little* and as the writer and director of the supernatural thriller *The Sixth Sense,* a huge hit that became one of the most talked-about films of the year. That film established his reputation as a maker of supernaturally themed films with twist endings, a reputation much of his subsequent work has reinforced. Shyamalan followed as the writer, director, and producer of *Unbreakable* (2000), a highly unusual superhero narrative that contains a number of sf elements. In 2002, he moved fully into science fiction territory as the writer, director, and producer of *Signs,* an **alien-invasion** narrative with strong religious resonances. Two lackluster supernatural thrillers followed, but Shyamalan again drew considerable attention (though lukewarm reviews) with *The Happening* (2008), an unusual environmentalist tale in which the earth itself appears to issue a warning to the human race that they had better start taking better care of their environment lest the environment be forced to defend itself against them. He is currently at work on an action-oriented fantasy, *The Last Airbender,* a live-action film adaptation of the **anime**-influenced American animated television series *Avatar: The Last Airbender.* See also ENVIRONMENTALISM.

SILENT RUNNING. (Dir. **Douglas Trumbull**, 1972.) Directed by **special-effects** master Douglas Trumbull and co-written by future big names Michael Cimino and Steven Bochco (along with Deric Washburn), *Silent Running* is typical of **American science fiction film** in the early 1970s in its pessimistic projection of a blighted future. It can be considered both a **dystopian** film and **postapocalyptic**, though it stands out for its special focus on **environmentalism**. In this film, we see little of the blighted earth, however. Instead, the film merely stipulates that environmental degradation on earth has made the planet unable to sustain forests and large-scale plant life. In response, huge space habitats have been set up in which humans and **robots** tend the last vestiges of the earth's forests, hoping to keep them alive toward the day when they can be returned to earth. There is no explanation of how humans can live on an earth that is essentially unable to sustain plant life, nor is there any explanation for the order that suddenly comes through for the forests to be destroyed and the ships that bear them returned to earth. This order triggers the main action of the film, in which nature-lover Freeman Lowell (Bruce Dern) undertakes a desperate effort (even resorting to murder) to save the forests. This effort makes Lowell appear a bit unhinged and ultimately leads to his death, but the film's sympathies are clearly with saving the forest, one module of which remains in operation in deep space as the film ends, tended by a lone, waddling robot, or "drone," the last of three (dubbed "Huey, Dewey, and Louie") that are one of the highlights of the film.

SITH. The Sith are a sinister order within the universe of the *Star Wars* films, essentially the evil counterparts of the **Jedi** knights, drawing their power from the dark side of the **Force**, just as the Jedi draw theirs from the light side. Devoted only to furthering their own power, the Sith thus serve as the antithesis of the Jedi, who use their power to serve others. The Sith order was originally founded by a group of renegade Jedi who were defeated by the Jedi in a confrontation that occurred thousands of years before the events of the *Star Wars* film sequence. The renegades were then exiled into deep space, eventually landing on the previously unknown planet of Korriban. There, they discovered a reptilian race known as the Sith who had a special affinity with the Force. The exiled Jedi nevertheless managed to subjugate the Sith and become the rulers of Korriban, using it as a base of power from which to build their order and taking the Sith name for their own. By the time of the events of the *Star Wars* film sequence, however, the Sith have been thought extinct for millennia. It turns out, however, that one Palpatine (Ian McDiarmid), a Senator of the Republic, is in fact secretly a surviving Sith lord, Sidious, backed by his apprentice, Darth Maul (Ray Park). Indeed, it seems that, at this point, only two Sith lords can exist at any given time, one master and one apprentice. Eventually, Palpatine rises to become the Supreme Chancellor of the Republic and then the Emperor of the new regime that supplants the Republic. Meanwhile, after Maul is killed by Jedi knight **Obi-Wan Kenobi (Ewan McGregor)**, Palpatine/Sidious finds a new apprentice in the former Jedi Count Dooku (Christopher Lee), who becomes Darth Tyranus but is later slain by Jedi knight **Anakin Skywalker. Anakin** then replaces Tyranus as Sidious's apprentice, becoming **Darth Vader**, now drawn to the dark side of the Force, his body almost entirely replaced by cybernetic parts.

SKYWALKER, ANAKIN. Anakin Skywalker is one of the key figures in the second *Star Wars* trilogy, while his later evil **cyborg** incarnation, **Darth Vader**, is the chief villain of the first *Star Wars* trilogy. In *Star Wars: Episode I—The Phantom Menace* (1999), Anakin is a young boy (played by Jake Lloyd) who is recognized as having great potential as a future **Jedi** knight because of his strong affinity with the **Force**. The apparent product of a virgin birth, he is suspected to be the "Chosen One" foretold by Jedi prophecy as fated to bring balance to the Force—and to wipe out the evil **Sith** order that has brought imbalance due to their use of the dark side of the Force. In *Star Wars: Episode II—Attack of the Clones* (2002), Anakin (now played by **Hayden Christensen**) is a young adult training to be a Jedi under the tutelage of **Obi-Wan Kenobi** (**Ewan McGregor**). However, Anakin is a strong-willed pupil who is showing signs of resistance to his training. He also seems increasingly to be falling under the influence of the sinister Palpatine, Supreme Chancellor of the Republic (Ian McDiarmid), while developing a growing attachment to the beautiful Padmé Amidala (Natalie Portman), Queen of the planet Naboo and a Senator of the Republic, for whom he and Kenobi serve as bodyguards. By the end of this film, Anakin has lost his right arm in a light saber battle with the evil Count Dooku (Christopher Lee), foreshadowing the later replacement of most of his body by cybernetic parts. He has also married Amidala in a clandestine ceremony, a union that will secretly produce the twin offspring **Luke Skywalker** and Princess **Leia Organa**; unfortunately, Amidala will die in childbirth and the twins will be separated and sent away with no knowledge of their background. By *Star Wars: Episode III—Revenge of the Sith* (2005), Palpatine has been revealed as the Sith lord Darth Sidious, and Anakin's anger and bitterness are clearly taking him toward the dark side. He is almost killed in a battle with Kenobi, but is reconstructed with a cybernetic body by Palpatine, in an act that is essentially the birth of Darth Vader.

SKYWALKER, LUKE. Luke Skywalker (played by Mark Hamill) is the central protagonist of *Star Wars: Episode IV—A New Hope* (1977) and a key protagonist in the next two *Star Wars* films as well. In *A New Hope,* he is a young man living on the remote desert planet of Tatooine, not realizing that he is the son of **Jedi** knight **Anakin Skywalker**. In the course of this first film, Luke joins up with **Obi-Wan Kenobi** (**Sir Alec Guinness**) and Princess **Leia Organa** (Carrie Fisher) in their battle against the evil Empire that has supplanted the once-novel Republic as the most powerful political entity in the galaxy. Like his father, Luke has an especially strong connection to the **Force** and shows immediate promise as a potential Jedi knight, though he is pure of heart and lacks his father's darkness; he ends the film by using his unique skills to destroy a giant Death Star, a new planet-killing weapon with which the Empire plans to enforce its rule. In the subsequent films, Luke and the audience learn that Leia is his twin sister and that the two were separated at birth for their own protection. He also learns, at the end of *Star Wars: Episode VI—The Return of the Jedi* (1983), that the evil **Sith** lord **Darth Vader** is, in fact, his father, Anakin, having now been drawn irrevocably to the dark side of the Force. In a last flash of humanity, however, Vader saves Luke from the evil Emperor Palpatine (who is, in fact, the Sith lord Darth Sidious, Vader's master) before meeting with his own death.

SLEEPER. (Dir. Woody Allen, 1973.) The most distinctive phenomenon in **American science fiction film** in the early 1970s was a cycle of dark, **dystopian** films that reflected the relatively pessimistic public atmosphere of the time. *Sleeper* was a response to these films, a comic parody of the dystopian film that turned many of the conventions of the genre and concerns of the time into objects of broad humor and proved that Americans could still laugh at themselves. At the same time, the film maintains certain dark undertones that make the humor seem a bit uneasy; indeed, the film's joking attitude suggests a strong skepticism that traditional realms of hope like science, religion, and politics can ever solve the problems of modern society. It even mocks the utopian potential of sexuality and poetry, two mainstays of oppositional energies in the dystopian tradition.

Something of a cross between **H. G. Wells**'s novel *When the Sleeper Wakes* (1899, rewritten in 1910 as *The Sleeper Wakes*) and Charlie Chaplin's 1936 film *Modern Times, Sleeper* includes many of the classic motifs of dystopian fiction, including the device of having protagonist Miles Monroe (played by Allen himself) frozen in 1973 to awake 200 years later in a future America. When Monroe finally awakes, he is questioned by a group of scientists (in a film made before many of the facts of the Watergate scandal had been revealed) about a mysterious individual named "Richard M. Nixon," about whom they have heard legends, but who seems to have been expunged from the historical record. Apparently, they tell Monroe, Nixon might once have been president, but might have done something so "horrendous" that he was expunged from the historical record. Discovering that he is to be brainwashed to ensure that he thinks in ways considered orthodox in this totalitarian future society, Monroe escapes from the scientists and (ludicrously) disguises himself as a **robot**, thus recalling in comic form the anxiety over the encroachment of technology into our humanity that informs many dystopian fictions. He then issues forth into the society of 2173 America, a society almost totally immersed in high-tech devices, junk food, fast and easy sex, and mind-numbing drugs (of which the most important is probably television).

Eventually, Monroe becomes embroiled in an underground political movement bent on overthrowing the repressive government of this future world, with its Big Brother–like "Leader." Though generally inept, these rebels manage to kill the Leader with a bomb. The Leader's nose survives, however, and a team of surgeons is preparing an elaborate high-tech operation to use the nose to clone a replacement Leader, who will then oversee the total extermination of the rebels. Monroe and rebel poet Luna Schlosser (Diane Keaton), a writer of popular but insipid verses, disguise themselves as doctors in an attempt to foil the procedure. The bumbling Monroe (mostly by accident) manages to destroy the nose, which is flattened by a steamroller. As the film ends, the way is clear for an eventual rebel victory and for Monroe and Schlosser to be together as lovers. On the other hand, *Sleeper* clearly implies that Monroe and Schlosser will not necessarily be happy together—and that the nation will not necessarily be better off under the new post-Leader regime.

SMITH, WILL (1968–). The American actor Will Smith first became a well-known figure in American popular culture as the rapper known as the "Fresh Prince," part of the duo "DJ Jazzy Jeff and the Fresh Prince," beginning in 1985. Although the duo was successful, Smith was nearly broke when he turned to acting in a sitcom built somewhat around his rapper persona, *The Fresh Prince of Bel-Air,* a hit that stayed on the air from 1990 to 1996. In the meantime, Smith had a critically acclaimed role in the film *Six Degrees of Separation* (1993) and achieved major commercial success with his starring role in *Bad Boys* (1995). Smith was thus poised to be catapulted into the top levels of Hollywood stardom when he appeared as a wise-cracking fighter pilot who helps to defeat an **alien invasion** in the sf blockbuster *Independence Day* (1996). From that point forward, he has been a major action star, with many of his most successful roles in science fiction films—all the while continuing his career as a solo rap artist, including producing music for many of his films. He followed his role in *Independence Day* with a starring turn the next year in ***Men in Black***, an alien-invasion comedy that is partly a spoof of films like *Independence Day*. Smith starred as James West in *Wild, Wild West* (1999), something of a science fiction–Western that was a bust both critically and commercially, but his rise to stardom continued unabated. After starring in the sequel to *Men in Black* in 2002, he starred in **Alex Proyas**'s big-budget, action-oriented **robot** film *I, Robot* (2004), and in 2007 he starred in *I Am Legend*, the third major film adaptation of the 1954 **Richard Matheson** novel of that title, solidifying his status in the top ranks of science fiction film stars and as the most successful African American science fiction star to date. He also served as a producer on both of the two latter films. Smith was nominated for an Academy Award for Best Actor for his role in *Ali* (2001).

SODERBERGH, STEVEN (1963–). The independent-spirited Steven Soderbergh is an American director and producer who first gained widespread attention with *sex, lies, and videotape* (1989), which he wrote and directed. He also directed such big-budget mainstream films as *Out of Sight* (1998), *Traffic* (2000), *Erin Brockovich* (2000), and *Ocean's Eleven* (2001) and its two sequels. Throughout his career, Soderbergh has shown a special interest in neo-noir filmmaking and in innovative filmmaking technologies, the latter of which has sometimes meshed with an interest in science fiction. In 2002, he wrote and directed the remake of *Solaris*. He also executive produced the experimental **green-screen** film *Able Edwards* (2004) and the innovative *A Scanner Darkly* (2006), based on a novel by **Philip K. Dick.**

SOLARIS. (Dir. **Andrei Tarkovsky**, 1972.) Andrei Tarkovsky's *So-laris* is widely regarded as one of the director's greatest films and as one of the high points of **Soviet/Russian science fiction film**. The film is based on **Stanisław Lem**'s classic 1961 sf novel of the same title, which is widely regarded as one of the most successful representations of an encounter with a truly alien intelligence in all of science fiction. Like the novel, the film focuses on a space station that has been placed in orbit around the planet Solaris in order to study the new planet. Attempts to study the enigmatic planet have proved oddly fruitless, and those sent from earth to study Solaris have suffered a variety of odd psychological symptoms. The film focuses on psychologist Kris Kelvin (Donatas Banionis), who travels to the station to investigate the situation there after decades of frustrated attempts to understand the planet. He finds only two men still alive in the station, both of whom seem to have been strangely affected by the nearby planet. He himself begins to suffer what seems to be a hallucination when his long-dead wife, Hari, appears to him on the station, but it soon becomes clear that the woman (played by Natalya Bondarchuk) is physically real and has apparently been materialized by the sentient planet below from information contained in Kelvin's memories. The others on the station have experienced similar manifestations, which they interpret as an attempt by the planet (or perhaps its ocean) to communicate with them. As these attempts continue, the film becomes a haunting meditation on the nature of memory, the nature of reality, and the possibility of human beings establishing communication with intelligences that are truly alien to them.

Tarkovsky's film premiered at the 1972 Cannes Film Festival, where it won the Grand Prix Spécial du Jury and was nominated for the Palme d'Or. It has since received substantial critical acclaim, though Lem himself expressed displeasure with the adaptation, which he felt diverged too extensively from the novel in its exploration of inner subjective experience as opposed to the novel's man-versus-the-cosmos theme. Lem's novel had also been adapted as a Soviet made-for-TV movie in 1968 and was adapted once again in a mid-budget American production in 2002, directed by **Steven Soderbergh**.

SOLO, HAN. The dashing smuggler Han Solo is a loveable rogue whom circumstances force to become a hero in the first *Star Wars* trilogy. Played by **Harrison Ford**, Solo first appears in the initial *Star Wars* film as a man who lives on the margins of society, accompanied only by his devoted Wookiee companion, Chewbacca. In debt to the dangerous intergalactic gangster Jabba the Hut, Solo is desperate for cash and thus willing to hire out his ship, the Millennium Falcon, when he is approached with a request to take **Obi-Wan Kenobi** and **Luke Skywalker** from the planet Tatooine to the planet Alderaan, along with the droids **C-3PO** and **R2-D2**. Solo is subsequently drawn essentially against his will into the colossal battle of good versus evil that constitutes the intergalactic politics of the *Star Wars* universe. He proves up to the task, becoming an important champion of the good and rising to the rank of general in the Rebel Alliance that opposes the evil Empire.

In the second film, *Star Wars: Episode V—The Empire Strikes Back,* Solo becomes a central figure in the plot when he is kidnapped, frozen in carbonite, and turned over to Jabba the Hut at the behest of the sinister **Darth Vader**. The third film, *Star Wars: Episode VI— The Return of the Jedi,* then narrates his rescue from captivity and subsequent rise to a position of leadership in the Rebel Alliance. The one-time self-serving loner has now completed his transformation into a man devoted to a larger cause. In 2003, the American Film Institute listed Solo as the 14th greatest movie hero of all time, second only to **Ellen Ripley** of the *Alien* sequence among sf film heroes.

SOVIET/RUSSIAN SCIENCE FICTION FILM. Led by cinema pioneers such as Sergei Eisenstein, Soviet film of the 1920s was among the most accomplished and innovative in the world, partly because the new Soviet regime felt that culture was a crucial means for conveying the ideals of socialism to the Soviet population, most of whom were at that time illiterate, making film a logical cultural form for this project. Among the classic Soviet films of that decade, one, Yakov Protazanov's *Aelita* (1924), is still an acknowledged classic of both silent film and science fiction film. Soviet film of the following years tended to focus on more realistic and historical subjects, while the successes of Soviet literacy program led to more emphasis on literature and less on film in the national culture. Scientist Konstantin Tsiolkovsky's vision of the possibilities of future space flight in *Kosmicheskiy reys: Fantasticheskaya novella* (1936, generally known in English as *The Space Ship* or *The Space Voyage*) was something of an exception.

Science fiction began to make something of a comeback in Soviet film by the late 1950s, though the unavailability of large budgets continued to plague the form in the Soviet Union. The Soviet space-race drama *Nebo zovyot* (*The Sky Is Calling,* 1960) was a low-budget but fairly effective effort, one of the few Soviet films to be adapted for American audiences. Unfortunately, it was made silly in **Roger Corman**'s American adaptation *Battle Beyond the Sun* (1960) via the gratuitous addition of an unconvincing alien monster. *Chelovek-Amfibiya* (*The Amphibian Man,* 1962) was a science fiction love story involving a boy who has been surgically modified to be able to live underwater. The space opera *Tumannost Andromedy* (1967, *Andromeda Nebula*) was an adaptation of Ivan Yefremov's 1957 novel *Andromeda*. **Andrei Tarkovsky**'s *Solaris* (1972), an eerie and thoughtful adaptation of **Stanisław Lem**'s 1961 novel of the same title, remains perhaps the greatest classic of Soviet science fiction film. Tarkovsky's *Stalker* (1979) is as thoughtful as *Solaris,* but a bit more ponderous as it explores the altered reality that reigns in a Soviet region that has apparently been visited by aliens.

In the meantime, Soviet science fiction film, following a strong satirical tradition in Soviet culture as a whole, took a turn toward humorous satire in the 1970s. Leonid Gaidai's *menyaet professiyu* (*Ivan Vasilevich Changes Professions,* 1973, released in the West as *Ivan Vasilievich: Back to the Future*), based on a play by master satirist Mikhail Bulgakov, was one of the highlights of the decade. Here, Engineer Shurik (Aleksandr Demyanenko) is working to develop a time machine when he accidentally sends building superintendent Ivan Vasilevich Bunsha (Yuriy Yakovlev), along with a small-time burglar, back to the 16th century, to the time of the notorious Tsar Ivan the Terrible. Meanwhile, Ivan is brought back to 1973, while the Bunsha impersonates Ivan in the 16th century. Much comic confusion ensues, though the entire plot is revealed at the end to have been a dream on the part of Shurik. The film was very popular in the Soviet Union, and the role of Bunsha became perhaps the best-known role of Yakovlev, one of the nation's most acclaimed film actors. Yakovlev also starred in Georgi Daneliya's *Kin-dza-dza!* (1986), little known in the West but a cult film in Russia; this film is a comic **dystopian** film that satirizes numerous aspects of Soviet life, though it satirizes the capitalist alternative as well.

More serious Soviet science fiction continued to be produced as well. For example, *Per Aspera ad Astra* (1981, later dubbed in English as *Humanoid Woman*) is a **space opera** involving **genetic engineering** that is far less silly than it appears in the English version, known to Western viewers primarily as an object of mockery in ***Mystery Science Theater 3000***. Russian science fiction film, like Russian culture as a whole, has seen a downturn in production since the fall of the Soviet Union in 1990.

SOYLENT GREEN. (Dir. **Richard Fleischer**, 1973.) *Soylent Green* is probably the best remembered of the several **dystopian** films that were produced in the United States in the early 1970s. **Environmentalism** is also an important theme. Based on the 1966 novel *Make Room! Make Room!* by Harry Harrison, *Soylent Green* depicts a future world in which overpopulation and environmental devastation have led to a drastically reduced standard of living for most citizens. Set in a 2022 New York City with a population of 40 million, the film features police detective Robert Thorn (**Charlton Heston**) as he investigates the recent murder of a prominent local citizen. This investigation leads him into the circles of the wealthy, who still live lives of luxury and plenty, even as the mass of the population struggles to survive. Food is particularly in short supply. Most of the world's food is produced by the Soylent **Corporation**, a huge conglomerate that manufactures various sorts of (presumably nutritious) processed foods. Their latest product is the Soylent Green of the film's title, which Thorn ultimately discovers is manufactured from the bodies of recently deceased humans, especially those sent from government-sponsored suicide facilities, which have been set up as a way of dealing with the overpopulation problem. (This sensational cannibalism theme, perhaps the biggest reason the film is so memorable, was added in the film and was not present in Harrison's novel. One of the last lines, a classic, is "Soylent Green is people!") Thorn also discovers that the corporation was responsible for the murder he is investigating; their hit men target him as well, but he survives to try to get out the truth about Soylent Green, though it is unclear as the film ends whether he will have any success taking on the powerful Soylent Corporation. The film also features Edward G. Robinson in his last film role, as Thorn's aging friend, Sol Roth, who commits suicide in one of the government facilities. Ironically, Robinson himself knew he was dying of cancer at the time; he passed away 12 days after shooting for the film was completed.

SPACE OPERA. During the years of the 1930s, when science fiction was still defining itself as a form, written science fiction was dominated by the pulp magazines and the most prominent science fiction works on film were the Buck Rogers and Flash Gordon **serials**. At this time, often melodramatic stories of adventure in outer space rose to the center of the genre, though the common term for such stories, *space opera,* was not suggested (by sf writer Wilson Tucker) until 1941. This term was originally meant to be derogatory, suggesting second-rate, formulaic stories produced by untalented hacks. Later, while the term continued to have pulpy connotations, it came to be associated with some of the best-known and most-loved works of the entire science fiction genre, from novels of the 1950s by writers such as **Isaac Asimov** and **Robert A. Heinlein**, to television series such as the various incarnations of *Star Trek,* to films such as the *Star Wars* sequence, which unapologetically looked back for inspiration to the serials of the 1930s.

Films featuring stories of travel into outer space began to appear as early as 1902, with **Georges Méliès**'s *Le voyage dans la lune* (*A Trip to the Moon*), which adapted an 1867 novel by **Jules Verne** into a brief silent film that features some of the first sf **special-effects** footage. The Soviet silent film *Aelita* (1924) adapts Alexei Tolstoy's similarly titled novel to silent film, dramatizing socialist ideals in an adventure set on **Mars**. Among other early films about flight into space was **Fritz Lang**'s German film *Frau im Mond* (1929), which is a serious sf film about a trip to the moon that introduces a number of future conventions for the cinematic representation of rocket launches. The plot of the first feature-length **American science fiction film**, *Just Imagine* (1930), centers around a trip to Mars, though the film is really more musical comedy than space opera.

Space opera in the purist sense of the term came to the fore with the serials of the 1930s, which featured simplistic plots aimed at younger audiences, but which were sometimes also able to stimulate the imaginations of and to instill a sense of wonder in their audiences. With the rise to prominence of science fiction as a film genre in the 1950s, space operas began to appear more frequently, though the era was dominated by **alien invasion** and **postapocalyptic** films. Indeed, two of the first major sf films released in the 1950s were narratives of adventure in outer space: *Destination Moon* (1950) and *Rocketship X-M* (1950). Other major space adventure films of the decade included *This Island Earth* (1955) and *Conquest of Space* (1955), while the ambitious *Forbidden Planet* (1956) might be considered the first truly great space opera on film.

By the end of the 1950s, Eastern bloc countries were producing science fiction films as well, such as the 1959 Soviet space-race drama *Nebo zovyot,* adapted to a U.S. version by **Roger Corman** in 1960 as *Battle Beyond the Sun.* The 1960 East German film *Der schweigende Stern* (*The Silent Star*) adapts **Stanisław Lem**'s novel to the screen. An expurgated version was released in the United States in 1962 as *First Spaceship on Venus.* Meanwhile, the Soviet space opera, *Tumannost Andromedy* (1967, *Andromeda Nebula*), adapts Ivan Yefremov's 1957 novel *Andromeda,* while **Andrei Tarkovsky**'s Soviet film *Solaris* (1972) is widely regarded as one of the truly great space operas on film.

Italy also produced space operas, including **Mario Bava**'s 1965 film *Terrore nello spazio* (released in the United States as *Planet of the Vampires*), which effectively combines horror and space opera, thus looking back to American films such as *It! The Terror from Beyond Space* (1958) and looking forward to later films such as *Alien* (1979). In general, however, the 1960s were a slow decade for the genre until **Stanley Kubrick**'s artistically ambitious *2001: A Space Odyssey* (1968) suddenly gained new respect for the space opera— and for science fiction film as a whole.

The early 1970s were dominated by **dystopian** film, though at least one of the films of the era, **Douglas Trumbull**'s *Silent Running* (1972) does take place in outer space. Meanwhile, **John Carpenter**'s *Dark Star* (1974) was a rare comic space opera, a form that reached its greatest success later in Mel Brooks's *Spaceballs* (1987), which had the advantage of being able to spoof the renaissance in space opera that began with *Star Wars* (1977), a film that nostalgically looked back to the grand adventure and simple good-versus-evil oppositions of the space operas of the 1930s. The success of that film ushered in a spate of space operas, including its own sequels. For example, 1979 saw the release of *Star Trek: The Motion Picture,* which brought the characters and scenario of the original 1960s television series to the big screen, becoming the first of what ultimately became an extensive franchise involving sequel films and even several additional television series set in the *Star Trek* universe. That year also saw the release of *The Black Hole,* a big-budget space opera for adults from **Disney,** previously known for children's and family films, thus indicating the extent to which the film industry as a whole was influenced by the success of *Star Wars,* as did the appearance in 1980 of such low-budget efforts as *Flash Gordon,* a campy feature-film reinvention of the 1930s serials, and ***Battle Beyond the Stars,*** Roger Corman's attempt to get on the bandwagon.

The first two *Star Wars* sequels appeared in 1980 and 1983, while *Star Trek* sequels appeared in 1982, 1984, 1986, and 1989. Meanwhile, these two dominant franchises were joined in 1986 by the ***Alien*** franchise, as **James Cameron**'s *Aliens* became the first sequel to the original *Alien.* Otherwise, space opera in the 1980s began to cool off as a genre, though a variety of space operas did continue to appear. *Space Raiders* (1983) was Corman's attempt at a kid-friendly, battle-based space opera, while *The Last Starfighter* (1984) featured a teenage protagonist able to win outer space battles because of his experience playing video games. ***Enemy Mine*** (1985) started out as a war story as well, but then turned to a story of interspecies cooperation between a human and an alien.

The *Star Trek* machine continued to turn out sequels through the 1990s, while the third and fourth *Alien* films appeared in 1992 and 1997. Meanwhile, the decade was topped off with the hugely successful release of *Star Wars: Episode I—The Phantom Menace* in 1999, after a gap of 16 years since the previous *Star Wars* films. Additional sequels were released in 2002 and 2005, carrying the franchise into the new millennium. Meanwhile, **Roland Emmerich**'s *Stargate* (1994) came up with a new twist on the space opera, with spaceships largely replaced by travel through wormholes accessed via special gateways—with some Egyptian mythology thrown in for good measure. Stuart Gordon's *Space Truckers* (1996) was a campy space opera that nevertheless included some effective action scenes and some serious satire. **Luc Besson**'s *The Fifth Element* (1997) also included some campy elements—and some Egyptian mythology—and was one of the most inventive space operas of the 1990s.

In 2000, two major films about journeys to Mars were released: Brian De Palma's *Mission to Mars* and Antony Hoffman's *Red Planet.* The **animated science fiction film** *Titan A.E.* was space opera in the grand mode, but a commercial failure, as American audiences had trouble taking an animated film seriously. In 2001, *Kaubôi bibappu: Tengoku no tobira (Cowboy Bebop: The Movie)* was an **anime** space opera about outer-space bounty hunters; that same year, an American remake of *Solaris* failed to capture the profundity of the Soviet original, while *Star Trek: Nemesis* was so unsuccessful that it almost killed off the franchise. **Joss Whedon**'s compelling space opera *Serenity* (2005) was one of the highlights of sf film in the first decade of the 21st century. **Danny Boyle**'s *Sunshine* (2007) concerns the attempts of a group of space travelers to reignite the dying sun.

SPACE TRUCKERS. (Dir. Stuart Gordon, 1996.) *Space Truckers* is a campy, tongue-in-cheek **space opera** that has a great deal of fun with the whole genre, though it reads most directly as a parody of the *Alien* franchise, the first film of which had originally been envisioned as being about "truckers in space." Here, aging independent space trucker John Canyon (Dennis Hopper) is unknowingly assigned to deliver a load of killer **robots** from Triton (a moon of Neptune) to the earth, where a corrupt **corporation** plans to use the superweapons to solidify its control of the planet. The robots even look a great deal like mechanized versions of the creature from *Alien.* Both the creature effects and the **special effects** in general are surprisingly good in *Space Truckers,* which is especially effective as a parody of outer space action movies because it is actually a fairly good action film in its own right. Virtually every aspect of *Space Truckers* is familiar from other films, but here each is pushed just slightly over the edge. Charles Dance (who had earlier played a major role in *Aliens³*) is particularly hilarious as the brilliant scientist who designed the robots, only to be nearly killed by one of the them on the orders of the company's evil CEO (played by Shane Rimmer); he then reconstructs his body using his knowledge of robotics, emerging as a **cyborg mad scientist** who is the leader of a gang of space pirates. Canyon ultimately defeats the pirates, the robots, and the CEO, then heads back into space, though he has in the meantime (gracefully) lost his beautiful young fiancée (Debi Mazar) to his youthful sidekick (Stephen Dorff). There is no indication that the real power of the corporation has been broken, however.

SPECIAL EFFECTS. Because science fiction cinema is inherently concerned with the representation on screen of technologies, settings, and creatures that do not exist in the real world, it can seldom depend on photographic realism but must typically employ a variety of special effects to create images of things that do not exist in reality. The French magician and pioneering filmmaker **Georges Méliès** is usually credited with having created the first cinematic special effects, and his short film *Le voyage dans la lune* (*A Trip to the Moon*), an adaptation of an 1867 novel by **Jules Verne**, is often considered the first science fiction film. In order to provide facilities for the production of the impressive special effects in his films, Méliès also constructed what is generally considered to be the fist motion picture studio. His films employed a variety of techniques, such as double exposure and overexposure of negatives; running films backwards; and fast, slow, and stop motion. He also achieved the first color effects in film, having color effects handpainted, frame by frame, onto some of his films.

The special photographic techniques used by Méliès have been used, in one way or another, by science fiction filmmakers ever since that time. However, through much of the history of science fiction film, special visual effects have been achieved simply by creating and then filming physical models of science fictional devices, setting, and creatures. Some of these physical techniques are as simple as employing painted backgrounds to create the illusion that the action being filmed is taking place in futuristic cities or distant planets. Techniques of back projection (projecting a moving image onto a screen behind the actors during filming) have similarly been used to create moving backgrounds. Makeup and costuming constitute an important part of this category of special effects, and any number of aliens and other science fictional creatures have been produced simply by placing human actors in elaborate makeup and costumes.

A particularly important breakthrough in physical special effects came in 1925, with the release of *The Lost World,* in which adventurers discover an enclave inhabited by a variety of exotic and prehistoric creatures that were produced by filming moveable physical models in **stop-motion animation**. These models were built by **Willis O'Brien**, who employed similar techniques to even better effect in producing the landmark creatures of *King Kong* (1933). O'Brien used the same technologies in *Son of Kong* (1933) and *Mighty Joe Young* (1949), helping to establish further the viability of stop-motion animation as a technique. The technique of stop-motion animation then reached its pinnacle in the work of O'Brien's protégé, **Ray Harryhausen**, who became the dominant figure in the world of special effects for American science fiction throughout the boom in science fiction cinema of the 1950s.

Harryhausen's elaborate models were used to create special effects via the stop-motion technique that came to be known as *Dynamation,* for such films as *The Beast from 20,000 Fathoms* (1953), *It Came from Beneath the Sea* (1955), *20 Million Miles to Earth* (1957), and *First Men in the Moon* (1964). Harryhausen's techniques had the advantage that they were relatively inexpensive, as were the techniques being used at the same time in Japan by artists such as **Eiji Tsuburaya** for the production of creature effects for films featuring **Godzilla** and other entries in the **monster-movie** subgenre. However, model-building for science fiction film reached a new level of sophistication (and costliness) with the release in 1968 of **Stanley Kubrick**'s *2001: A Space Odyssey,* which employs a variety of highly complex (and convincing) futuristic spacecraft and other futuristic hardware, including the representation of the interior and exterior of the spacecraft *Discovery* in unprecedented detail. Special photographic-effects director **Douglas Trumbull** and other crew members achieved these effects partly through the simple expedient of building large, complex models, which they were able to do because of the availability of an unusually large budget for the film. However, a number of innovative strategies were also used to film these models, including the use of front-projection (aka *retroflective matting*), a technique that allowed for the creation of much more detailed and believable backgrounds than could have been achieved by painted backdrops or back-projection. This technique had never before been used so extensively, but has been widely used ever since. It involves placing a separate scenery projector at right angles to the camera. A special mirror splits the light coming out of the projector, with about half of it reflected forward onto a backdrop, which then reflects the image back to the camera, where it is combined in-camera with the actual scene being filmed.

Trumbull went on to supervise special effects for a number of other sf films, including *The Andromeda Strain* (1971), *Silent Running* (1972, which he also directed), *Close Encounters of the Third Kind* (1977), *Star Trek: The Motion Picture* (1979), and *Blade Runner* (1982). However, he turned down an offer from **George Lucas** to supervise the special effects for *Star Wars* (1977) because he was busy with other projects. That film, with effects supervised by Trumbull's former assistant **John Dykstra**, became the next major landmark in the history of special effects for science fiction film. *Star Wars* employed a number of complex models filmed using computer-controlled cameras. But it became best known for its pioneering use of blue-screen technologies, in which action was filmed in front of a blank blue screen, the background images to be filled in later. The blue screens of *Star Wars* were soon replaced by the use of a **green screen**, but the basic technique remained the same and has since become a staple of science fiction film, largely supplanting the front-projection techniques of *2001: A Space Odyssey*.

Star Wars also made unprecedented use of **computer-generated imagery (CGI)**, which had been pioneered in the films *Westworld* (1973) and *Future World* (1976). From that point forward, CGI became more and more dominant as a technique for the generation of special effects for science fiction film, with Lucas's own **Lucasfilm** and its special-effects arm **Industrial Light & Magic** leading the way, producing effects not just for Lucas's *Star Wars* films, but for hundreds of other films as well. As computer technology itself improved, the sophistication with which computer-generated special effects could be produced improved as well, to the point that, in 1995, the new studio, **Pixar** (a spin-off of Lucasfilm), produced an entire film (*Toy Story*) using computer animation. Pixar has gone on to become the industry leader in the production of computer-animated family films, while computer animation itself has largely supplanted traditional hand animation as a technique for producing such films. Pixar's films, meanwhile, often include a number of science fictional elements, and one of their films, *WALL-E* (2008), is pure science fiction.

By 2001, with the release of the big-budget, joint U.S.-Japanese production, *Final Fantasy: The Spirits Within*, science fiction filmmakers were fast approaching the ability to produce entire photorealistic films by computer animation, though the human characters in this film still look a bit more like video-game characters than real actors. For example, 2004 saw the release of such films as the Japanese *Casshern*, the French *Immortel (ad vitam)*, and the American *Able Edwards* and *Sky Captain and the World of Tomorrow* (the latter actually a joint British-Italian-American production), all of which were shot entirely in front of green screens, using live actors, with all backgrounds added later by computer. *Immortel* even made extensive use of computer-generated human characters to supplement the characters portrayed by human actors, while *Sky Captain* used one computer-generated character (based on recorded images of legendary actor Laurence Olivier) as well. With the release of *WALL-E*, computer generation of science fictional backgrounds and hardware reached a new level of sophistication (though the film made no attempt at photorealistic depiction of human characters), suggesting a bright future for computer animation of science fiction films, a future that was already becoming a reality with the release of such films as **James Cameron**'s *Avatar*, one of the most complex, sophisticated (and expensive) films ever made. *See also* ANIMATED SCIENCE FICTION FILMS.

SPIELBERG, STEVEN (1946–). Though his work spans many different genres, Steven Spielberg is still arguably the most important and successful director and producer in the history of science fiction film. Spielberg began his career in television, directing numerous episodes of various programs for **Universal Studios**, beginning with "L.A. 2017," a science fiction episode of the series *The Name of the Game* set in a dystopian future that aired in 1971. Having moved into feature films (again working initially for Universal), Spielberg began his career as a director of science fiction films with the alien-invasion classic *Close Encounters of the Third Kind* (1977), which he also wrote. This film, along with *Star Wars,* ushered in one of the most productive periods in the history of science fiction film, a period that also included *E.T. the Extra-Terrestrial* (1982), which was both directed and produced by Spielberg. A huge hit, this film, following on Spielberg's success as the director of *Raiders of the Lost Ark* (1981), solidified his reputation as box-office gold. Though he produced or executive produced several more films with sf themes in the coming years, it was not until 1993, with the much-hyped release of *Jurassic Park,* that Spielberg returned to the helm as director of a science fiction film, though this one was a **monster movie**, a genre whose relation with science fiction is sometimes considered tenuous. Spielberg returned to all-out science fiction, both scripting and directing the Pinocchio-inspired robot story *Artificial Intelligence: AI* in 2001, completing a project originally conceived by **Stanley Kubrick,** who died before he was able to begin the film. Spielberg followed as the director of *Minority Report* (2002), a stylish futuristic thriller that was another major box-office hit. Spielberg's remake of *War of the Worlds* in 2005 was greeted with lukewarm response by critics, but was another commercial success. In 2008, Spielberg released his fourth Indiana Jones film, *Indiana Jones and the Kingdom of the Crystal Skull,* this time taking the archaeological adventurer into the realm of the **alien-invasion** narrative. Spielberg has also executive produced such high-profile science fiction film sequences as the *Back to the Future* films and the *Men in Black* films. *See also* DYSTOPIAN FILM.

SPOCK. Spock is the iconic half-human, half-Vulcan science officer and first mate of the starship *Enterprise* in the original *Star Trek* television series (1966–1969). Played by **Leonard Nimoy,** Spock is the son of Sarek, a Vulcan diplomat (played by Mark Lenard), and the human woman Amanda Grayson (Jane Wyatt). As a hybrid of the two races, Spock is the ultimate outsider, never quite fitting in on either side, a trait that helped to make him an icon for young science fiction fans who often felt similarly alienated. However, it is clear that Spock seems to value his Vulcan heritage more than his human one, and he consistently strives to be coldly logical and unemotional, in the Vulcan manner, while his often sardonic view of human foibles presents an important outsider's viewpoint on the human condition. Spock, with his trademark pointy ears and short-cropped bangs, looks almost entirely Vulcan. Further, in addition to his superhuman ability to think logically, he also has a number of other Vulcan abilities that humans do not possess, including superhuman strength (which helps him to immobilize opponents via the "Vulcan nerve pinch") and certain telepathic abilities (which allow him to merge his consciousness with that of other sentient beings via the "Vulcan mind meld.")

Spock teamed with the all-too-human Captain **James T. Kirk (William Shatner)** and Dr. **Leonard McCoy (DeForest Kelley)** to form one of the most effective character groupings in science fiction history. Indeed, much of the success of the *Star Trek* franchise can be attributed to the sometimes uneasy, but always sincere camaraderie that developed among these three very different characters. The chemistry among these characters (and actors) helped them to carry the first six *Star Trek* feature films, including the second, *Star Trek: The Wrath of Khan,* which sees Spock die in the end, sacrificing himself to save his shipmates, and the third, *Star Trek III: The Search for Spock* (directed by Nimoy), in which he is restored to life. The young Spock, played by Zachary Quinto, is also a major figure in the 2009 *Star Trek* reboot/prequel, which features a **time-travel** motif that allows the older Spock (still played by Nimoy) to appear as well. All in all, Spock is one of the most recognizable characters, not just in science fiction film and television, but in American popular culture as a whole.

STALKER. (Dir. **Andrei Tarkovsky**, 1979.) A brooding meditation on the nature of memory, desire, and reality, *Stalker* is a masterpiece of philosophical, thought-provoking science fiction. The film is based on the 1971 novel *Roadside Picnic,* by Boris and Arkadi Strugatsky, who also wrote the screenplay. In the film, the Stalker of the title (played by Aleksandr Kaidanovsky), is a professional guide who takes two clients, a Writer (Anatoli Solonitsyn) and a Professor (Nikolai Grinko), into the strange, forbidden area known as "The Zone," where the very laws of physics seem to have been modified, perhaps as the result of an earlier alien visitation. The trip is an extended encounter with a world in which human beings are decidedly not at home, making The Zone something of a microcosmic commentary on humanity's difficult relation to the world as a whole. The film also lends itself to a variety of other interpretations, such as a psychoanalytical one, in which The Zone became an analog for the unconscious mind. The main goal of the trip in the film is to reach a special room where one's deepest wishes can be fulfilled, though sometimes this room reveals that one's deepest wishes are not at all what one thought they were. The three men make it back alive from the dangerous Zone, but, in keeping with the strangeness and unde-cideable nature of the Zone, the eerie film remains enigmatic and inconclusive to its very end, after a running time of more than two and one-half hours.

***STAR TREK* AND SEQUELS.** (Various directors, 1979–2009.) Given its own longevity and its inspiration of a vast media franchise, the original *Star Trek* television series (1966–1969) might rightly be regarded as the most important single work of science fiction in history. It is certainly the case that the *Star Trek* film franchise is the most extensive (in terms of duration and number of films) in sf film history. Partly inspired by the recent commercial and technical success of *Star Wars, Star Trek: The Motion Picture* (1979), directed by sf veteran **Robert Wise**, was an attempt to update the original *Star Trek* for a new generation of fans, building upon recent dramatic advances in **special-effects** technology. With nearly three times the budget of *Star Wars* and with special-effects wizards such as **Douglas Trumbull** and **John Dykstra** on board, *Star Trek* is indeed an impressive-looking film, even if it is not really groundbreaking in the way *Star Wars* had been. Moreover, the first *Star Trek* film puts more emphasis on visual grandeur than on interpersonal relationship among the crew of the USS *Enterprise,* especially the key figures of Captain **James T. Kirk (William Shatner)**, the half-Vulcan first mate **Spock (Leonard Nimoy)**, and the irascible doctor **Leonard McCoy (DeForest Kelley)**. The plot is a bit weak as well, and as a whole the film was something of a disappointment. Still, the built-in audience from loyal fans of the original series made the first *Star Trek* film a substantial commercial success, leading to the longest series of sequels in sf film history.

For most fans (and critics), *Star Trek: The Wrath of Khan* (1982), directed by **Nicholas Meyer**, was a great improvement over the first film, returning more to the spirit of the original series. Indeed, the second *Star Trek* film is a direct sequel to one of the episodes of the original series. It is also science fiction in the grand manner, featuring a number of key sf tropes, including **genetic engineering**, the terraforming of planets for human colonization, and the requisite space battles. The real emphasis, though, is on character. We discover, for example, that Kirk has a son. Most importantly, the film features the death of Spock, who sacrifices himself to save the *Enterprise* and its crew. Spock is resurrected, however, in *Star Trek III: The Search for Spock* (1984), though the *Enterprise* is destroyed. This was the first numbered *Star Trek* film (suggesting the expectation of a long sequence of films) and the first of two consecutive *Star Trek* films directed by Nimoy.

Star Trek IV: The Voyage Home (1986) follows directly on that film, completing a sort of trilogy. Here, the earth is nearly accidentally destroyed by an alien probe that is attempting to communicate with the planet's humpback whales, which are unfortunately extinct in the 23rd-century setting of the film. The film then becomes a **time-travel** narrative in which the original *Enterprise* crew, now piloting a stolen Klingon Bird of Prey, travels back to the 1980s to retrieve a pair of the whales to take back to the future. They succeed, of course, in the meantime experiencing a number of humorous misadventures due to their unfamiliarity with the culture and language of the 1980s.

This turn to more humor continues in *Star Trek V: The Final Frontier* (1989) and *Star Trek VI: The Undiscovered Country* (1991), in which serious plots are supplemented by comic interactions among Kirk, Spock, and McCoy. Indeed, the original cast was by this time growing so old that their advancing age itself became a key object of humor in the films. *Star Trek: Generations* (1994) then handed the mantle over to the younger cast of television's *Star Trek: The Next Generation,* who continued the film series in *Star Trek: First Contact* (1996), one of the more interesting of the *Star Trek* films. However, *Star Trek: Insurrection* (1998), and *Star Trek: Nemesis* (2002) were not big hits with critics or fans, and the series fell dormant until it was resurrected in 2009 with **J. J. Abrams**'s *Star Trek,* a prequel featuring an all-new cast of actors playing young versions of the original characters, freshly out of Starfleet Academy—though Nimoy plays a prominent role as the older Spock as well. That film was the most commercially successful of all the *Star Trek* films, though some purists thought the turn to more high-energy special-effects action represented a departure from the thoughtfulness of the *Star Trek* franchise as a whole.

STAR WARS **AND SEQUELS.** (Dir. **George Lucas** et al., 1977– 2008.) The original *Star Wars* (now conventionally referred to as *Star Wars: Episode IV—A New Hope*) caused a sensation upon its release in 1977, helping to initiate an explosion of production in science fiction film over the next several years. Moreover, the innovative **special effects** of *Star Wars* were on the cutting edge of a revolution in the **computer-generated imagery** that continues to this day and that has had a dramatic impact on the visual texture of science fiction film. However, despite its technical innovations, *Star Wars* is at heart a nostalgic film that looks back to the science fiction **serials** of the 1930s, featuring a simple narrative of good versus evil in which good triumphs against all odds.

Star Wars also introduced some of the best-known characters in the history of science fiction film, including its center trio of protagonists, the young and gifted **Luke Skywalker**, the courageous Princess **Leia Organa** (Carrie Fisher), and the heroic smuggler **Han Solo (Harrison Ford)**, who remained the central figures in the other films of the original trilogy, *Stars Wars: Episode V—The Empire Strikes Back* (1980) and *Star Wars: Episode VI—The Return of the Jedi* (1983). Even the supporting cast of *Star Wars* have become icons of popular culture, from wise old **Obi-Wan Kenobi (Sir Alec Guinness)** to Solo's sidekick, the towering Wookie Chewbacca (Peter Mayhew), to the loveable, bickering **robots** (referred to as *droids*) **C-3PO** (Anthony Daniels) and **R2-D2** (a mechanical costume with dwarf Kenny Baker inside and electronic "voice" effects created by Ben Burtt). Beginning with the second film, the **Jedi** sage **Yoda** (voiced by puppeteer Frank Oz) also became an iconic figure. Ultimately, however, the best-known figure from the original trilogy might be its central villain, the black-clad **cyborg Darth Vader** (voiced by James Earl Jones, but physically played by champion bodybuilder David Prowse).

Part of the secret of the success of the original *Star Wars* trilogy lay in its ability to create a compelling and gradually expanding mythology that made its fictional context (famously set "long, long ago in a galaxy far, far away") seem believable, despite the sometimes farfetched or muddled nature of its narrative. Thus, as the trilogy proceeds, we learn that Luke and Leia are twin brother and sister and that their father is **Anakin Skywalker**, a talented Jedi Knight who eventually evolved into the sinister Vader due to his turn to the dark side of the seemingly part-physical and part-mystical "**Force**" that is the secret to the power of the Jedi knights. Meanwhile, the lives of all of the characters are intimately entwined with the political situation that prevails in this fictional galaxy, with the forces of an evil Empire opposed by rebel Republicans.

The *Star Wars* sequence was in hiatus from 1983 to 1999, when the release of *Star Wars: Episode I—The Phantom Menace* became one of the most anticipated events in global film of the late 20th century. This film also initiated a second "prequel" trilogy of *Star Wars* films that also went on to include *Star Wars: Episode II—Attack of the Clones* (2002) and *Star Wars: Episode III—Revenge of the Sith* (2005). In keeping with the focus of the first three *Star Wars* films on building a detailed mythological framework, the prequel trilogy does a great deal to fill in the backgrounds of the characters and political oppositions of the first trilogy. In particular, the prequel trilogy focuses on the gradual slide of the promising Anakin Skywalker (portrayed as a young adult by **Hayden Christensen** in the second and third prequel films) into the dark side, despite the best efforts of his mentor, the young Obi-Wan Kenobi (**Ewan McGregor**), to steer him onto the proper course.

A seventh *Star Wars* film, the computer-animated *Star Wars: The Clone Wars,* was only a modest success in 2008, but together the seven *Star Wars* films have taken in nearly $2 billion at the box office (over $3.5 billion adjusted to 2005 dollars), making *Star Wars* the most lucrative film franchise of all time. *Star Wars* is also the center of a multimedia empire, having inspired one of the most successful licensing and merchandising campaigns in film history. In addition to toys and other merchandise, the *Star Wars* "expanded universe" now includes an extensive sequence of video games, comic books, novels, fan fiction, animated television series, and made-for-TV films.

STEWART, PATRICK (1940–). In 1987, the British actor Patrick Stewart had a distinguished stage career (including work with the

Royal Shakespeare Company) and had made a number of television appearances. He had even had substantial roles in science fiction film as Gurney Halleck in **David Lynch**'s *Dune* (1984) and as Dr. Armstrong in the 1985 space vampire film *Lifeforce*. But he was still a relative unknown to American audiences when he was tapped for the role of Captain Jean-Luc Picard in *Star Trek: The Next Generation* in 1987, bringing new episodes of the *Star Trek* franchise back to television for the first time in 18 years. The success of *The Next Generation* quickly made Stewart a familiar face (and voice) to American audiences, and he will forever be associated with Picard, especially after playing the character for seven years on television and then in three *Star Trek* feature films: *Star Trek: Generations* (1994), *Star Trek: First Contact* (1996), and *Star Trek: Insurrection* (1998). *Insurrection* appeared to be his last film as Picard, but, lest he be regarded as a one-role actor, it should also be noted that he has subsequently had major success as Professor Xavier in the three *X-Men* films (released in 2000, 2003, and 2006), superhero narratives that include strong science fiction elements. Stewart also played Captain Nemo in a 2005 made-for-TV adaptation of **Jules Verne**'s *Mysterious Island* and lent his distinctive booming voice to three **animated science fiction films**, *Nausicaä of the Valley of the Wind* (1984, the English-dubbed version of *Kaze no tani no Naushika*), *Jimmy Neutron: Boy Genius* (2001), and *Chicken Little* (2005).

STOP-MOTION ANIMATION. Stop-motion animation is an animation technique in which posable models are repeatedly photographed, then moved into a slightly different position and rephotographed, creating a series of still images that can then be combined sequentially to create the illusion of continuous movement. **Willis O'Brien** was the first great practitioner of this technique, using it to particularly good effect in the original movie version of *King Kong* (1933). O'Brien's protégé, **Ray Harryhausen**, is easily the most famous stop-motion animation artist; he used the technique in a variety of science fiction **monster movies** of the 1950s, as well as in other films. Harryhausen also developed the "**Dynamation**" process through which he combined live-action with stop-motion animation.

There are many varieties of stop-motion animation. Some applications, for example, use manipulated models made of clay, in the so-called clay animation or "claymation" process. Another, more sophisticated, variation, called *go motion,* combines traditional hand manipulation of models with computer-controlled movement of the models. All in all, however, stop motion has been supplanted in recent years by **computer-generated imagery,** though some film-makers (notably **Tim Burton** and Henry Selick) still prefer the look produced by traditional stop-motion animation. In addition, some computer-generated features—such as the **postapocalyptic** film *9* (2009)—have intentionally been designed to mimic the look of stop-motion animation.

SUTHERLAND, DONALD (1935–). The Canadian-born actor Donald Sutherland was propelled to stardom via his role as Hawk-eye Pierce in Robert Altman's antiwar film, *MASH* (1970), and he quickly followed with a lead role in another classic film, *Klute* (1971). In 1978, Sutherland began his career in science fiction film when he starred as San Francisco health inspector Matthew Bennell in the remake of the 1956 classic **alien-invasion** film *Invasion of the Body Snatchers.* That same year he was made an Officer of the Order of Canada to honor him for his achievements, though they were in fact at that time just beginning. He has now appeared in dozens of films spanning virtually every genre, including science fiction. In 1994, for example, he returned to science fiction as the star of *The Puppet Masters,* an adaptation of the 1951 novel of the same title by **Robert A. Heinlein** that features a scenario very similar to that of *Invasion of the Body Snatchers.* That same year he turned toward roles as villains when he starred in the made-for-TV sf film *The Lifeforce Experiment* playing a scientist who develops a computer that can read the dreams of sleeping people. In *Outbreak* (1995), Sutherland plays a general who is willing to bomb an en-tire American town to cover up his and the military's involvement in clandestine biological weapons development. In *Virus* (1999), Sutherland is a sea captain who, in order to further his own ends, is willing to make common cause with an alien bent on wiping out the human race. In 2000, he returned to a kinder and gentler role as one of a group of aging astronauts in *Space Cowboys* (2000). He has not since appeared on screen in a science fiction film, but he does provide the voice for characters in the 2001 animated film *Final*

Fantasy: The Spirits Within and the 2009 animated film *Astro Boy,* based on a popular Japanese manga series.

– T –

TARKOVSKY, ANDREI (1932–1986). Andrei Tarkovsky was one of the giants of Soviet cinema, though his relatively short life and his problematic relationship with the Soviet cinema establishment (somewhat analogous to Orson Welles's difficulties with the Hollywood establishment) caused his total output to be fairly small. He made only two science fiction films, *Solaris* (1972) and *Stalker* (1979), but both are among the great achievements of Soviet science fiction film. His other best-known work is the 1966 film *Andrei Rublev,* which is loosely based on the life of the eponymous 15th-century Russian painter of religious icons, though that controversial film (like Welles's *Citizen Kane*) saw only very limited release in the director's home country. Neither *Solaris* nor *Stalker* was widely seen in the Soviet Union either, and Tarkovsky ended his career working in Italy, where Welles had spent much of his eight-year European exile as well.

TAYLOR, ROD (1930–). Born and raised in Australia, Rod Taylor came to the United States in 1954 to pursue a career as a film actor. One of his first major roles was in the **postapocalyptic** film *World Without End* (1956), in which he plays one of a group of astronauts who are inadvertently catapulted into a future ravaged by nuclear war, thus making it a **time-travel** film as well. Four years later, he starred in what remains in many ways the prototypical time-travel film when he played the unnamed time traveler in **George Pal**'s film adaptation of **H. G. Wells**'s novel *The Time Machine.* That role and his star turn in Alfred Hitchcock's horror classic *The Birds* (1963) are the ones for which Taylor is most remembered. He did, however, have a substantial career as a leading man in Hollywood films in a variety of genres and on American television, usually playing American characters, but sometimes affecting a British accent. In 1998, he returned to science fiction with a supporting role in *The Warlord:*

Battle for the Galaxy, a made-for-TV film that was the pilot for a series that never materialized.

THE TERMINATOR AND SEQUELS. (Dir. **James Cameron** et al., 1984–2009.) *The Terminator* (1984) was a relatively low-budget film whose director and star were virtually unknown at the time. However, the film helped to propel director James Cameron and star **Arnold Schwarzenegger** to the top ranks of sf film stardom. *The Terminator* is a **time-travel** narrative about the "terminator" of the title, a killer **cyborg** (Schwarzenegger) that travels back to the present time of the film in order to kill young **Sarah Connor (Linda Hamilton)** before she can give birth to the child (**John Connor**) who will go on to lead the human resistance movement in a future in which machines have virtually wiped out the human race and established their dominion over the earth. It is thus partly a **postapocalyptic** film, though we see only a few glimpses of this machine-ruled future. Instead, the focus is on the 1980s, where Connor attempts to elude the cyborg with the help of Kyle Reese (**Michael Biehn**), a resistance fighter from the future, sent back by John Connor to protect his mother. In the kind of twist that is typical of time-travel narratives, Reese manages to save Sarah, dying in the effort, but not before he becomes the father of the child who will become John Connor.

The role of the muscular, laconic terminator was a perfect match for Schwarzenegger's particular set of acting skills, propelling him to stardom. Meanwhile, Cameron's effective use of the limited resources available to him to construct a compelling narrative set him on the road to stardom as well. However, *The Terminator* was only a moderate box-office success. Though it won the **Saturn Award** as the year's best science fiction film, it otherwise got little in the way of immediate critical recognition. Yet this relatively simple film, strongly rooted in the tropes of pulp science fiction, went on to be named by *Esquire* magazine as "the film of the eighties" and has now received attention from academic film critics exceeded by that accorded only a handful of sf films.

The basic scenario of *The Terminator* also made it a prime candidate for the development of sequels, of which there have been three as of this writing. *Terminator 2: Judgment Day* (1991), also directed by Cameron, builds upon the scenario of the first film by having Schwarzenegger (now a major star) return as a benevolent terminator sent back in time by John Connor to protect his childhood self from the murderous attentions of a much more advanced terminator that has been sent back to kill him. This transformation was compelling enough that, in 2003, the American Film Institute ranked this "good" Terminator as one of only four sf characters on its list of 50 Greatest Movie Heroes—while ranking the "bad" Terminator of the first film among the 50 Greatest Movie Villains. In addition to Schwarzenegger's shift from villain to hero, this film is also remarkable for Sarah Connor's transformation from a relatively conventional young woman to a tough, muscular resistance fighter, determined to defend her son (and, ultimately, the human race) both from terminators and from the ignorance of the society around them. The camaraderie between Schwarzenegger's terminator and young John Connor (Edward Furlong) also leads to a number of memorable (often humorous) scenes. With Schwarzenegger and Cameron both now among the elite of sf film, *Terminator 2* was able to command a huge budget, which allowed for vastly improved **special effects** relative to the first film.

Schwarzenegger returned as a benevolent terminator in *Terminator 3: Rise of the Machines* (2003), in his last film before his turn to politics. This film is notable for the fact that the advanced killer cyborg sent back to kill John Connor this time is female, but, with Cameron and Hamilton (Sarah Connor has died of cancer) no longer involved, most critics felt that *Terminator 3* was uninspired and that the *Terminator* franchise may have run its course, even though the film was a box-office hit. A television series, set roughly in the same time period as *Terminator 3* featured Sarah Connor (now played by Lena Headey), now resurrected via time-travel manipulation of the past, again in a lead role. *The Sarah Connor Chronicles* (2008–2009) ran on the Fox network for two seasons. Still another film sequel, *Terminator Salvation,* appeared in 2009, this time with Schwarzenegger joining Cameron and Hamilton on the sidelines. However, this film's shift to a focus on the man-machine war of the future takes the franchise in a new direction, though the interrogation of the relationship between men and their machines (and of the boundary between the two) that marks the first three films remains. Meanwhile, with top draw **Christian Bale** in the lead role as the adult John Connor, the film was a commercial success, if less so than the second and third *Terminator* films.

TEZUKA, OSAMU (1928–1989). The pioneering manga artist and animator Osamu Tezuka is often referred to as the "Father of Manga" and the "Father of **Anime**" for his own groundbreaking contributions to the development of comics art, animated film, and animated television in Japan, as well as for his incalculable influence on numerous artists and filmmakers who came after him. In the realm of science fiction, Tezuka is probably best known as the creator of the manga *Tesuwan Atom* (*Astro Boy*), which appeared from 1951 to 1968, and which has been the basis of several animated television series, including an initial series (which ran from 1963 to 1966) that was the first Japanese-produced animated series to appear on television in that country. In 2009, an American-produced, computer-animated *Astro Boy* feature-length film was released, bringing the **robot** hero to a new generation of viewers. *See also* JAPANESE SCIENCE FICTION FILM.

THEM! (Dir. Gordon Douglas, 1954.) *Them!* is essentially a giant bug **monster movie**, though it is especially important because of the way it addressed topical issues of the day due to the fact that its giant, man-eating ants were produced by nuclear testing in the New Mexico desert. These ants seem to pose a genuine threat to the entire United States before they are finally defeated (in the storm sewers of Los Angeles) by an alliance of scientists, police, and the military, ultimately reassuring audiences that the military-industrial complex is there to protect them from such dangers, even if the dangers are, in fact, produced by that complex in the first place. Scientists are treated especially well in the film; on the other hand, the police and military, while ultimately playing a positive role, are more problematic in their willingness to suspend civil liberties to further their efforts to defeat the ants or to keep the existence of the ants a secret from the general public in order to prevent a panic. For example, when an individualistic pilot (played by Fess Parker) spots one of the queen ants flying toward Los Angeles and wants to announce his sighting to the world, the authorities order the pilot detained in a psychiatric ward in order to keep him quiet, even though they know perfectly well that he is sane.

As insects, the ants of the film have little in common with human beings and are the objects of little sympathy. As matriarchal insects, they are even more foreign and threatening. And, as highly organized, communal insects whose every activity is orchestrated by central planning, they served as a perfect metaphor for the 1950s fear of regimentation, either communist or capitalist.

THEY LIVE. (Dir. **John Carpenter**, 1988.) Though a low-budget effort, *They Live* is one of the most satirically effective science fiction works of the 1980s, a decade that was marked by a satirical turn in science fiction in general. Here, former professional wrestler **Roddy Piper** plays Nada, an itinerant workman who accidentally stumbles on the fact that an earlier **alien invasion** has already put aliens in control of the United States, which they are secretly manipulating for profit even as they move to take over the rest of the world as well. Nada, using special glasses manufactured by an underground resistance group, is able to see through the mass illusion that has been imposed on the general population, thus not only seeing the true appearance of the gruesome aliens (who look like normal humans to those who are in their thrall), but also seeing the true content of the various subliminal messages that are being promulgated through the media to ensure the continuing subjugation of the general population. Nada ultimately strikes an important blow against the aliens by knocking out the main signal with which they mesmerize the general population, even as he himself is shot down, though it remains unclear whether this step will lead to the defeat of the aliens, especially as many wealthy and powerful humans are knowingly working hand in hand with the aliens.

If this last aspect of the film can be taken as a strong criticism of the selfishness and ruthlessness of America's corporate elite, the film as a whole is even more effective due to the fact that the strategies of the aliens so closely resemble those that we already know are in use by American corporate capitalism, exploiting and manipulating the bulk of the population largely through concealing its true nature by careful control of the media. The film thus joins contemporaneous

Hollywood productions such as Oliver Stone's *Wall Street* (1987) in satirizing the corporate practices of the Reaganite 1980s, though its science fictional context allows for a more sweeping indictment of the capitalist system. *See also* CORPORATION.

THE THING FROM ANOTHER WORLD. (Dir. Christian Nyby and Howard Hawks, 1951.) Opening in April 1951, *The Thing from Another World* was the first of the many **alien-invasion** films of the 1950s, serving as something of a prototype for the genre. The Thing of the title is a single alien invader that survives the crash of its flying saucer near the North Pole, then undertakes what appears to be a project to colonize the planet for itself and its fellow vegetable creatures, planning to use the human race as a source of its favorite plant food, blood. Luckily, it is defeated fairly easily by the personnel of an arctic scientific outpost.

Crucial to this film is the opposition between Captain Patrick Hendry (**Kenneth Tobey**), leader of an air force contingent sent to investigate the saucer crash, and Dr. Arthur Carrington (Robert Cornthwaite), a famous scientist (stipulated to be a Nobel Prize winner), who heads the research team at the outpost. Carrington is all intellect and wants to preserve the alien for study, seeing it as an unprecedented source of scientific knowledge. Moreover, he also admires the creature as an advanced being, believing that it operates on pure logic, with no interference from human emotions, especially sexual ones. Hendry, meanwhile, is more moderate (and more human), and his common-sense view is that the invader must be killed to protect humanity, a position that the film clearly supports, preferring Hendry over the extremist Carrington, who becomes a typical image of the 1950s suspicion of scientists as not sharing the concerns of ordinary humans and of being devoted to cold logic in ways that were vaguely associated with communism and the Soviet Union. The film thus sets the tone for many of the alien-invasion films of the 1950s, in which the alien invaders were consistently associated, in one way or another, with the Soviet threat.

The Thing from Another World was remade by **John Carpenter** as *The Thing* in 1982 with much better visual effects, but the remake is actually less interesting than the original.

THINGS TO COME. (Dir. **William Cameron Menzies**, 1936.) The first major feature-length science fiction film of the sound era, *Things to Come* was scripted by science fiction pioneer **H. G. Wells** based on his book *The Shape of Things to Come* (1933). The film illustrates Wells's belief late in his life that a utopian future was attainable, but only after the current order of civilization had been destroyed, clearing the way for a new era of technological progress and global government.

The film focuses on the city of Everytown, beginning in 1940, when a cataclysmic war breaks out and the city (along with most of human civilization) is virtually destroyed by a deadly plague that sweeps the globe as the result of the use of biological weapons. The plague rages on for decades; in 1970 it is declared over, but civilization still lies in ruins. Much of the film is set in 1970, as an envoy from an organization known as "Wings Over the World" arrives in a high-tech plane, announcing that his group has rebooted civilization and is making great technological advances. When the local warlord spurns the envoy's efforts to negotiate, the organization bombs the city with the "gas of peace," tranquilizing everyone and then forcing the city to join their new global order. The city is then rebuilt under the leadership of this visionary group of aviators and engineers who use technology (and superior air power) to enforce their vision of an enlightened world government. Conflicts remain, however, and by 2036, many citizens are dissatisfied with the new order and its devotion to technological progress. Angry crowds protest a new project to colonize outer space, beginning with an initial flight to the moon. The flight is launched nevertheless, and the film seems to imply that this is the beginning of an exciting new adventure for humanity—and that humanity needs such adventures to flourish. However, it is also possible to see the space colonization project as a sign of an insatiable drive for progress that only threatens to undermine the now idyllic life in Everytown. A thoughtful work of science fiction, the film is also quite impressive for its time in its use of futuristic sets to portray the Everytown of the 21st century.

THIS ISLAND EARTH. (Dir. Joseph Newman, 1955.) In one of the most ambitious science fiction films of the 1950s, *This Island Earth* varies the **alien-invasion** theme by depicting a group of alien scientists (from the besieged planet of Metaluna) who have come to earth to recruit earth scientists to help them develop better sources of nuclear power so they can fight off their enemies on the neighboring planet of Zahgon. The Matalunans are apparently desperately in need of brainpower, most of their own scientists having already been killed in the war with Zahgon. On the other hand, Metalunan science seems much more advanced than that of earth, so the notion that earth scientists could really be of help is a bit farfetched. In any case, he-man scientist Cal Meacham (Rex Reason) and beautiful female scientist Ruth Adams (**Faith Domergue**) are making some useful progress, then are spirited off via flying saucer to the blighted planet of Metaluna as a crisis approaches, moving the film into the realm of **space opera**. The film suggests that the Metalunans may be the victims in the war, but the American scientists do not appreciate being forcibly conscripted; they are especially alarmed when the Metalunans reveal that they plan to abandon their planet and resettle on earth. Meacham and Adams escape and manage to return to earth on the Matalunan ship, with the help of a sympathetic Metalunan, who drops them off safely before crashing into the ocean. The film ends with Metaluna destroyed but with romance blooming, Hollywood style, for the two scientists.

Though a comparatively high-budget effort for its day, *This Island Earth* had neither the budget nor the technology to pursue its ambitious premise entirely successfully; its wooden acting, bad dialogue, and cheap effects made it the featured object of parody in the 1996 theatrical film version of *Mystery Science Theater 3000,* though the commentary there makes *This Island Earth* seem a good deal sillier than it really is.

THE TIME MACHINE. (Dir. **George Pal**, 1960.) One of the finest of the many film adaptations of works by science fiction great **H. G. Wells,** *The Time Machine* details a trip from the Victorian era to the far-distant future by a time traveler (unnamed in the Wells novel) who is identified in the film as Wells himself (played by **Rod Taylor**). The film version of *The Time Machine* is a reasonably faithful adaptation of Wells's novel, though at one point it does have the time traveler (who begins his journey on New Year's Eve, 1899) stop off in 1966, where he is nearly killed in a nuclear assault on London. Therefore, when he subsequently travels into the far future (he ends up in the year 802,701, just as in Wells's book), the depiction of the dystopian environment of that future is given a postapocalyptic cast dating back to the cold war. As in Wells's book, the time traveler discovers that the human race has evolved (actually, devolved) into two separate species, a motif that in the original novel was clearly a commentary on the separation of the classes in Victorian England. The passive and indolent Eloi live on the gardenlike surface of the planet, enjoying lives of mindless leisure. Meanwhile, the aggressive and animalistic Morlocks live beneath the surface, where they still have at least some operating technology. The Morlocks, as it turns out, are raising the Eloi essentially as cattle, taking them at full maturity beneath the surface to be slaughtered for food. The time traveler manages to evade the Morlocks and return to his own time, but, as the film ends, he returns to 802,701 to help lead the Eloi in their attempt to build a new world and regenerate their ability for creative action, thus suggesting that whatever horrors have been introduced into humanity's future can still be corrected. In this sense, *The Time Machine* is typical of the science fiction films of the 1950s in its attempt ultimately to calm the very fears that it draws upon for its central energies. *See also* DYSTOPIAN FILM; TIME TRAVEL.

TIME TRAVEL. Time-travel narratives have long been a favorite subgenre of science fiction. They offer numerous possibilities for inventive plotting, including sudden twists, turns, and reversals. They also offer considerable attractions that stimulate the imaginations of their readers or viewers, including the ability to see into the future or to revisit (and possibly change) the past. Indeed, the majority of science fiction stories, being set in the future, involve imaginative time travel of a sort, in which the reader or viewer must place him- or herself within the context of a different time. Time-travel narratives also potentially present opportunities for speculation on the fundamental nature of time—and of reality itself, potentially making them one of the most thoughtful forms of science fiction. Finally, the time-travel motif presents extensive opportunities for humor and satire, giving the subgenre a wide range.

H. G. Wells's *The Time Machine* (1895) was the first genuinely science fictional exploration of time travel in book-length form. That novel has exercised an extensive influence on the time-travel genre, including the production of **George Pal**'s 1960 film adaptation of the novel, one of the classic science fiction films of its era. It was also one of the first time-travel films, such films not having been a major subgenre during the sf explosion of the 1950s. Occasional 1950s films did explore the motif, however, as in **Edward Bernds**'s *World without End* (1956), in which a crew of astronauts on earth's first mission to **Mars** (in 1957) encounters strange turbulence in space and is hurtled forward in time into the early 26th century as they return to a postapocalyptic earth. This combination of time-travel film and **postapocalyptic** film occured again in the classic *Planet of the Apes* (1968), indicating the extensive potential of the time-travel trope to join with other sf motifs in the same narrative.

Nicholas Meyer's *Time After Time* (1979) is an effective "spin-off" of *The Time Machine* in which Wells himself travels from Victorian London to modern-day San Francisco in order to prevent Jack the Ripper, who has similarly time-traveled, from going on a murder spree there. It was quickly followed by Jeannot Szwarc's *Somewhere in Time* (1980), which demonstrates the romantic and sentimental possibilities of time travel as its protagonist travels back in time to seek a young woman with whose photograph he has fallen in love. *Forever Young* (1992), starring **Mel Gibson**, also explores romantic territory in its story of a cryogenically frozen pilot who awakens after more than 50 years of suspended animation. *Frequency* (2000), meanwhile, includes the sentimental expedient of a man communicating with the past to warn his father of an accident that is about to kill him, but then becomes a thriller as this action also saves the life of a would-be serial killer.

More genuinely science fictional time-travel narratives came to the fore in sf film with the release of *The Terminator* in 1984, initiating a franchise whose central premise involves travel in time from a postapocalyptic future back into the preapocalyptic present times of the films. The high stakes (including the very survival of the human race) that are central to the *Terminator* sequence are typical of time-travel films, as when the crew of the *Enterprise* must retrieve whales from the 20th-century earth in order to save their 23rd-century earth from destruction in *Star Trek IV: The Voyage Home* (1986), or when they must travel back to the 21st century to save earth from the Borg in *Star Trek: First Contact* (1996). Time travel also ultimately plays a major role in the 2009 *Star Trek* reboot. In *Millennium* (1989) agents from a future so polluted that humans have all become sterile travel to the past to retrieve fertile humans in the hope of repopulating the planet in some far future time when the pollution has abated—but meanwhile must seek to avoid changing the past itself. In Terry Gilliam's *Twelve Monkeys* (1995), scientists from a postapocalyptic future send agents back to the past to try to find a cure for the virus that caused the apocalypse that ruined their world. And, in **Donnie Darko** (2001), a troubled teen travels into the past and sacrifices himself in order to prevent the catastrophic end of the world.

Despite such dark scenarios, *Twelve Monkeys* and *Donnie Darko* have their comic moments. Indeed, the time-travel motif has often been effectively played for **comedy** in films such as Gilliam's *Time Bandits* (1981), though here the comedy is rather dark. Lighter comedy reigns in one of the most charming and successful of all time-travel sequences, the **Back to the Future** films of **Robert Zemeckis** (1985, 1989, 1990). The combination of time travel and teen comedy that informs this trilogy was also used to good effect in *Bill & Ted's Excellent Adventure* (1989) and its sequel *Bill & Ted's Bogus Journey* (1991).

In recent years, time travel has often served as a pretext for the production of plot-twisting action films and thrillers such as **Peter Hyams**'s *Timecop* (1994), Richard Donner's *Timeline* (2003, based on a novel by **Michael Crichton**), *The Butterfly Effect* (2004), and Tony Scott's Denzel Washington vehicle *Deja Vu* (2006). More thoughtful uses of the motif have also continued to appear, however, including such low-budget independent films as *The Sticky Fingers of Time* (1997) and *Primer* (2004). Meanwhile, the time-travel motif has continued to show its versatility via such films as *Freejack* (1992), which involves travel into a dystopian future, the Korean **2009: Lost Memories** (2002), which explores the potential of time-travel narratives to explore **alternate-history** narratives, and **Disney**'s *Meet the Robinsons* (2007), a lighthearted time-travel adventure for children. The time-travel motif was used to good effect in the Japanese animated teen drama *Toki o kakeru shôjo* (2006, *The Girl Who Leapt* *through Time*), while the subgenre has also continued to demonstrate its potential for telling romantic stories in the Bollywood production *Love Story 2050* (2008) and in *The Time Traveler's Wife* (2009).

TITAN A.E. (Dir. Don Bluth and **Gary Goldman**, 2000.) Excellent animation, interesting characters, and a rousing *Star Wars*–style **space opera** narrative could not stop *Titan A.E.* from being a bust at the box office, proving just how difficult it is to sell an **animated science fiction film** to American audiences. Part of the problem is one of generic recognition: *Titan A.E.* features a science fiction narrative that addresses a number of mature themes (including the destruction of the entire earth by an **alien invasion**). But American audiences tend to think of animated films as being for children. Indeed, the animation style of *Titan A.E.*, while allowing for elaborate sf **special effects**, is still reminiscent of the earlier children's films made by Bluth and Goldman, including *The Secret of N.I.M.H.* (1982), which features the sf theme of animals given super-intelligence by scientific experiments.

In *Titan A.E.*, the son of a human scientist seeks the *Titan*, a special high-tech spaceship hidden by his scientist father from the alien Drej after the Drej have destroyed the earth to try to prevent the development of precisely the technologies that are hidden aboard the *Titan*. Eventually, the ship is found and its technology activated: it draws upon raw materials in space to build a duplicate earth, populating it with animal species created from the DNA samples in its extensive files. Surviving humans from around the galaxy flock to the new planet, giving the race a new start and the film a happy ending—though this ending fails to address the potential colonialist implications of the Titan technology, which would allow humans to build duplicate earths for colonization anywhere in the galaxy. Perhaps the Drej had good reason to be concerned. *Titan A.E.* has become something of a cult favorite among sf fans in the years since its release, and the film does suggest considerable potential for animated sf, even if it was not a commercial success at the box office.

TOBEY, KENNETH (1917–2002). The American actor Kenneth Tobey had an extensive career on Broadway and in television. He also acted in a variety of films, but it is almost certainly for his performances in several science fiction films that he will be best remembered. Perhaps the most important of these performances was his first one, as Captain Patrick Hendry, who leads the effort to kill the title monster in the early **alien-invasion** drama *The Thing from Another World* (1951), opposing the efforts of scientists to preserve the creature for study. Tobey carried this same persona—the tough, no-nonsense military man who sometimes has to rescue (or shove aside) idealistic but unrealistic scientists in order to save the human race from a terrible monster—into his next two major sf roles, in *The Beast from 20,000 Fathoms* (1953) and *It Came from Beneath the Sea* (1955). After that, as scientists, rather than military men, became more popular as sf film heroes, leading-man roles for Tobey were hard to come by, though he continued to work extensively in television. In 2005, he starred (again as Hendry) posthumously in *The Naked Monster* (actually filmed in the mid-1980s), a campily nostalgic look back at the **monster movies** of the 1950s that also featured 1950s sf star **John Agar**.

TOHO STUDIOS. Toho Company, Ltd. (more often referred to as "Toho Studios") is a Japanese film and television production and distribution company widely known for its production of *kaiju* **monster movies** (including the **Godzilla** franchise) and effects-driven *tokusatsu* science fiction movies. However, the company has also produced a number of television series (especially in the superhero genre), as well as the critically acclaimed films of Akira Kurosawa. In addition, they are the distributors of many of the much-admired **anime** films produced by Studio Ghibli and **Hayao Miyazaki**, as well as the producers of numerous anime films of their own.

Founded as a live theater company in 1932, Toho soon moved into film production, then burst onto the international scene with the success of *Gojira* (1954, *Godzilla*), followed by its English-language version *Godzilla, King of the Monsters* (1956). Godzilla went on to become one of the most successful movie monsters of all time, eventually being joined in the Toho stable by such additional popular monsters as Rodan and Mothra. Toho soon moved into other genres of science fiction film as well, as in the effects-driven **alien-invasion** drama *Chikyû Bôeigun* (1957, *The Mysterians*) and its sequel *Uchu daisenso* (1959, *Battle in Outer Space*). Toho's output in the 1960s was dominated by monster movies, though some of these, such as *Kaijû daisenso* (1965, *Invasion of Astro-Monster*) had especially strong science fictional elements. In addition to their ongoing output of monster movies—especially Godzilla movies, now spiced up by the introduction of an evil **mecha** version of the legendary monster—Toho films of the 1970s included the **disaster** film *Nihon chinbotsu* (1973, *Japan Sinks,* remade with the same title in 2006) and the alien-invasion film *Wakusei daisenso* (1977, *The War in Space*).

The company's most notable efforts of the 1980s were anime films and Kurosawa films—including the classic *Ran* (1985), though they did produce their 17th Godzilla film in *Gojira vs. Biorante* (1989, *Godzilla vs. Biollante*). The 1990s were again dominated by monster movies, including no less than six additional entries in the Godzilla franchise. The first decade of the 21st century saw an increased output from the company in anime, including an anime remake of the classic science fiction film *Metropolis* in 2001 and the big-budget animated steampunk film *Suchîmubôi* (2004, *Steamboy*). Still, five more Godzilla films remained their core product in the first years of the new century. However, Toho announced that the franchise has been temporarily retired after the *Gojira: Fainaru uôzu* (*Godzilla: Final Wars*), a 2004 film released in conjunction with the celebration of the franchise's 50th anniversary. *See also* JAPANESE SCIENCE FICTION FILM.

TOTAL RECALL. (Dir. **Paul Verhoeven**, 1990.) "Inspired" by the **Philip K. Dick** short story, "We Can Remember It for You Wholesale," *Total Recall* was a big-budget production that combined the over-the-top sf satire for which its director is well known with plenty of action scenes for its star, **Arnold Schwarzenegger**, then at the height of his box-office appeal. Set in 2084, the film centers on the colonization of **Mars**, where both the planet and the human colonists are brutally exploited in the interest of extracting a valuable mineral for transport to earth. This mining operation is run by one Vilos Cohaagen (Ronny Cox), who is able to maintain his power through his control of the colony's air supply, though there is a growing resistance movement among the colonists. The film's protagonist, Douglas Quaid (Schwarzenegger), seemingly begins the film as an ordinary construction worker on earth, but ends up traveling to Mars and becoming involved in the (ultimately successful) resistance movement, of which he had apparently been a key member once before, though his memories of that earlier life have been erased.

Along the way, this basic plot is supplemented by a number of science fiction conceits and technologies, as when the rebel victory on Mars is facilitated by the discovery of an underground Martian machine that is able to generate a breathable atmosphere for the planet. But the most important technologies in the film involve the ability to either erase real memories or implant artificial ones, which leads Quaid (and the audience) into Dick's own favorite fictional situation: confusion concerning what is real and what is a mere simulation. This confusion facilitates numerous plot twists throughout the film and remains even at the end, leaving open the possibility of varying interpretations of what has actually happened and what was mere fakery. As such, the film is much more thoughtful than a quick look at its numerous hyperviolent fight scenes, questionable science, and fancy **special effects** might at first indicate.

TRUMBULL, DOUGLAS (1942–). The American film director and **special-effects** artist Douglas Trumbull has supervised special effects for some of the most important sf films in history, including *2001: A Space Odyssey* (1968), *The Andromeda Strain* (1971), *Close Encounters of the Third Kind* (1977), *Star Trek: The Motion Picture* (1979), and *Blade Runner* (1982), working with many of the leading directors in sf film history. He was nominated for Best Visual Effects Oscars for the latter three of these, though he won no Oscars. In addition, he turned down an offer from **George Lucas** to supervise the special effects for *Star Wars* (1977). In 1993 he was given a Special Scientific and Engineering Oscar for his role as the conceptual designer of the CP-65 Showscan Camera System. Trumbull was also the director, producer, and photographic effects supervisor for the important sf film *Silent Running* (1972). In 1983, he produced and directed the sf thriller *Brainstorm*. In 1996, Trumbull was given the President's Award from the American Society of Cinematographers, a lifetime achievement award.

TSUBURAYA, EIJI (1901–1970). During his career, Eiji Tsuburaya was the leading **special-effects** artist in **Japanese science fiction**

film, directing the effects for numerous **Toho Studios** films, including **monster movies** such as those featuring **Godzilla**. Tsuburaya had already begun to break new ground in the development of special effects technologies (setting up a special-effects department at Toho in 1939) when his career was interrupted by the outbreak of World War II, during which he directed numerous propaganda films at the behest of the Japanese government. This work made him something of a persona non grata during the postwar occupation years, making it difficult for him to work in the film industry. He finally returned to Toho as the head of the special-effects department he himself had created, soon making a major contribution as the special-effects director for the first *Godzilla* film (1954). Though Tsuburaya has identified *King Kong* (1933) as his most important inspiration for the effects in this film (and for his own interest in special effects as a whole), Godzilla did not use **stop-motion** effects but was instead realized via an actor wearing a rubber suit, in the technique now sometimes known as *suitmation*. Though hampered by low budgets and sometimes looking almost comically cheap, Tsuburaya's special effects were oddly effective, propelling Godzilla to international fame and himself to a prolific career in special-effects artistry.

He supervised the special effects for many Toho monster movies, as well as for more purely science fictional films such as *Chikyû Bôeigun* (1957, *The Mysterians*), *Bijo to Ekitainingen* (1958, *The H-Man*), and *Sekai daisenso* (1961, *The Last War*). In 1963, Tsuburaya founded his own special-effects laboratory, which went on to produce the effects for numerous films as well as television series. He himself ultimately worked on the special effects for over 200 films.

TWELVE MONKEYS. (Dir. Terry Gilliam, 1995.) One of the most interesting and unusual science fiction films of the 1990s, *Twelve Monkeys* combines the quirky vision of its director with the talents of an A-list Hollywood cast to produce a thoughtful and entertaining film that deals with a number of important issues and combines a number of science fiction genres. It begins as a **postapocalyptic** film, set in a future in which most of the world's population has been killed by the release in late 1996 of a deadly experimental virus. This **plague** has driven humanity's survivors into grim underground habitats, while the surface world grows wild, ruled by animals that are immune to the virus. The film gives us very few details about this subterranean world, though Gilliam, through the effective use of a few sets of images (most of them echoing his 1985 **dystopian** film *Brazil*), makes it clear that this is also a dystopian film, depicting a dark world devoid of joy, ruled by heartless scientists and bureaucrats. The only denizens of this future world that we see in the film are these rulers and a group of prisoners, entrapped in cages from which they are periodically extracted so that they can "volunteer" for various dangerous missions, including trips to the surface to gather biological samples to enable the scientists to monitor conditions there.

The future scientists, seeking a cure for the now-mutated virus, decide that they need a sample of the virus in its original unmutated form. Luckily, they have also developed the technology for **time travel**, so they select one of the prisoners, James Cole (**Bruce Willis**), for the special—and especially dangerous—mission of traveling back to 1996 to gather data and to try to recover a specimen of the original virus. Unfortunately, the time-travel technology has not quite been perfected, and all sorts of things go wrong, leading, among other things, to Cole's incarceration in a Baltimore mental hospital in 1990. There he meets patient Jeffrey Goines, played by Brad Pitt, who won an Academy Award nomination for Best Supporting Actor for the role. Goines turns out to be the son of Nobel Prize–winning virologist Dr. Goines (Christopher Plummer), who developed the virus, which eventually adds a number of complications to the plot. The plot is complicated further when Cole, after several tries, finally lands in 1996 and decides that he loves the preapocalypse world so much that he wants to stay there permanently. He also falls in love with psychiatrist Kathryn Railly (Madeleine Stowe), whom he originally met in 1990 in the Baltimore hospital, and the two work frantically to try to prevent the release of the virus. They do not succeed, and Cole is killed in the effort. He has, however, gotten important information about the release of the virus back to the future, and the film ends as one of the scientists from the future is seen sitting on an airplane beside the scientist (and assistant to Dr. Goines). It is not clear, however, what the scientist plans to do, and there are no indications in the film that the scientists seek to prevent the release of the virus. They may be, in fact, trying to ensure its release, thus protecting their position of power and authority in the future. Then again, this enigmatic ending is appropriate given the nature of this unusual film, whose twisting plot offers a number of opportunities for meditation on the nature of time, memory, reality, and perception.

TWOHY, DAVID (1955–). The American screenwriter and director David Twohy got his start in science fiction with the minor film *Timescape* (1992). He had his breakthrough into the Hollywood mainstream as the co-writer of the 1993 **Harrison Ford** vehicle *The Fugitive.* Twohy moved into big-budget science fiction as the co-writer of the **postapocalyptic** film *Waterworld* (1995), which he followed as the writer and director of the **alien-invasion** film *The Arrival* (1996). In 2000, he directed and co-wrote the sf action film *Pitch Black,* perhaps his most important contribution to science fiction film to date. Twohy also wrote and directed the less successful sequel to that film, *The Chronicles of Riddick* (2004).

– U –

ULMER, EDGAR G. (1904–1972). The Austrian-born director Edgar G. Ulmer first came to Hollywood as an assistant to famed director F. W. Murnau in 1926, working on set design for the film *Sunrise* (1927). He subsequently had a long career in Hollywood as a director of low-budget B movies, during which he became known as a master of getting the maximum mileage out of limited resources. His 1934 horror film *The Black Cat,* for example, is one of the classics of that genre, while his 1945 film noir *Detour* has achieved near-legendary status. He was a master of low-budget science fiction as well. His 1951 **alien-invasion** film *The Man from Planet X,* while a bit technically crude, has some interesting noirish visuals and is a thoughtful meditation on the kind of paranoid xenophobia that was fueling the cold-war arms race. Ullmer also directed *The Amazing Transparent Man* (1960), a less interesting **mad-scientist** film. That same year, he directed *Beyond the Time Barrier,* an enjoyable little **postapocalyptic** film in which a pilot is accidentally transported into a future world plagued by infertility, so that the ruler wants the pilot to impregnate his daughter. In 1961, Ulmer directed the sf **adventure** film *L'Atlantide,* a French-Italian co-production made in Italy.

UNDERSEA ADVENTURE. It has long been common within the realm of science fiction to think of the world beneath the earth's oceans as a strange, unexplored frontier somewhat analogous to outer space. And, while sf narratives of undersea adventure have never been as popular as narratives of the exploration of outer space, numerous sf films have, in fact, involved undersea adventure. The first major film in this category was Disney's *20,000 Leagues Under the Sea* (1954), which made **Jules Verne**'s 1870 novel into a glossy entertainment, updated for American audiences of the 1950s, though still set in the 19th century. This film was particularly timely in that it was released in the same year that the USS *Nautilus* (named after the high-tech sub in Verne's novel) became the first real-world nuclear-powered submarine. Actually, Verne's novel had been adapted to silent film as early as 1916, and it underwent numerous subsequent adaptations as well, including animated films in 1973, 1985, and 2002, and two made-for-TV films in 1997.

Though Verne's novel remains the prototype for science fictional undersea adventures, numerous other sf films have involved undersea exploration as well. *The Atomic Submarine* (1959, spearheaded by British-born producers Richard and Alex Gordon) built on the possibilities offered by real-world technologies such as that used in the *Nautilus*. **Irwin Allen**'s *Voyage to the Bottom of the Sea* (1961) was a relatively successful undersea narrative that ultimately spawned a television series of the same title that ran on the ABC network in the United States from 1964 to 1968. In addition, a number of monster films have involved monsters that emerge from beneath the mysterious depths of the ocean to do most of their damage on dry ground, ranging from *The Beast from 20,000 Fathoms* (1953) and *It Came from Beneath the Sea* (1955) to *Deep Rising* (1998). The *Godzilla* films could be placed in this category as well. Still, partly due to the difficulty of filming underwater sequences (or of convincingly simulating such sequences), undersea adventure remained a relatively secondary genre of science fiction for many years.

All of that changed dramatically in 1989, with the release of the B-grade undersea **monster movie** *DeepStar Six* and George Cosmatos's more effective *Leviathan,* a claustrophobic monster movie reminiscent of the *Alien* films, but set underwater. More importantly, the same year saw the release of **James Cameron**'s *The Abyss,* which pushed the envelope of available underwater filmmaking technology to become perhaps the most technically sophisticated film made to that date. Cameron's film, meanwhile, combined the subgenre of undersea adventure with an **alien-invasion** narrative, making it the direct forerunner of Barry Levinson's *Solaris*-inflected *Sphere* (1998), another big-budget effort that involves the discovery of an alien spacecraft deep beneath the ocean. Renny Harlin's *Deep Blue Sea* (1999) topped off the 1990s with what is essentially another underwater monster film, with the added sf twist that the monsters in question are sharks made more dangerous by a genetic experiment gone wrong. The undersea adventure seemed to fall out of favor with filmmakers about that time.

UNIVERSAL STUDIOS. Founded in 1912 as the Universal Film Manufacturing Company under the leadership of Carl Laemmle, Universal Studios is one of the world's oldest film studios. The company was incorporated as Universal Pictures Company, Inc., in 1925, by which time it had already been on the forefront of numerous innovations, such as giving on-screen credit to performers in films, thus facilitating their marketing as "brand" names. Though lacking the resources (especially extensive company-owned theater chains) to compete directly with the biggest studios, Universal carved out a niche for itself as the major studios gained increased power in the early sound era. In particular, it produced a series of distinctive and now-classic **monster movies** in the early 1930s, including *Dracula* (1931), *Frankenstein* (1931), *The Mummy* (1932), *The Black Cat* (1934), and *The Bride of Frankenstein* (1935). In 1933, Universal produced *The Invisible Man,* based on the 1897 novel by **H. G. Wells**. That film and the *Frankenstein* films can be considered to be science fiction, given that they deal centrally with the consequences of scientific research.

Much of the company's output in the 1940s involved sequels to the classic monster movies of the 1930s, making the company a pioneer in the development of the phenomenon of film franchises. During this period and through the 1950s, the company also developed such franchises as the low-budget "Francis the Talking Mule" and "Ma and Pa Kettle" sequences, as well as a series of films starring comedians Lou Abbott and Bud Costello, several of which were spoofs of science fiction or of the company's own monster movies, including *Abbott and Costello Meet Frankenstein* (1948), *Abbott and Costello Meet the Invisible Man* (1951), and *Abbott and Costello Go to Mars* (1953). The company, now operating as Universal-International, was also a central force in the science fiction film boom of the 1950s, producing such classic films as **It Came from Outer Space** (1953), the **Creature from the Black Lagoon** trilogy (1954–1956), and **The Incredible Shrinking Man** (1957). By the late 1950s, however, the financially troubled company was concentrating on increasingly low-budget efforts such as *The Thing That Couldn't Die* (1958) and *The Leech Woman* (1960); in 1963 they served as the U.S. distributor for **Toho Studios'** 1962 film *Kingu Kongu tai Gojira* (*King Kong vs. Godzilla*). Indeed, their activity in science fiction film in the 1960s was mostly limited to the U.S. distribution of Toho products and other international productions, such as **Fahrenheit 451** (1966). By the 1970s, now under the ownership of the entertainment conglomerate MCA, Universal was primarily a television production company.

However, among the films they produced in this era were several that contributed to the minor sf film boom of the early 1970s, including *Colossus: The Forbin Project* (1970), **The Andromeda Strain** (1971), *Slaughterhouse-Five* (1972), and **Silent Running** (1972). The company also participated in the **disaster** film cycle of the 1970s, producing such works as *Airport* (1970) and its three sequels of the decade, as well as *Earthquake* (1974). Interestingly, though, the company largely sat out the major **Star Wars**-fueled sf film boom of 1977–1984, concentrating its efforts in science fiction during this period on television productions such as *Battlestar Galactica* (1978–1979) and *Buck Rogers in the 25th Century* (1979–1981), the former being so similar to *Star Wars* that it triggered a lawsuit from **20th Century Fox**, the producers of *Star Wars*. Universal did co-produce (with **Steven Spielberg**'s Amblin Entertainment) *E.T. the Extra-Terrestrial* (1982) during this period, also working with Amblin to co-produce the immensely successful **Back to the Future** trilogy later in the decade (1985–1990).

Most of Universal's efforts in sf film during the early 1980s again largely involved U.S. distribution of international films, such as *Flash Gordon* (1980) and **Dune** (1984). They were also the U.S. distributor for *Brazil* (1985). Their own early 1980s productions included *The Incredible Shrinking Woman* (1981), a spoofy gender-reversed remake of *The Incredible Shrinking Man*, and the teen-oriented *The Last Starfighter* (1984), co-produced with Lorimar Productions. Universal was also the U.S. distributor for much of **John Carpenter**'s work in the 1980s, including *The Thing* (1982, a remake of the 1951 classic *The Thing from Another World*) and *They Live* (1988).

In recent years, Universal has remained a relatively minor player in sf film, participating mostly in co-productions (as in their co-production of the *Jurassic Park* trilogy with Amblin) and as a distributor for films produced by others. Highlights in recent years have included the co-production and U.S. distribution of *Twelve Monkeys* (1995), *Waterworld* (1995), *King Kong* (2005), and *Children of Men* (2006). As of this writing, Universal is part of the media conglomerate NBC Universal, a subsidiary of the General Electric Corporation whose holdings include the Syfy (formerly Sci Fi) cable television network.

UTOPIAN. Utopian thinking involves attempts to envision future improvements in human life, especially including visions of ideal societies in which the social, political, and economic problems of the present have been solved. There are few actual representations of utopian societies in science fiction films, though such films often contain certain utopian elements, as when they typically assume that technology will become significantly more advanced as time moves forward. Scripted by science fiction pioneer **H. G. Wells** based on his book *The Shape of Things to Come* (1933), the film *Things to Come* (1936) well illustrates Wells's belief late in his life that a utopian future was attainable, but only after the current order of civilization had been destroyed. *Things to Come* looks at the future of the city of Everytown, which is virtually destroyed by a deadly **plague** that sweeps the globe as the result of the use of biological weapons. Nevertheless, the city is rebuilt under the leadership of a visionary group of aviators and engineers who use technology (and superior air power) to enforce their vision of an enlightened world government. Conflicts remain, however, and the film leaves open whether a project to colonize outer space, launched in the year 2036, represents an exciting new utopian adventure for humanity or an insatiable drive for progress that threatens to undermine the now idyllic life in Everytown.

This inclusion of the possibility of seeing *Things to Come* as a **dystopian** film indicates the embattled nature of utopian imagery in science fiction film, which can partly be attributed to the simple fact that filmmakers believe they can create more interesting narratives within settings that involve significant social and political problems. However, it should be pointed out that all of modern science fiction film is in many ways rooted in the science fiction film boom of the cold-war 1950s, during a time in which utopianism was consistently associated with communism and thus regarded in the West as discredited and disreputable. Partly as a result of this suspicion of utopian thought, the science fiction films of the 1950s are typically either set in the present time or in a future that has been ravaged by nuclear war or some other sort of apocalyptic destruction, leaving little room for the depiction of future utopian societies. More recent films, especially since the strikingly effective visuals of *Blade Runner* (1982), have turned more often to the depiction of future societies, but usually in a dystopian mode, often involving future dystopian societies that were designed according to someone's utopian ideals, only to go badly wrong. Even when generally utopian societies are depicted, as in the city of Olympus in Japan's *Appleseed* television and film **anime** franchise, these utopias tend to be situated within dystopian or postapocalyptic surroundings that threaten to engulf or destroy them.

The *Star Trek* franchise, in five live-action television series and 11 feature films (as well as a variety of works in other media), represents science fiction's most extended attempt to imagine a utopian future. This franchise is set in a future world in which it is stipulated that all of earth's social, political, and economic problems have been solved, largely thanks to a universal affluence brought about by technological progress. Contact with the cerebral and highly logical aliens of the planet Vulcan has also led to a philosophical enlightenment that has helped the people of earth to make the most of their newfound prosperity. Even in *Star Trek,* however, we see relatively little of this utopian society and instead have to piece together its details from passing mentions in the dialogue. In order to create more drama, the series focuses on the dangers and difficulties of outer-space exploration and on encounters and conflicts with civilizations in other parts of the galaxy that might not be so enlightened or utopian. Indeed, certain moments in the *Star Trek* franchise (especially episodes such as "This Side of Paradise" and "Return of the Archons" from the original 1960s television series) seem to question conventional notions of utopia, arguing instead that humans must have problems to solve and obstacles to overcome in order to live fulfilling lives. Tellingly, however, the half-Vulcan first mate of the USS *Enterprise*, Mr. **Spock**, typically offers a counter-view in these series, arguing the advantages of a strife-free existence, as opposed to the view of Captain **James T. Kirk**, the series' principal spokesman for the value of struggle and strife.

– V –

VADER, DARTH. The **Sith** lord Darth Vader, a **cyborg** whose body has been almost entirely replaced by synthetic parts, is the chief villain of the first *Star Wars* trilogy. In the course of that trilogy, we learn that Vader had once been **Anakin Skywalker**, who was in turn the father of both **Luke Skywalker** and Princess **Leia Organa**, two of the principal protagonists of the first trilogy. The second *Star Wars* trilogy, which is a prequel to the first, narrates the series of events through which Anakin was transformed from a promising **Jedi** knight to a Sith lord, drawn to the dark side of the **Force**. Though he shows a brief moment of humanity in saving Luke from the evil Emperor Palpatine (who is Vader's own Sith master) at the end of *Star Wars: The Return of the Jedi* (1983), Vader is generally a sinister and imposing figure, made more frightening by his black cape and the black helmet and mask that cover his cybernetic face and head. Meanwhile, his hulking physical presence (provided by champion bodybuilder David Prowse wearing the Vader suit) is supplemented by his stentorian voice (supplied by actor James Earl Jones) and the trademark swooshing sound of his mechanical breathing apparatus. In 2003, the American Film Institute listed Darth Vader as the third greatest movie villain of all time.

VAUGHN, ROBERT (1932–). Though he will probably always be best remembered for his role as the dashing Napoleon Solo in the 1960s television series *The Man from U.N.C.L.E.,* Robert Vaughn has made many other appearances on television and has also had a long and varied career in film. In 1958, Vaughn played the title character in **Roger Corman**'s *Teenage Cave Man,* though he quickly moved on to more prestigious fare and was nominated for a Best Supporting Actor Oscar for his role in *The Young Philadelphians* a year later. Vaughn also made an important appearance as a hired gunman in *The Magnificent Seven* (1960), a role he essentially reprised in 1980 in the Corman-produced sf film *Battle Beyond the Stars.* That same year he starred in the B-grade UFO-coverup drama *Hangar 18,* after starring in another science fiction film three years earlier, the rather obscure Canadian film *Starship Invasions.* Also in 1977, Vaughn supplied the voice of Proteus IV, a computer that seeks to remake the human race in *Demon Seed.* In 1978, he starred in *The Lucifer Complex,* a drama about Nazi clones. Vaughn was thus fairly busy during the sf renaissance of 1977–1984, though he was never able to break into the first rank of science fiction film roles. In 1986, he had an important role as the lead villain in the sf-oriented action film *Black Moon Rising,* written by **John Carpenter**, but his subsequent appearances in sf film have been rather obscure, including the little-known 1997 **virtual-reality** thriller *Menno's Mind* and the 1998 B-grade sf thrillers *The Sender* and *Visions.*

VENUS. The planet Venus ranks second only to **Mars** as the site of extraterrestrial adventure and exploration in science fiction, including science fiction film. Largely because it is named after the Roman goddess of love, Venus has often been depicted in science fiction film as a planet dominated by beautiful (and typically scantily clad) women. For example, the early spoof *Abbott and Costello Go to Mars* (1953), despite the title, involves a trip by the comedy team of the title to the planet Venus, where they encounter an all-female society. The 1958 film *Queen of Outer Space* is also typical of the conceit of Venus as a woman-ruled planet. The German-Polish film *Der schweigende Stern* (1960) is a much more serious treatment of Venusian exploration, based on a novel by **Stanisław Lem**. This film was later adapted to a less-serious English-language version as *First*

Spaceship on Venus (1962). The Soviet film *Planeta Bur* (1962) depicts Venus as a wild and savage planet inhabited by dinosaurs; it, too, was later adapted to English versions as *Voyage to the Prehistoric Planet* (1965) and *Voyage to the Planet of Prehistoric Women* (1968), both produced by **Roger Corman** and **American International Pictures**.

VERHOEVEN, PAUL (1938–). The Dutch director Paul Verhoeven was almost entirely unknown in the United States when he was tapped to direct **Robocop** (1987), a science fiction satire for which Verhoeven's over-the-top style was well suited. Verhoeven followed that film with the **Arnold Schwarzenegger** vehicle *Total Recall* (1990), another sf film with strong satirical components. Verhoeven then scored a mainstream success with the neo-noir thriller *Basic Instinct* (1992), followed by controversy and critical derision for *Showgirls* (1995). The director has never shied away from controversy, however, and in 1997 he directed the film adaptation of *Starship Troopers,* **Robert A. Heinlein**'s most controversial novel. The film was controversial as well: it seemed to want to critique the violence and militarism of Heinlein's novel via Verhoeven's trademark satire, but was taken by many as a violent, militaristic film in its own right. Verhoeven followed with *Hollow Man* (2000), a sort of combination of an invisible man narrative with a Jeckyll and Hyde **mad-scientist** narrative. That film features superb **special effects** but is otherwise unremarkable. In 1999, his film *Turkish Delight* (1973) was named the best Dutch film of the 20th century at the Netherlands Film Festival.

VERNE, JULES (1828–1905). The French writer Jules Verne was one of the founders of modern science fiction, authoring a number of works that were eventually adapted to film. Verne's work—including the novels *De la terre à la lune* (1865, *From the Earth to the Moon*) and *Vingt mille lieues sous les mers* (1869–1870, *20,000 Leagues Under the Sea*)—was particularly important as a source of material for the pioneering French filmmaker **Georges Méliès**. Verne's work was particularly popular as a source during the science fiction explosion of the 1950s, when it served as material for a number of unusually high-budget productions aimed at family audiences. **Disney's**

20,000 Leagues Under the Sea (1954) is a particularly well-known adaptation of the latter novel, which has, in fact, been filmed several times. The Verne adaptation *Around the World in Eighty Days* (1956) was also a popular success, though it is not strictly science fictional. *Journey to the Center of the Earth* (1959), based on Verne's 1864 novel of the same title, is also a classic adaptation. In 1961, *Master of the World,* scripted by **Richard Matheson**, and *The Mysterious Island* topped off this early cycle of Verne-inspired sf films. Film and television adaptations of Verne's work have continued to appear regularly worldwide, including such loose adaptations as *Rocket to the Moon* (1967), which was "inspired by the writings of" Verne, and *Mysterious Planet* (1982), which moves *Mysterious Island* into outer space. A 2008 remake of *Journey to the Center of the Earth* features 3-D **special effects**.

VIRTUAL REALITY. Although the term *virtual reality* seems to have been first used by playwright and drama theorist Antonin Artaud in the 1930s to describe the imaginative power of the theater, it has now come to be used almost exclusively to describe computer-generated simulated environments with which humans can interact. As a science fiction concept, virtual reality rose to prominence in the 1980s, when it was a key trope of the **cyberpunk** movement. Science fiction films, which have increasingly relied on **computer-generated imagery (CGI)** for their visual effects, are themselves a sort of virtual reality, but virtual reality has also become an important theme in science fiction film—often in films that have made particularly effective use of CGI. The video game–inspired *Tron* explored virtual reality as early as 1982, followed by the film *Brainstorm* in 1983. By the 1990s, however, the growing importance of computers and the Internet as part of the texture of everyday life opened the way for the production of a number of virtual-reality films.

Virtual reality was often used as an important theme in Japanese **anime** sf films such as *Kôkaku kidôtai* (1995, **Ghost in the Shell**). Early films in this category from the United States include *The Lawnmower Man* (1992), *Johnny Mnemonic* (1995), *Strange Days* (1995), and *Virtuosity* (1995). Films such as **Alex Proyas's** **Dark City** (1998), **David Cronenberg's** *eXistenZ* (1999), and Josef Rusnak's *The Thirteenth Floor* (1999) used virtual-reality concepts even more effectively, though by far the most important dramatization of the possibilities of virtual reality in sf film has been Andy and Larry Wachowski's **dystopian** film *The Matrix* (1999), which was followed by two sequels in 2003, *The Matrix Reloaded* and *The Matrix Revolutions*. Here, most human beings live their lives in a virtual-reality environment, unaware that in the physical world they are entrapped in small pods where the machines that now rule the world use them as a power source. The Japanese-Polish co-production *Avalon* (2001) is another dystopian film that makes important use of virtual reality, this time following *eXistenZ* in drawing upon the important theme of video gaming as a form of virtual reality. Finally, **Andrew Niccol**'s *Simone* (2002) may prefigure the future of sf film with its vision of a virtual-reality starlet who is transparently inserted into live-action films.

VIRUS. *See* PLAGUE.

– W –

WACHOWSKI, LARRY (1965–) AND ANDY (1967–). Generally referred to in the collective as the "Wachowski Brothers" because they work together so closely as a team, Larry and Andy Wachowski (as of 2010, Larry appears to have changed his name to Lana and is rumored to be undergoing sex reassignment) had worked primarily as comic book writers until their screenplay (written with Brian Helgeland) for the film *Assassins,* a thriller directed by Richard Donner, was produced in 1995. In 1996, the brothers wrote and directed the excellent erotic thriller *Bound* (1996), but it was with the release of *The Matrix* (1999), which they wrote, directed, and produced, that the brothers were propelled into Hollywood and science fiction stardom. That film, one of the highlights of science fiction film in the 1990s, was followed by two sequels, *The Matrix Reloaded* and *The Matrix Revolutions,* both released in 2003, and both also written, produced, and directed by the Wachowskis. The brothers wrote and produced the 2006 **dystopian** film *V for Vendetta,* directed by James McTeigue, and they contributed (though without on-screen credit) to the script for the 2007 **alien-invasion** film *The Invasion,* essentially an update and

remake of the classic *Invasion of the Body Snatchers* (1956). They
returned to writing, producing, and directing for *Speed Racer* (2008),
a live-action film whose innovative visuals attempted to capture the
spirit of the 1960s Japanese **anime** television series. That film, which
includes strong sf elements, was not a critical or commercial success.

WALL-E. (Dir. Andrew Stanton, 2008.) Though a charming film that
children seem to love, *WALL-E* is a genuine work of science fiction
cinema that participates in a number of science fiction subgenres,
including the **dystopian** and the **postapocalyptic** film, with a dash
of **space opera** included as well. Important themes include **environmentalism** (particularly the danger posed to the environment by
runaway consumerism) and the loss of humanity that might come
about through excessive reliance on technology. The film envisions a
future earth that has been rendered uninhabitable by an environmental collapse in which most of the earth's surface seems to have been
covered by garbage generated by excessive consumption, encouraged
by the global hegemony of the "Buy N Large" (BNL) megacorporation, which dominates every industry (including government services)
at the time of the collapse. The remnants of the human race then take
up residence in outer space in gigantic ships, leaving behind a fleet of
robots to clean up the mess toward the day when humanity can return.
BNL projects that this cleanup will take five years, but the film itself is
set 700 years after humanity's departure from earth, by which time it
is clear that BNL's original plan has gone badly awry. Humanity still
lives in space, while the fleet of cleanup robots seems to have worn out
and ceased to function, except for one lone robot (the WALL-E of the
title). This robot, which seems to have gained intelligence and humanity in its hundreds of years of operation, still labors away alone in an
abandoned city (vaguely similar to New York), compacting trash into
cubes that it then stacks into huge towers, waiting to be picked up and
incinerated by other equipment that no longer functions.

Meanwhile, the humans in space live in luxury with every need
met by automated systems. As a result, the humans seem to have lost
the ability to think or act for themselves. They still routinely send
periodic probes back to earth to check on conditions there, seeking in
particular to find signs of plant life that suggest that life is now sus-
tainable on the planet, but otherwise they are content to remain where

they are. Their bodies have become fat and bloblike, with atrophied limbs, and they have become so accustomed to having every need automatically met by machines that they have even lost the ability to walk, moving about instead on automated recliners. Humans, in short, have lost much of their humanity, even as the WALL-E robot back on earth has grown more human.

Ultimately (after the beginning of a sentimental love story involving WALL-E and a female robot), WALL-E accompanies one of the probes back to the *Axiom* with a sample of plant life that presumably proves that the earth is again inhabitable. The *Axiom* eventually returns to earth to start life there anew, after an extended sequence in which the ship's soulless autopilot robot (AUTO) attempts to prevent the return because it has been programmed to do so and because it, unlike WALL-E, lacks the imagination to go beyond its programming. In the process of relating this narrative, *WALL-E* is filled with references to earlier science fiction films, many of which will probably be recognizable only to adults. Meanwhile, *WALL-E* itself can be considered a landmark in the history of science fiction film simply because its animation is so good that it points toward a future in which **computer-generated imagery** will be used more and more effectively (and ubiquitously) in sf film, freeing filmmakers to explore any territory that they can imagine, confident that these imaginary worlds can be realized on film via computer.

THE WAR OF THE WORLDS. (Dir. **Byron Haskin**, 1953.) A relatively high-budget Technicolor adaptation of **H. G. Wells**'s pioneering 1898 **alien-invasion** novel, *The War of the Worlds* was the first sf film to team up producer **George Pal** and director Byron Haskin. In this updated and Americanized version, the Martian invasion seems concentrated in the United States, where it is quickly opposed by the military, which has been alerted to the threat by physicist Clayton Forrester (Gene Barry), the film's protagonist. Stomping about the countryside in high-tech war machines protected by force fields, the Martians prove invulnerable to conventional attack, so the top American brass order a nuclear strike, but the Martians prove impervious even to a bomb that is "ten times more powerful than anything used before." All seems lost, when the Martians suddenly die off due to their lack of resistance to the germs that inhabit earth's atmosphere, as they had in the original novel. Tellingly, the film adds a religious twist to this classic ending, having the Martians fall dead only after they have had the audacity to attack humans hiding in churches, suggesting that the invaders have been killed off by divine intervention. As the film closes, church bells ring and a chorus sings "amen," while the narrator informs us that the Martians have been killed by "the littlest of things, which God in His wisdom had put upon this earth."

Despite its scientist protagonist, *The War of the Worlds* is typical of the early 1950s in its expressed fears over the possible drawbacks of scientific advancement. The Martians are far more scientifically advanced than their earthling opponents, but their technology cannot protect them from their own physical weakness. Nor can their technological superiority serve as a substitute for spiritual strength, and the religious tones of the film's ending suggests that an excessive devotion to scientific and technological progress can lead to spiritual, as well as physical degeneration.

The War of the Worlds was remade by **Steven Spielberg** in 2005, with state-of-the-art **special effects** and some compelling drama, though many critics found the film a disappointment in its failure fully to explore the post-9/11 implications of its traumatic invasion, now centered on New York City. *See also* MARS.

WEAVER, SIGOURNEY (1949–). The American actress Sigourney Weaver was still virtually unknown when she was cast in the role of Ripley in **Ridley Scott**'s *Alien* (1979). Her performance in that role made the character an icon of both science fiction and feminism; she became a model for strong, heroic female characters in subsequent movies, science fiction or otherwise. Weaver went on to reprise the role in three sequels, gradually building out various aspects of the character (and acquiring a first name, "Ellen") in the process. This role made Weaver herself an iconic sf actress; she and Ripley will forever seem virtually synonymous, despite Weaver's appearances in several other notable roles. Her association with science fiction is such that she was a natural for casting in major roles in both *Galaxy Quest* (1999), a spoof of sf fandom, and **James Cameron**'s long-awaited *Avatar* (2009). In another case of what might be referred to as *allusive casting,* Weaver also supplied the voice of the ship's computer in the animated film *WALL-E* (2008), essentially reprising the role she had had as the voice of the Planet Express Ship in an episode of the animated sf TV comedy *Futurama* in 2002.

WELLER, PETER (1947–). The American actor Peter Weller got his start in science fiction as the star of *The Adventures of Buckaroo Banzai Across the Eighth Dimension* (1984), a campy film that was not a hit at the time but that has gained a certain cult following over the years. This following has been enhanced by Weller's subsequent appearance as the title character in the high-profile *Robocop* (1987), one of the highlights of 1980s science fiction film. Weller returned to play the same character in the first sequel, *Robocop 2* (1990). Between these two *Robocop* films, Weller played the lead role in the **undersea adventure** *Leviathan* (1989), and then followed the *Robocop* roles as the lead character in **David Cronenberg**'s *Naked Lunch* (1991), a surreal film that includes a heavy dose of science fictional elements. Weller also starred in *Screamers* (1995), a science fiction action thriller based on a short story by **Philip K. Dick**.

WELLS, H. G. (1866–1946). Herbert George Wells is widely regarded as the father of modern science fiction, thanks to the enduring presence and influence of a number of "scientific romances" he wrote in the late 19th and early 20th centuries. These include *The Time Machine* (1895), *The Island of Dr. Moreau* (1896), *The Invisible Man* (1897), *The War of the Worlds* (1898), *The First Men on the Moon* (1901), and *The Food of the Gods and How It Came to Earth* (1904), all of which have been adapted to film at least once, most of them multiple times. These collective adaptations make Wells the single sf author whose work has most often been adapted to film, and particular adaptations such as *The War of the Worlds* (1953) and *The Time Machine* (1960) are genuine landmarks in the history of sf film. Wells is such a prominent figure in the history of sf that he has even appeared as a character in several sf films, most notably *Time After Time* (1979), though the 1960 adaptation of *The Time Machine* also presents its protagonist (unnamed in the novel) as a figure of Wells. In addition, lesser-known Wells novels such as *When the Sleeper Wakes* (1899, rewritten in 1910 as *The Sleeper Wakes*) and *A Modern Utopia* (1905) were important contributions to turn-of-the-century socialist and utopian thought. Indeed, Wells was a well-known public intellectual whose thoughts on history and politics had an important impact on the course of many subsequent debates in those fields, while his meditations on utopia, dystopia, and the growing technologization of modern society were crucial in forming the modern Western mindset. *See also* DYSTOPIAN FILM; TIME TRAVEL; UTOPIAN FILMS.

WEYLAND-YUTANI CORPORATION. The Weyland-Yutani **Corporation** is the evil conglomerate whose ruthless quest for profit drives much of the action in the *Alien* sequence of films. In the first *Alien* film (1979), the corporation is generally referred to simply as *the Company,* though the name *Weylan-Yutani* does appear fleetingly. Here, it becomes clear that the company is heavily involved in managing the human colonization of outer space, which they do strictly in the interest of making money, with little sense of the noble mission of exploration and discovery that had previously driven so many previous science fictional forays into space. The company owns and operates the mining vessel *Nostromo* that is central to the film; they also employ the ship's crew, but treat their employees as their property as well, regarding them as expendable in the quest for profit. They also tend to use human-looking androids to spy on their human employees. The representation of the company's willingness to endanger their own employees and the colonists for whom those employees sometimes provide support services gradually evolves through the *Alien* series until it becomes clear that the company is willing to endanger the earth itself in its greedy grab for profits. This corporate attitude is most clearly seen in the company's willingness to explore the use of the deadly alien creatures that give the film sequence its title as weapons that they can breed and sell for gain.

In *Aliens* (1986), the second film in the sequence, the corporate name "Weyland-Yutani" is foregrounded for the first time. Here, especially in **James Cameron**'s extended DVD director's cut, it becomes clear that the company is involved in a vast range of enterprises, from the manufacture of consumer goods (including toys), to mining, to arms trading. They even employ their own private army, which they use to further their corporate goals in outer space, where they apparently answer to no higher authority. *Alien³* (1992) focuses on the company's role in still another shady enterprise, the management of private prisons, which they do with their typical ruthlessness and irresponsibility. Most of the film, in fact, is set in one such prison, located in a remote outpost in space but now abandoned by the company (while still full of inmates). Weyland-Yutani does not figure in *Alien Resurrection* (1997), in which their former military activities and their activities in weapons research and distribution seem to have been assumed by the "United Systems Military." Though there is no explanation in the theatrical cut of this film for the absence of Weyland-Yutani, the extended DVD director's cut of the film includes a scene in which one character explains that the former Weyland-Yutani has now been taken over by Wal-Mart, apparently an even more predatory corporation.

Weyland-Yutani also figures centrally in *Alien vs. Predator* (2004), a sort of spin-off of the *Alien* film series that is not generally considered a member of the sequence proper. In this film, we see Charles Bishop Weyland, the founder of the company, played by Lance Henriksen, who had played the android Bishop in *Aliens* and *Alien³*. The film thus suggests that the android was modeled on the company's founder, perhaps indicating the heights of his ego. Weyland-Yutani has also entered into popular culture outside the *Alien* films. For example, it is referenced in the *Angel* and *Firefly* television series, both of which were created by **Joss Whedon**, who wrote the screenplay for *Alien Resurrection*.

WHALE, JAMES (1889–1957). The British-born James Whale became a major figure in Hollywood as the director of a series of groundbreaking horror films for **Universal Studios** in the 1930s. *Frankenstein* (1931), *The Old Dark House* (1932), *The Invisible Man* (1933), and *Bride of Frankenstein* (1935) are all classics of their kind, and all but *The Old Dark House* (which revitalized the "dark house" subgenre of horror films) have science fiction themes and feature scientists whose unbridled search for knowledge pushed them to the edge of the **mad-scientist** subgenre. Whale was one of the few openly gay directors working in Hollywood at the time. Among his numerous films outside the genres of horror and science fiction was the 1936 version of the classic musical *Show Boat*. Christopher Bram's 1995 novel *Father of Frankenstein* is based on the final years of Whale's life. It brought the director newfound prominence, especially after it was adapted to film as *Gods and Monsters* in 1998.

WHEDON, JOSS (1964–). The American writer, director, and producer Joss Whedon is doubtless best known as the creator and executive producer for the *Buffy the Vampire Slayer* television series (1997–2003) and its spinoff *Angel* (1999–2004). However, Whedon has been a prolific writer, creator, director, and producer of television series, films, and comic books (including those based on his own television series as well as substantial contributions as a writer for the *X-Men* comics). Among film scripts co-written by Whedon is that for the **Pixar** children's film *Toy Story* (1995), the first film composed entirely of **computer-generated imagery**, and one that includes a number of science fictional elements. Whedon wrote the screenplay for the mainstream sf film *Alien: Resurrection* (1997) and co-wrote the script for the **animated science fiction film** *Titan A.E.* (2000). Whedon was the creator and principal writer for the short-lived "science fiction–Western" *Firefly* (2002–2003), which was canceled by Fox television midway through its first season, though it gained considerable critical praise. Whedon then wrapped up *Firefly* with the successful feature film *Serenity* (2005), which he wrote and directed. His latest science fictional effort is the ongoing series *Dollhouse* (2009–), about a group of young "actives" who have their identities erased, then replaced with a series of substitute identities tailored to the various missions on which they are sent by the mysterious agency that handles them.

WHEN WORLDS COLLIDE. (Dir. Rudolph Maté, 1951.) Produced by **George Pal** as a followup to **Destination Moon**, *When Worlds Collide* (1951), based on the 1932 serial novel by Philip Wylie and Edwin Balmer, helped to set the stage for the many apocalyptic and **postapocalyptic** films of the 1950s, while also anticipating the natural-disaster films that became popular in the 1970s. Here, the earth is ultimately destroyed by a collision with a runaway planet that happens to have swerved into our solar system. Meanwhile, anticipating the collision, a team of scientists scrambles to develop a spacecraft that will allow at least a few humans to escape to the planet Zyra, which is also, rather conveniently, passing near earth at the time. As in *Destination Moon,* the development of the spacecraft is supported by private funding because the government is simply too hidebound to mobilize in time. In this case, the plan succeeds, giving this story of global destruction an oddly happy ending as a shipload of healthy young technologists (plus a cute kid and a pregnant female dog, along with numerous other animals) manages to escape to Zyra to begin life anew. There is even a utopian (if somewhat troubling) suggestion that the outcome is all for the best and that the handpicked young, educated, intelligent, clean-cut, white American colonists seem fated to build a better world on Zyra than the one they left. Meanwhile, the entire story is accompanied by vaguely religious trappings, complete with on-screen Biblical quotations, and the notion that the destruction of the earth has a therapeutic, cleansing effect is supported by the film's continual comparisons of the spaceship with Noah's ark.

WILLIAMS, JOHN (1932–). The American composer John Williams had scored numerous films before his now-classic score for *Star Wars* (1977) became some of the best-known music in movie history. He followed with an equally stirring and majestic (some would say melodramatic) score for *Superman* (1978) and went on to score a number of the most commercially successful films in history. Many of these were science fiction films, and Williams's music became so thoroughly associated with the genre that even sf films not scored by Williams have often had scores that were intentionally crafted to sound as if Williams had written them. In addition to all five *Star Wars* sequels, sf films scored by Williams include all of the science fiction films directed by **Steven Spielberg**: *Close Encounters of the Third Kind* (1977), *E.T. the Extra-Terrestrial* (1982), *Jurassic Park* (1993), *The Lost World: Jurassic Park* (1997), *Artificial Intelligence: AI* (2001), *Minority Report* (2002), and *War of the Worlds* (2005). Altogether, Williams has garnered 45 Academy Award nominations, winning five Best Score awards.

WILLIS, BRUCE (1955–). The American actor Bruce Willis leapt into the national spotlight with his comic role as detective David Addison Jr. in the innovative television series *Moonlighting* (1985–1989), a success that propelled him into several lead roles in film, mostly in comedies, though he also became a major action star with his role as John McClane in *Die Hard* (1988) and its sequels. He moved into science fiction film as the protagonist of Terry Gilliam's *Twelve Monkeys* (1995), then quickly followed with a starring role in another distinctive sf film, **Luc Besson**'s *The Fifth Element* (1997). These two roles can both be taken as somewhat ironic commentaries on his status as an action star in other films, such as the *Die Hard* sequence. Willis also had a more conventional lead role in **Michael Bay**'s sf **disaster** film *Armageddon* (1998). He did not return to sf film for more than a decade, although he remained a highly visible presence in a number of genres, especially via the ongoing *Die Hard* series. Then, in 2009, he starred in *Surrogates,* a comic-book adaptation the premise of which is based on the popular phenomenon of adopting online personae—only in this case the surrogate personalities can be sent out into the real world in remote-controlled robotic bodies.

WINSTON, STAN (1946–2008). The **special-effects** and makeup artist Stan Winston produced some of the most impressive visuals in the history of science fiction film, working extensively with such major directors as **James Cameron**, **Steven Spielberg**, and **Tim Burton**. Though he began to move into digital effects at the end of his career, most of his work was done with physical props, such as puppets, models, and makeup. After several early efforts, he made his big-time Hollywood debut with his impressive effects for **John Carpenter**'s *The Thing* (1982). Winston was then hired to do the effects for Cameron's *The Terminator* (1984) and *Aliens* (1986), the latter of which won him an Academy Award for Best Visual Effects. He returned to work with Cameron on *Terminator 2: Judgment Day* (1991), for which he won another Best Visual Effects Oscar, as well as an Oscar for Best Makeup. Winston won still another Best Visual Effects Oscar for his work on Spielberg's *Jurassic Park* (1993). In addition, he was nominated for Academy Awards for his effects work on the **robot** comedy *Heartbeeps* (1981), *Predator* (1987), Burton's *Edward Scissorhands* (1990) and *Batman Returns* (1992), and Spielberg's *The Lost World: Jurassic Park* (1997) and *Artificial Intelligence: AI* (2001). Other sf films to which Winston contributed either effects or makeup include *Invaders from Mars* (1986), *The Island of Dr. Moreau* (1996),

Galaxy Quest (1999), *Jurassic Park III* (2001), *Terminator 3: Rise of the Machines* (2003), and *Terminator Salvation* (2009).

WISE, ROBERT (1914–2005). Robert Wise began his Hollywood career working as a film editor on such illustrious works as Orson Welles's *Citizen Kane* (1941) and *The Magnificent Ambersons* (1942). Wise had also started as a director, though somewhat inauspiciously, on the latter film, when RKO Radio Pictures asked him to direct a new, more upbeat ending for the film while Welles was away in South America on another project. Wise directed the sequence, which was the ending ultimately released in theaters, though many subsequent critics have felt this ending undermined the entire film. Wise continued his career with two early horror films for producer Val Lewton that are still worth watching today, *The Curse of the Cat People* (1944) and *The Body Snatcher* (1945). He also directed several competent Westerns and was the director of at least one film, *The Set-Up* (1949), that is now considered a film noir classic and one of the best boxing dramas ever made. He thus had substantial credentials when he was tapped to direct **The Day the Earth Stood Still** (1951), which still stands as one of the most important classics of the genre of sf film. Wise went on to direct still another important film noir, *Odds Against Tomorrow* (1959), as well as a number of truly classic films, including *West Side Story* (1961), *The Sound of Music* (1965), and *The Sand Pebbles* (1966); he was never someone who could be simply slotted as a director of science fiction films. However, he did go on to further build his science fiction credentials as the director of two of the most important sf films of the 1970s, **The Andromeda Strain** (1971) and **Star Trek: The Motion Picture** (1979).

– Y –

YATES, GEORGE WORTHING (1901–1975). The American screenwriter George Worthing Yates began his career writing for **serials** such as *The Lone Ranger* (1938). Though a fairly obscure figure, he wrote widely for the sf films of the 1950s, often working with director **Bert I. Gordon**. This phase of Yates's career began with his writing of the story for **Them!** (1954), though his script for that film required so much reworking by others that he did not receive on-screen credit for it. In 1955, he co-wrote the screen adaptation for *Conquest of Space,* based on the book by **Chesley Bonestell** and Willy Ley. That same year, Yates wrote the story and co-wrote the screenplay for *It Came from Beneath the Sea.* He co-wrote the screenplay for *Earth vs. the Flying Saucers* (1956) and also contributed to the screenplay for Gordon's *The Amazing Colossal Man* (1957), though he did not receive on-screen credit. In 1958, he co-wrote the "original screenplay" for **Edward Bernds**'s *Space Master X-7,* though that film is highly derivative of *The Quatermass Xperiment* (1955). That same year, Yates wrote the story for the little-known sf film *The Flame Barrier* (1958) and wrote the screenplays for *Attack of the Puppet People* (1958) and *War of the Colossal Beast* (1958), both of which were directed by Gordon. One of his most interesting scripts was for the horror film *Tormented* (1960), again directed by Gordon, who also wrote the story.

YEAWORTH, IRVIN S. (1926–2004). Irvin S. Yeaworth had only a brief career in the Hollywood film industry, spending most of his professional life in other endeavors, such as making private religious films and designing and building amusement parks. He did, however, make a substantial contribution to sf film as the director of *The Blob* (1958), a memorable **alien-invasion** narrative that is also a key **monster movie**, as well as an important marker of the turn toward teenage audiences in sf film in the late 1950s. He followed as the director and producer of *4D Man* (1959), an interesting and unusual **mad-scientist** tale, then ended his brief career in sf film as the director and producer of the rather forgettable sf **adventure** *Dinosaurus!* (1960), in which an undersea explosion unleashes a **dinosaur** attack on a Caribbean island.

YESTERDAY. (Dir. Jeong Yun-su, 2002.) *Yesterday* is a slickly produced, big-budget action thriller from South Korea that grafts a dark, gritty murder mystery onto a basic science fiction premise. In the film (set in a unified Korea in the year 2020), a series of murders of aging scientists gradually leads the Korean police into a complex investigation that ultimately reveals the killer to be one "Goliath" (Choi Min-su), who had been involved as a young boy in a series of illicit genetic experiments 30 years earlier. Goliath, deranged as a result of the experiments, is now seeking revenge upon the scientists who were involved in those experiments, though it turns out that his real goal is to bring about his own death. One of the principal investigators is Hui-su, a brilliant criminologist (played by Kim Yoon-jin, known to American audiences as Yunjin Kim, one of the stars of the *Lost* television series). In the course of the investigation, Hui-su discovers that she herself is actually a clone produced by the same experiments in which Goliath had been involved. *Yesterday* is, by Western standards, a rather slow-paced film that devotes a great deal of its runtime to building its characters, even though it also involves a number of spectacular, ultraviolent, hyperkinetic action sequences. *See also* KOREAN SCIENCE FICTION FILM.

YODA. Yoda is a diminutive green alien who appears in all but the first of the main sequence of six *Star Wars* films. Though small, cute, and somewhat comical, Yoda is represented in the films as an incredibly wise **Jedi** master, partly because he has studied the Jedi way for hundreds of years. He is thus the most important teacher and trainer of neophyte Jedis. It also turns out that he is a formidable Jedi knight in his own right, a swift and deadly warrior who is particularly adept in the use of the trademark Jedi light saber. He is also a mysterious figure, and many of the details of his background remain unknown throughout the series. In *Star Wars: Episode VI—The Return of the Jedi* (1983), he dies in a touching scene at the age of 900. However, in keeping with the quasimystical nature of Jedi power, his death is more of an ascension as he leaves his physical body to become one with the **Force**. Here and in *Star Wars: Episode V—The Empire Strikes Back* (1980), Yoda is represented by a puppet, operated and voiced by Frank Oz. He is mostly represented by a (younger look-ing) puppet in *Star Wars: Episode I—The Phantom Menace* (1999) as well, though the puppet is supplemented in this film by some use of **computer-generated imagery**. In *Star Wars: Episode II—Attack of the Clones* (2002) and *Star Wars: Episode III—The Revenge of the Sith* (2005), Yoda is rendered entirely via computer animation, with Oz still supplying the voice. Yoda also plays a prominent role in the *Star Wars: Clone Wars* animated series and the *Star Wars: The Clone*

Wars animated series and animated feature film, in all of which he is voiced by Tom Kane.

YORK, MICHAEL (1942–). The Oxford-educated British actor Michael York began his career on the Shakespearean stage; he also figured prominently in two of Franco Zeffirelli's film adaptations of Shakespeare's plays in the late 1960s. Through much of the 1970s, York seemed on the verge of major Hollywood stardom, though in later years he has become something of a journeyman, making numerous guest appearances on television programs (including sf programs such as *Babylon 5*) and doing a significant amount of voiceover work for animated television programs, including *Star Wars: The Clone Wars*. He also lent his distinctive voice to *Transformers: Revenge of the Fallen* (2009). His most prominent roles in the latter part of his career have been as the spy handler Basil Exposition in the *Austin Powers* sequence of films (which spoof the James Bond films), beginning in 1997.

Near the height of his popularity as an actor, York played the title role in the 1976 **postapocalyptic-dystopian** film *Logan's Run*, still his best-known role in a science fiction film. He followed in 1977 with a major role as Andrew Braddock in *The Island of Dr. Moreau*, adapted from the 1896 novel by **H. G. Wells**. Neither of these films was especially successful, though *Logan's Run* has developed a certain cult following over the years. He subsequently worked widely in other genres (including supernatural thrillers and literary adaptations). In a sign of the arc taken by his career between the 1970s and the 1990s, York returned to sf film in 1995, starring in a vaguely comedic remake of **Roger Corman**'s 1957 **alien-invasion** vampire thriller *Not of This Earth* (which had already been remade once earlier in 1988). That same year, he played Merlin in *A Young Connecticut Yankee in King Arthur's Court*, based on the vaguely science fictional 1889 **time-travel** novel by Mark Twain. In 1996, York had a major role in the relatively low-budget **space opera** *Dark Planet*. He was made an Officer of the Order of the British Empire (OBE) in 1997.

– Z –

ZEMECKIS, ROBERT (1951–). The Chicago-born Robert Zemeckis has been one of the most commercially successful American film directors of his generation. Also active as a writer and producer on many of his directorial projects, Zemeckis moved into science fiction (and into Hollywood stardom) with the **time-travel** teen **comedy** *Back to the Future* (1985), which ultimately had sequels in 1989 and 1990. This trilogy of films remains the work for which Zemeckis is best known and one of the central works of American popular cinema in the period 1985–1990. Zemeckis subsequently won an Academy Award for Best Director for *Forrest Gump* (1994), which itself won a Best Picture Oscar. He moved back into science fiction as the producer and director of *Contact* (1997).

Bibliography

CONTENTS

INTRODUCTION

Though science fiction cinema has long been regarded as a relatively low-brow cultural form, it has received a certain amount of serious critical attention since the very beginning. Now, more than four decades after *2001: A Space Odyssey* and *Planet of the Apes* brought new respect to science fiction film when they were released in 1968, there exists an extensive critical literature that includes everything from fan guides and "companions" (especially for hugely popular phenomena such as the *Star Wars* franchise) to extremely sophisticated book-length studies by academic critics and high-powered theoretically informed essays in respected critical journals. Meanwhile, these critical discussions cover essentially the same territory as film criticism as a whole, though they often place special emphasis on technical aspects such as special effects or on the effectiveness of individual films as works of science fiction, which are designed to produce thoughtful reactions in viewers.

One might locate the beginnings of truly serious critical discussion of science fiction cinema in Susan Sontag's essay "The Imagination of Disaster," included in her important collection *Against Interpretation and Other Essays,* published in 1966. Here, Sontag argued that the science fiction films of the 1950s, typically until then regarded as low-brow products of a mindless "mass" culture, were actually among our most valuable and insightful reflections of the popular American psyche in that anxious decade. Carlos Clarens followed in 1967 with the publication of *An Illustrated History of the Horror Film,* which is, in fact, a sensitive and serious historical study of both horror and science fiction films. Indeed, it was republished in 1997 as *An Illustrated History of Horror and Science-Fiction Films: The Classic Era, 1895–1967.*

Drawing directly on the work of Clarens, and with the intervening appearance of *Planet of the Apes* and *2001: A Space Odyssey* in 1968 drawing new critical attention to science fiction film, John Baxter published *Science Fiction in the Cinema* (1970), another book-length work that treated science fiction cinema as a serious cultural phenomenon, providing what was essentially a historical survey of the development of the form. When it was followed in short order by Denis Gifford's *Science Fiction Film* (1971) and William Johnson's edited volume *Focus on the Science Fiction Film* (1972), it was clear that a new critical industry had been born. University courses in science fiction and science fiction film began to be offered more and more widely, furthering the academic study of the form. Other book-length critical studies appeared in the decade as well, including John Brosnan's *Future Tense: The Cinema of Science Fiction* (1978). Meanwhile, in 1976, Vivian Sobchack graduated from the University of California in Los Angeles with an MA in critical studies that included a thesis on science fiction film, which eventually evolved into a book entitled *The Limits of Infinity: The American Science Fiction Film 1950–1975* (1980). By the time that book was reworked and republished in significantly expanded form as *Screening Space: The American Science Fiction Film* in 1987 (a second edition was published in 1997), Sobchack was emerging as a major film critic and theorist of the phenomenology of film. In this book, which remains one of the most important critical statements on science fiction cinema, Sobchack explores the visual and aural conventions of science fiction film from the 1950s to the time of her writing, looking closely at specific films as complex aesthetic objects. In so doing, she not only seeks to validate science fiction film as an object of serious critical inquiry, but also to validate genre studies as a whole.

The evolution of Sobchack's work is indicative of the way in which, during the decades of the 1980s and 1990s, science fiction in general got more and more attention from academic critics, including major figures such as Fredric Jameson, who made science fiction a key component in his trenchant Marxist analysis of contemporary world culture. Many of Jameson's essays on science fiction (including film) would eventually be collected in the volume *Archaeologies of the Future* (2005), which also includes a lengthy meditation on the utopian potential of science fiction as a genre. Jameson's discussions of science fiction through the 1980s and 1990s were also closely related to his interest in postmodernism, as when he suggests that cyberpunk science fiction might be the quintessential example of postmodernist culture. Other leading theorists of postmodernism have employed science fiction film as central examples as well, as when David Harvey, in *The Condition of Postmodernity* (1990), suggests *Blade Runner* as one of the key examples of the new figuration of time and space that for him characterizes postmodern cinema.

By the 1990s, critical analyses of science fiction film were proliferating at a pace so rapid that it is impossible to mention here all of the important individual examples. One might, however, single out the work of J. P. Telotte, who, with the publication of *Replications: A Robotic History of the Science Fiction Film* (1995), emerged as a leading academic critic of science fiction cinema with a particular interest in the key subject of how science fiction examines the ways in which humans relate to their own science and technology. Telotte has since published widely in the field, including two additional book-length studies, *A Distant Technology: Science Fiction Film and the Machine Age* (1999), published by Wesleyan University Press, and *Science Fiction Film* (2001), published by the prestigious Cambridge University Press. The latter includes a useful review of criticism on science fiction film to that point, noting the wide variety of critical approaches that have been taken to the genre, including historical, political, and psychoanalytic. He concludes, however, that reading science fiction film within the context of postmodernism has, at the time of his writing, become the most important way to approach the genre for academic critics, thanks to the influence of Jameson, among others.

A number of book-length studies and essay collections on science fiction cinema have now appeared, including several volumes devoted to the analysis of individual films or film franchises. The British pop culture critic Roz Kaveney addresses fairly recent developments in science fiction film in *From Alien to The Matrix: Reading Science Fiction Film* (2005). My own *Alternate Americas: Science Fiction Film and American Culture* (2006) provides a historical survey of American science fiction film in the second half of the 20th century through detailed discussions of 15 major films, from *The Day the Earth Stood Still* (1951) to *The Matrix* (1999). I also attempt to place these films in their historical and political contexts and to explore the ways in which they engage those contexts in productive dialogue.

Given the scope and variety of criticism that has now been published on the science fiction film, this bibliography cannot hope to be comprehensive, but is instead designed to point to some of the most valuable resources in a variety of categories. Beginning with general studies of science fiction cinema as a cultural phenomenon such as those just mentioned, the bibliography continues with a list of important anthologies of criticism on the topic. All of these are useful and contain many valuable entries. In the interest of saving space, individual essays within these volumes have not generally been listed in this bibliography. The bibliography then moves into a listing of a number of recommended thematic studies that focus on particular aspects of science fiction cinema rather than discussing the phenomenon as a whole. It then includes a number of cross-media studies that are relevant to science fiction film within a broader context that includes television and written science fiction as well.

The bibliography then continues with a listing of recommended studies that are relevant primarily within the context of particular national cinemas. Included in this section are studies of individual films, though broader studies have generally been given precedence in making the selections to be listed. National cinemas covered in this listing include those from France, Germany, Great Britain, Italy, Japan, South Korea, and the United States. The next section of the bibliography contains a listing of published works that discuss the contributions to science fiction film of specific individuals, including actors, artists (including special effects artists), directors, producers, and writers (both screenwriters and writers on whose work a significant number of sf films has been based). The bibliography then concludes with a listing of a few general reference works and a number of Internet sites that are relevant to science fiction cinema. Together, the works listed in this bibliography provide a wealth of basic information about science fiction cinema. Many of them also provide interesting and even provocative points of view on science fiction film.

GENERAL STUDIES

Baxter, John. *Science Fiction in the Cinema.* New York: Paperback Library, 1970.

Booker, M. Keith. *Alternate Americas: Science Fiction Film and American Culture.* Westport, Conn.: Praeger, 2006.

Brosnan, John. *Future Tense: The Cinema of Science Fiction.* New York: St. Martin's Press, 1978.

Clarens, Carlos. *An Illustrated History of Horror and Science-Fiction Films: The Classic Era, 1895–1967.* 1967. New York: De Capo Press, 1997.

Gifford, Denis. *Science Fiction Film.* London: Studio Vista, 1971.

Johnson, William, ed. *Focus on the Science Fiction Film.* Englewood Cliffs, N.J.: Prentice Hall, 1972.

Kaveney, Roz. *From* Alien *to* The Matrix: *Reading Science Fiction Film.* London: I. B. Tauris, 2005.

King, Geoff, and Tanya Krzywinska. *Science Fiction Cinema: From Outerspace to Cyberspace.* London: Wallflower, 2000.

Scalzi, John. *The Rough Guide to Sci-Fi Movies.* London: Rough Guides, 2005.

Sobchack, Vivian. *The Limits of Infinity: The American Science Fiction Film 1950–1975.* South Brunswick, N.J.: A.S. Barnes, 1980.

———. *Screening Space: The American Science Fiction Film.* 2nd ed. New Brunswick, N.J.: Rutgers University Press, 1997.

Telotte, J. P. *Replications: A Robotic History of the Science Fiction Film.* Urbana: University of Illinois Press, 1995.

———. *Science Fiction Film.* Cambridge: Cambridge University Press, 2001.

ANTHOLOGIES OF CRITICISM

Johnson, William, ed. *Focus on the Science Fiction Film.* Englewood Cliffs, N.J.: Prentice Hall, 1972, 78–90.

Kuhn, Annette, ed. *Alien Zone: Cultural Theory and Contemporary Science Fiction Cinema.* London: Verso, 1990.

———, ed. *Alien Zone II: The Spaces of Science Fiction Cinema.* London: Verso, 1999.

Redmond, Sean, ed. *Liquid Metal: The Science Fiction Film Reader.* London: Wallflower, 2004.

Rickman, Gregg, ed. *The Science Fiction Film Reader.* New York: Limelight Editions, 2004.

Sardar, Ziauddin, and Sean Cubitt, eds. *Aliens R Us: The Other in Science Fiction Cinema.* London: Pluto, 2002.

THEMATIC STUDIES

Berger, Albert I. "Love, Death, and the Atom Bomb: Sexuality and Community in Science Fiction, 1935–55." *Science-Fiction Studies* 8, no. 3 (1981): 280–295.

Clifton, Michael. "Cinematic Aliens: Moving toward the Child." In *Genre at the Crossroads: The Challenge of Fantasy,* edited by George Slusser and Jean-Pierre Barricelli, 158–166. Riverside, Calif.: Xenos, 2003.

Dubeck, Leroy W., Suzanne Moshier, and Judith E. Boss. *Fantastic Voyages: Learning Science through Science Fiction Films.* New York: Springer, 2009.

Evans, David H. "Alien Corn: *The War of the Worlds, Independence Day,* and the Limits of the Global Imagination." *Dalhousie Review* 81, no. 2 (2001): 7–23.

Evans, Joyce A. *Celluloid Mushroom Clouds: Hollywood and the Atomic Bomb.* Boulder, Colo.: Westview Press, 1998.

Faden, Eric S. "The Cyberfilm: Hollywood and Computer Technology." *Strategies: A Journal of Theory, Culture, and Politics* 14, no. 1 (2001): 77–90.

Frayling, Christopher. *Mad, Bad, and Dangerous?: The Scientist and the Cinema.* London: Reaktion, 2006.

Freedman, Carl. "Marxism, Cinema, and Some Dialectics of Science Fiction and Film Noir." In *Red Planets: Marxism and Science Fiction,* edited by Mark Bould and China Miéville, 66–82. Middletown, Conn.: Wesleyan University Press, 2009.

Gifford, Denis. *Movie Monsters.* London: Studio Vista, 1969.

Hayward, Philip, ed. *Off the Planet: Music, Sound and Science Fiction Cinema.* London: John Libbey, 2004.

Hendershot, Cyndy. *Paranoia, the Bomb, and 1950s Science Fiction Films.* Bowling Green, Ohio: Bowling Green University Popular Press, 1999.

Lane, Christina. *Feminist Hollywood: From* Born in Flames *to* Point Break. Detroit, Mich.: Wayne State University Press, 2000.

Mank, Greogry William. *It's Alive! The Classic Cinema Saga of Frankenstein.* New York: A. S. Barnes, 1981.

McKee, Gabriel. *The Gospel According to Science Fiction: From* The Twilight Zone *to the Final Frontier.* Louisville, Ky.: Westminster John Knox Press, 2007.

Meehan, Paul. *Tech-Noir: The Fusion of Science Fiction and Film Noir.* Jefferson, N.C.: McFarland, 2008.

Milner, Andrew. "Darker Cities: Urban Dystopia and Science Fiction Cinema." *International Journal of Cultural Studies* 7, no. 3 (2004): 259–279.

Nama, Adilifu. *Black Space: Imagining Race in Science Fiction Film.* Austin: University of Texas Press, 2008.

Penley, Constance, et al., eds. *Close Encounters: Film, Feminism, and Science Fiction.* Minneapolis: University of Minnesota Press, 1991.

Rushing, Janice Hocker, and Thomas S. Frentz. *Projecting the Shadow: The Cyborg Hero in American Film.* Chicago: University of Chicago Press, 1995.

Sanders, Steven M. *The Philosophy of Science Fiction Film.* Lexington: University Press of Kentucky, 2007.

Seed, David. *American Science Fiction and the Cold War: Literature and Film.* Chicago: Fitzroy Dearborn, 1999.

Shapiro, Jerome F. "Atomic Bomb Cinema: Illness, Suffering, and the Apocalyptic Narrative." *Literature and Medicine* 17, no. 1 (1998): 126–148.

Shaw, Debra Benita. "Systems, Architecture and the Digital Body: From *Alphaville* to *The Matrix.*" *Parallax* 14, no. 3 (2008): 74–87.

Shelton, Robert. "The Utopian Film Genre: Putting Shadows on the Silver Screen." *Utopian Studies* 4, no. 2 (1993): 18–25.

Short, Sue. *Cyborg Cinema and Contemporary Subjectivity.* New York: Palgrave Macmillan, 2005.

Skal, David J. *Screams of Reason: Mad Science and Modern Culture.* New York: W. W. Norton, 1999.

Telotte, J. P. *A Distant Technology: Science Fiction Film and the Machine Age.* Middletown, Conn.: Wesleyan University Press, 1999.

———. "Human Artifice and the Science Fiction Film." *Film Quarterly* 36, no. 3 (Spring, 1983): 44–51.

CROSS-MEDIA STUDIES

Barrett, Michèle, and Duncan Barrett. Star Trek: *The Human Frontier.* New York: Routledge, 2001.

Bernardi, Daniel Leonard. Star Trek *and History: Race-ing Toward a White Future.* New Brunswick, N.J.: Rutgers University Press, 1998.

Booker, M. Keith. *Monsters, Mushroom Clouds, and the Cold War: American Science Fiction and the Roots of Postmodernism, 1946–1964.* Westport, Conn.: Greenwood Press, 2001.

———. *Science Fiction Television.* Westport, Conn.: Praeger, 2004.

Booker, M. Keith, and Anne-Marie Thomas. *The Science Fiction Handbook.* Oxford: Wiley-Blackwell, 2009.

Butler, Andrew M. *The Pocket Essential Cyberpunk.* Harpendon: Pocket Essentials, 2000.

Cartmell, Deborah, et al., eds. *Alien Identities: Exploring Difference in Film and Fiction.* London: Pluto Press, 1999.

Decker, Kevin S., and Jason T. Eberl, eds. Star Trek *and Philosophy: The Wrath of Kant.* Chicago: Open Court, 2008.

Espenson, Jane, ed. *Serenity Found: More Unauthorized Essays on Joss Whedon's* Firefly *Universe.* Dallas, Tex.: BenBella Books, 2007.

Harrison, Taylor, et al., eds. *Enterprise Zones: Critical Positions on* Star Trek. Boulder, Colo.: Westview Press, 1996.

Harvey, David. *The Condition of Postmodernity: An Enquiry into the Origins of Cultural Change.* Oxford: Blackwell, 1990.

Jameson, Fredric. *Archaeologies of the Future: The Desire Called Utopia and Other Science Fictions.* London: Verso, 2005.

Luckhurst, Roger. *Science Fiction.* London: Polity, 2005.

McConnell, Frank. *The Science of Fiction and the Fiction of Science: Collected Essays on SF Storytelling and the Gnostic Imagination.* Jefferson, N.C.: McFarland, 2009.

Sherman, Fraser A. *Cyborgs, Santa Claus and Satan: Science Fiction, Fantasy and Horror Films Made for Television.* Jefferson, N.C.: McFarland, 2009.

Suvin, Darko. *Metamorphoses of Science Fiction: On the Poetics and History of a Literary Genre.* New Haven, Conn.: Yale University Press, 1979.

Telotte, J. P., ed. *The Essential Science Fiction Television Reader.* Lexington: University of Kentucky Press, 2008.

Westfahl, Gary. *Science Fiction, Children's Literature, and Popular Culture: Coming of Age in Fantasyland.* Westport, Conn.: Praeger, 2000.

Westfahl, Gary, and George Edgar Slusser, eds. *Nursery Realms: Children in the Worlds of Science Fiction, Fantasy, and Horror.* Athens: University of Georgia Press, 1999.

NATIONAL SCIENCE FICTION CINEMAS

France

Anshen, David. "*Alphaville:* A Neorealist, Science Fiction Fable about Hollywood." In *Italian Neorealism and Global Cinema*, edited by Laura E. Ruberto and Kristi M. Wilson, 91–110. Detroit, Mich.: Wayne State University Press, 2007.

Buckland, Warren. "Video Pleasure and Narrative Cinema: Luc Besson's *The Fifth Element* and Video Game Logic." In *Moving Images: From Edison to the Webcam,* edited by John Fullerton and Astrid Widding, 159–164. Sydney, Australia: Libbey, 2000.

Chamarette, Jenny. "A Short Film about Time: Dynamism and Stillness in Chris Marker's *La jetée.*" In *Rhythms: Essays in French Literature, Thought and Culture,* edited by Elizabeth Lindley and Laura McMahon, 217–231. Oxford: Peter Lang, 2008.

Darke, Chris. Alphaville *(Jean-Luc Godard, 1965).* London: I. B. Tauris, 2005.

Geoffroy-Menoux, Sophie. "Enki Bilal's Intermedial Fantasies: From Comic Book *Nikopol* Trilogy to Film *Immortals (Ad Vitam)*." In *Film and Comic Books,* edited by Ian Gordon, Mark Jancovich, and Matthew P. McAllister, 268–283. Jackson: University Press of Mississippi, 2007.

Hawk, Byron. "Hyperrhetoric and the Inventive Spectator: Remotivating *The Fifth Element*." In *The Terministic Screen: Rhetorical Perspectives on Film,* edited by David Blakesley, 70–91. Carbondale: Southern Illinois University Press, 2003.

Ott, Brian L. "Counter-Imagination as Interpretive Practice: Futuristic Fantasy and *The Fifth Element*." *Women's Studies in Communication* 27, no. 2 (2004): 149–176.

Thiher, Allen. "Postmodern Dilemmas: Godard's *Alphaville* and *Two or Three Things that I Know about Her*." *Boundary 2: An International Journal of Literature and Culture* 4, no. 3 (1976): 947–964.

Woolfolk, Alan. "Disenchantment and Rebellion in *Alphaville*." In *The Philosophy of Science Fiction Film,* edited by Steven M. Sanders, 191–205. Lexington: University Press of Kentucky, 2008.

Germany

Berger, James. "From 'After' to 'Until'" Post-Apocalypse, Postmodernity, and Wim Wenders's *Until the End of the World*." *Genre: Forms of Discourse and Culture* 28, no. 1–2 (1995): 1–16.

Cowan, Michael. "The Heart Machine: 'Rhythm' and the Body in Weimar Film and Fritz Lang's *Metropolis*." *Modernism/modernity* 14, no. 2 (2007): 225–248.

Elsaesser, Thomas. *Metropolis*. London: BFI, 2000.

Grob, Norbert. "'Life Sneaks out of Stories': *Until the End of the World*." In *The Cinema of Wim Wenders: Image, Narrative, and the Postmodern Condition,* edited by Roger F. Cook and Gerd Gemünden, 191–204. Detroit, Mich.: Wayne State University Press, 1997.

Haase, Christine. *When Heimat Meets Hollywood: German Filmmakers and America, 1985–2005*. Rochester, N.Y.: Camden House, 2007.

James, Nick. "The Greatest Show on Earth: Herzog." *Sight and Sound* 16, no. 2 (2006): 22–26.

Minden, Michael, and Holger Bachmann. *Fritz Lang's* Metropolis: *Cinematic Visions of Technology and Fear*. Rochester, N.Y.: Camden House, 2000.

Murphy, Richard. "Modernism and the Cinema: *Metropolis* and the Expressionist Aesthetic." *Comparative Critical Studies* 4, no. 1 (2007): 105–120.

Rieder, John. "Spectacle, Technology and Colonialism in SF Cinema: The Case of Wim Wenders' *Until the End of the World*." In *Red Planets: Marxism and*

Science Fiction, edited by Mark Bould and China Miéville, 83–99. Middletown, Conn.: Wesleyan University Press, 2009.

Great Britain

Atkinson, Barry. *You're Not Old Enough Son: An Irreverent Recollection of the Horror/Science Fiction/Fantasy Scene in British Cinema, 1954–1970.* Baltimore, Md.: Midnight Marquee Press, 2006.

Banerjee, Suparno. *"2001: A Space Odyssey:* A Transcendental Trans-Locution." *Journal of the Fantastic in the Arts* 19, no. 1 (2008): 39–50.

Bizony, Piers. *2001: Filming the Future.* London: Aurum Press, 2000.

Cook, John R. "Adapting Telefantasy: The *Doctor Who and the Daleks* Films." In *British Science Fiction Cinema*, edited by I. Q. Hunter, 113–127. London: Routledge, 1999.

Freedman, Carl. "Kubrick's *2001* and the Possibility of a Science-Fiction Cinema." *Science Fiction Studies* 25, no. 2 (1998): 300–319.

Fry, Carrol L. "From Technology to Transcendence: Humanity's Evolutionary Journey in *2001: A Space Odyssey.*" *Extrapolation: A Journal of Science Fiction and Fantasy* 44, no. 3 (2003): 331–343.

Hunter, I. Q., ed. *British Science Fiction Cinema.* London: Routledge, 1999.

Hutchings, Peter. *Hammer and Beyond: The British Horror Film.* Manchester: Manchester University Press, 1993.

Jones, Robert A. "Science Fiction, Solid Fact and Social Formation in *Spaceways.*" *Foundation: The International Review of Science Fiction* 35 (Autumn 2006): 44–57.

Kolker, Robert, ed. *Kubrick's* 2001: A Space Odyssey. New York: Oxford University Press, 2006.

Kuberski, Philip. "Kubrick's *Odyssey:* Myth, Technology, Gnosis." *Arizona Quarterly: A Journal of American Literature, Culture, and Theory* 64, no. 3 (2008): 51–73.

Maland, Charles. *"Dr. Strangelove* (1964): Nightmare Comedy and the Ideology of Liberal Consensus." In *Hollywood as Historian: American Film in a Cultural Context,* rev. ed. Edited by Peter C. Rollins, 190–210. Lexington: University Press of Kentucky, 1998.

Rhodes, Gary D. "Believing Is Seeing: Surveillance and *2001: A Space Odyssey.* In *Stanley Kubrick: Essays on His Films and Legacy,* edited by Gary D. Rhodes, 94–104. Jefferson, N.C.: McFarland, 2008.

Rolinson, Dave. "'Bring Something Back': The Strange Career of Professor Bernard Quatermass." *Journal of Popular Film and Television* 30, no. 3 (2002): 158–165.

Wheat, Leonard. *Kubrick's 2001: A Triple Allegory.* London: Scarecrow Press, 2000.

Italy

Paul, Louis. *Italian Horror Film Directors*. Jefferson, N.C.: McFarland, 2004.

Japan

Bolton, Christopher. "The Mecha's Blind Spot: *Patlabor 2* and the Phenomenology of Anime." *Science Fiction Studies* 29, no. 3 (2002): 453–474.
Bolton, Christopher, Istvan Csicsery-Ronay Jr., and Takayuki Tatsumi, eds. *Robot Ghosts and Wired Dreams: Japanese Science Fiction from Origins to Anime*. Minneapolis: University of Minnesota Press, 2007.
Fisch, Michael. "Nation, War, and Japan's Future in the Science Fiction Anime Film *Patlabor 2*." *Science Fiction Studies* 27, no. 1 (2000): 49–68.
Galbraith, Stuart, IV. *Japanese Science Fiction, Fantasy and Horror Films: A Critical Analysis and Filmography of 103 Features Released in the United States, 1950–1992*. Jefferson, N.C.: McFarland, 2007.
———. *The Toho Studios Story: A History and Complete Filmography*. Lanham, Md.: Scarecrow Press, 2008.
Kalat, David. *A Critical History and Filmography of Toho's* Godzilla *Series*. Jefferson, N.C.: McFarland, 2007.
Napier, Susan J. *Anime from* Akira *to* Howl's Moving Castle: *Experiencing Contemporary Japanese Animation*. Updated ed. New York: Palgrave Macmillan, 2005.
Orbaugh, Sharalyn. "Frankenstein and the Cyborg Metropolis: The Evolution of Body and City in Science Fiction Narratives." In *Cinema Anime: Critical Engagements with Japanese Animation,* edited by Steven T. Brown, 81–111. New York: Palgrave Macmillan, 2006.
Standish, Isolde. *A New History of Japanese Cinema: A Century of Narrative Film*. New York: Continuum, 2005.
Tsutsui, William M. *Godzilla on My Mind: Fifty Years of the King of Monsters*. New York: Palgrave Macmillan, 2004.
Tsutsui, William M., and Michiko Ito. *In Godzilla's Footsteps: Japanese Pop Culture Icons on the Global Stage*. New York: Palgrave Macmillan, 2006.
Tucker, John A. "Anime and Historical Inversion in Miyazaki Hayao's *Princess Mononoke*." *Japan Studies Review* 7 (2003): 65–102.

South Korea

Choi, Jinhee. *The South Korean Film Renaissance: Local Hitmakers, Global Provocateurs*. Middletown, Conn.: Wesleyan University Press, 2010.

Leong, Anthony C. Y. *Korean Cinema: The New Hong Kong: A Guidebook for the Latest Korean New Wave.* Victoria, B.C.: Trafford, 2003.

United States

Abrams, Nathan. "'Are You Still You?': Memory, Identity and Self-Positioning in *Total Recall.*" *Film and Philosophy* 7 (2003): 48–59.

Agel, Jerome, ed. *The Making of Kubrick's* 2001. New York: Signet-New American Library, 1970.

Allen, Louise. "Monkey Business: *Planet of the Apes* and Romantic Excess." *FEMSPEC: An Interdisciplinary Feminist Journal Dedicated to Critical and Creative Work in the Realms of Science Fiction, Fantasy, Magical Realism, Surrealism, Myth, Folklore, and Other Supernatural Genres* 3, no. 2 (2002): 3–15.

Arnold, Robert F. "Termination or Transformation: The *Terminator* Films and Recent Changes in the U.S. Auto Industry." *Film Quarterly* 52, no. 1 (1998): 20–30.

Aronstein, Susan. "Who's Your Daddy?: Politics and Paternity in the *Star Wars* Saga." In *The Legend Returns and Dies Harder Another Day: Essays on Film Series,* edited by Jennifer Forrest, 158–177. Jefferson, N.C.: McFarland, 2008.

Badmington, Neil. "Pod Almighty! Or, Humanism, Posthumanism, and the Strange Case of *Invasion of the Body Snatchers.*" *Textual Practice* 15, no. 1 (Spring 2001): 5–22.

Barone, Dennis. "Klaatu Was No Angel: A Historical-Contextual Analysis of *The Day the Earth Stood Still.*" *Studies in the Humanities* 23, no. 2 (1996): 202–212.

Bellin, Joshua David. "Us or Them!: *Silent Spring* and the 'Big Bug' Films of the 1950s." *Extrapolation: A Journal of Science Fiction and Fantasy* 50, no. 1 (2009): 145–168.

Biskind, Peter. *Seeing Is Believing: How Hollywood Taught Us to Stop Worrying and Love the Fifties.* New York: Pantheon, 1983.

Brin, David, and Matthew Woodring Stover, eds. Star Wars *on Trial: Science Fiction and Fantasy Writers Debate the Most Popular Science Fiction Films of All Time.* Dallas, Tex.: BenBella Books, 2006.

Brooker, Will, ed. *The* Blade Runner *Experience: The Legacy of a Science Fiction Classic.* London: Wallflower Press, 2005.

Bruno, Giuliana. "Ramble City: Postmodernism and *Blade Runner.*" *October* 41 (1987): 61–74. Reprinted in *Alien Zone: Cultural Theory and Contemporary Science Fiction Cinema,* edited by Annette Kuhn, 183–195. London: Verso, 1990.

Buchanan, Judith. "*Forbidden Planet* and the Retrospective Attribution of Intentions." In *Retrovisions: Reinventing the Past in Film and Fiction*, edited by Deborah Cartmell, I. Q. Hunter, and Imelda Whelehan, 148–162. London: Pluto, 2001.

Bukatman, Scott. *Blade Runner*. London: BFI, 1997.

Clover, Joshua. *The Matrix*. London: British Film Institute, 2004.

Cox, Alexander. "*Star Wars:* Decoding the Spectacle of Myth." *Foundation: The International Review of Science Fiction* 33 (Autumn 2004): 17–30.

Decker, Kevin S., Jason T. Eberl, and William Irwin, eds. *Star Wars and Philosophy: More Powerful Than You Can Possibly Imagine*. Chicago: Open Court, 2005.

Del Rio, Elena. "The Remaking of *La jetée*'s Time-Travel Narrative: *Twelve Monkeys* and the Rhetoric of Absolute Visibility." *Science Fiction Studies* 28, no. 3 (2001): 383–398.

DeSalle, Rob, and David Lindley. *The Science of* Jurassic Park *and* The Lost World, *or, How to Build a Dinosaur*. New York: Basic Books, 1997.

Devlin, William J. "Some Paradoxes of Time Travel in *The Terminator* and *12 Monkeys*." In *The Philosophy of Science Fiction Film*, edited by Steven M. Sanders, 103–117. Lexington: University Press of Kentucky, 2008.

Dillman, Joanne Clarke. "*Minority Report:* Narrative, Images, and Dead Women." *Women's Studies: An Interdisciplinary Journal* 36, no. 4 (2007): 229–249.

Doherty, Thomas. "Genre, Gender and the *Aliens* Trilogy." In *The Dread of Difference: Gender and the Horror Film*, edited by Barry Keith Grant, 181–199. Austin: University of Texas Press, 1996.

———. *Teenagers and Teenpics: The Juvenilization of American Movies in the 1950s*. Boston: Unwin Hyman, 1988.

Dragunoiu, Dana. "Neo's Kantian Choice: *The Matrix Reloaded* and the Limits of the Posthuman." *Mosaic: A Journal for the Interdisciplinary Study of Literature* 40, no. 4 (2007): 51–67.

Drakakis, John. "*Terminator 2 1/2:* Or, Messing with Canons." *Textual Practice* 7, no. 1 (1993): 60–84.

Duckenfield, Mark. "*Terminator 2:* A Call to Economic Arms?" *Studies in Popular Culture* 17, no. 1 (1994): 1–16.

French, Sean. *The Terminator*. London: BFI, 1996.

Galipeau, Steven A. *The Journey of Luke Skywalker: An Analysis of Modern Myth and Symbol*. Chicago: Open Court, 2001.

Gallardo, Ximena, and C. Jason Smith. *Alien Woman: The Making of Lt. Ellen Ripley*. New York: Continuum, 2004.

George, Susan A. "Invaders of the Cold War: Generic Disruptions and Shifting Gender Roles in *The Day the Earth Stood Still*." In *Why We Fought:*

America's Wars in Film and History, edited by Peter C. Rollins and John E. O'Connor, 349–366. Lexington: University Press of Kentucky, 2008.

Geraghty, Lincoln. "Creating and Comparing Myth in Twentieth-Century Fiction: *Star Trek* and *Star Wars.*" *Literature Film Quarterly* 33, no. 3 (2005): 191–200.

Greene, Eric. Planet of the Apes *as American Myth: Race, Politics, and Popular Culture.* Middletown, Conn.: Wesleyan University Press, 1996.

Gunkel, David J. "The Virtual Dialectic: Rethinking *The Matrix* and Its Significance." *Configurations: A Journal of Literature, Science, and Technology* 14, no. 3 (2006): 193–215.

Haspel, Paul. "Future Shock on the National Mall: Washington, D.C. as Disputed Ideological Space in Robert Wise's *The Day the Earth Stood Still.*" *Journal of Popular Film and Television* 34, no. 2 (2006): 62–71.

Henthorne, Tom. "Boys to Men: Medievalism and Masculinity in *Star Wars* and *E. T. : The Extra Terrestrial.*" In *The Medieval Hero on Screen: Representations from Beowulf to Buffy,* edited by Martha Driver and Sid Ray, 73–89. Jefferson, N.C.: McFarland, 2004.

Hills, Matt. "*Star Wars* in Fandom, Film Theory, and the Museum: The Cultural Status of the Cult Blockbuster." In *Movie Blockbusters,* edited by Julian Stringer, 178–189. London: Routledge, 2003.

Hobby, Teresa Santerre. "*Independence Day:* Reinforcing Patriarchal Myths about Gender and Power." *Journal of Popular Culture* 34, no. 2 (2000): 39–55.

Instrell, Rick. "Blade Runner: the Economic Shaping of a Film." In *Cinema and Fiction: New Modes of Adapting, 1950–1990,* edited by John Orr and Colin Nicholson, 161–179. Edinburgh: Edinburgh University Press, 1992.

Irwin, William. The Matrix *and Philosophy: Welcome to the Desert of the Real.* Chicago: Open Court, 2002.

Jenkins, Henry. "Looking at the City in the *Matrix* Franchise." In *Cities in Transition: The Moving Image and the Modern Metropolis,* edited by Andrew Webber, Andrew and Emma Wilson, 176–192. London: Wallflower, 2008.

Kapell, Matthew, and William G. Doty, eds. Jacking in to the Matrix *Franchise: Cultural Reception and Interpretation.* New York: Continuum, 2004.

Kapell, Matthew Wilhelm, and John Shelton Lawrence, eds. *Finding the Force of the* Star Wars *Franchise: Fans, Merchandise, and Critics.* New York: Peter Lang, 2006.

Kerman, Judith B., ed. *Retrofitting* Blade Runner: *Issues in Ridley Scott's* Blade Runner *and Philip K. Dick's* Do Androids Dream of Electric Sheep? 2nd ed. Madison: University of Wisconsin Press, 1997.

Kimball, A. Samuel. "Conceptions and Contraceptions of the Future: *Terminator 2, The Matrix,* and *Alien Resurrection.*" *Camera Obscura: A Journal of Feminism, Culture, and Media Studies* 17 (May 2002): 69–107.

Krämer, Peter. "'It's Aimed at Kids—the Kid in Everybody': George Lucas, *Star Wars*, and Children's Entertainment." In *Action and Adventure Cinema*, edited by Yvonne Tasker. London: Routledge, 2004, 358–370.

Lancashire, Anne. "*Attack of the Clones* and the Politics of *Star Wars*." *Dalhousie Review* 82, no. 2 (2002): 235–253.

Landsberg, Alison. "Prosthetic Memory: *Total Recall* and *Blade Runner*." In *The Cybercultures Reader*, edited by David Bell and Barbara M. Kennedy, 190–201. London: Routledge, 2000.

Lawrence, Matt. *Like a Splinter in Your Mind: The Philosophy Behind the* Matrix *Trilogy*. Oxford: Blackwell, 2004.

Lerer, Seth. "*Forbidden Planet* and the Terrors of Philology." *Raritan: A Quarterly Review* 19, no. 3 (Winter 2000): 73–86.

Lerner, Neil. "Nostalgia, Masculinist Discourse, and Authoritarianism in John Williams' Scores for *Star Wars* and *Close Encounters of the Third Kind*." In *Off the Planet: Music, Sound and Science Fiction Cinema*, edited by Philip Hayward, 96–108. London: Libbey, 2004.

Luckhurst, Roger. "'Going Postal': Rage, Science Fiction, and the Ends of the American Subject." In *Edging into the Future: Science Fiction and Contemporary Cultural Transformation*, edited by Veronica Hollinger and Joan Gordon, 142–156. Philadelphia: University of Pennsylvania Press, 2002.

Mair, Jan. "Rewriting the 'American Dream': Postmodernism and Otherness in *Independence Day*." In *Aliens R Us: The Other in Science Fiction Cinema*, edited by Ziauddin Sardar and Sean Cubitt, 34–50. London: Pluto, 2002.

Mann, Katrina. "'You're Next!': Postwar Hegemony Besieged in *Invasion of the Body Snatchers*." *Cinema Journal* 44, no. 1 (Fall 2004): 49–68.

McConnell, Kathleen. "Creating People for Popular Consumption: Echoes of *Pygmalion* and 'The Rape of the Lock' in *Artificial Intelligence: AI*." *Journal of Popular Culture* 40, no. 4 (2007): 683–699.

McCullough, John. "The Exile of Professionals: John Glenn, *Planet of the Apes*, and *2001: A Space Odyssey*." *Canadian Journal of Film Studies/Revue Canadienne d'Etudes Cinématographiques* 10, no. 2 (2001): 36–58.

McHugh, Susan Bridget. "Horses in Blackface: Visualizing Race as Species Difference in *Planet of the Apes*." *South Atlantic Review* 65, no. 2 (2000): 40–72.

McNamara, Kevin R. "*Blade Runner*'s Post Individual Worldspace." *Contemporary Literature* 38, no. 3 (1997): 422–446.

Moberly, Kevin. "Revising the Future: The Medieval Self and the Sovereign Ethics of Empire in *Star Wars*." In *Medievalism in Technology Old and New*, edited by Karl Fugelso and Carol L. Robinson, 159–183. Cambridge: Brewer, 2008.

Park, Jane. "Virtual Race: The Racially Ambiguous Action Hero in *The Matrix* and *Pitch Black*." In *Mixed Race Hollywood,* edited by Mary Beltrán and Camilla Fojas, 182–202. New York: New York University Press, 2008.

Pask, Kevin. "Cyborg Economies: Desire and Labor in the *Terminator* Films." In *Postmodern Apocalypse: Theory and Cultural Practice at the End,* edited by Richard Dellamora, 182–198. Philadelphia: University of Pennsylvania Press, 1995.

Pyle, Forest. "Making Cyborgs, Making Humans: Of Terminators and Blade Runners." In *The Cybercultures Reader,* edited by David Bell and Barbara M. Kennedy, 124–137. London: Routledge, 2000.

Rinzler, J. M. *The Making of* Star Wars: *The Definitive Story Behind the Original Film.* New York: Del Rey, 2007.

Roth, Marty. "Twice Two: *The Fly* and *Invasion of the Body Snatchers*." In *Dead Ringers: The Remake in Theory and Practice,* edited by Jennifer Forrest and Leonard Koos. New York: State University of New York Press, 2002.

Ruben, Matthew. "*12 Monkeys,* Postmodernism, and the Urban: Toward a New Method." In *Keyframes: Popular Cinema and Cultural Studies,* edited by Matthew Tinkcom and Amy Villarejo, 312–332. London: Routledge, 2001.

Russell, Patricia Read. "Parallel Romantic Fantasies: Barrie's Peter Pan and Spielberg's *E. T.: The Extraterrestrial*." *Children's Literature Association Quarterly* 8, no. 4 (1983): 28–30.

Russo, Joe, and Larry Landsman. Planet of the Apes *Revisited: The Behind-the-Scenes Story of the Classic Science Fiction Saga.* New York: St. Martin's, 2001.

Sammon, Paul M. *Future Noir: The Making of* Blade Runner. New York: HarperPrism, 1996.

Sanders, Steven M. "Picturing Paranoia: Interpreting *Invasion of the Body Snatchers*." In *The Philosophy of Science Fiction Film,* edited by Steven M. Sanders, 55–72. Lexington: University Press of Kentucky, 2008.

Sebeok, Thomas A. "Enter Textuality: Echoes from *the Extraterrestrial*." *Georgetown University Round Table on Languages and Linguistics* (1984): 175–180.

Shay, Don, and Jody Duncan. *The Making of* Jurassic Park. New York: Ballantine Books, 1993.

Silvio, Carl, and Tony M. Vinci, eds. *Culture, Identities and Technology in the* Star Wars *Films: Essays on the Two Trilogies.* Jefferson, N.C.: McFarland, 2007.

Skoble, Aeon J. "Technology and Ethics in *The Day the Earth Stood Still*." In *The Philosophy of Science Fiction Film,* edited by Steven M. Sanders, 91–101. Lexington: University Press of Kentucky, 2008.

Smith, Paul. "*Terminator* Technology: Hollywood, History, and Technology." In *Keyframes: Popular Cinema and Cultural Studies,* edited by Matthew Tinkcom and Amy Villarejo, 333–342. London: Routledge, 2001.

Sontag, Susan. "The Imagination of Disaster." In *Against Interpretation and Other Essays* by Susan Sontag, 209–225. New York: Farrar, Straus and Giroux, 1966.

Tarratt, Margaret. "Monsters from the Id." In *Film Genre Reader,* edited by Barry Keith Grant, 104–114. Austin: University of Texas Press, 1986.

Telotte, J. P. "Heinlein, Verhoeven, and the Problem of the Real: *Starship Troopers.*" *Literature/Film Quarterly* 20, no. 3 (2001): 196–202.

Trushell, John. "A Postmodern (Re)Turn to *Forbidden Planet.*" *Foundation: The International Review of Science Fiction* 69 (Spring 1997): 60–67.

Warren, Bill. *Keep Watching the Skies! American Science Fiction Movies of the Fifties: Vol. 1, 1950–1957.* Jefferson, N.C.: McFarland, 1982.

———. *Keep Watching the Skies! American Science Fiction Movies of the Fifties: Vol. 2, 1958–1962.* Jefferson, N.C.: McFarland, 1986.

Wells, Paul. "The Invisible Man: Shrinking Masculinity in the 1950s Science Fiction B-Movie." In *You Tarzan: Masculinity, Movies, and Men,* edited by Pat Kirkham and Janet Thurman, 181–199. New York: St. Martin's, 1993.

Wetmore, Kevin J. Jr. *Empire Triumphant: Race, Religion and Rebellion in the* Star Wars *Films.* Jefferson, N.C.: McFarland, 2005.

Wilson, Rob. "Cyborg America: Policing the Social Sublime in *Robocop* and *Robocop 2.*" In *The Administration of Aesthetics: Censorship, Political Criticism, and the Public Sphere,* edited by Richard Burt, 289–306. Minneapolis: University of Minnesota Press, 1994.

Yeffeth, Glen, ed. *Taking the Red Pill: Science, Philosophy, and Religion in* The Matrix. Chichester, England: Summersdale, 2003.

Youngs, Tim. "Cruising against the Id: The Transformation of Caliban in *Forbidden Planet.*" In *Constellation Caliban: Figurations of a Character,* edited by Nadia Lie and Theo D'haen, 211–229. Amsterdam, Netherlands: Rodopi, 1997.

PERSONNEL

Actors

Duke, Brad. *Harrison Ford: The Films.* Jefferson, N.C.: McFarland, 2005.

Freedman, Carl. "Polemical Afterword: Some Brief Reflections on Arnold Schwarzenegger and on Science Fiction in Contemporary American Culture." *PMLA: Publications of the Modern Language Association of America* 119, no. 3 (2004): 539–546.

Goldberg, Jonathan. "Recalling Totalities: The Mirrored Stages of Arnold Schwarzenegger." *Differences: A Journal of Feminist Cultural Studies* 4, no. 1 (1992): 172–204.

Herzog, Peter, and Gene Vazzana. *Brigitte Helm: From* Metropolis *to* Gold Portrait of a Goddess. New York: Corvin, 1994.

Jenkins, Garry. *Harrison Ford: Imperfect Hero.* Secaucus, N. J.: Carol Publishing Group, 1998.

Morton, Andrew: *Tom Cruise: An Unauthorized Biography.* New York: St. Martin's, 2008.

Parker, John. *Bruce Willis: The Unauthorised Biography.* London: Virgin Books, 1997.

Rovin, Jeff. *The Films of Charlton Heston.* Secaucus, N.J.: Citadel Press, 1977.

Weaver, Tom. *They Fought in the Creature Features: Interviews with 23 Classic Horror, Science Fiction, and Serial Stars.* Jefferson, N.C.: McFarland, 1995.

Artists

Dalton, Tony. *Ray Harryhausen: An Animated Life.* London: Billboard, 2004.

Duncan, Jody. *The Winston Effect: The Art and History of Stan Winston Studio.* London: Titan, 2006.

Harryhausen, Ray, and Tony Dalton. *The Art of Ray Harryhausen.* London: Billboard, 2006.

Miller, Ron, and Frederick C. Durant. *The Art of Chesley Bonestell.* London: Paper Tiger, 2001.

Ragone, August. *Eiji Tsuburaya: Master of Monsters: Defending the Earth with Ultraman, Godzilla and Friends in the Golden Age of Japanese Science Fiction Film.* San Francisco: Chronicle Books, 2007.

Rickitt, Richard. *Designing Movie Creatures and Characters: Behind the Scenes with the Movie Masters.* Amsterdam: Elsevier Focal Press, 2006.

———. *Special Effects: The History and Technique.* New York: Billboard Books, 2000.

Vaz, Mark Cotta. *Industrial Light & Magic: Into the Digital Realm.* New York: Del Rey, 1996.

Directors

Baxter, John. *Stanley Kubrick: A Biography.* London: HarperCollins, 1997.

Beard, William. *The Artist as Monster: The Cinema of David Cronenberg,* rev. ed. Toronto: University of Toronto Press, 2006.

Cooper, Sarah. *Chris Marker.* Manchester: Manchester University Press, 2008.

Cumbow, Robert C. *Order in the Universe: The Films of John Carpenter.* Metuchen, N.J.: Scarecrow Press, 1990.

Ezra, Elizabeth. *Georges Méliès: The Birth of the Auteur.* Manchester: Manchester University Press, 2000.

Frazer, John. *Artificially Arranged Scenes: The Films of Georges Méliès.* Boston: G. K. Hall, 1979.

Gordon, Andrew M. *Empire of Dreams: The Science Fiction and Fantasy Films of Steven Spielberg.* Lanham, Md.: Rowman & Littlefield, 2007.

Grant, Michael, ed. *The Modern Fantastic: The Films of David Cronenberg.* Westport, Conn.: Praeger.

Gunning, Tom. *The Films of Fritz Lang: Allegories of Vision and Modernity.* London: BFI, 2000.

Haskin, Byron, and Joe Adamson. *Byron Haskin.* Metuchen, N.J.: Scarecrow Press, 1984.

Hayward, Susan. *Luc Besson.* Manchester: Manchester University Press, 1998.

Hearn, Marcus. *The Cinema of George Lucas.* New York: Harry N. Abrams, 2005.

Herzogenrath, Bernd, ed. *Edgar G. Ulmer: Essays on the King of the B's.* Jefferson, N.C.: McFarland, 2009.

Hutchings, Peter. *Terence Fisher.* Manchester: Manchester University Press, 2002.

Keegan, Rebecca Winters. *The Futurist: The Films of James Cameron.* New York: Crown, 2009.

Keller, Alexandra. *James Cameron.* London: Routledge, 2006.

Kendrick, James. "Marxist Overtones in Three Films by James Cameron." *Journal of Popular Film and Television* 27, no. 3 (1999): 36–44.

Kowalski, Dean, ed. *Steven Spielberg and Philosophy: We're Gonna Need a Bigger Book.* Lexington: University Press of Kentucky, 2008.

Leggett, Paul. *Terence Fisher: Horror, Myth, and Religion.* Jefferson City, N.C.: McFarland, 2002.

Lewis, Jon. "The Perfect Money Machine(s): George Lucas, Steven Spielberg, and Auteurism in the New Hollywood." In *Looking Past the Screen: Case Studies in American Film History and Method,* edited by Jon Lewis and Eric Smoodin, 61–86. Durham, N.C.: Duke University Press, 2007.

Lucas, Tim. *Mario Bava: All the Colors of the Dark.* Cincinnati, Ohio: Video Watchdog, 2007.

Mathijs, Ernest. *The Cinema of David Cronenberg: From Baron of Blood to Culture Hero.* London: Wallflower, 2008.

McGilligan, Patrick. *Fritz Lang: The Nature of the Beast.* New York: St. Martin's, 1997.

McGowan, Todd. *The Impossible David Lynch.* New York: Columbia University Press, 2007.

Muir, John Kenneth. *The Films of John Carpenter.* Jefferson, N.C.: McFarland, 2000.

Nelson, Thomas Allen. *Kubrick, Inside a Film Artist's Maze.* Bloomington: Indian University Press, 1982.

Olson, Greg. *David Lynch: Beautiful Dark.* Lanham, Md.: Scarecrow Press, 2008.

Pollock, Dale. *Skywalking: The Life and Films of George Lucas.* New York: Harmony Books, 1983.

Reemes, Dana M. *Directed by Jack Arnold.* Jefferson, N.C.: McFarland, 1988.

Rhodes, Gary D., ed. *Stanley Kubrick: Essays on His Films and Legacy.* Jefferson, N.C.: McFarland, 2008.

Sammon, Paul. *Ridley Scott.* London: Orion, 1999.

Schwartz, Richard Alan. *The Films of Ridley Scott.* Westport, Conn.: Praeger, 2001.

Sheen, Erica, and Annette Davison. *The Cinema of David Lynch: American Dreams, Nightmare Visions.* London: Wallflower Press, 2004.

Skotak, Robert. *Ib Melchior: Man of Imagination.* Baltimore, Md.: Midnight Marquee Press, 2000.

Van Scheers, Rob. *Paul Verhoeven.* London: Faber, 1997.

Producers

Alexander, David. Star Trek *Creator: The Authorized Biography of Gene Roddenberry.* New York: Roc, 1994.

Cochran, David. "The Low-Budget Modernism of Roger Corman." *North Dakota Quarterly* 64, no. 1 (1997): 19–40.

Hickman, Gail Morgan. *The Films of George Pal.* South Brunswick, N.J.: A.S. Barnes, 1977.

Kezich, Tullio, and Allessandra Levantesi. *Dino: The Life and Films of Dino De Laurentiis.* New York: Hyperion, 2004.

Law, John W. *Master of Disaster: Irwin Allen, The Disaster Years.* San Francisco: Aplomb, 2008.

McGee, Mark Thomas. *Roger Corman, the Best of the Cheap Acts.* Jefferson, N.C.: McFarland, 1988.

Morris, Gary. *Roger Corman.* Boston: Twayne, 1985.

Naha, Ed. *The Films of Roger Corman: Brilliance on a Budget.* New York: Arco, 1982.

Writers

Butcher, William. *Jules Verne: The Definitive Biography.* New York: Thunder's Mouth Press, 2006.

Butler, Andrew. "Science Fiction as Postmodernism: The Case of Philip K. Dick." In *Impossibility Fiction: Alternativity, Extrapolation, Speculation,* edited by Derek Littlewood and Peter Stockwell, 45–56. Amsterdam: Rodopi, 1996.

Cavallaro, Dani. *Cyberpunk and Cyberculture: Science Fiction and the Work of William Gibson.* London: Athlone Press, 2000.

Costello, Peter. *Jules Verne: Inventor of Science Fiction.* New York: Scribner, 1978.

Downing, Crystal. "Deconstructing Herbert: *The War of the Worlds* on Film." *Literature Film Quarterly* 35, no. 4 (2007): 274–281.

Franklin, H. Bruce. *Robert A. Heinlein: America as Science Fiction.* New York: Oxford University Press, 1980.

Grazier, Kevin Robert. *The Science of Michael Crichton: An Unauthorized Exploration into the Real Science Behind the Fictional Worlds of Michael Crichton.* Dallas, Tex.: BenBella Books, 2008.

Gunn, James. *Isaac Asimov: The Foundations of Science Fiction,* rev. ed. Lanham, Md.: Scarecrow Press, 1996.

Havens, Candace. *Joss Whedon: The Genius Behind Buffy.* Dallas, Tex.: BenBella Books, 2003.

Hillegas, Mark. *The Future as Nightmare: H. G. Wells and the Anti-Utopians.* New York: Oxford University Press, 1967.

Hollow. John. *Against the Night, the Stars: The Science Fiction of Arthur C. Clarke.* San Diego, Calif.: Harcourt Brace Jovanovich, 1983.

McConnell, Frank. *The Science Fiction of H. G. Wells.* New York: Oxford University Press, 1981.

Palumbo, Donald. *Chaos Theory, Asimov's Foundations and Robots, and Herbert's Dune.* Westport, Conn.: Greenwood Press, 2002.

Patrouch, Joseph F. *The Science Fiction of Isaac Asimov.* Garden City, NY: Doubleday, 1974.

Robinson, Kim Stanley. *The Novels of Philip K. Dick.* Ann Arbor, Mich.: UMI Research Press, 1984.

Slusser, George Edgar. *The Space Odysseys of Arthur C. Clarke.* San Bernardino, Calif.: Borgo Press, 1977.

Smith, Don G. *H. G. Wells on Film: The Utopian Nightmare.* Jefferson, N.C.: McFarland, 2002.

Sutin, Lawrence. *Divine Invasions: A Life of Philip K. Dick.* New York: Harmony Books, 1989.

Suvin, Darko. "Artifice as Refuge and World View: Philip K. Dick's Foci." In *Philip K. Dick,* edited by Martin Harry Greenberg and Joseph D. Olander, 73–95. New York: Taplinger, 1983.

Swirski, Peter. *The Art and Science of Stanisław Lem.* Montreal: McGill-Queen's University Press, 2006.

————. *Between Literature and Science: Poe, Lem, and Explorations in Aesthetics, Cognitive Science, and Literary Knowledge.* Montreal: McGill-Queen's University Press, 2000.

Trembley, Elizabeth. *Michael Crichton: A Critical Companion.* Wesport, Conn.: Greenwood Press, 1996.

Wiater, Stanley, Matthew Bradley, and Paul Stuve. *The Twilight and Other Zones: The Dark Worlds of Richard Matheson.* New York: Citadel Press, 2009.

Ziegfeld, Richard E. *Stanisław Lem.* New York: Ungar, 1985.

REFERENCE WORKS

Clute, John, and Peter Nicholls, eds. *The Encyclopedia of Science Fiction.* New York: St. Martin's Griffin, 1995.

Hardy, Phil, ed. *The Overlook Film Encyclopedia: Science Fiction.* Woodstock, N.Y.: Overlook Press, 1994.

Henderson, C. J. *The Encyclopedia of Science Fiction Movies from 1897 to the Present.* New York: Facts on File, 2001.

Okuda, Michael, and Denise Okuda. *The* Star Trek *Encyclopedia: A Reference Guide to the Future.* New York: Pocket Books, 1999.

Sansweet, Stephen J., et al. *The Complete* Star Wars *Encyclopedia.* New York: Del Rey, 2008.

Westfahl, Gary, ed. *The Greenwood Encyclopedia of Science Fiction and Fantasy: Themes, Works, and Wonders,* 3 vols. Westport, Conn.: Greenwood Press, 2005.

INTERNET RESOURCES

The Academy of Science Fiction, Fantasy & Horror Films. http://www.saturn awards.org/ (accessed November 5, 2009).

Dirks, Tim. "Science Fiction Films." *Filmsite.* http://www.filmsite.org/sci-fi films.html (accessed November 5, 2009).

The Encyclopedia of Fantastic Film and Television. http://www.eofftv.com/ (accessed November 5, 2009).
"Honor Roll: Science Fiction Films." *Award Annals.* http://www.awardannals .com/wiki/Honor_roll:Science_Fiction_films (accessed November 5, 2009).
Science Fiction Films and Shows. http://www.windows.ucar.edu/tour/link=/ art_and_music/films.html&br=graphi&edu=elem (accessed November 5, 2009).
Science Fiction Filmsite. http://www.umich.edu/~umfandsf/film/ (accessed November 5, 2009).
Sci Fi Movies.com. http://www.scifimovies.com/ (accessed November 5, 2009).
SF Site. http://www.sfsite.com/ (accessed November 5, 2009).
Westfahl, Gary. *Gary Westfahl's Biographical Encyclopedia of Science Fiction Film.* http://www.sfsite.com/gary/ww-encyclopedia.htm (accessed November 5, 2009).
World Science Fiction Society. http://www.wsfs.org/ (accessed November 5, 2009).

About the Author

M. Keith Booker is the James E. and Ellen Wadley Roper Professor of English at the University of Arkansas, where he is also the director of the Program in Comparative Literature and Cultural Studies. Before devoting himself to literary and cultural studies, Professor Booker spent 14 years on the scientific research staff of the Oak Ridge National Laboratory. He is the author or editor of dozens of books on literature, popular culture, and literary and cultural theory. His books on science fiction include *Monsters, Mushroom Clouds, and the Cold War: American Science Fiction and the Roots of Postmodernism, 1946–1964* (2001), *Strange TV: Innovative Television Series from* The Twilight Zone *to* The X-Files (2002), *Science Fiction Television* (2004), *Alternate Americas: Science Fiction Film and American Culture* (2006), and *The Science Fiction Handbook* (co-authored with Anne-Marie Thomas, 2009). Other books include *Joyce, Bakhtin, and the Literary Tradition: Toward a Comparative Cultural Poetics* (1995); *A Practical Introduction to Literary Theory and Criticism* (1996); *Colonial Power, Colonial Texts: India in the Modern British Novel* (1997); *The African Novel in English: An Introduction* (1998); *The Post-Utopian Imagination: American Culture in the Long 1950s* (2002); *Postmodern Hollywood: What's New in Film and Why It Makes Us Feel So Strange* (2007); and *"May Contain Graphic Material": Comic Books, Graphic Novels, and Film* (2007).